DECOLONIZING JOURNALISM

DECOLONIZING JOURNALISM

A Guide to Reporting in Indigenous Communities

Duncan McCue

OXFORD
UNIVERSITY PRESS

Oxford University Press is a department of the University of Oxford.
It furthers the University's objective of excellence in research, scholarship,
and education by publishing worldwide. Oxford is a registered trade mark of
Oxford University Press in the UK and in certain other countries.

Published in Canada by Oxford University Press
8 Sampson Mews, Suite 204, Don Mills, Ontario M3C 0H5 Canada

www.oupcanada.com

Copyright © Oxford University Press Canada 2023

The moral rights of the authors have been asserted

Database right Oxford University Press (maker)

First Edition published in 2022

All rights reserved. No part of this publication may be reproduced, stored in a retrieval system,
or transmitted, in any form or by any means, without the prior permission in writing of Oxford
University Press, or as expressly permitted by law, by licence, or under terms agreed with the
appropriate reprographics rights organization. Enquiries concerning reproduction outside the scope
of the above should be sent to the Permissions Department at the address
above or through the following url: www.oupcanada.com/permission/permission_request.php

Every effort has been made to determine and contact copyright holders.
In the case of any omissions, the publisher will be pleased to make
suitable acknowledgement in future editions.

Library and Archives Canada Cataloguing in Publication
Title: Decolonizing journalism : a guide to reporting in Indigenous communities / Duncan McCue.
Names: McCue, Duncan, 1971- author.
Description: First edition. | Includes bibliographical references and index.
Identifiers: Canadiana (print) 20220174504 | Canadiana (ebook) 20220174881 | ISBN 9780190164263
(softcover) | ISBN 9780190164287 (loose-leaf) | ISBN 9780190164270 (EPUB)
Subjects: LCSH: Indigenous peoples—Press coverage—Canada. | LCSH: Race relations and the press—
Canada. | LCSH: Racism in the press—Canada. | LCSH: Journalism—Objectivity—Canada. | LCSH:
Journalism—Social aspects—Canada. | LCSH: Journalism—Canada—Textbooks. | LCGFT: Textbooks.
Classification: LCC PN4914.I553 M33 2022 | DDC 070.4/49305897071—dc23

Cover image: Joshua Mangeshig Pawis-Steckley
Cover and interior design: Sherill Chapman

Oxford University Press is committed to our environment.
This book is printed on Forest Stewardship Council® certified paper
and comes from responsible sources.

Printed and bound in Canada

Table of Contents

About the Author vii
Foreword viii
Acknowledgements xii
Contributors xiii
A Brief History of Indigenous Relations in Canada xv

Part 1   **At the Desk**   **1**

     1.1   First Contact   3

     1.2   Historical News Stereotypes of Indigenous Peoples   7

     1.3   Beyond Victims and Warriors: Choosing Indigenous News Stories   18

     1.4   Positive versus Negative Stories   26

     1.5   Searching for Solutions   31

     1.6   How to Pitch a Story Successfully   35

     1.7   "Where Are You From?" Rethinking Objectivity   39

Part 2   **In the Field**   **49**

     2.1   Indian Time   51

     2.2   Indigenous Customs and Protocols   56

     2.3   Who Represents the "Indigenous Perspective"?   68

     2.4   White Characters and Indigenous Agency   71

     2.5   Trauma-Informed Reporting   74

     2.6   Story-Takers: How to Deal with 500+ Years of Rage   87

     2.7   Breaking News: Indians Are Funny!   91

Part 3   **On the Air**   **97**

     3.1   Terminology and Lexicon   99

     3.2   Context and Colonial Amnesia   109

     3.3   Accountability, Reciprocity, and Criticism   112

     3.4   Social Media: The New Moccasin Telegraph   115

     3.5   Reconciliation and Journalism   122

Part 4 Teachings 129

4.1 Becoming Trauma-Informed: A Conversation with Connie Walker 131

4.2 Lessons in Humility: A Conversation with Waubgeshig Rice 141

4.3 "In Love with My People": A Conversation with Mark Trahant 151

4.4 Northern Reflections: A Conversation with Juanita Taylor 162

4.5 Respect and Relationships: A Conversation with Tanya Talaga 172

4.6 In Pursuit of Truth: A Conversation with Karyn Pugliese 182

4.7 Punching Up: A Conversation with Tim Fontaine 194

4.8 The Need for Knowledge-based Journalism: A Conversation with Merelda Fiddler-Potter 205

4.9 Asking Hard Questions: A Conversation with Tristan Ahtone 215

Conclusion: The Last Word 227
Appendix 1: UNDRIP Articles Relating to Media 229
Appendix 2: TRC Calls to Action Relating to Media 230
Appendix 3: OCAP® Principles for Indigenous Research and Data Collection 232
Appendix 4: Residential School Apology 234
Additional Resources 237
Bibliography 244
Index 254

About the Author

Source: Photo by Sinisa Jolic, CBC Radio and used with permission of Duncan McCue.

Duncan McCue is an award-winning journalist, author, and journalism professor. His radio and television career at the Canadian Broadcasting Corporation (CBC) spans over two decades, most recently serving as host of CBC Radio's national phone-in program *Cross Country Checkup* and *Kuper Island*, a CBC podcast about Canada's Indian residential schools. In addition to teaching at the UBC Graduate School of Journalism and Toronto Metropolitan University, he has delivered Indigenous cultural competency training to reporters and journalism students in Canada, the United States, Europe, and Australia. A proud Anishinaabe from the Chippewas of Georgina Island First Nation in southern Ontario, Duncan is the recipient of an Indspire Award for Public Service and an honorary doctorate from the University of King's College.

Foreword

I'm pretty sure Tonto was the first Indian I ever saw on TV.

The Lone Ranger's sidekick was a lousy role model for a little Indigenous lad. Tonto wore buckskin, spoke in pidgin English, and existed to serve the needs of "Ke-mo Sah-bee." Adding insult to injury, his name translates into "dummy" in Spanish.

But, no question, Tonto was indispensable to his masked companion.

I can't count how many times as a journalist I wished I had a "Tonto" when venturing into an unfamiliar Indigenous community. A partner—who offers advice on the lay of the land, provides wise counsel, helps make my stories better.

Every reporter—Indigenous or non-Indigenous—needs a guide.

It's been over a decade since I wrote those words, as an introduction to my online guide www.riic.ca, or Reporting in Indigenous Communities (RIIC).

My tongue was planted firmly in cheek with the *Lone Ranger* reference, but I had Tonto's generous spirit in mind when I approached the John S. Knight Journalism Fellowships at Stanford University in 2010 with the notion of developing a toolkit for reporters covering Indigenous communities.

I got the idea from a summit of Indigenous and non-Indigenous journalists working at the Canadian Broadcasting Corporation (CBC). It was one of many such meetings I've attended seeking to improve news coverage of Indigenous issues. At that one, it dawned on me why Indigenous communities had been so badly served by the media: many non-Indigenous reporters felt uncomfortable when visiting Indigenous communities and disliked being assigned stories on Indigenous subjects.

I heard tales of non-Indigenous reporters hiding under desks when the assignment editor was hunting for somebody to cover a First Nations story. Was it because Indigenous folks so often didn't return their calls? Did they feel out of place, rolling up in a shiny news truck on a dusty reserve? For whatever reason, reporters often cursed their fate (more than usual) when asked to file on Indigenous issues. No wonder so many Indigenous stories were thin on content and persistently filled with stereotypes.

By offering an online education resource, free for any journalist or newsroom to use, I figured at least reporters wouldn't be able to blame their objectionable journalism on a lack of education about Indigenous issues.

The guide was intended to provide practical solutions to the real-life challenges journalists face in the field, addressing everything from common news stereotypes of Indigenous Peoples to Indigenous customs and protocols. In short, I wanted to help journalists tell better Indigenous news stories.

When www.riic.ca launched in 2011, it was one of a kind. I was pleased as punch to watch the site become a go-to resource in Canadian journalism classrooms and attract tens of thousands of visitors from around the globe.

But times change.

In 2012, about a year after RIIC launched, four women from Saskatchewan started grassroots teach-ins to raise awareness about Indigenous sovereignty, Indigenous rights, and respect for treaties. "Idle No More" quickly became a rallying cry for protests and demonstrations that spread across Canada and the world, fuelled by hashtags and viral videos on social media.

Though the round-dance flash mobs ultimately faded away, there was no mistaking the lasting effect of Idle No More on Indigenous engagement with the mainstream media. Journalists could no longer responsibly choose to cover Ikea monkeys instead of Indigenous Peoples without having their Twitter and Facebook accounts flooded by Indigenous audiences demanding responsible coverage.

In 2015, Canada's Truth and Reconciliation Commission into Indian Residential Schools (TRC) delivered another wake-up call to the country's mainstream media. The TRC drew attention to the role journalists have played in entrenching inequities in Canada, citing contemporary media coverage of Indigenous issues as persistently fraught with misinformation and stereotypes.

"To ensure that the colonial press truly becomes a thing of the past in twenty-first-century Canada, the media must engage in its own acts of reconciliation with Aboriginal peoples," urged the TRC.[1]

While a handful of news outlets responded by making sincere attempts to improve relationships with Indigenous communities, and some Canadian journalism schools began to Indigenize curricula, change has been painfully slow.

In 2020, Black Lives Matter demonstrations swept across the United States and around the globe, and lack of diversity in Canadian media was once again in the spotlight. Racialized journalists shared uncomfortable truths about racism in their newsrooms, and major news outlets promised to do better. Some have called it a reckoning—we'll see if leads to more Indigenous journalists and more cultural competency training for non-Indigenous journalists.

That, dear readers, is a prolonged introduction to this new iteration of www.riic.ca.

Welcome to *Decolonizing Journalism: A Guide to Reporting in Indigenous Communities*—a text intended to offer you useful ideas and practical methods for finding and developing news stories in "Indian Country" (as we NDNs sometimes refer to the lands we inhabit).

It's rooted in the Canadian experience, but journalists around the globe may find it useful when covering Indigenous communities from the Americas to Australia.

The guide is structured into three areas of reporting where journalists face challenges when producing news stories about Indigenous Peoples.

1) **AT THE DESK** – how to research and pitch stories;
2) **IN THE FIELD** – how to gather information for these stories; and
3) **ON THE AIR** – how journalists present stories about Indigenous Peoples.

Those familiar with the original online RIIC guide will observe significant and necessary updates in *Decolonizing Journalism*.

The chapters on news stereotypes and terminology have been updated, in line with changing times and emerging scholarship. There are new chapters on trauma-informed

---

[1] Truth and Reconciliation Commission of Canada. *Canada's Residential Schools: Reconciliation: The Final Report of the Truth and Reconciliation Commission of Canada, Volume 6.* (McGill-Queen's University Press, 2015), 194.

reporting, rethinking journalistic objectivity, how to use social media in Indigenous communities, and reconciliation journalism.

I'm especially excited about a new section called "Teachings." The advice and lessons in the original guide were drawn largely from my experiences as a television and radio reporter, but this edition includes my conversations with some of Turtle Island's top Indigenous journalists about how they do their jobs. I spoke with them via Zoom from January to April 2021.

During one interview, my friend Tristan Ahtone questioned whether it's possible to "decolonize journalism." I understand his desire to radically overhaul the news business. It's the kind of world-changing, chaotic break from settler colonialism envisioned by Franz Fanon in *Wretched of the Earth*. By contrast, "decolonization" is too often used casually in online chat, in the media, in academic discourse, or in social justice circles without reference to Indigenous self-determination or Indigenous lands. So—let me be clear. I define "decolonizing journalism" as the process of deconstructing and dismantling the structures and practices in the media that perpetuate colonial ideals and privilege Western ways of doing. Decolonization means addressing power imbalances in newsrooms and news organizations, by valuing Indigenous knowledge and weeding out Western biases that impact Indigenous ways of being.

If you closely examine Indigenous journalists' methods, you'll see we are doing that work, pushing back against problematic norms in our industry in order to practise our craft "in a good way." What is emerging is transformative: a journalism more in keeping with Indigenous ways of knowing and doing. In my opinion, it's not only possible to decolonize journalism, it's becoming a reality: change is afoot, thanks to the tireless efforts of Indigenous journalists in newsrooms around the world.

Here are some things this guide is *not*.

Reading this book from cover to cover does not mean you are officially "reconciled." Instant reconciliation does not exist. Reconciliation is an ongoing process, which involves efforts by individual journalists and media organizations to raise awareness about colonial history and its present-day impacts on Indigenous Peoples. Reconciliation also involves media and Indigenous Peoples building new relationships. Most importantly, reconciliation means newsrooms must take concrete steps to change biased behaviour. Without action, reconciliation is an empty and meaningless buzzword.

Another thing: *Decolonizing Journalism* is not Indigenous 101. If you want to learn about the *Indian Act* or Inuit art or the *Royal Proclamation of 1763* or the Sixties Scoop or Michif place names or how to make deadly beaded moccasins, those are admirable goals. But this is primarily a journalism textbook, in which I examine the craft of journalism in an Indigenous context.

Of course, the text is full of resources and references that will point you in the right direction to learning more about Indigenous culture, politics, and history. However, I trust you'll consider this text but a stepping stone in that much longer journey.

Decolonizing Journalism will help writers, journalists, and journalism students understand there is no "one-size-fits-all" approach to covering diverse Indigenous Peoples. It offers guidance on how to respect Indigenous Peoples' customs and traditions, and to recognize, above all else, the importance of nurturing relationships.

It will help you to feel more confident when you tackle Indigenous stories, to build stronger audiences, and, ultimately, to tell better stories. If we improve the quality of our news coverage, we will better serve Indigenous communities. In the end, this country will be better for it.

A note about the often informal, sometimes wry, language in the guide. Gatherings of Indigenous folks are generally full of laughter. Journalists can also be darkly humorous. Academics, on the other hand, are a rather solemn crowd. This is a textbook, but I try to err on the side of funny.

Finally, a word about that thorny issue of terminology.

I'm Anishinaabe, as my people call ourselves, from the Chippewas of Georgina Island First Nation in southern Ontario in the country now known as Canada. I use the terms Native-Indian-Aboriginal-First Nations-Indigenous fluidly, depending on the context. I've opted for conversational usage within. Should you do the same? Check the Terminology and Lexicon chapter for some advice.

—Duncan McCue, Toronto/Treaty 13 and Williams Treaties Territory, May 2022

Acknowledgements

This textbook would not have been possible without the support of many.

The original online guide was born at Stanford University. I'm indebted to Jim Bettinger, Dawn Garcia, and Pam Maples of the John S. Knight Fellowships at Stanford University, for recognizing value in my idea in its infancy and offering a year's worth of endless encouragement. Special thanks to my fellow Fellows (Class of 2011) for your friendship and advice during our transformative Fellowship year.

I couldn't have taken a sabbatical from the newsroom's unrelenting pace without the backing of Jennifer McGuire and Jonathan Whitten of the Canadian Broadcasting Corporation.

During this book's first iteration, many friends and colleagues shared their time and wisdom as I bombarded them with rough drafts—Shannon Avison, Don Bain, Jeff Bear, David Beers, Kelly Crichton, Kathryn Gretsinger, Rick Harp, Jennifer Leask, Minelle Mahtani, Brenda Nadjiwan, Tracy Seeley, Connie Walker, David Wiwchar, and Mary Lynn Young.

Jon Christensen of Stanford University's Bill Lane Center for the American West made it financially possible to transform the original guide into a website. Geoff McGhee, Wendy Norris, Mike Marcotte, and Jacob Beaton offered patient counsel on how to do so. Chantelle Bellrichard at the UBC Graduate School of Journalism enthusiastically helped me maintain and update the RIIC site over the years.

When it came time to transform the website into this text, Susan Marjetti and Seema Patel of the Canadian Broadcasting Corporation wholeheartedly backed my request to step away from the mic for a time. It wouldn't have been possible without support from the William Southam Journalism Fellowships, run by Massey College at the University of Toronto.

A big *miigwech* to those who acted as peer reviewers for this text, including Melissa Ridgen (APTN), Trina Roache (University of King's College), Charles A. Hays (Thompson Rivers University), Shannon Avison (First Nations University of Canada), Shenaz Kermalli (Toronto Metropolitan University), Heather Y. Shpuniarsky (Trent University), Patti-Ann Finlay (Wilfrid Laurier University), Jeanelle Mandes (University of Regina), Miranda Brady (Carleton University) and Sonya Fatah (Toronto Metropolitan University).

Nmaamkaadenmaag e-debaajmajig. I celebrate Indigenous journalists, past and present, who show such dedication to sharing the truths of our Peoples, under often difficult circumstances. We're building stronger Nations—one story at a time.

I reserve my deepest gratitude for my mom Sharon for her unwavering love, my children Samantha and Cas who have always reminded me there's so much more to life than work, and *nbazgim* Pichi for her support.

I dedicate this to my father Waubageshig, the original Professor McCue. *Gnitaakinoomaage*—you are a good teacher.

Contributors

Tristan Ahtone
Tristan Ahtone is a member of the Kiowa Tribe and is editor-in-chief at the *Texas Observer*. He has reported for multiple outlets including *PBS NewsHour, National Native News, NPR, Al Jazeera America*, and *High Country News*, where he served as Indigenous Affairs editor. Tristan is a director of the Muckrock Foundation and is a former president of the Native American Journalists Association (NAJA).

Merelda Fiddler-Potter
Merelda Fiddler-Potter is a proud Métis woman whose ancestors fought in both the 1869–70 Red River Resistance and the 1885 Battle of Batoche. Merelda is a sessional lecturer at First Nations University of Canada and the University of Regina. Before entering academia, Fiddler-Potter was an award-winning current affairs producer and reporter for CBC Saskatchewan. She is currently a PhD candidate at the Johnson Shoyama Graduate School of Public Policy in Regina.

Tim Fontaine
Tim Fontaine is a journalist-turned-satirist who founded Walking Eagle News, a website that parodies Canadian and Indigenous news, in 2017. Before becoming a pretend journalist, he was a real-life journalist for almost two decades, working for CBC and APTN. Tim is a member of the Sagkeeng First Nation, an Anishinaabe community in Manitoba.

Karyn Pugliese
Karyn Pugliese is best known for her work as a Parliament Hill reporter and as the executive director of News and Current Affairs at APTN (Aboriginal Peoples Television Network), where she ran the news department for seven years. In 2022, she became the editor-in-chief of the *National Observer*. Karyn is the past president of the Canadian Association of Journalists (CAJ). A citizen of the Pikwàkanagàn First Nation in Ontario, Karyn is of mixed Algonquin and Italian descent.

Waubgeshig Rice
Waubgeshig Rice is an author and journalist from Wasauksing First Nation on Georgian Bay. He spent most of his journalism career with the Canadian Broadcasting Corporation (CBC) as a video journalist, web writer, producer, and radio host. His latest novel, *Moon of the Crusted Snow*, was a national bestseller and received widespread critical acclaim, including the Evergreen Award.

Tanya Talaga
Tanya Talaga is an Anishinaabe journalist. Tanya's mother's family is from Fort William First Nation, and her father was Polish-Canadian. For more than 20 years, she was a journalist at the *Toronto Star*, and she is now a regular columnist at the *Globe and Mail*. She is the award-winning author of two national bestsellers, *Seven Fallen Feathers* and *All Our Relations: Finding the Path Forward*. Tanya heads up Makwa Creative Inc., a production company focused on amplifying Indigenous voices through documentary films, TV, and podcasts.

Juanita Taylor
Juanita Taylor is originally from Arviat, Nunavut, and has also lived in Saskatchewan, Iqaluit, and Rankin Inlet. Juanita got her start as a journalist at APTN in Nunavut, where she became co-host of *APTN National News* in Winnipeg, before

moving to CBC North in Yellowknife. Now, Juanita is a senior reporter and national correspondent for the North with CBC News Network.

Mark Trahant

Mark Trahant is the editor of *Indian Country Today* (ICT). Known for his election reporting in Indian Country, Mark was the editorial page editor of the *Seattle Post-Intelligencer* and has worked for *The Arizona Republic, Salt Lake Tribune, The Seattle Times, The Navajo Times Today*, and the *Sho-Ban News*. Mark has held an endowed chair at the University of North Dakota and University of Alaska Anchorage. He is a member of the Shoshone-Bannock Tribes.

Connie Walker

Connie Walker is an award-winning investigative reporter, podcast host, and producer of the podcast *Stolen: The Search for Jermain* for Gimlet Media. Connie worked for CBC, hosting the acclaimed podcast series *Missing & Murdered*, which focuses on missing and murdered Indigenous women and girls. She was the lead reporter for CBC Indigenous, and a reporter for the flagship CBC news show *The National*. Connie is from the Okanese First Nation in Saskatchewan.

A Brief History of Indigenous Relations in Canada

While Indigenous Nations have their own origin stories and histories – and no timeline can be exhaustive – this chronology highlights some key events in the relations between Indigenous Nations and settlers in the land now known as Canada.[1]

1400s	**Doctrine of Discovery**: The Papal Bulls of *Romanus Pontifex* (1455) and *Inter Caetera* (1493) purport to give European monarchs the rights to lands and jurisdiction over any lands that they discover. The "Doctrine of Discovery" becomes the means which Europeans claim legal title to the "New World," including Canada.
1613	The **Two-Row Wampum** (Kaswentha) establishes the Covenant Chain, a series of alliances and treaties between the Haudenosaunee Confederacy and European settlers.
1725–1761	On the East Coast, **Peace and Friendship Treaties** are signed with the Mi'kmaq, Wolastoqiyik (Maliseet), and Passamaquoddy.
1763–1766	**Pontiac's War**: Under the leadership of Odawa chief Obwandiyag (Pontiac), an Indigenous alliance tries to oust the British from Indigenous lands in the Great Lakes region. The uprising fails, but forces British authorities toward a recognition of Indigenous rights.
1763	King George III of Britain issues the **Royal Proclamation of 1763**, recognizing Indian land rights and establishing guidelines for negotiating treaties on a nation-to-nation basis. It has been called an "Indian Magna Carta."
1812	In the **War of 1812**, tens of thousands of First Nations and Métis warriors fight for their land, independence, and culture. Some side with American forces, but most strategically ally with Great Britain. Tecumseh's Confederacy, also led by Tenskwatawa, plays a critical role in protecting Canada from American invasion.
1850–1854	The **Robinson-Superior** and **Robinson-Huron treaties** are signed in what is now Ontario, as are the **Douglas treaties** in what is now British Columbia.
1867	The *British North America Act* creates the Dominion of Canada. Responsibility for "Indians and the Lands reserved for Indians" is transferred to the federal government.
1869	**Red River Resistance**: Led by Louis Riel, the Métis and First Nations allies defend the Red River Colony from white settlers and government encroachment on their lands, which results in the creation of the province of Manitoba.

---

[1] I drew from multiple sources to prepare this timeline, but I must acknowledge the very helpful "Indigenous Peoples Timeline" by The Canadian Encyclopedia and "Key Moments in Indigenous History Timeline" by Historica Canada.

1876	The ***Indian Act*** is passed by the Government of Canada. The Act aims to assimilate Indigenous Peoples, turning them into wards of the state and controlling their social, economic and political lives.
1883	Prime Minister John A. Macdonald authorizes the creation of church-run **residential schools**, designed to separate Indigenous children from their families and assimilate them into Euro-Canadian culture.
1885	The Métis and their First Nations allies lead the five-month **Northwest Resistance** against the federal government in what is now Saskatchewan and Alberta. Federal troops prevail, and Louis Riel is sentenced to death.
1871–1921	The 11 **Numbered Treaties** are signed by the Crown and First Nations, covering the territories from present-day Ontario to Alberta and portions of British Columbia and the Northwest Territories.
1914–1918	**WWI**: Between 4,000 and 6,000 Indigenous people serve in the Canadian military during the First World War. First Nations veterans are denied veterans' benefits on their return.
1939–1945	**WWII**: Over 4000 Indigenous soldiers fight for Canada in the Second World War. Most do not receive the same support or compensation as other veterans upon returning home.
1951	***Indian Act* amendments**: Some of the more oppressive sections of the *Indian Act* are amended and removed. The ban on the potlatch and sun dances is lifted, women have the right to vote in band elections, and elected band councils are given more powers.
1953	**Inuit Relocation**: The federal government forcefully moves 87 Inuit from Inukjuak in northern Québec to Ellesmere and Cornwallis Islands, in an effort to secure northern territorial sovereignty during the Cold War. The relocated Inuit are not given sufficient support and endure many hardships.
1960	Status Indians receive the **right to vote** in federal elections, no longer losing their status or treaty rights in the process.
1960s	**Sixties Scoop**: Thousands of Indigenous children are taken from their families and communities by provincial social workers and placed in foster homes, often with non-Indigenous families.
1969–1970	A federal **White Paper** proposes abolishing the *Indian Act*, eliminating Indian status, and transferring responsibility for Indian Affairs to the provinces. **Nêhiyaw** (Cree) leader Harold Cardinal responds with the Red Paper, calling for recognition of First Nations as "Citizens Plus."
1973	***Calder* decision**: Named for Nisga'a chief Frank Calder, the Supreme Court of Canada agrees that Indigenous Peoples held title to land before European contact. The *Calder* decision forces the federal government to adopt a new process to negotiate land claims with Indigenous Peoples not covered by treaty.

1974	The **Native Women's Association of Canada** is established to advocate for the social, economic, cultural and political well-being of Indigenous women and girls.
1982	The **Assembly of First Nations** is formed out of the National Indian Brotherhood to promote the political interests of First Nations.
1982	The **Canadian Constitution** is patriated. Indigenous groups fight to protect their rights, resulting in Section 35 of the *Constitution Act*, which recognizes and affirms Aboriginal title and treaty rights.
1990	**Oka Crisis**: Kanien'kehá:ka (Mohawk) protesters clash with Québec provincial police and the Canadian military for 78 days.
1990	The **Meech Lake Accord** collapses when Manitoba MLA Elijah Harper blocks its passage, citing the accord's failure to consult First Nations or recognize their constitutional rights.
1993	Inuit and the governments of the Northwest Territories and Canada sign the **Nunavut Land Claims Agreement**. Nunavut is created in 1999, from the central and eastern portions of the Northwest Territories.
1996	The final report of the **Royal Commission on Aboriginal Peoples** is published. It recommends a public inquiry into the effects of residential schools and a complete restructuring of the relationship between Indigenous and non-Indigenous peoples in Canada.
1997	*Delgamuukw* **decision** – Supreme Court of Canada finds that Aboriginal title to land exists and cannot be extinguished by a provincial government.
2008	Prime Minister Stephen Harper issues a formal **apology to former students of residential schools** for Canada's role in the operation of the schools.
2012	Four women in Saskatchewan start **Idle No More** as a national movement of marches and teach-ins, raising awareness of Indigenous rights and advocating for self-determination.
2015	The Indian Residential School **Truth and Reconciliation Commission** (TRC) delivers its final report. After examining the experiences of 150,000 residential school students and Survivors, the TRC characterizes Canada's treatment of Indigenous Peoples as "cultural genocide."
2016	*Daniels* **decision**: Supreme Court of Canada rules that Métis and non-status Indians are "Indians" within the meaning of s. 91(24) of the *Constitution Act, 1867*. However, like Inuit, they are not granted status under the *Indian Act*.
2016	Canada officially supports the 2007 **UN Declaration on the Rights of Indigenous Peoples**, which recognizes Indigenous Peoples' rights, from land and language rights to self-determination.

2019 The **Missing and Murdered Indigenous Women and Girls National Inquiry** report is published. The inquiry concludes persistent and deadly violence against Indigenous women and girls is a form of genocide.

2021 The discovery of 200 unmarked graves at the Kamloops Indian Residential School in B.C. draws widespread attention to the thousands of deaths of children at residential schools. Hundreds of unmarked graves are subsequently confirmed at former residential school sites across Canada.

DECOLONIZING JOURNALISM

Part I
At the Desk

✦ 1.1 ✦

First Contact

In this chapter, students will learn to:
- identify cultural appropriation in an Indigenous context; and
- recognize the importance of reporting ethically on Indigenous communities.

So. You want to file a news story on Indigenous issues.

You've done some research. You've identified an Indigenous person perfect for your story. It's essential you land this interview. But you feel a bit nervous. Much like Leif Erikson or Jacques Cartier, you're not sure what to expect when you make "first contact." How do you proceed?

Let's begin with the critically important first step—learning the sacred Indian handshake. The sacred Indian handshake goes like this: When you first meet an Indigenous person, hold out your left hand. NEVER, ever extend your right hand—I can't emphasize this enough. Now, lift your thumb, on your left hand, to a 90-degree angle, then extend your index finger . . .

I'm kidding.

There is no sacred Indian handshake. Nope. There's no magic way to sweep back the "buckskin curtain," revealing a mother lode of news scoops secretly hidden in Indigenous communities. Reporting news from Indigenous communities is like reporting on any subject. It's hard work.

So, let's begin again. I'm going to write down a word. I'd like you to note the first thing that pops into your head when you read it. Here's the word.

INDIAN

Okay. What went through your mind? When I first started teaching journalism (in the late Aughts, around about the time Apple Inc., introduced a newfangled electronic device called the iPhone), I performed this exercise with my journalism students. I wrote "Indian" on the chalkboard, and they'd shout words at me like crazy. After a couple minutes, the list looked something like this:

Tomahawk Chop. Reserves. Pocahontas. Curry. Feathers. Mohawk. Buckskin. Totem pole. Powwow. Land claims. Columbus. Drunk. Headdress. Culture. Cleveland. Welfare. Self-government. Suicide. Hunting. Spiritual. Poverty. Jeep.

The list went on and on. It's a list heavy on images of "Indians" in Canadian popular culture. Invariably, the list did *not* include many, many different things being talked about "around the water cooler" in contemporary Indigenous communities,[1] such as

Daycare. Water polo. Auto mechanic. Sex. Baby Yoda. Vacuuming. Tooth decay. School supplies. Millionaire. Diapers. Piano lessons. Cheerios. Duvet covers. Happiness. Internet. Journalism professor.

What's my point? The word "Indian" has all kinds of images associated with it. And those images are far from a complete picture of life for Indigenous people in Canada. "The Indian began as a White man's mistake, and became a White man's fantasy," writes Daniel Francis in his very helpful book *The Imaginary Indian*.[2] Francis argues there is no such thing as an Indian; rather, the Indian is an image of Indigenous people that Euro-Canadians "manufactured, believed in, feared, despised, admired and taught their children," an image which continues to shape public policy in Canada today.

Inuit also know what it's like to contend with such manufactured imagery, having long been referred to as "Eskimos," depicted wearing parkas, paddling kayaks, building igloos, surrounded by polar bears and seals.

Who created those images of Indians and Eskimos? Anthropologists, explorers, missionaries, photographers, historians, medical researchers, artists, and filmmakers, to name a few.

There's a long history of non-Indigenous people coming to Indigenous communities, asking about people's lives, requesting their stories, then *leaving*. Those visitors interpreted what they saw and heard—in books, reports, studies, films, or photos. Indigenous people had little say in how those stories were told; in many cases, the story never even made it back to them.

Some of those images were accurate representations of Indigenous people. Many were not. Indigenous people know what happened with *those* stories. Nowadays, the whole world has an image of what an Indian/Eskimo looks like. How an Indian/Eskimo acts. What an Indian/Eskimo is. Often those representations are stereotypical. Sometimes they're harmful. What does this have to do with journalists?

You are the latest in a long line of storytellers, requesting permission to portray Indigenous Peoples to the world. If you are calling, or going to meet, an Indigenous person for an interview for the first time, that Indigenous person may have an image of *you* in their head. You may be a story-taker—someone who is going to take their story away. And, if history is a guide, there's a good chance that a) that Indigenous person is correct, and b) you're going to get that story wrong.

But I'm different, you protest. I'm a capital-J Journalist, whose guiding principles are Truth, Independence, Accountability, and Minimizing Harm.

Maybe so. But, in the next chapter, I'll examine how long-standing stereotypes of Indigenous people continue to be repeated in contemporary news broadcasts and on the front pages of newspapers.

And, remember this. If the Indigenous person you hope to interview seems angry, standoffish, uncommunicative—well, we've got hundreds of years of contact to thank for that. It's up to us, as skilled journalists, to be aware of the patterns, appreciate the frustration, and persevere.

EXERCISE 1   First Impressions Worksheet

You have ten minutes, in class, to complete this "First Impressions" worksheet. The purpose of this worksheet is to encourage you to examine your current beliefs about Indigenous people. I assume many of you already know quite a bit. This will not be graded or distributed publicly, so please be candid.

Don't worry about being "politically correct." There are no right or wrong answers.

NAME:

First Impressions Worksheet

Please use <u>one-word</u> responses to complete these statements:

In the past, Indigenous Peoples were _____.

Now, many are _____.

Three characteristics that I think describe Indigenous Peoples are _____ _____ _____.

Sometimes, I feel _____ when preparing to interview a person who is of Indigenous descent.

I think the biggest problem for Indigenous Peoples here in Canada is _____.

I think their greatest strength is _____.

One thing journalists need to do is to be more _____ when working with Indigenous people.

It is _____ to answer these questions.

On a scale of 1–10 (1 low, 10 high), I rank my knowledge of Indigenous issues as _____.

This worksheet is adapted from the Indigenous Cultural Competency curriculum developed by the Provincial Health Service Authority in B.C.

Discussion Questions

1. If Indigenous Peoples are imagined or stereotyped as "stuck in the past," how do these ideas impact Indigenous Peoples themselves? Who benefits from these stereotypes?
2. Do you typically imagine yourself as a storyteller? How do your perceptions about your role change if you imagine a journalist as a "story-taker"?
3. What do you recall learning or hearing about Indigenous Peoples in your elementary and secondary schooling?

Additional Readings and Resources

APTN's *First Contact*: A Canadian docuseries aimed at unpacking the hard-baked stereotypes and preconceived notions White Canadians hold about Indigenous people and communities. https://www.aptn.ca/firstcontact/

Daniel Francis, *The Imaginary Indian: The Image of the Indian in Canadian Culture* (Vancouver, B.C: Arsenal Pulp Press, 1992).

Neil Diamond, Rezolution Pictures Inc., et al, *Reel Injun*. Lorber Films, 2010.

Thomas King, *I'm Not the Indian You Had in Mind*. National Screen Institute, 2012. http://www.nsi-canada.ca/2012/03/im-not-the-indian-you-had-in-mind/

Endnotes

1 Yes, conversations about such matters actually do take place around water coolers in many First Nation communities, given that's still the only way to access clean drinking water.

2 Daniel Francis, *The Imaginary Indian: The Image of the Indian in Canadian Culture* (Vancouver, B.C: Arsenal Pulp Press, 1992), 5.

✦ 1.2 ✦
Historical News Stereotypes of Indigenous Peoples

> *In this chapter, students will learn to:*
> - *identify common stereotypes of Indigenous Peoples in the news;*
> - *examine the narrative lens through which news stories are told; and*
> - *evaluate what representations of Indigenous Peoples have formed their worldviews.*

The myth of the drunken Indian has been retired in favour of the legend of the crooked band council.[1]

– Stephen Hume

An Elder once told me the only way an Indian[2] would make it into the news is if they were one of the four Ds:

- Drumming;
- Dancing;
- Drunk; or
- Dead.

C'mon, I said, that's simplistic. I can show you all kinds of different news stories—about Indigenous workers running a forestry operation, an Indigenous student winning a scholarship, or an Indigenous group repatriating a sacred artifact.

But after that encounter, I got to thinking more about what he said, as you often do with Elders' stories. I started looking more closely at Indigenous people in the news. Those four Ds sure do show up an awful lot (if that repatriation event has some drumming and dancing goin' on, the reporter is bound to squeeze both into the story). Actually, if you take that Elder's four Ds and add one more, you could make it a rule on how Indians (or Inuit or Métis) can make the news.

The "Five Ds Rule" on How Indians Make the News

#1 Act Defiantly

It's a photo so iconic it has a title. "Face to Face." A baby-faced soldier staring down a masked warrior. Shaney Komulainen's snapshot during the Oka Crisis in 1990 so perfectly captured longstanding racial and national tensions that *The Beaver* magazine named it one of the Top Five News Photos That Changed Canada. The photo personifies Indigenous defiance.

Face to Face.
Canadian soldier Patrick Cloutier and Brad Larocque (alias "Freddy Krueger," an Anishinaabe university student from Saskatchewan who drove to Quebec to support the Mohawk Warriors), come face to face in a tense standoff at the Kanesatake reserve in Oka, Que., on Sept. 1, 1990.

But consider a different photo, also captured during the Oka Crisis, one that doesn't have a title. Maybe it should. I'd suggest "Media Circus." It is equally telling, about how the media actively *shapes* perceptions about confrontation and conflict between Canada and Indigenous people.

Why does direct action by Indigenous groups, such as marches, blockades, or occupations, receive disproportionate attention from the news media? Yes, protests often meet the test of whether a story is "newsworthy," because they're unusual, dramatic,

Media Circus.
Over 4,000 soldiers took up positions in and around Kanestake and Kahnawake, along with armoured vehicles, helicopters, artillery and police boats, in order to confront roughly 40–50 Mohawks and supporters. When the army began to advance on September 1, 1990, there were multiple face-to-face confrontations, with large numbers of media present.

or involve conflict. Yes, Indigenous activists, who understand the media's hunger for drama, also play a role by tailoring protests in ways that guarantee prominent headlines and lead stories.

But does today's front-page news of some traffic disruption in the name of Indigenous land rights actually have its roots in a much older narrative—of violent and "uncivilized" Indians who represent a threat to "progress" in Canada? Are attitudes of distrust and fear underlying our decisions to dispatch a crew to the latest Indigenous blockade? Are there no iconic photos of *reconciliation*, because no one from the newsrooms believes harmony between Indigenous Peoples and settlers is "newsworthy"?

#2 Beat Your Drum

It's easy to laugh, these days, at those ridiculous Hollywood Indian stereotypes of yesteryear: Indians wearing feathers, grunting in monosyllables, "circling the wagons." But contemporary news stories continue to reproduce the mainstay of those old Westerns—the Indian drums.

Even if you're not a fan of cowboy movies, you probably learned that "Indian" beat in the schoolyard—BMMM bmmm bmmm bmmm BMMM bmmm bmmm bmmm BMMM bmmm bmmm bmmm. Indians about to ride over the hill, on the warpath. Indians doing a rain dance. That sort of thing.

Well, how many broadcast news stories start with Indigenous drumming? Reporters seem entranced by those drums, whether they be Indigenous protests or Indigenous celebrations. (And if there are no drums around, heaven forbid, then hurry up and find some flute music for the background track!)

Sure, I get it. You need sound and action to start your piece with a kick.

But do you ask the purpose and meaning of the song? Is it an honour song, a prayer song, a memorial song? Do you request a translation of the lyrics, or just describe it as "chanting"? Or do you just let those frozen-in-time Indians beat their drums, leaving it to your audience to interpret? (I'll bet many viewers heave a mighty sigh and groan, "Oh, drums. Indians on the warpath. What do they want *this time*?")

#3 Start Dancing

The dancing thing goes hand-in-hand with drumming. Indians in traditional regalia fit a popular but superficial interpretation of Canadian multiculturalism. Please, share your entertaining costumes and dances, and, yes, we'd love to taste your exotic food!

Actually, Indians outfitted in buckskin and feathers (whether real Indians like Pauline Johnson or fake Indians like Grey Owl) have long been objects of fascination and even admiration. To many Canadians, an Indigenous person wearing a button blanket or beaded vest represents a bygone era. Dressed-up Indians are benign, without all those messy contemporary problems—suicides and land claims, mouldy houses, and tax exemption.

Newsrooms, in the same way, are not immune to this nostalgia for "Indians." Why are chiefs so often portrayed wearing traditional regalia, rather than dashing through airports, barking into cellphones? How many TV newscasts use an over-the-shoulder graphic of a feather to signify an "Indian" story? Is it powwow time again? Get a camera over there!

Trust me. If you're an Indigenous person and you want to make the news, haul out your headdress (or give one to the Prime Minister).

#4 Get Drunk

No question, alcohol is at the root of many stories reporters cover in Indigenous communities—car accidents, murders, assaults, and the like.

But does that age-old stereotype of the "drunken Indian" have any basis in reality?

No, asserted the Royal Commission on Aboriginal Peoples (RCAP), after examining several studies that show abstinence is twice as frequent among Indigenous Peoples as it is in non-Indigenous communities. Heavy drinking is more prevalent among Indigenous people than it is in the mainstream, but the proportion of people who drink on a daily basis is seven times higher among non-Indigenous people than among Indigenous people. "The widely held belief that most Indigenous people consume excessive amounts of alcohol on a regular basis appears to be incorrect," RCAP concluded.[3]

Do the countless stories we cover about Indigenous people involving alcohol help reinforce the myth of the "drunken Indian"? Ask yourself: is alcohol relevant to the story, and why? The media often stays mum about the drinking habits of notable Canadian politicians—would alcohol be part of your story if this was about a non-Indigenous person?

#5 Be Dead

Go to a news search engine such as Google News and search "dead" and "Indigenous" (or equivalent terms such as "Aboriginal" or "First Nations" or "Inuit"). I'll bet my grandmother's dreamcatcher your cup overfloweth with news from across the country.

Newsrooms have this thing for death, anywhere it's happening. "It bleeds, it leads," right? Sadly, in Canada, there's a disproportionate amount of death happening in Indigenous communities. Maybe that explains why we see so many dead Indigenous people in the news.

But what does this constant barrage of dead Indigenous people tell our audiences about Indigenous communities in Canada? That Indigenous life in Canada is, to quote philosopher Thomas Hobbes and one infamous judge in British Columbia, "nasty, brutish and short"?[4] Or, nefariously, that "the only good Indian is a dead Indian"?[5]

Okay, I admit I'm trying to stir the pot with the Five Ds Rule. Still, research shows news reports from Indigenous communities tend to follow extremely narrow narratives based on pre-existing stereotypes of Indians. For a far more sophisticated analysis, I strongly recommend you read *Seeing Red: A History of Natives in Canadian Newspapers* by history professors Mark Anderson and Carmen Robertson. *Seeing Red* is a comprehensive piece of scholarship that provides ample evidence that colonial imagery has not only thrived but dominates depictions of Indigenous Peoples in Canadian newspapers. I'll get to their analysis in a moment.

But first, let's take a step back and ask—what is a stereotype anyway?

Indigenous Stereotypes in Media

Whether we're aware of it or not, reporters use stereotypes. A lot. News happens fast, and we need quick ways to simplify our storylines to make sure our audience "gets it."

Stereotypes act like codes, giving audiences an instant, common understanding of a person or group of people—usually relating to their class, ethnicity or race, gender, sexual orientation, social role, or occupation (for example, "NHL hockey players have physical stamina" is a safe assumption, even if it's not based on statistical fact).

Things get problematic when stereotypes are based on untruths. Unfortunately, there's ample evidence of reporters basing stereotypes about Indigenous Peoples on false assumptions. By repeating stereotypes, journalists have the power to transform assumptions about Indigenous Peoples into "realities" that reinforce discrimination and prejudice.

Media stereotypes of Indigenous Peoples have tended to shift depending on the concerns of the age. In fact, there's evidence the Five Ds Rule is being replaced by more complex, more refined stereotypes.

In 1996, when the RCAP examined representations of Indigenous Peoples in the media, they concluded that many Canadians know Indigenous people only as the Pathetic Victim, the Noble Environmentalist, or the Angry Warrior:

> Aboriginal people are portrayed in a historical past reconstructed in present stereotypes: the noble Red Man roaming free in the forest; the bloodthirsty savage attacking the colony or the wagon train; the drunken Indian; the Aboriginal environmentalist; and, most recently, the warrior in para-military dress, wielding a gun. . . . As with all stereotypes, there is a kernel of truth in the images, which assume a dramatic profile and become etched in the popular consciousness. But stereotypes block out complexity of context and diversity of personality and perspective.[6]

In 2002, Crystal Maslin used her master's thesis to examine how Saskatchewan newspapers have constructed portrayals of Indigenous people,[7] identifying the two used most frequently:

- The "Troublemaker"—politically active Indigenous Peoples portrayed as advocating for recognition of rights and the promise of government funds, *at the expense of other Canadians*; and
- The "Good Indian"—individuals who are successful according to the standards of dominant society by *not* relying on welfare and paying income tax, *despite* their racial background (implying that it is personal deficiencies rather than structural barriers that prevent widespread Indigenous success).

In 2005, social work professor Robert Harding found the "Native-as-environmentalist" stereotype to be on the wane, while a new stereotype was emerging: Indigenous people as "incompetent or corrupt financial managers." Harding suggested this pattern of news discourse "protects the status quo while limiting the potential for Indigenous self-determination." While self-governance may be the ultimate goal for many Indigenous Peoples, Harding wrote, "others may see these aspirations primarily in terms of the threat they pose to their lifestyle and standard of living."[8]

There are many other ways media frame news stories about Indigenous Peoples, and there are certainly regional variations (for example, "Native-as-gangster" news stories abound in the Prairies, just as "casino-rich Natives" stories are common in the United States).

However, there was little qualitative analysis of media representations of Indigenous people in Canada until Robertson and Anderson published *Seeing Red*, a ground-breaking study of how Canadian English-language newspapers portrayed Indigenous Peoples between 1869–2011.[9]

After investigating a wide range of news coverage on topics ranging over a century of Canadian history, Robertson and Anderson concluded that contemporary stereotypes of Indigenous people (the moribund Native, the savage, the Indian princess, the stoic Native, the childish Native, the drunken Indian) are in fact, colonial archetypes. That is to say, these negative characteristics describing Indigenous Peoples remain widely held views today, in part, *because* they've been popping up in news stories for a very long time.

The authors suggest Canadian newspapers have consistently expressed ideas and representations that boil down to three overlapping "essentialisms" purportedly exhibited by Indigenous people:[10]

1) **moral depravity** (such as poor parenting, laziness, and a tendency toward violence and sexual debauchery);
2) **inherent racial inferiority** (which leads to poor decision-making and childish, frequently irrational, behaviour such as violent crime or tendency toward mayhem); and
3) **resistance to progress** (often expressed as remaining stubbornly mired in an unprogressive and non-evolving past).

Seeing Red argues Canadian media have "long identified and championed alleged Native inferiority"[11] and provide examples of 140 years of mainstream news coverage to back it up. What may be surprising to some Canadians is that these colonial narratives haven't changed or improved over time. Certainly, news prose is no longer overtly racist—no journalist in the twenty-first century would use the term "squaw" to refer to an Indigenous woman. But the kinds of stereotypes Robertson and Anderson found in newspapers in the late-nineteenth century, in news reports and editorials regarding the sale of Rupert's Land or the Northwest Rebellion, were still being reproduced in the late-twentieth century, in reports about Bill C-31 and the Oka Crisis.

"Colonialism has always thrived in Canada's press,"[12] write Robertson and Anderson. By perpetuating an imagined Native inferiority, the authors argue that Canadian journalists have been anything but objective. Instead, according to Robertson and Anderson, journalists have reflected their own biases in their reportage and helped prop up the colonial project, serving as "a kind of national curriculum" that paved the way for Indian treaties and residential schools:

> Canada's mainstream newspapers have aided and abetted the marginalization of Aboriginals in Canada. Overall, the results can only have been deleterious for the million-plus Canadians today of Aboriginal heritage, though it is impossible to tease out the specific media effects when the press operates as just one among many influences. Yet clearly the printed press has, since the sale of Rupert's Land, operated as a principal voice of and for Canadian-style colonialism.[13]

Fast forward a few more years. In 2015, the Truth and Reconciliation Commission (TRC) observed that the historical pattern of stereotypes and colonial journalism persists: "Media coverage of Aboriginal issues remains problematic; social media and online commentary are often inflammatory and racist in nature."[14] In keeping with its broad conclusion that the path to reconciliation would be achieved through better education, the TRC called for journalism schools to educate the next generation of journalists on everything from the history of residential schools to the United Nations Declaration on the Rights of Indigenous Peoples and Indigenous law. (See Appendix 2 for full text of TRC Calls to Action 84 to 86, which deal with Media and Reconciliation.)

Lest you consider stereotypes a thing of the past, take a look at the editorial cartoons published in Canadian newspapers at the height of the SNC-Lavalin scandal in 2019.

The conflict pitted Prime Minister Justin Trudeau against his former justice minister Jody Wilson-Raybould, who happens to be of Kwakwaka'wakw descent. Several cartoonists were criticized for offensive depictions of Wilson-Raybould, the most egregious being a piece by Yannick Lemay of *le Journal de Québec/Journal de Montréal*. He portrayed Wilson-Raybould in buckskin and feathers, wielding a tomahawk.

Lemay later apologized. "The next time I have to draw an Indigenous person, I will have to ask myself what are the appropriate ways to imagine someone of Indigenous ancestry now. I admit that I have not found it for the moment but it will come."[15]

Cartoon of Jody Wilson-Raybould and Prime Minister Justin Trudeau.
On March 1, 2019, after Justice Minister Jody Wilson-Raybould had resigned from cabinet alleging undue pressure from the Prime Minister's Office over the SNC-Lavalin affair, *Le Journal de Montréal* published this cartoon by Yannick Lemay (who draws under the name Ygreck). Lemay later apologized, saying "If I offended someone with this drawing, obviously I'm sorry."

Here's the bottom line: when it comes to representations of Indigenous Peoples in our stories: as journalists, our first obligation is to the truth. We need to convey accurate facts in context. That means that when covering Indigenous communities, we need to resist the shortcut of stereotypes.

Be conscious of your own personal and cultural biases. Examine what you were taught in school about Indigenous Peoples, and, just as importantly, what was *missing* from your education. Finally, verify the information you report. Otherwise, you risk undermining the accuracy of your work and adding fuel to the fire of existing stereotypes.

> **EXERCISE 1** Imaginary Indians
>
> In this exercise, you'll be telling a story about an Indian from your childhood.
>
> Perhaps it's a fictional Indian in a book or a movie, or a real person you heard or saw or met. That Indian (or Indigenous person) needs to have made an impression on you.
>
> Share with your classmates, orally, a two-minute story about that Indian/Indigenous person. Bring him or her (or them) to life for us. What did they look like? What kind of impact did this person (or people) have on you?
>
> Though you may plan how you want to tell this story, and you may rehearse if you wish, you don't need to write it out, and you will *not* be allowed to read off paper in class.
>
> Try to dig deep into your memory for this exercise. If your story seems embarrassing or even racist today, please don't let that stop you from sharing. The idea here is to explore the imaginary "Indians" we all have buried in our consciousness, and try to understand how they shape our present-day lives.

Discussion Questions

1. Has anyone ever made an assumption about you because of a stereotype that was untrue? How did you react to the situation? Did you express how you felt to the person who made the erroneous assumption?

2. What are effective ways to respond when you or someone you know is the target of stereotyping?

3. Take a close look at and describe some of the elements of Shaney Komulainen's famous photograph during the Oka Crisis, "Face to Face," shown earlier in this section. What story does it tell about the two men in the photograph? Why do you think it became so iconic? How is this single image symbolic of the larger relationship between Canada and Indigenous Peoples?

4. Find a photo in a news story that involves an Indigenous person. Be prepared to discuss it in class. What interests you about the photo? What do you think of the photo's technical quality (i.e., composition, story, creativity, light, impact)? What do you think of how Indigenous cultural elements are portrayed?

5. Sports team names, such as the Blackhawks and Braves, as well as brand names such as Pontiac automobiles, are well known and are part and parcel of the cultural and economic landscape. Why do sports teams, in particular, use First Nations names and figures? Do these names and terms affect people's perceptions of Indigenous Peoples? How?

6. As you journey to Indigenous communities, you may find that Indigenous people sometimes encourage, expand, and even exploit stereotypes. For example, it's not uncommon to encounter First Nation baseball teams sporting jerseys with a Chicago Blackhawks logo, or First Nation hockey teams dubbed the Chiefs. How should a reporter respond to or present stereotypical Indigenous imagery if it is displayed by Indigenous people themselves?
7. How have stereotypical images and ideas in the news supported colonialism?
8. What other stereotypes have you seen in the news media? How are different ethnic or cultural groups portrayed? What about women? LGBTQ2SIA+ folks? Immigrants?

Additional Readings and Resources

Mark Anderson and Carmen Robertson, *Seeing Red: A History of Natives in Canadian Newspapers* (Winnipeg, Manitoba: University of Manitoba Press, 2011).

Thomas King, *The Inconvenient Indian: A Curious Account of Native People in North America* (Toronto: Doubleday, 2012).

David Treuer, *The Heartbeat of Wounded Knee: Native America from 1890 to the Present* (New York: Riverhead Books, 2019).

Jody Wilson-Raybould, *"Indian" in the Cabinet: Speaking Truth to Power* (Toronto: Harper Collins, 2021).

Rima Wilkes et al, "Packaging Protest: Media Coverage of Indigenous People's Collective Action." *Canadian Review of Sociology* 47 (2010), 349–379.

Jennifer Wells, "A Warrior, a Soldier and a Photographer." *Toronto Star* (August 22, 2015). https://www.thestar.com/news/insight/2015/08/22/a-warrior-a-soldier-and-a-photographer-remembering-the-oka-crisis.html

Helen Knott, "The Indigenous People I Read About as a Kid Were Nothing Like Me—So I Became a Writer." *Chatelaine* (June 21, 2017). https://www.chatelaine.com/living/indigenous-representation-literature/

American Indians in Children's Literature (AICL) provides critical perspectives and analysis of Indigenous peoples in children's and young adult books. https://americanindiansinchildrensliterature.blogspot.com/p/about.html

Endnotes

1. Stephen Hume, "Seems No One's Without Sin in the Practice of Self-Government," *Vancouver Sun*, March 1, 2006.
2. I use the term "Indian" throughout this textbook in a variety of contexts. In this instance, it is used conversationally, between two Indigenous people. I offer some specific advice in the Terminology and Lexicon chapter on how and when the term "Indian" should be used by journalists. I'm from a generation of Indigenous people who use the word colloquially, but be aware that some Indigenous people may be offended if the word is used inappropriately by non-Indigenous people.
3. Canada, Georges Erasmus, and René Dussault, *Report of the Royal Commission on Aboriginal Peoples: Volume 3—Gathering Strength* (Ottawa: The Commission, 1996), 150.
4. In 1991, the B.C. Supreme court issued a decision in the landmark Aboriginal title claim of the Gitxsan and Wet'suwet'en peoples. Denying their claim, Chief Justice Allan McEachern described pre-contact life of the Gitxsan and Wet'suwet'en as

"nasty, brutish, and short." The decision has been criticized for both its treatment of oral evidence and its tone. It was overturned by the Supreme Court of Canada in 1997.

5. Prior to his election as U.S. President, Theodore Roosevelt said in a speech in New York in 1886, "I don't go so far as to think that the only good Indians are the dead Indians, but I believe nine out of every 10 are. And I shouldn't like to inquire too closely into the case of the tenth." The phrase has also been attributed to Phillip Henry Sheridan, a U.S. Army general who fought in the Indian Wars in the mid-19th century.

6. Canada, Georges Erasmus, and René Dussault, *Report of the Royal Commission on Aboriginal Peoples: Volume 3—Gathering Strength* (Ottawa: The Commission, 1996), 581.

7. Crystal Lynn Maslin, "Social construction of aboriginal people in the Saskatchewan print media." Unpublished thesis, 2002. https://harvest.usask.ca/handle/10388/etd-06202008-130404

8. Robert Harding, "The Media, Aboriginal People, and Common Sense," *The Canadian Journal of Native Studies* 25.1 (2005), 331.

9. Mark Anderson and Carmen Robertson, *Seeing Red: A History of Natives in Canadian Newspapers* (Winnipeg, Manitoba: University of Manitoba Press, 2011).

10. Ibid., 7.
11. Ibid., 275.
12. Ibid., 4.
13. Ibid., 274.
14. Truth and Reconciliation Commission of Canada, *Truth and Reconciliation Commission of Canada Interim Report* (Winnipeg: Truth and Reconciliation Commission of Canada, 2012), 275.
15. Ka'nhehsí:io Deer, "Quebec Political Cartoonist 'Sorry' for Feathers and Fringe Portrayal of Wilson-Raybould," *CBC Indigenous*, March 1, 2019. https://www.cbc.ca/news/indigenous/quebec-cartoon-jody-wilson-raybould-denounced-1.5038862

✦ 1.3 ✦

Beyond Victims and Warriors: Choosing Indigenous News Stories

> In this chapter, students will learn to:
> - use wide-ranging methods of finding Indigenous news stories;
> - discover new story sources that include Indigenous publications and newsmakers; and
> - conduct research in person, when possible.

> *Indian Country is more than a legal entity and a state of mind. It is a place journalism must find—by going there—walking the ground, encountering the people, asking questions, listening to the answers.*[1]
>
> – Victor Merina

Bingo!

With stereotypes of Indigenous people so discouragingly common in American media, the Native American Journalists Association (NAJA) decided it needed an innovative and engaging way to prompt discussion about the harmful tropes about Indigenous Peoples that keep recurring in news stories.

In 2017, NAJA issued a tongue-in-cheek Reporting in Indian Country bingo card, filled not with numbers but with clichés and stereotypes about Indigenous Peoples. If a reporter has one of these words or phrases in their copy, the reporter has to mark that square. If the story gets a BINGO, it's time to go back to the drawing board, explained then vice-president of NAJA Tristan Ahtone:

> Because news organizations often refuse to commit time, energy or resources to covering Indigenous communities in real or meaningful ways, coverage is often shallow and formulaic. The bingo board is designed to draw attention to stereotypes and cultural bias reporters employ when framing their stories. It's the responsibility of journalists to combat clichés in order to ensure that information is accurate, fair and thorough.[2]

The Native American Journalists Association Bingo card.
The Native American Journalists Association (NAJA) produced the Reporting in Indian Country bingo card in 2017 to encourage reporters to identify stereotypes in their stories and improve storytelling in Indigenous communities.

Unfortunately, Canadian newsrooms give their American neighbours a run for their money when it comes to scoring a bingo on stereotypes.

If you want to avoid stereotypical news coverage from Indigenous communities, the trick is not to parrot back the latest press conference called by the government or some Indigenous group. It's time to start digging up different stories that don't fall into tired victim/warrior narratives. Simple enough, right? You just need to have your ears to the ground in Indigenous communities. Here are a few ways to do that:

- Check in regularly with Indigenous news websites (some suggestions are listed at the end of this chapter and in the Additional Resources chapter).
- Use social media (such as Facebook, Twitter, Instagram, or TikTok) to reach out and get connected with Indigenous users.
- "Colour balance" your Rolodex by developing a database of Indigenous contacts, and nurture relationships with those contacts over time.
- Establish a database to catalogue research and ideas for future stories (those little snippets of conversation that may not make news today but could be a story down the road).
- Consult Indigenous colleagues in your newsroom.[3]

How Research Can Build Trust

But let's not kid ourselves. Finding those unique stories in Indigenous communities is hard work. You need to develop sources, know your history, and be doggedly persistent. You need to listen, listen, listen.

More often than not, it takes a "pre-research" trip to the rez to build trust (or, in the case of an urban Indigenous community, a trip to *that* side of town). Indeed, you'll have greater success finding stories in Indigenous communities if you get off the phone and do your research in person. The distrust of mainstream media that's built up over years (referred to by one reporter as "guilty until proven innocent" syndrome) often dissolves when a reporter simply finds the time to *meet* a story subject.

Many people—not just Indigenous people—prefer face-to-face interviews because it's easier to gauge a person's sincerity and understand their motives. Doors will start to open for you when an Indigenous person discovers you're willing to show respect for Indigenous culture and listen to what they are saying.

But to really listen, you'll need to set aside (at least momentarily) frames of storytelling hardwired into most news reporters: negative news and the search for conflict. More on that in the next chapter.

EXERCISE 1 "The Land You Live On" Worksheet

Whose land are you on?

It may seem like a simple question, with a quick and easy answer. However, in many cases, colonial history in Canada has silenced Indigenous voices and erased Indigenous identities from the land where we all live. If the relationship between

Indigenous and non-Indigenous Peoples is to improve, it's important that all Canadians understand more about the land they live on through an Indigenous perspective.

Use this worksheet to learn more about the Indigenous Peoples in the city/town where you live and practise journalism. In your research, consider both the historical and contemporary context of the Indigenous group(s). (This sheet is adapted from a similar exercise on the Historica Canada website.)[4]

As a starting point, check out these websites documenting Indigenous territories:

- Native land. https://Native-land.ca/
- Whose land. https://www.whose.land/en/
- *Teacher tip: This activity can be completed in pairs or in small groups.*

Table 1.1 The Land You Live On

Peoples • List the Indigenous groups originally inhabiting the territory where you live. • How do the members of the Indigenous group identify themselves? (For example, some Ojibways prefer to be called Anishinaabe, and some Shuswap may prefer the term Secwépemc.)	
Geography • Give a basic description of the traditional territory of the group(s) (e.g., topography, unique geographical features). • Include a map of the territory or the wording of a territorial acknowledgement.	
Languages • List traditional languages/dialects spoken by the group(s). • Do the languages/dialects belong to a larger language family? Additional: How many people speak that language today? List three words in this language/dialect, with accompanying translations.	
Treaties • Has the Indigenous group signed a treaty or treaties with the federal government? Is the land you are living on subject to any treaties? If not, is the land "unceded" or subject to a comprehensive land claim? • What are some of the terms of the treaty/treaties? Additional: What are some of the impacts of the treaty on the Indigenous group?	

continued

Governance • How is the Indigenous group governed (e.g., Indian Act band council, traditional chiefs, tribal or hamlet council)? • How does the Indigenous group create and enact laws? • What types of governmental services does the Indigenous group provide?	
Culture and Economy • List some notable members of the Indigenous group, living or deceased, and their achievements.	
Other Interesting Facts • Use this space to jot down any other bits of information that you find interesting or important.	

EXERCISE 2 Indigenous "Beat" Presentations

Teacher tip: the geographical parameters of this exercise depend on how many diverse Indigenous communities are near your classroom.

Expanding on what you learned from The Land You Live On worksheet, this assignment is designed to introduce you to an Indigenous community and to help you educate your classmates about this place. Choose an Indigenous community either a) near your city/town, or b) in your province/territory.

Pretend you are a producer, and you are preparing a very thorough PowerPoint brief on this community for your network's chief correspondent, who is preparing to visit this community on assignment.

This should be more than a Wikipedia entry. Yes, we want to know vital information such as the community's history, political system, population, languages, etc. But what are the key issues facing the community today?

This should be presented in a creative and entertaining manner. We definitely want to see visuals. Help us understand how this community looks and feels.

You will make your presentation in class for 8–10 minutes.

Discussion Questions

1. List three resources available on your campus and in your community where you could learn more about Indigenous Peoples.
2. Time to play bingo! Find two news stories about Indigenous Peoples, and see how they stack up for stereotypes, using NAJA's Reporting in Indian Country bingo card

(shown earlier). If the story checks multiple boxes, it's a sign it could be cliché. If it gets a BINGO (a full line of checks in any direction), that story needs a major rewrite.

3. What are the advantages and disadvantages of interviewing an Indigenous person in person, rather than via email or over the phone?

Additional Readings and Resources

One of the best ways to become more familiar with covering Indigenous communities is to read Indigenous media regularly. It's a good idea to review Indigenous news outlets daily, looking for news ideas of your own, sources for future reference, or unique treatments. Here's a list of regional, national, and international Indigenous media outlets that will act as a starting point for you.

Regional
Anishinabek News: This monthly community newspaper is produced by the Communications Unit of the Anishinabek Nation at the head office in Nipissing First Nation. https://anishinabeknews.ca/
Eagle Feather News: A leading source of Indigenous news in Saskatchewan. https://www.eaglefeathernews.com/
First Nations Forward: A collection of special reports on Indigenous issues in the *National Observer*. https://www.nationalobserver.com/special-reports/first-nations-forward
Ha-Shilth-Sa: *Ha-Shilth-Sa* is one of Canada's oldest First Nations newspapers and is the newspaper of record of the Nuu-chah-nulth people on Vancouver Island. It has been published by the Nuu-chah-nulth Tribal Council since 1974. https://hashilthsa.com/
IndigiNews: IndigiNews is a partnership between APTN and *The Discourse* to cover Okanagan Valley and Vancouver Island community news. https://indiginews.com/
Ku'ku'kwes: Ku'ku'kwes is a news website dedicated to covering Indigenous news in Atlantic Canada. http://kukukwes.com/
Métis Voyageur: This is a newsletter of the Métis Nation of Ontario. https://www.metisnation.org/news-media/the-metis-voyageur/
Muskrat Magazine: MUSKRAT is an online Indigenous arts and culture magazine that honours the connection between humans and our traditional ecological knowledge by exhibiting original works and critical commentary. http://muskratmagazine.com/
Native Communications Society of the NWT: This organization provides the most extensive Dene-language programming in the world, broadcasting from northern Alberta to the Arctic Ocean. https://ncsnwt.com/
Northern News Services Limited: This aggregator provides access to several community newspapers published by Northern News Services, including *Northwest Territories News*, *Nunavut News*, *The Yellowknifer*, and more. https://www.nnsl.com/
Nunatsiaq News: *Nunatsiaq News* is the newspaper of record for Nunavut and the Nunavik territory of Quebec. It has been published since 1975, and issues from 1997 to the present are available online. https://nunatsiaq.com/
The Discourse: *The Discourse* provides community-powered journalism to underserved communities, including Indigenous communities in British Columbia. https://thediscourse.ca/
The Eastern Door: This is a community-based newspaper from Kahnawake Mohawk Territory in Quebec. https://www.easterndoor.com/
The Nation: *The Nation Magazine* is an independent Indigenous news source serving the Cree of James Bay, including Northern Quebec and Ontario, since 1993. http://nationnews.ca/
The Two Row Times: *The Two Row Times* is a free weekly news publication aimed at Ontario Indigenous communities as well as Haudenosaunee communities in the United States. https://tworowtimes.com/

Tusaayaksat Magazine: *Tusaayaksat Magazine* covers news for the Inuvialuit People with a focus on arts, culture, and history. https://books.apple.com/us/author/tusaayaksat-magazine/id1501900928

TVO Indigenous: Television Ontario (TVO) is a publicly funded English-language educational television network and media organization serving Ontario. https://www.tvo.org/current-affairs/tag/indigenous

Wawatay News: This organization publishes in English and Indigenous languages of northern Ontario, including Ojibway, Oji-Cree, and Cree. It also publishes multimedia content including videos and podcasts. https://www.wawataynews.ca/

National

Aboriginal Peoples Television Network (APTN) National News: National news that provides comprehensive coverage of Indigenous news stories. https://www.aptnnews.ca/

CBC Indigenous: The latest news and current affairs from Indigenous communities across Canada. http://www.cbc.ca/news/indigenous

CBC Unreserved: CBC's radio space for Indigenous community, culture, and conversation. https://www.cbc.ca/listen/live-radio/1-105-unreserved

First Nations Drum: Billed as "Canada's largest First Nations newspaper." http://www.firstnationsdrum.com/

Media Indigena: A weekly Indigenous current affairs podcast. http://www.mediaindigena.com

Uvagut TV: Canada's first Inuktitut television channel, broadcasting a rich 24/7 slate of programming from Inuit producers across Inuit Nunangat. http://www.isuma.tv/es

Windspeaker: Published by the Aboriginal Multi-Media Society (AMMSA), Windspeaker is Edmonton-based and includes national content. windspeaker.com

International

ABC Indigenous (Australia): Australian Broadcasting Corporation's news portal for Aboriginal and Torres Strait Islander people. https://www.abc.net.au/indigenous/

Indian Country Today (USA): This national news site features the work of Indigenous news journalists and aggregated news content with an Indigenous focus. https://indiancountrytoday.com/

National Indigenous Times (Australia): *National Indigenous Times* (NIT) strives to be the most comprehensive Indigenous online news site in Australia by offering rigorous reporting on the issues that affect Aboriginal and Torres Strait Islander peoples. https://nit.com.au/

NITV (Australia): Bills itself as home of Indigenous storytelling, with TV programs that inspire, instill pride, and lead to a greater respect for Indigenous Australians and Aboriginal culture. https://www.sbs.com.au/nitv/

NRK Sápmi (Norway): A unit of the Norwegian Broadcasting Corporation (NRK) that produces Sápmi-language news and other programs. https://www.nrk.no/sapmi/

Te Ao Māori News (New Zealand): The latest news from Māori Television, New Zealand's Indigenous broadcaster. https://www.teaomaori.news/

The Circle News (USA): *The Circle* is a community newspaper that publishes from an Indigenous perspective and is located in Minneapolis, Minnesota. https://thecirclenews.org/

Endnotes

1   Victor Merina, "The Internet: Continuing the Legacy of Storytelling." *Nieman Reports,* September 15, 2005. https://niemanstoryboard.org/articles/the-internet-continuing-the-legacy-of-storytelling/

2   Mike Howell, "Media called out for cliched First Nations coverage." *Vancouver Is Awesome,* September 26, 2017.

3   Before you consult an Indigenous colleague, ensure you've taken as many steps as possible

to do your research. Indigenous journalists are busy with their own work. It's not in the job description for Indigenous journalists to educate their colleagues, yet this kind of "invisible labour" is commonplace. Similarly, don't expect an Indigenous journalist to hand over contacts for your story. Building relationships with sources is hard work—no journalist wants to see their relationships with sources unwittingly harmed by another journalist.

4 Historica Canada, *Indigenous Perspectives Education Guide,* https://fb.historicacanada.ca/education/english/indigenous-perspectives/IndigenousPerspectives/assets/common/downloads/publication.pdf

✦ 1.4 ✦
Positive versus Negative Stories

> *In this chapter, students will learn to:*
> - *produce news coverage balanced between "positive" and "negative" news by expanding their evaluation of "newsworthy" Indigenous stories; and*
> - *create a range of stories, by including Indigenous people in "non-Indigenous" stories, avoiding "calendar journalism," and looking beyond conflict.*

> *The fundamental nature of news and news reporting depends on bad news to garner ratings, which means that tragedies, conflicts and crises get reported and success stories rarely do. With this in mind, it is easy to understand why a non-Indigenous audience might come to the conclusion that Indigenous people are a troubled, plagued and contentious people.*[1]
>
> – MediaSmarts

It's a common tale among Indigenous people of a certain age who grew up watching Western movies: when it came time to play "Cowboys and Indians," Indigenous kids often opted for the role of cowboy. Who would want to play the Indian—that violent and inept tomahawk-wielding savage whose appearances were marked by ominous drum themes?

Beyond Negative Stories

News stories from Indigenous communities, so often negative in tone and subject matter, aren't unlike that evil Hollywood Indian. Who would blame Indigenous people for being weary of "disaster coverage" from their communities? What impact does a relentless stream of negative news have on the self-esteem of Indigenous youth? If non-Indigenous audiences form their impressions about Indigenous Peoples from the news, who would be surprised if they develop unfavourable opinions?

That said, it's hard to fight the prevailing wisdom of most newsrooms: bad news is sexy. Years of experience have taught us that news about conflict, disaster, and death gets clicks, grabs eyeballs, and sells papers.

However, if we don't attempt to strike a balance in our coverage—between the positive and negative—we risk alienating our Indigenous audience and, over time, contributing to an unbalanced perspective of Indigenous communities.

Tell a Range of Stories

Hard news, human interest, and features. If you have a track record of presenting a variety of Indigenous perspectives—solutions as well as problems, reconciliation as well as discord—Indigenous people will notice, and you'll discover that almost any subject is fair game.

Include Indigenous People in "Non-Indigenous" Stories

Don't seek out only Indigenous people for "Indigenous" stories (whether those stories are "good" or "bad"). Consult Indigenous people for their take on any sort of local, provincial, national, and international story. What do Indigenous folks think about the weather, the trade mission to China, or interest rates? When searching for parents for your annual back-to-school story, can you interview an Attagutaluk and a Longclaws, as well as a Smith and a Singh?

Avoid "Calendar Journalism"

Some newsrooms, in an attempt to portray minorities more equitably, roll out annual stories about multicultural celebrations, such as Chinese New Year or Diwali. The Indigenous versions of this "calendar journalism" are the annual stories on pow-wows, cultural gatherings, and National Indigenous Peoples Day. These events are undoubtedly important to Indigenous people, but studies of minority news audiences show they want more than fluffy stories about food and festivals. They want up-to-date, accurate, and factual coverage of events that reflect and impact on their lives. In other words, they want journalism—so don't pitch your journalistic principles out the window just to meet a diversity quota.

Don't Bury the "Good News"

Most newsrooms regularly shop for human-interest and "feel-good" stories to balance out all that violence and tragedy our audiences tell us they dislike. In fact, it's not too hard to find "good news" or "success" stories involving Indigenous people, but these stories often get buried—at the back end of newscasts or in the lifestyle sections of newspapers. Don't let "bad news" grab all the attention. Take credit for that strong human-interest story (and balance out your audience's perception of Indigenous Peoples) by using promotional spots at your disposal—whether it's an ad on your website, or targeted tweets, or "bumpers" early on in a broadcast to promote stories that the audience might otherwise overlook.

Don't Shy Away from "Bad News"

In an effort to achieve balanced coverage of Indigenous communities, journalists shouldn't pussyfoot around controversial issues or neglect their role as watchdogs. It's our job to ask accountability questions. Indigenous people themselves want to know if there's corruption or mismanagement within their own organizations, or if individuals are being mistreated within their community. Negative media attention can be a powerful catalyst for positive social change. But investigative and adversarial stories represent a quandary for journalists from powerful media corporations, according to journalism professor John Hartley, in his examination of media portrayal of Indigenous Peoples in Australia:

> *Good* journalism requires fearless critique, impartial treatment and no allegiance to party or faction—it requires professional *indifference*. But this is exactly what looks like unethical journalism to people in an outsider group whose organizations and leaders are dragged over the coals on what seems like a routine basis. To them, such journalism looks like part of the control strategies of a regime in which they have no independent stake. Fearless reporting isn't experienced as a cleansing agent in "our" body politic, but as a toxic weapon in "their" arsenal.[2]

There's no easy solution to that, but if we treat Indigenous stories with kid gloves, we can be sure they won't resonate with our audience.

Look beyond Conflict

From war zones to squabbles over potholes at city hall, journalists are drawn to conflict. Why? At the heart of every conflict lies a key feature of most good stories—change. Where there's change, there's often disagreement. Some people like the change. Some people do not. Some people want more change, others oppose it. To journalists, change (read: conflict) is news.

Indigenous groups, as savvy as any other interest group when it comes to promoting their cause, employ blockades and marches and standoffs to attract media attention. But news outlets respond with coverage disproportionate to the size and frequency of such confrontations, according to the Royal Commission on Aboriginal Peoples:

> Media images that focus predominantly on conflict and confrontation make communication more difficult and reconciliation more elusive. Too often, media treatment of Aboriginal people and issues reinforces old and deeply embedded notions of 'Indians' as alien, unknowable and ultimately a threat to civil order.[3]

Our stories can be *destructive*—by promoting fear and feuds, by reinforcing notions of "us" versus "them," and by placing Indigenous groups in binary opposition to the "rest of Canada." Conversely, our stories can be *constructive*, by helping citizens be better informed and promoting dialogue.

The late journalist and educator Ross Howard, in his work on conflict-sensitive journalism,[4] suggests key questions that you should ask yourself the next time you're reporting on a conflict involving an Indigenous group:

- Does your reporting frame the conflict as consisting of only two opposing sides?
- Do you quote only leaders who make familiar demands? Are you interviewing "ordinary" community members who are being impacted by the conflict? Are you using first-hand sources?
- Are you asking questions that may reveal common ground? Are you reporting on the shared interests or goals of groups involved?

These are the questions of a reporter aiming to go beyond conflict to solutions.

> **EXERCISE 1** Indigenous Playlist
>
> Using your favourite music-sharing platform, create a playlist that features at least ten songs by Indigenous artists. Develop an annotated bibliography of each song that explains your reason for selecting the piece (one sentence per song will suffice). What kinds of social and political issues are Indigenous artists raising? What types of ideas for news stories do the songs inspire? Post your playlist so that you can share it with others in your class.

Discussion Questions

1. How could a news story about a dispute over Indigenous land rights be framed in a way that promotes dialogue rather than exacerbates conflict?

2. The key to finding ideas for news stories is to be curious, but allowing algorithms to dictate what we read online can result in a personal echo chamber of news and ideas. Hearing and reading the different perspectives of Indigenous people is really important if you're going to pitch Indigenous news. Do you have Indigenous perspectives in your social media feed?

   To start diversifying your online news sources, read through the list of Indigenous media compiled for the #Next150Challenge (https://next150.indianhorse.ca/challenges/diversify-your-news). Choose five to ten Indigenous media makers you don't know and follow them on your social media.

3. Why should journalists balance coverage of tragedies and conflicts facing Indigenous communities with positive stories about Indigenous successes and prosperity?

Additional Readings and Resources

Chelsea Vowel, *Indigenous Writes: A Guide to First Nations, Métis & Inuit Issues in Canada* (Winnipeg: Highwater Press, 2016).

Tristan Ahtone, "Telling Indigenous Stories." *Nieman Reports*, June 7, 2017. https://niemanreports.org/articles/telling-indigenous-stories/

Emilee Gilpin, "Indigenous journalists speak up." *National Observer*, December 11, 2018. https://www.nationalobserver.com/2018/12/11/indigenous-journalists-talk-about-past-present-and-future-journalism

Endnotes

1 ©2022 MediaSmarts, Ottawa, Canada, *Indigenous People in the News*, http://www.mediasmarts.ca. Quoted with permission.

2 John Hartley, "Their own media in their own language," in Catharine Lumby and Elspeth Probyn (eds.), *Remote Control: New Media, New Ethics* (New York: Cambridge University Press, 2003), 42–66.

3 Canada, Georges Erasmus, and René Dussault, *Report of the Royal Commission on Aboriginal Peoples: Volume 3—Gathering Strength* (Ottawa: The Commission, 1996), 581.

4 Ross Howard, *Conflict Sensitive Journalism: A Handbook* (International Media Support/IMPACS: Vancouver, 2009), 16.

✦ 1.5 ✦

Searching for Solutions

> In this chapter, students will learn to:
> - recognize how Indigenous Peoples have been problematized by colonial policymakers; and
> - generate ideas for producing solutions-oriented journalism.

How many stories about Indigenous people start this way? "The statistics paint a bleak picture of Indigenous life in Canada. Young Indigenous males with three times the national youth suicide rate; prison populations seven times the national average; diabetes and tuberculosis levels at epidemic proportions; fifty percent of the children in welfare care in Canada are Indigenous," etcetera, etcetera, etcetera . . .

Study after study gets released listing these shocking statistics. Journalists dutifully report them to offer context to the shameful living conditions facing Indigenous people in Canada.

Why do we repeat those statistics? Because we witness evidence of them, up close and personal. We travel to the reserves to see the rotten houses and lousy drinking water. We interview Indigenous people in the inner city who are struggling with drug problems.

Do the bleak statistics paint a full picture of Indigenous life in Canada? Of course not. Ill-health, lack of education, and poor job prospects are not the sum total of Indigenous experience.

However, if that's all the media reports, it's easy to see why our viewers and readers might develop that opinion. When the media repeatedly focus on problems in Indigenous communities, we send an underlying message to our audience: Indigenous people are a problem people.

Should a reporter pretend those troubling statistics don't exist? Only tell stories about happy, proud, wealthy, healthy Indigenous folks? No—that's not a true picture either. Indigenous communities face a host of socio-economic crises, and these stories need to be told. These tragic statistics aren't just numbers: they are grannies and grandpas, aunties and uncles, sisters and brothers, mothers and fathers.

Enter solutions-oriented journalism.

Look for Solutions

> If muckraking asks "what went wrong yesterday, and who is to blame?" then future-focused journalism asks "what might go right tomorrow and who is showing the way?"[1]
>
> – David Beers

Solutions-oriented journalism, future-focused journalism, development journalism, catalytic journalism—call it what you like. The key tenet of this approach is that journalists need to look for constructive, solution-oriented activities that inform, intrigue, and inspire an audience.

Rather than taking a traditional investigative approach and asking "whodunnit," a solutions-oriented journalist asks "howdunnit?" For example, instead of digging to find out who is behind corruption on a First Nation band council or who is to blame for the death of a child in care, a journalist could be digging to find out whether there are First Nations governments or Indigenous child welfare agencies that have solved that problem.

That's because for every problem faced by an Indigenous community, there's likely an Indigenous community *somewhere* out there (in the province, in the country, or in other countries) that's working toward—or has found—a way to resolve that challenge.

Journalists, with our expertise in research and communication, are well equipped to share and promote possible alternatives by reporting firsthand on experiments, sharing data, and involving audiences in dialogue and debate. Old-school journalists may pooh-pooh this approach, calling it "advocacy journalism." But is it advocacy to look for common interests shared by Indigenous Peoples and the rest of Canada?

Instead of creating a sense of desolation and despair about Indigenous communities, solutions-oriented journalism can give viewers and readers a sense of hope. As David Beers, the founder of a solutions-oriented online news publication called *The Tyee*, says, "When editors do green-light those stories, the results allow citizens to imagine and debate alternative futures, and to mobilize support for the versions they support."[2]

Reporting solutions, rather than problems, is complicated. Solutions are rarely simple, and rarely happen during a 24-hour news cycle. In short, you may need more time. But fight for that time by telling your senior editor or producer your story is going to make a difference.

Indigenous People as Problem Solvers

> I want to get rid of the Indian Problem . . .[3]
>
> – Duncan Campbell Scott, Deputy Supt. Of Indian Affairs, 1920

Oh, the "Indian problem." Entire departments of Indian agents, missionaries, and Mounties (and frankly, many an editorial writer) have asked, "Why won't those Indians behave like white men?" Politicians and bureaucrats designed legislation and policy, particularly the *Indian Act*, with the express purpose of assimilating First Nations people in order to fix the "Indian problem." The *Indian Act* effectively treats First Nations people as children or wards of the state, incapable of taking on the responsibilities of the "white" world. In effect, the *Indian Act* condemned generations of First Nations people to a state of dependence. Similarly, the forced settlement of Inuit in permanent communities across the North led to increasing Inuit reliance on the government for education, health care, and other services.

Today, Indigenous and non-Indigenous people alike decry that culture of dependence. That's why it's critical to go beyond government officials and non-Indigenous experts when reporting on Indigenous issues.

Always ask: What are Indigenous people themselves doing to try to solve the problem? Maybe they don't believe there's a problem. That's important to know. Or perhaps they believe there's a problem, but they're doing nothing. Or maybe they're demanding that the government fix their problem. But, in many cases, either Indigenous people are working toward solutions to challenges in their own community, or Indigenous people in a different community are trying to tackle similar challenges.

Ask Indigenous leaders what steps they're taking to solve their community's problems. Ask community members what they think the solutions might be. If your story includes Indigenous people as problem solvers, you'll be helping to transform Indigenous-as-victim narratives into stories of self-reliance and self-determination.

Discussion Questions

1. Why is it important to have Indigenous characters who are solving problems in your story?
2. Many solutions journalism stories are positive in nature, but that doesn't mean that journalists should forget to question the claims of their sources. How can you ensure that your story is not "hero worship"?
3. Find two stories on Indigenous issues in the news. What sorts of solutions-oriented approaches could you take to those stories?

Additional Readings and Resources

The Solutions Journalism Network. https://www.solutionsjournalism.org/
Solutions Journalism Online Course. https://learninglab.solutionsjournalism.org/courses/curriculum-builder
Wilson Lievano, "How to Write Compelling Solutions Journalism Stories." *The Groundtruth Project*, January 31, 2019. https://thegroundtruthproject.org/write-compelling-solutions-journalism-stories/
David Venn, "Searching for Solutions." *Ryerson Review of Journalism*, October 30, 2019. https://rrj.ca/searching-for-solutions/
John Dyer, "Is Solutions Journalism the Solution?" *Nieman Reports*, June 11, 2015. https://niemanreports.org/articles/is-solutions-journalism-the-solution/

Antonia Gonzales and Sarah Gustavus, "For Stories on Solutions to Native Health Problems, Reporters Take Pains to Avoid Outside-Looking-In Trap." USC Annenberg Centre for Health Journalism, December 2017. https://centerforhealthjournalism.org/resources/lessons/stories-solutions-native-health-problems-reporters-take-pains-avoid-outside

Endnotes

1. David Beers, "A Truly Influential Question: What Might Go Right Tomorrow?" *SPARC BC News*, Spring 2005, 5–7. https://thetyee.ca/Documents/2020/03/02/Future-Focused.pdf
2. Ibid, 6.
3. National Archives of Canada, Record Group 10, vol. 6810, file 470-2-3, vols. 7, 55 (L-3), and 63 (N-3).

✦ 1.6 ✦
How to Pitch a Story Successfully

> *In this chapter, students will learn to:*
> - conduct research that emphasizes the human elements of the story;
> - search for stories about Indigenous Peoples that have impact and bring understanding to audiences; and
> - demonstrate how diverse voices in news stories can increase audiences.

Assignment editors are the gatekeepers of our industry. Every day, they're faced with an enormous task: fill the news program or news site with stories that are new, relevant, and edgy. Most days, there are too many stories to cover and not enough reporters.

That means there's a lot riding on the pitch. Give a lousy pitch and your idea will get spiked before you even get to work on it.

Maybe you make a great pitch, but your assignment editor is one of those Five D Rule types, only interested in Indigenous news stories that deal with Big Tragedy, Big Hope, or Big Money.

Here are three tips on how to present your story idea to your assignment editor—and remember, as that ancient Indigenous saying goes, "If at first you don't succeed, try, try again." (Okay, maybe that's not an ancient Indigenous saying. But I imagine generations of hunters following that advice.)

Research Strong Stories

Pitching a story about Indigenous issues successfully is no different than pitching any other story. **A good news story needs to be about people.**

"Hey, that kid in custody died.... We should do something on Indigenous child welfare agencies" is not a great pitch. Your long-suffering assignment editor knows your audience is interested in people, not *issues*.

Oprah Winfrey (who may not be a journalist per se, but knows a thing or two about storytelling) says everyone has a story—the question is how to make it *pop* for your audience. Do some research so you can explain why your particular story is going to "pop":

- Who are the people involved in this story?
- What's at stake for them?
- Why is this story important?
- Does it have strong visuals or scenes?

If you can answer all (or some) of those questions, and summarize the story in a couple sentences, you're more likely to pique your assignment editor's interest.

Find the News Hook

Residential schools, land claims, hunting and fishing rights—these subjects have been around for a hundred years or more. They are recurring stories because they go to the core of Indigenous–settler relations. They are part of Canada's narrative, part of our national consciousness.

But are they news? You may not appreciate or even be offended by your assignment editor's patronizing, bored tone when they ask, "What's new about mouldy Indian reserve houses?" But it's up to you to find a new angle, or brainstorm a different treatment.

If you apply a formula to a story about residential schools—find a suffering former student, pull out some archive photographs, mix in a lawyer and a politician or two—who would blame your audience for tuning out? The story isn't tired and hackneyed. The storyteller is.

What can you bring to this story that will make me sit up and pay attention? Maybe it's youth involvement, or a business angle, or a technology solution. Can you offer special access to something I haven't seen before? Is there a compelling character who presents this story in a fresh way?

Search for stories that will have impact and bring understanding to your audience. Find something that interests *you*. If it interests you, you'll share that passion with your assignment editor—and your audience.

Diversity Sells

In today's fragmented news environment, diversity sells. (Hopefully, your assignment editor got that memo—if not, tell them there's also this newfangled thing called the internet.) Every media outlet needs to reach as broad an audience as possible, and that means reflecting the entirety of your community, your province, your country. We need to tell stories about all kinds of different people—including Indigenous Peoples.

Studies and polling show your non-Indigenous audience wants to learn more about Indigenous people.[1] In some markets, Indigenous people represent significant audience share—ignoring them is a sure-fire way to see your numbers shrink.

Keeping this in mind, "diversity" should be one of the buzzwords (such as "exclusive," "inside access," or "enterprise") that make an assignment editor's ears perk up. Remind your assignment editor that, in *addition* to being a fantastic enterprise story about fascinating characters involved in real struggles regarding a pressing public policy issue, this story you're pitching will present a "diverse" and "under-reported" community (or whatever buzzwords your newsroom uses). If your newsroom is progressive enough to have a diversity audit, then your story will provide some much-needed checkmarks on that balance sheet.

Discussion Questions

1. Come up with two strong story ideas about Indigenous issues for each of the following news outlets:
   - your local campus news organization;
   - your local newspaper or online news site; and
   - a national broadcaster.
2. Identify two major issues covered in the news today. What kind of Indigenous angle could you develop for each of them?
3. If you are reporting for a media outlet (whether it be a student or professional news organization), does that newsroom have a diversity audit? If yes, how many of the stories involve Indigenous people? People of colour? Women? LGBTQ2SIA+ folks? Disabled folks? If the newsroom does not have a diversity audit, audit your own sources over the past six months. What can you do right now to make your journalism more inclusive?

Additional Readings and Resources

Shelby Lisk, "Rewriting Journalism: 'Get Indigenous Voices Involved.'" *TVO*, September 3, 2020. https://www.tvo.org/article/rewriting-journalism-get-indigenous-voices-involved

Sarah Scire, "Five Do-Them-Now Steps to Making Your Newsroom (and Coverage) More Representative." *Nieman Lab*, June 12, 2020. https://www.niemanlab.org/2020/06/five-simple-steps-to-making-your-newsroom-and-coverage-more-representative/

Taylor Blatchford, "A More Diverse Student Newsroom Will Make Your Publication Stronger. Here's How to Get Started." *Poynter Institute*, June 17, 2020. https://www.poynter.org/newsletters/2020/a-more-diverse-student-newsroom-will-make-your-publication-stronger-heres-how-to-get-started/

Alison Macadam, "What Makes a Good Pitch? NPR Editors Weigh In." *NPR Training*, January 24, 2017. https://training.npr.org/2017/01/24/what-makes-a-good-pitch-npr-editors-weigh-in/

Tim Herrera, "How to Successfully Pitch *The New York Times* (or, Well, Anyone Else)," *Nieman Lab*, October 22, 2018. https://www.niemanlab.org/2018/10/how-to-successfully-pitch-the-new-york-times-or-well-anyone-else/

Tom Huang, "6 Questions Journalists Should Be Able to Answer Before Pitching a Story," *Poynter Institute*, August 22, 2012. https://www.poynter.org/reporting-editing/2012/6-questions-journalists-should-be-able-to-answer-before-pitching-a-story/

Endnotes

1. In 2016, Environics conducted a survey of Canadian public opinion about Indigenous issues. Three in four Canadians said they are paying a great deal of (22%) or some attention (51%) to news and stories about Indigenous Peoples. Furthermore, most non-Indigenous Canadians expressed a desire to know more about Indigenous cultures. Eight in ten strongly (39%) or somewhat (40%) agreed that they would be personally interested in learning more about Indigenous cultures. https://www.environicsinstitute.org/docs/default-source/project-documents/public-opinion-about-aboriginal-issues-in-canada-2016/final-report.pdf?sfvrsn=30587aca_2

✦ 1.7 ✦
"Where Are You From?" Rethinking Objectivity

> *In this chapter, students will learn to:*
> - understand the standards of journalism that are designed to minimize the influence of individual and group biases;
> - recognize how cultural biases affect the way people perceive the world around them, including the information they encounter; and
> - identify some of the challenges of dispassionate, "objective" reporting.

How do journalists know what they know? How do we decide what is good journalism? And who gets to decide?[1]

– Candis Callison and Mary Lynn Young

"Where are you from?"

Invariably, it's one of the first questions you'll get asked when you meet an Indigenous person for the first time, whether you travelled thousands of kilometres to an isolated Indigenous community or simply took a walk in any big city's downtown core.

On one hand, it's a pretty basic question. A journalist may think there's an easy answer: it's where they live or work. But when an Indigenous person asks where you're from, they are typically attempting to determine something more meaningful than where you hang your hat.

What they really want to find out is who your people are. Where did you grow up? Who are your parents? Your grandparents? Your great-grandparents? What clan do you belong to?[2] Who do you know that I know?

The true import of the inquiry is to find out how you're connected to your community and your ancestry and what values you've inherited. Among many Indigenous Peoples, this is essential information in the early stages of building a relationship with another human being.

This deeper aspect of the "where-are-you-from" question makes some journalists uncomfortable. It demands reporters disclose what so many assiduously avoid in their news stories—explaining who they are and how they know what they know.

In fact, how much of yourself to reveal to your subjects—and more importantly, to your audience—is something journalism has been wrestling with for over a century, ever since journalists first started using a complex contraption known as "objectivity" as a way to legitimize their craft.

What Is Journalistic Objectivity?

Here's a fun exercise. Ask fifteen journalists what "objectivity" means. You'll likely get fifteen different answers. For an ideal so deeply entrenched in contemporary journalistic standards and practices, the principle of objectivity is pretty loosely defined.

Journalistic objectivity is more properly described as a notion, as opposed to an absolute standard, which may include (but is not limited to)

- fairness;
- impartiality;
- factuality; and
- non-partisanship.

Journalists learn all about objectivity at the outset of their careers, whether in the classroom or in their first job. In pursuit of truth, young reporters are taught to seek out differing views and opinions, regardless of their own personal standpoint or preferences, and present them in a balanced way, without prejudice.

That's no easy task. Journalists are a civically engaged and opinionated bunch. Given that, you'd be hard-pressed to find any journalist who agrees it is possible to be *entirely* objective. We are only human, after all. We choose what stuff to put in a story and what stuff to leave out. When we take pictures, we choose how they're framed, cropped, exposed. We make these types of subjective decisions every day. For that reason, some argue objectivity is a false ideal, even a myth.

Yet, most journalists get in a huff at any suggestion their reportage is biased. So, what is this debate all about? Let's look back at the roots of the concept of objectivity. The term came into use among American journalists in the early twentieth century, at a time when Western society was turning away from religion toward science to explain the world. It was also a time when journalism was beginning to define itself as a "profession" that required special skills and training. An American journalist named Walter Lippmann was the first to call for a "scientific" approach toward gathering and reporting news, in 1919, as a way to combat what he perceived as a glut of sensational news coverage. Lippmann and others began to look for ways for a journalist "to remain clear and free of his irrational, his unexamined, his unacknowledged prejudgments in observing, understanding and presenting the news."[3]

The idea caught on. By 1923, the American Society of Newspaper Editors had canonized the concept of impartiality, adopting a code of ethics that declared: "News reports should be free from opinion or bias of any kind."[4]

The principle of objectivity has always had critics who balk at any suggestion that a good reporter never has an opinion. Media theorist Jay Rosen argues journalism went awry when it began to adopt "the view from nowhere," a term he borrowed from philosopher Thomas Nagle:

> ["The view from nowhere"] says that human beings are, in fact, capable of stepping back from their position to gain an enlarged understanding, which includes the more limited view they had before the step back. Think of the cinema: when the camera pulls back to reveal where a character had been standing and shows us a fuller tableau. To Nagel, objectivity is that kind of motion. We try to "transcend our particular viewpoint and develop an expanded consciousness that takes in the world more fully." But there are limits to this motion. We can't transcend all our starting points. No matter how far it pulls back the camera is still occupying a position.[5]

Rather than acting as a wide-angle lens, Rosen argues objectivity has translated into reporters developing bad habits.

Take, for example, that old newsroom adage "There are two sides to every story." When on deadline, journalists often settle for presenting "both sides" of an issue, trusting the public to make up its mind about what is true and what is false. The reporter may not have betrayed any bias, but they haven't pushed the story toward a deeper understanding of the truth, either.

This extreme view of balance also tends to worsen reporters' inclination to rely on official sources, such as government or police, because it's the quickest way to get a "he said, she said" version of events. Furthermore, journalists without time or energy to verify claims often hide behind the neutral voice, in a manner that damages journalism's credibility: "We're not saying the world is flat. We're saying that HE SAID the earth is flat."[6]

By 1996, with a growing chorus of media scholars such as Rosen lambasting objectivity as misleading, even deceitful, and the 24-hour news cycle amping up the appetite for interpretative and point-of-view reportage, the Society of Professional Journalists in the U.S. finally revised its code of ethics to remove the word "objectivity."

Still, many newsrooms have held fast to concepts such as distance and impartiality. That is, until 2020, the year objectivity broke into the mainstream.

How Objectivity Can Be Harmful

When an unarmed Black man named George Floyd was killed at the hands of Minneapolis police on May 25, 2020, Black Lives Matter demonstrations spread across the United States and around the world. Racism in all facets of society was called out and white privilege challenged. The demographics of newsrooms became part of the debate, and people began to look more closely at how journalistic objectivity was operating in a way that caused harm to those on the outside.

One of those critiques came from Waubgeshig Rice, an Anishinaabe journalist for nearly two decades and celebrated author of fiction. Rice chose to hang up his reporter's hat in 2020. Not long after he left journalism behind, he penned an open letter to aspiring young Indigenous journalists, revealing systemic racism was a major reason for his departure from the newsroom.

The overwhelming whiteness of Canadian newsrooms, wrote Rice, "means the default reader/viewer/listener perspective is that of a White Canadian." He continued,

> The entire industry binds itself to an archaic fallacy of neutrality that silences and limits journalists of colour . . . the whiteness default drives the journalistic objectivity that's been idealized, and in this way, it further marginalizes perspectives outside of the dominant newsroom voice.[7]

It would be difficult to dispute Rice's contention that Canadian newsrooms are largely white. BIPOC individuals account for nearly 30 per cent of Canada's population, yet this diversity isn't reflected in Canadian media. It's not easy to put a hard number on under-representation, given that statistics documenting race in Canadian newsrooms are sparse at best.[8, 9] What little data exists clearly demonstrates the "persistent whiteness" of Canada's newsrooms, according to journalism professors Candis Callison, Tahltan, and Mary Lynn Young, a white settler. They highlight the following:

- A 1998 study by scholars David Pritchard and Florian Sauvageau showed that the vast majority (97%) of journalists in Canada were white.[10]
- A 2004 study of diversity at Canadian newspapers by John Miller at Ryerson University found that visible minority journalists accounted for only 4.1 per cent of the staff at large papers.[11]
- A 2010 study of journalists and diversity in the major journalism organizations in the Greater Toronto Area (GTA) by Wendy Cukier, John Miller, Kristen Aspevig, and Dale Carl found that 4.8 per cent of media decision-makers were visible minorities.[12]
- The CBC's 2019 employment equity annual report identified that Indigenous employees accounted for 2.1% of permanent staff, while visible minorities made up 13.3 per cent.[13]

How does this enduring whiteness impact the news? Let me count the ways.

Leave aside (for a moment) how race factors into what types of stories are deemed newsworthy. Consider, instead, the small acts of bias in news stories every day. For example, naming whiteness is unusual in most reports. Can you recall a time you've seen Canada's prime minister described as "white"? Not often, unless photos surface of him wearing blackface. Yet, it is common for the media to use a racial identifier if the subject is Indigenous—an Innu senator, a Kwakwaka'wakw judge, a Métis minister. This seemingly benign act has the effect of reinforcing whiteness as normal and neutral. Anyone who is not white is thereby Othered.

Similarly, our word choices matter. Think of the values embedded in a term such as "land claim," used commonly in Canadian media to describe everything from modern treaty negotiations (known as "comprehensive land claims") to specific claims (which deal with specific grievances against the Crown).

On a plain reading, it's easy to see why the average Canadian might misunderstand the term. Use of the word "claim" implies First Nations are asking the government to give them more land. On the contrary, "land claims" flow from Indigenous Peoples' original occupation: First Nations are asking the government to honour previous promises regarding lands and resources, or where Indigenous lands are unceded, negotiate a debt settlement plan. Yet, the term "land claim" remains ubiquitous, reinforcing a status quo in which Canada has never been called upon by a court to validate its claim to sovereignty.

Style guides can become a heated battleground. It took a concerted effort from Indigenous staff at the CBC in 2015 to convince the public broadcaster to permit journalists to refer to "former residential school students" as "survivors."[14] More recently, Indigenous activists have called upon media outlets to stop using the term "protester," suggesting "land defender" is a more accurate and less loaded phrase.[15]

These few examples illustrate one of the troubles with objectivity as it has come to be practised: while earnestly striving to be fair and balanced, newsroom decision-makers consistently fail to identify their race and culture—or social class—as a source of potential bias.

Is Objectivity Useful?

Should this long-overdue moment of reckoning in journalism mark the end of objectivity? It's certainly time for a rethink, if we take public trust seriously.

Social media has turned the world into a more polarized place, where "fake news" is a rallying cry and journalists are constantly under attack for being biased. In this hyper-partisan environment, misinformation spreads like a virus, threatening everything from public health to social order. We are awash in a flood of false, misleading, or misinterpreted information.

Facts have always been central to journalism's brand. Facts matter. Still, as journalists increasingly use lively, opinionated style to distinguish themselves as sense-makers, the line between accuracy and activism blurs.

In a post-truth era, journalists must work harder than ever to live up to the standards we profess to follow. As journalism ethics expert Stephen Ward has put it, "There is no better antidote to fake news than real news, objectively tested. Fake news and alternate facts are just other terms for biased, subjective belief."[16]

Note that Ward draws attention to objectivity of journalistic *methods*, not tone. In their seminal work *The Elements of Journalism*, Bill Kovach and Tom Rosenstiel argue journalists have strayed from Walter Lippmann's goal for introducing scientific rigour to newsrooms. The original concept, they argue, was about the discipline of fact verification:

> Being impartial or neutral is *not* a core principle of journalism. Because the journalist must make decisions, he or she is not and cannot be objective. But journalistic *methods* are objective. When the concept of objectivity originally evolved, it did not imply that journalists were free of bias. It called, rather, for a consistent method of testing information—a transparent approach to evidence—precisely so that personal and cultural biases would not undermine the accuracy of the work. The method is objective, not the journalist.[17]

Think how objectivity operates in the legal or scientific realm. In a court of law, judges rely upon rules of evidence to assist in fact-finding. In laboratories, scientists have methods of observation when conducting experiments. Similarly, journalism needs standards for testing the truth of information. Otherwise, what is to distinguish news from propaganda, advertising, fiction, or entertainment?

Ward has proposed a revision to the old ways of journalism, what he calls "pragmatic objectivity." In this view, objectivity about facts is retained as a requirement, but the journalist is not required to be detached in his stance. Ward suggests that "objective engagement does not require an all-encompassing neutrality which precludes expressing a view or coming to a conclusion." He continues:

> Objectively engaged journalists are impartial or disinterested because they do not let their partialities or interests undermine objective judgment and inquiry. They do not prejudge the story before fairly weighing all relevant evidence. But after such inquiry, journalists are free to draw an informed conclusion. Such is the method of investigative journalism. Objectivity is not a value-free zone.[18]

A cornerstone of journalism has always been context and analysis. If we've done the work, there's nothing biased about truth-telling.

How Can Journalists Be Fair?

If you're the type of reporter whose eyes glaze over during these kinds of newsroom debates, consider how Vox journalist Johnny Harris sums up a journalist's duty to fairness, once they have gathered a bunch of facts about a thing and come to a conclusion about it.

> What you can do as a fair journalist is *be generous to the other side*. You can present the best version of the other sides' argument. That, to me, is what healthy journalism has: generosity to the other side. (*emphasis added*)[19]

Harris' notion of generosity dovetails with Indigenous principles of respect that I return to over and over in this guide. But if you're looking for other ways to practise "new objectivity," here are a few more suggestions.

The View from Somewhere

If the trouble with objectivity is that "the view from nowhere" has operated to exclude Indigenous Peoples and other marginalized groups by affirming status quo positions in predominantly white newsrooms, a cornerstone of "new objectivity" will consist of journalists being up front with their subjects and their audiences about where they come from.

Rather than hide behind The View from Nowhere, this is journalism that trumpets a View from Somewhere. Callison and Young call this "situated knowledge," drawing on the work of feminist scholar Donna Haraway, which they assert is a form of expertise, not bias. In their book *Reckoning*,[20] they argue it's essential for journalists to be transparent about what forms their epistemology (what they know). With a nod to the work of anthropology professor Kim TallBear, Callison has explained that we have all walked through life and shouldn't try to pretend there isn't "mud on our shoes": identifying and acknowledging our own experiences makes us work harder to counter them and figure out what we actually think is the truth.

Former journalist and activist Desmond Cole has been blunter about it. When offering advice to journalists who are not members of a visible minority but want to write about race or issues affecting racialized communities, Cole has said: "Talk about whiteness and talk about your damn selves."[21]

Practically speaking, there are many ways to situate oneself. When introducing yourself to an Indigenous subject, you can explain your racial background, state whether there are Indigenous people involved in your story production, and describe how much experience you have reporting on Indigenous issues. You should also take time to clarify your journalistic process to people you want to interview. This gives them the chance to understand your motivations, so they can choose whether or not to engage with you.

With regard to situating yourself for your audience, journalists have been experimenting for a long while with ways to be more up front about their journalistic perspective. It can be as simple as including more detailed biographical information in a tag. A step further would be point-of-view reportage, in which you insert yourself into the story.

Question What Makes a Story Newsworthy

Every day, editors and executive producers are tasked with figuring out what is newsworthy and deciding what makes "the news." There are no firm rules about this. Often, it's as simple as whether a story is significant, interesting, and new. Of course, determining whether a thing is significant, interesting, and new is a matter of perspective—hence, the often-passionate debates at assignment/lineup meetings.

Indigenous perspectives have long been absent from these debates. The result? The question of what makes Indigenous Peoples newsworthy has been judged through a colonial lens, as I discussed in Chapters 1.2 through 1.4. The cure for this newsroom myopia is thinking more expansively about what makes an Indigenous news story, by doing better at listening to what Indigenous communities consider newsworthy. That means applying more rigour to those assignment/lineup meetings by consciously and explicitly naming the factors that go into deciding what is "news."

Transparency

If objective methods of journalism help assure our audiences we are trustworthy, we must explain whom we have chosen as "experts" in our story and why we trust their expertise. This is critical when covering Indigenous issues, because studies have repeatedly shown that most Canadians lack awareness about Indigenous issues.[22] If our audiences don't have an appreciation of the history between Canada and Indigenous Peoples or of the constitutionally protected rights of Indigenous Peoples, they may not understand who the people are in our stories and what their roles or functions are.

If we've invested time researching and verifying facts, we should explain our assessments of trustworthiness with our audiences. Transparency adds more weight to our reportage. It also pushes us to justify our choices, and to recognize that some Indigenous people may not be suitable to speak on all things Indigenous. For example, an Indigenous person who grew up in the city and works for an urban Indigenous organization may not be the best choice to comment about a report on First Nation drinking water standards. An elected *Indian Act* band councillor may not be able to explain the roles and expectations of traditional governance. A First Nations person may not be the ideal guest to discuss Inuit cultural property or Métis hunting rights.

Try *Not* Observing from a Distance

Journalists have an almost pathological fear of being seen as biased, but it's worthwhile to consider Kim TallBear's extensive critique of how distanced objectivity serves to reinforce power imbalances.

As a Dakota anthropologist, TallBear has thought long and hard about how to bridge the divide between researchers and their subjects (i.e., those from whom knowledge is extracted.) She envisions her research methodology as a relationship-building process. Instead of thinking of research as data gathering from "subjects," she describes it as an opportunity for sharing knowledge with *colleagues*. For example, in a research project on Indigenous bioscientists, she develops collaborative relationships with the people she studies, describing them as "subjects/colleagues/friends/teachers/mentees." She enthusiastically accepts the invitation to join the board of an Indigenous science organization, seeing it as a way to build capacity within the Indigenous community.[23]

Drawing from the work of feminist and Indigenous scholars, TallBear terms this "objectivity in action"—a mode of inquiry where she becomes invested in the lives and experiences of her research subjects, which, she argues, produces "empirically more accurate and theoretically richer" insights into the topic at hand:

> Inquiring not at a distance, but based on the lives and knowledge priorities of subjects—helps open up one's mind to working in non-standard ways. It may take you to new and surprising places.[24]

TallBear acknowledges not everyone can replicate her approach, and certainly, journalists adhere to different ethical guidelines than academic researchers.

But, if our goal is to seek truth, how would it change our journalistic process to centre the needs and priorities of the Indigenous people we report on? Only you can determine how deep your relationship with your subject gets, but in Chapter 3.3, I explore further how this dovetails with Indigenous understandings of reciprocity.

A Final Word on Objectivity

Before you set out to report in Indigenous communities, recognize this: on your journey to seek truth, you *do* have a point of view. And that point of view is valuable, so long as it's grounded in verifiable facts. Before communicating with a wider audience, it's your job as a journalist to ensure you've done your best to challenge your point of view—instead of pretending it doesn't exist.

Discussion Questions

1. Is it possible to be objective? Why or why not?
2. How does journalistic objectivity contribute to harm?
3. How can reporters go about "locating" themselves?
4. Where and how do you draw the line between activism and journalism?

Additional Readings and Resources

Candis Callison and Mary Lynn Young, *Reckoning: Journalism's Limits and Possibilities* (New York: Oxford University Press, 2020).
Waubgeshig Rice, "Letter to a Young Indigenous Journalist," *The Walrus*, August 31, 2020. https://thewalrus.ca/terra-cognita-letter-to-a-young-indigenous-journalist/
Denise Balkissoon, "Objectivity: Trust and Truth in an Age of Disinformation," 2020 Atkinson Lecture at Ryerson University. https://www.ryerson.ca/journalism/news-events/2020/10/atkinson-2020-objectivity-trust-and-truth-in-an-age-of-disinformation/
Alexandria Neason, "On Atonement," *Columbia Journalism Review*, January 28, 2021. https://www.cjr.org/special_report/apologies-news-racism-atonement.php
The View from Somewhere podcast. https://www.lewispants.com/

Endnotes

1. Candis Callison and Mary Lynn Young, *Reckoning: Journalism's Limits and Possibilities* (New York: Oxford University Press, 2020), 200.
2. Clan membership is an important aspect of some First Nations cultures. Others do not have clans.
3. American Press Institute, "The Lost Meaning of 'Objectivity.'" https://www.americanpressinstitute.org/journalism-essentials/bias-objectivity/lost-meaning-objectivity/
4. American Society of Newspaper Editors, "Statement of Principles." (1923), https://accountablejournalism.org/ethics-codes/american-society-of-newspaper-editors-statement-of-principles
5. Jay Rosen, "The View from Nowhere: Questions and Answers." *Press Think*, November 10, 2010. https://pressthink.org/2010/11/the-view-from-nowhere-questions-and-answers/
6. Tom Warhover, "Against Objectivity." *Poynter*, June 15, 2017. https://www.poynter.org/ethics-trust/2017/against-objectivity/
7. Waubgeshig Rice, "Letter to a Young Indigenous Journalist." *The Walrus*, August 31, 2020. https://thewalrus.ca/terra-cognita-letter-to-a-young-indigenous-journalist/
8. Canadian broadcasters are required by law to report workplace demographics, but there is no similar requirement for newspapers or digital publications. What few studies exist on race in Canadian newsrooms have been hampered by low participation rates from print and online outlets.
9. The situation is similarly bleak in the United States when it comes to Indigenous representation in newsrooms. A 2017 survey by the American Society of News Editors found that Indigenous journalists made up about 0.5 per cent of the industry's workforce, while Indigenous people, including those "mixed with other races," make up about 1.7 per cent of the U.S. population.
10. David Pritchard and Florian Sauvageau, "The Journalists and Journalisms of Canada," in David Weaver (ed.), *The Global Journalist: News People Around the World* (Cresskill, NJ: Hampton Press, 1998), 373–393.
11. John Miller, "Who's Telling the News? Racial Representation Among News Gatherers in Canada's Daily Newsrooms."

The International Journal of Diversity in Organizations, Communities, and Nations: Annual Review 5.4 (2006), 133–142.

12. Wendy Cukier, John Miller, Kristen Aspevig, and Dale Carl, "Diversity in Leadership and Media: A Multi-perspective Analysis of the Greater Toronto Area, 2010." *The International Journal of Diversity in Organizations, Communities, and Nations: Annual Review* 11.6 (2012), 63–78.

13. CBC-Radio Canada Employment Equity Annual Report 2019. https://cbc.radio-canada.ca/en/impact-and-accountability/diversity-and-inclusion/equity-reports

14. Alanna Brousseau, "Wab Kinew: The Politics of Power and Language." Blog, October 17, 2015. https://www.theeditingco.com/blog/10188/wab-kinew-the-power-and-politics-of-language; Joseph Brean, "'The Experiment of Colonization in Canada, It Damaged You Too': Wab Kinew on His New Memoir." *National Post*, September 18, 2015

15. Rhea Rollmann, "Protesters? Or Land Protectors." *The Independent*, October 28, 2016. https://theindependent.ca/2016/10/28/protesters-or-land-protectors/

16. Stephen J.A. Ward. "Engagement and Pragmatic Objectivity." Centre for Journalism Ethics, March 27, 2017. https://ethics.journalism.wisc.edu/2017/03/27/engagement-and-pragmatic-objectivity/

17. American Press Institute, "What is Journalism?" https://www.americanpressinstitute.org/journalism-essentials/what-is-journalism/elements-journalism/

18. Ward, *ibid.*

19. Johnny Harris, "7 Things I've Learned about Journalism in 7 Years of Being a Journalist." https://www.youtube.com/watch?v=Rr7povAInwQ&feature=youtu.be

20. Candis Callison and Mary Lynn Young, *Reckoning: Journalism's Limits and Possibilities* (New York: Oxford University Press, 2020).

21. Sukaina Jamil, "How Journalists Should Reframe Their Perspectives on Objectivity." *Ryerson Review of Journalism*, November 26, 2019. https://rrj.ca/how-journalists-should-reframe-their-perspectives-on-objectivity/

22. Environics Institute, "Canadian Public Opinion on Aboriginal Peoples: Final Report, June 2016." https://www.environicsinstitute.org/docs/default-source/project-documents/public-opinion-about-aboriginal-issues-in-canada-2016/final-report.pdf?sfvrsn=30587aca_2

23. Kim TallBear, "Indigenous Bioscientists Constitute Knowledge across Cultures of Expertise and Tradition: An Indigenous Standpoint Research Project," in Johan Gärdebo, May-Britt Öhman, and Hiroshi Maruyama (eds.), *Re:Mindings: Co-Constituting Indigenous, Academic, Artistic Knowledges* (Uppsala: The Hugo Valentin Centre, Uppsala University, 2014), 173–191.

24. Kim TallBear, "Standing with and Speaking as Faith: A Feminist-Indigenous Approach to Inquiry." *Journal of Research Practice* 10.2 (2014), Article N17.

Part 2
In the Field

✦ 2.1 ✦

Indian Time

> In this chapter, students will learn to:
> - recognize the concept of "Indian Time"; and
> - modify their reporting practice to operate in different cultural environments.

To report this story well, we needed to slow down. I don't mean we needed to work slowly; we just needed to understand that some of what we needed to tell this story was going to come when it came.[1]

– Michael Moore

Indian Time

It's 9 A.M. The assignment editor hands you a press release: Funding announcement by the Minister of Indigenous Affairs. Big money to refurbish a decrepit school at a nearby reserve. Event starts at 12 P.M. You grab a coffee, race to the vehicle, and make the one-hour drive to the community. You arrive at the school gym with time to spare. But the event unfolds something like this:

12:15 The event has not yet started (media is there, minister is there, schoolkids are there, but things still haven't started). Chief busy talking with principal.
12:30 Ceremony starts. Principal makes introductions, including everyone on band council, school board, and all the teachers.
12:40 Principal invites an Elder to bless the gathering. She speaks passionately for twenty minutes about her traumatic experience at residential school, then prays.
1:15   Performance by a traditional singer, honouring the educational achievements of last year's high school graduates.
1:30   Principal introduces education counsellor, who gives a speech.

1:45   Education counsellor introduces Chief, who gives a speech.
1:15   Minister finally makes The Announcement.

The whole time, your phone is buzzing nonstop. The assignment editor wants an update—is this a story, she wonders, and what should she tell the 4:00 production meeting? The news service wonders if you can do a short hit. The promo people want a piece of you too.

Two hours after the initial start time, you have your 15-second clip from the Minister of Indigenous Affairs—but you still have to gather interviews from community members and drive back to the city to edit the piece. Welcome to "Indian Time."

It's not easy to explain what Indian Time is.[2] It's more complicated than assuming everything will be late (though that's often a safe bet). I've heard Indian Time jokingly described as "the time it takes for moss to grow on a stone," or as one Elder put it, "the time it takes to do things in a good way."

Here's what Anishinaabe author and humourist Drew Hayden Taylor had to say about Indian Time:

> It's an enigmatic idea based on a uniquely cultural relationship with time. Simply put, things happen when they happen. There are not 24 hours in a day. Time is unlimited, impossible to cut up into chunks.
>
> If something is to happen at 11 am, it might happen at 11:01 am or 12:26 or 1:11 pm. It will happen when it will happen. The universe has its own heartbeat, and who are we to speed it up or slow it down? To some, it's an excuse to be late. To others, it's a way to avoid ulcers.[3]

Kanien'kehá:ka (Mohawk) psychiatrist Dr. Clare Brant also tried to explain Indian Time, after observing Kanien'kehá:ka steelworkers who sometimes appear to be "lazy" or dragging their feet—but suddenly react in a burst of energy to finish a job:

> It means when the time is right . . . when the time, the seasons, the conditions, the feelings, the Manitou, the spirit and everything are correct, then you proceed; pull out all the stops and get the work done.[4]

In the school press conference scenario above, an anxious reporter may perceive the schedule as a loosey-goosey disaster when, in fact, the introductions and speeches and performances are highly structured in terms of local manners and protocol. Process (which includes honouring people) is considered as important as the product or result. It's part of how things are done in "a good way," or "the right way."

Make no mistake: *Indian Time is not Newsroom Time.* You have a deadline, and you need to fill a hole in a lineup with material—and Indian Time is likely going to be an obstacle.

Here are some ways to tackle it.

Plan for Indian Time

Build extra time into *your* schedule to allow for events to be delayed, for interviewees to be late, or for the appropriate introductions to be made. If this is not a "today" story, start your research sooner rather than later, to allow time for First

Nation communities to discuss the story and decide who would be appropriate to interview.

On the day of a shoot, if you need to book a cameraman or a photographer, ask for extra time both before and after the shoot. Put in an overtime request, if that helps. Do your best not to squeeze a lot of interviews into a small period of time. Allow for the all-important cup of tea.

Explain to your assignment editor that it may take twice as long to get your work accomplished in an Indigenous community—and if they can cut you some slack (whether by extending research time or pushing your deadline), the story will be a lot better.

Indian Time May Mean Early

Indian Time, especially when it relates to excursions on the land, does not always mean "running late" or that things will take longer. Things happen when they happen, and sometimes that means *earlier* than planned. If the origins of Indian Time hearken back to an age when Indigenous people's activities revolved around the seasons, the sun, and the migratory patterns of animals (though who really knows what the origins of Indian Time are), then allowances must always be made for changes to your plans.

So, if you're set up to go out in a boat at 8 A.M. to film your character fishing, you may find them knocking on your door at 4 A.M. if an earlier departure is dictated by a) weather patterns, b) the behaviour of the fish, c) the advice of an Elder, or d) all of the above.

Not All Indigenous People Run on Indian Time

Some days, YOU might be running late, thanks to a traffic jam or that senior editor who took forever to sign off on the item. "It's okay if I'm late," you say to yourself. "It's an Indigenous story—they'll understand. They're on Indian Time." Maybe yes, maybe no.

Indigenous people are just as busy as anyone else in this fast-paced world, and many have hectic and demanding schedules. You run the risk of offending someone—or worse, losing an interview—if you don't show up or call at the agreed-upon time. Treat Indigenous folks the same as you would anyone else—if you're running late, make a quick call to advise them and apologize.

Expect Delays, If Cultural Events Are Happening

If your story happens to fall on a day when the salmon are running, or there is a funeral for an Elder, or some other significant cultural event is occurring (such as hunting, gathering, harvesting, spiritual ceremonies, funerals, births, or family gatherings), you may find it difficult to get hold of anyone. That doesn't necessarily mean the person you're trying to contact doesn't want to talk to you. It does mean they have different priorities than you.

Your Deadline Is Your Problem

You may wish the rest of the world understood how important it is for you to make your deadline, and perhaps, if you explain your deadline, the Indigenous folks you're dealing with will bend over backwards to help. But you will likely win respect—and may wind up with a bigger and better story—if you try to forget your deadline (as difficult as that is) and recognize that it often takes a little longer to do things in Indigenous communities.

Instead of thinking of Indian Time as a reporter's worst enemy, why not think of it as a friend? If you're successful in getting your editors to understand that your story will take a little longer but it will be worth it, your story is only going to improve. Use the time to do research and develop story leads. What reporter doesn't want *more* time to work on a story?

What if your assignment editor wants a story, come hell or high water? Well, maybe you can try to find a different story, one that you know you can deliver on—and put this one and the contacts you've made in your story bank. Or maybe you're stuck, and you just file the story with the limited information and sound bites you can get. But if all you wind up with is a quote from the Chief—and, for the unlucky TV reporter, wide shots of the reserve and file footage—don't blame the Indians.

Discussion Questions

1. When comparing cultures, attitudes toward time can be very different. Western cultures often run their lives by the clock. Are you aware of other cultures/countries where the approach to time tends to be more laid back?

2. You are likely familiar with the urgency of the "time is money" mindset that is common in North America. What are some of the advantages and disadvantages of a slower pace of life?

3. How can you adjust your reporting practices to account for "Indian Time" when you encounter it in Indigenous communities?

Additional Readings and Resources

John Hopkins, "A Look at Indian Time." *Indian Country Today*, September 13, 2018. https://indiancountrytoday.com/archive/a-look-at-indian-time

Robert Joseph, "Use These Culturally Offensive Phrases, Questions at Your Own Risk." *Indigenous Corporate Training Blog*. https://www.ictinc.ca/blog/culturally-offensive-phrases-you-should-use-at

Samantha Chisholm Hatfield, Elizabeth Marino, et al. "Indian Time: Time, Seasonality, and Culture in Traditional Ecological Knowledge of Climate Change." *Ecological Processes* 7.25 (2018). https://link.springer.com/content/pdf/10.1186/s13717-018-0136-6.pdf

Endnotes

1. Michael Moore, "Taking Time to Understand the Story to Be Told," *Nieman Reports*, September 15, 2005. https://niemanreports.org/articles/taking-time-to-understand-the-story-to-be-told/

2. Exercise caution when using the term "Indian Time." Many Indigenous people may consider this a slur if used by non-Indigenous people. For example, on October 6, 2016, Québec's Indigenous Affairs Minister Geoffrey Kelly

used "Indian time" when asked why it took eight years to write a piece of legislation. The term wasn't received well. See: https://www.aptnnews.ca/national-news/is-indian-time-a-real-thing-time-to-weigh-in/ The concept of "Indian Time" is also applicable amongst the Inuit. See: https://canadianmysteries.ca/sites/franklin/archive/text/TimeAfterTime_en.htm

3 Drew Hayden Taylor, "Ipperwash, on Indian time," *NOW Magazine*, January 3, 2008. https://nowtoronto.com/news/ipperwash-on-indian-time

4 Dr. Clare Brant, "Native Ethics and Principles," Lecture, 1982. https://www.cbu.ca/indigenous-affairs/mikmaq-resource-centre/mikmaq-resource-guide/essays/native-ethics-principles/

✦ 2.2 ✦

Indigenous Customs and Protocols

In this chapter, students will learn to
- examine and explain some common Indigenous cultural customs such as participating in ceremonies and deciding whether to film them, giving and receiving gifts, understanding the role of Elders, and reporting on deaths in Indigenous communities; and
- discover how to navigate Indigenous customs and protocols in a news-gathering context.

My friend . . . has said for decades that if she were running a Canadian newspaper, she would treat coverage of Aboriginals and Aboriginal issues as a foreign bureau, complete with foreign correspondent and travel budget.

The reporter would be posted to, say, Regina for three years, with the mandate to write about this country's reserves, isolated and not, about Natives, rural and urban, and to move around the country with the same set of fresh eyes and wonder that often distinguishes the best work of a correspondent posted to Beijing or London or Washington.

Only then . . . would the story of Canada's Natives get the hearing and attention it deserves; only then might it be properly and fully told.[1]

– Christie Blatchford

I didn't see eye-to-eye with everything the late Christie Blatchford wrote about "Canada's Natives" during her rare journalistic forays into First Nation communities (for example, it would have been helpful if she had observed some of the tips in the Terminology chapter in this book Chapter 3.1), but how revealing it was, back in 2008, for Blatchford to imagine a reporter on a national or regional Indigenous beat as a *foreign correspondent*. Not only does it hint at the extra resources required to properly cover isolated Indigenous communities, but it also helps us appreciate how many reporters feel like fish out of water when visiting them.

Like foreign correspondents, who literally journey to new countries, reporters covering Indigenous communities may find themselves in places where the language, food, and customs aren't what they're used to (and may not have electricity, clean drinking water, or—gasp!—cell phone coverage). It may feel like a different planet to you. If you're non-Indigenous, you may feel like an adventurous explorer, or you may feel awkward because you are the minority and you stick out like a sore thumb.

Journalists are trained to ask questions, but, oddly enough, cultural differences make us nervous to ask the most important ones.

The thing is, unlike tourists, reporters have the responsibility of finding the "truth" about a given place—and relating it to the rest of the world. That's why it's important to acknowledge that all journalists have biases, and that we bring them to work every day. They show up in our story choices, the ways in which we frame those stories, and the decisions we make about what words, pictures, and video to include.

In this chapter, I'll explain some common Indigenous customs and offer tips on how to navigate them. Just as a foreign correspondent relies on a "fixer" to help translate local language and customs, your travels to Indigenous communities will run more smoothly if you have a trusted advisor who can explain why that old guy expects payment for that ride on his snowmobile, or what to do when you're invited to a feast. After all, the Lone Ranger didn't go far without his faithful Indian guide.

Here's the bottom line on Indigenous customs and protocols: If you're ever unsure about your interpretation of an Indigenous custom, or whether it's appropriate for you to participate in, write about, or record, an Indigenous ceremony, dance, or song, *ask your host*. They will appreciate your care and concern (though you may well get teased for it).

Participating in Ceremonies/Feasts

As a reporter in Indian Country, it won't be long before you come across spiritual ceremonies. From sweat lodges to sun dances, from memorial feasts to spirit dancing, different Indigenous Peoples have different ceremonies—and they're an important contemporary connection to ancient cultural traditions.

To Indigenous Peoples, ceremony is about community. Ceremony is a way to acknowledge the interconnectedness of everything. Ceremony is how values and beliefs are taught and reinforced. Some ceremonies are sacred and private. But sometimes, at Indigenous gatherings, everyone present is asked to participate in a cultural ceremony, a prayer, a dance, or a feast.

For reporters who see themselves as objective observers of events, it can be unnerving to join a ceremony for the first time. If it makes you feel uncomfortable, ask your host to explain the process. If all else fails, follow the lead of the person in front of you.

It's imperative to remain non-judgmental throughout the process. The idea behind a smudge, for example, is to wipe away negative thoughts, tension, and anxiety. If participating in the ceremony contradicts your own cultural or religious beliefs, just politely explain that.

Ceremonies: To Film or Not to Film

Indigenous ceremonies are always intriguing to visitors, sometimes colourful, perhaps even mystical. But how important is this ceremony to your story?

Maybe it is critical, especially if it tells us something about the motivations of a person you are interviewing or profiling. If it doesn't, ask yourself why you're trying to record it. Does the ceremony fit an image you or your audience have of "Indians" or "Eskimos" as mysterious or exotic?

When you request permission to film or photograph a ceremony, be prepared for differing opinions. Indigenous spiritual traditions and protocols are based on oral custom; there is no official handbook. Different people may give you different answers. For example, smudging (using the smoke of sweetgrass, tobacco, cedar, or sage to cleanse the mind, body, heart, and spirit) is a common ceremonial act you may encounter. While some Indigenous people don't object to a smudge being photographed or filmed, some do.

Who do you ask? In some Indigenous communities, you may be introduced to an Elder's helper, or a person appointed to speak on behalf of a ceremonial leader. Or you may be directed to the person leading the ceremony. If not, you should try to locate that person—not everyone who is attending has the authority to grant you permission to film or photograph, no matter their stature in the community.

If, after asking politely, you're told "No. This ceremony is off-limits to cameras," consider whether there's an alternative. Do you have to explain this moment with photos or video? For example, if you're a TV reporter, can you discuss a ceremony you're forbidden to film in a live hit, the same way a radio reporter might?

Try explaining to your hosts *why* the ceremony is important to your story, and how you intend to present it in your report. (For example, will it be sound only? If it's a video, will it be edited? If it's a photo, what sort of caption will run underneath?) Perhaps only a small part of the ceremony cannot be described or filmed and you can use other parts instead. Once your subjects have a better understanding of why it is important to you to describe or film this ceremony, you may be able to find common ground.

If you do get permission to film or write about a ceremony, explain to your audience what's going on and why. In an abbreviated news story, it's tough to relay the complex stories and beliefs behind a particular ceremony, but help your audience appreciate that each ceremony has a purpose, that "chants" contain words. Think about explaining the ceremony in a contemporary context—these days, "medicine-men" use cellphones and "shamans" are as likely to call a gathering using Facebook as a "sacred drum."

If you agree not to film certain portions of a ceremony, camera operators should turn their cameras off and point the lenses toward the ground, or in another direction, so participants are clear the camera isn't rolling.

If you're asked *not* to record a ceremony, it's unwise to ignore that request. If you really feel you must proceed and film surreptitiously, be aware that you may jeopardize your story, or future stories about that First Nation by you or anyone else in your newsroom. You may also hurt relationships with other First Nations who hear about your transgression or learn that you've exposed something that shouldn't have been made public.

Stealing Souls

The Lakota leader Crazy Horse is one of the most famous Native Americans in history, but there are no pictures of him. As legend has it, he refused to be photographed because he believed the camera would steal his soul.

The "Crazy Horse School of Photography" still has some subscribers, those who refuse to allow cameras because they believe a photograph literally captures an element of the life force of its subject. Certainly, many people—not just Indigenous people—find cameras intrusive.

But, historically, many Indigenous people didn't object to pictures and eagerly posed for cameras. These days, cameras are ubiquitous. Indeed, most Indigenous people, using their cellphones and digital cameras, are as fond of taking pictures as the next person. Lots of Indigenous people like to see themselves on TV or in the newspaper. At powwows or other public celebrations, if you ask politely, most Indigenous participants will usually cooperate—unless there are cultural or spiritual reasons for not doing so.

Additionally, a growing number of Indigenous cultural leaders recognize that a camera (and the person operating it) can be an important witness to cultural events. Capturing images of people and events "for the record" (and portraying them with dignity) is becoming an increasingly important tool for education, healing, and growth.

Giving Gifts

Media organizations often forbid reporters from paying a source for their participation in a story, the theory being that payment may potentially taint the truth. But, in some Indigenous cultures, it is considered appropriate to offer a storyteller a gift as a sign of respect. A gift is a way to acknowledge the willingness of the storyteller to share their time and knowledge, and to recognize that knowledge has value.

Other Indigenous people may take offence if a visitor brings a gift, seeing it as a bribe—a version of Europeans landing on the shores of the New World, smiling, and saying, "We come bearing gifts."

Should a reporter walk into a community bearing gifts, and if so, what kind? The easy answer: Ask your Indigenous host whether a gift for an interview subject is appropriate, and if so, what type. The gift certainly need not be lavish. Among many First Nations, tobacco is a common gift for an Elder, as it's considered sacred medicine. Traditionally, the gift would be tobacco leaves; today, it's acceptable to give a pouch of commercial rolling tobacco. A package of cigarettes will also do in a pinch, but generally, the tobacco is burned in ceremony, not smoked. Note that this practice has become widespread, but not all Indigenous Peoples put the same significance on tobacco.

If you're uncomfortable presenting tobacco, any small token will do—a homemade jar of canned peaches, a tin of Tim Horton's coffee. If the person drives a car, offer to contribute gas money. You may also feel it appropriate to offer an interview subject an honorarium. However, be aware that if you work for a large media organization, this can get complicated—you may need to provide the person's Social Insurance Number, mailing address, etc.

Receiving Gifts

Sharing and generosity are integral parts of Indigenous culture. Visitors, journalists included, are often offered small gifts and keepsakes or invited to eat when visiting an Indigenous person's home. Try to accept such gifts—rarely will they be offered with the intention of bribing you.

If you don't know what the meaning of the gift is, you should ask. A feather or blanket may seem innocuous to you, but in some instances, the gift may carry weighty cultural expectations akin to obligations. Do your best to understand what you're being gifted, and what it means if you decline to accept it.

Ethics policies in some newsrooms put a dollar limit on gifts that can be accepted ($25 is common), and most gifts you'll be offered will fall below that line. However, you may find it helpful to discuss these boundaries in your newsroom. One approach is to return the favour by sharing pens and baseball caps and buttons emblazoned with your news brand; however, this could also be construed as tacky. If you're offered cash in a potlatch or a giveaway, accept it and use the money to buy gifts for people in the community or redistribute it to community members.

What goes for gifts goes doubly for a host's offers of food and beverages. If someone pours you a cup of tea, take the time to drink it. Avoid rejecting reasonable offers of food, whether or not they seem delicious to you (moose nose, for example—don't knock it until you've tried it), unless you have a health reason for declining. (I will say, it's lonely being a vegetarian in Indian Country.)

The Role of Elders

Elders are treated with immense respect in Indigenous communities. Elders aren't just old people. They are considered repositories of history and cultural teachings, and they're often looked to for guidance and wisdom.

Reporters should take great pains to avoid annoying Elders. An Elder's blessing can make a reporter's visit to a community run smoothly; an Elder's disapproval can signal the demise of a story.

Still, the realities of our business often conflict with expectations of how an Elder should be treated, especially when it comes to interviewing protocol and clips. When speaking in public at gatherings in Indigenous communities, Elders will often be given as much time as they need to speak. Similarly, when in private discussion with an Elder, it's considered rude to interrupt them. Don't ask an Elder for their opinion if you're on deadline and don't have time to listen to it respectfully.

Interviewing Elders can be a frustrating and puzzling experience to the non-initiated. Traditional Indigenous storytelling is elliptical, and, sometimes, it's difficult to pry specific information out of an Elder. "How do you feel about XYZ?" may result in a half-hour tale about a childhood experience. If you're only looking for a 10-second clip or a short quote, explain the conventions of your medium; at least that person will be forewarned that you plan to reduce their teachings to a sound bite.

Finally, Indigenous Elders are busy folks. Far from relaxing in their golden years, a community's oldest and most respected Elders are often in high demand, with a steady schedule of ceremonial functions to attend and requests to share traditional knowledge. "Consultation burnout" is not uncommon in Indigenous communities, particularly among Elders.

If you've requested the involvement of an Elder in your story, be prepared to offer a gift that acknowledges that person's time and commitment to your project.

Death

Death is often a journalist's bread-and-butter.

Get your hands on the home video of the father of two who died in the car crash, dig up the high school yearbook photo of the boy shot in a drive-by gang slaying, find a Facebook snapshot of the toddler who was smothered to death by her foster parents.

Letting our audience visualize a dead person, via either still photos or video, helps them appreciate the gravity of the situation and empathize with larger public policy issues—so the thinking goes. It's uncomfortable work, no matter what culture or community you're in, and you've likely developed your own approach for broaching such a difficult subject with grieving friends and family.

But, be aware that Indigenous cultures have their own customs for dealing with death. Some First Nations cultures forbid showing pictures of the deceased for at least a year after the death. Other cultures find it extremely disrespectful to show *any* images of a deceased person, or even mention their names.

This custom of "putting away" the name and image of the deceased can be extremely problematic for a journalist whose objective is the opposite: to put a human face on a tragedy. What do you do when an Indigenous community has cultural objections to you using images?

The Aboriginal Peoples Television Network (APTN) news and current affairs division has an answer, in a section of its journalistic policy called "Cultural Considerations":

> We will take care to respect and acknowledge ceremonial conduct and customs of a Nation. Certain ceremonies should not be named or shown for broadcast....
> In respect for certain Inuit culture, when a person dies every effort will be made not to say the name of the person or show their image in a news story or program for at least one year.[2]

Mainstream news reporters may balk at such restrictions, but our newsrooms regularly make editorial decisions based on cultural considerations. Many media outlets restrict reports about suicide, in part because the details are often unpleasant, but also for fear of triggering more suicides. Similarly, Canadian broadcasters hesitate to show graphic and brutal images of war, such as body parts, out of concern that these may be upsetting to audiences.

These are matters of journalistic policy and ethics, based upon assumptions about cultural mores of our audience. Indigenous traditions relating to death may not follow mainstream Canadian practice, but they should also be respected.

In Australia, the government, broadcasters, and filmmakers have all taken steps to sensitize reporters and producers on cultural protocols relating to coverage of deaths of Indigenous people. Among Indigenous societies in Australia, grieving traditions strictly prohibit the use of the name of a deceased person. (Customs vary from region to region, but among some groups, this may last for as long as 15 years.) Ignoring protocols can cause immense grief and sorrow for the bereaved family.

In 2008, the Australian government encouraged the media to respect local grieving protocols when reporting Indigenous deaths, issuing the following advice:

- When a well-known individual passes away, the local community or media group may issue instructions on how the name, voice or images of this person can be used.
- If names or images are to be used, written permission should be obtained from the person's family and/or community. When contacting the community, care

should be taken to avoid using the person's name. The context in which the request is made should make it clear who is being referred to.
- If permission is granted, it is usually restricted to the particular media outlet that applied for it—it does not mean that other media agencies can publish the name or image without seeking permission.[3]

Australia's public broadcaster, ABC, went a step further, developing comprehensive guidelines instructing its journalists and documentary makers.[4] The policy advises journalists that using images and voices of long-dead people—such as archival footage and photographs—may cause distress. Now, at the beginning of ABC programs, and on its website, this caution appears:

> WARNING: Aboriginal and Torres Strait Islander viewers are warned that the following program may contain images and voices of deceased persons.

These may be complicated matters for mainstream Canadian media to wrestle with. Who owns archival images? How do you report a death without mentioning the name of the deceased? What if your competitor makes a different decision? However, tackling these issues, whether on a case-by-case basis or by developing a Code of Conduct, is key to showing respect for and reciprocity to Indigenous cultural traditions.

Eye Contact

Eye contact is considered a basic component of social interaction in Canada. "Look me in the eye," we tell our children. "Make eye contact," we advise students learning to speak in public. Typically, in social situations, Canadians make eye contact when first beginning to speak, then look away, then, periodically, return to the eyes of the person with whom we're talking (the average duration of eye contact among North Americans is about three seconds). Someone who won't make eye contact may be considered shy, rude, bored, or untrustworthy.

But staring directly into someone's eyes is *not* the cultural norm among some Indigenous groups. If you find that an Indigenous person isn't looking at you, it may be related to cultural teachings, gender roles, or the after-effects of imbalanced relationships with authority figures at residential schools.

Be aware of your own biases when interpreting facial cues. Cross-cultural training manuals advise non-Indigenous judges, for example, to be cautious about interpreting an Indigenous defendant's unwillingness to make eye contact as an admission of guilt.[5]

This can be especially challenging for a reporter during an interview. There's no easy answer about whether to make eye contact and for how long. Pay attention to your interviewee's face, and do your best to use facial behaviour that makes them feel comfortable.

Indigenous Languages

If you are a foreign correspondent, working with an interpreter is an essential skill any time you are in a country where the primary language is one you don't speak. It's no different when you travel to Indigenous communities. You will encounter many people whose mother tongue is not English or French, and you should make every effort to allow them to share their story in the language they feel most comfortable.

First and foremost, you should consider an interpreter an essential part of your journalism, and budget to pay that person fairly for their time. Indigenous-language interpreters may not have professional qualifications, but that person is providing you with a valuable service and likely invaluable cultural knowledge that deserves compensation. Relying on the goodwill of a source or someone in the Indigenous community to translate for you is unfair and potentially insulting.

The biggest challenge faced by all journalists who work with interpreters is accuracy.[6] Reporters cannot afford to get facts wrong or misquote someone simply because it was "lost in translation." You should explain this to your interpreter before you begin, to make sure they understand the importance of getting words right, even when they may seem like small details. It helps to review your questions with the interpreter before an interview, so that they know what to expect. Finally, working in a different language always takes longer, so make sure to allow for more time during an interview, and in the writing/production of your story afterwards.

If adding Indigenous languages to your "to-do" list seems a burden, consider how much more expressive your Indigenous interviewee will be with you if they are able to engage in their mother tongue. Ask yourself how you would feel in a courtroom or a hospital if staff did not speak your language and you didn't have an interpreter—why should engaging with the media be any different?

Furthermore, it's important to recognize that many Indigenous languages around the world are threatened or endangered, often as a result of intentional efforts to eradicate them. Offering to interview someone in their mother tongue is not only a measure of respect, it's also a matter of reconciliation: your media platform can amplify efforts by Indigenous communities to preserve or revitalize heritage languages.

Inuit Qaujimajatuqangit

When a journalist heads to the far North, they would do well to be familiar with a timeless set of Inuit societal values that are now an important part of contemporary Nunavut.

From its start in 1999, the government of Nunavut pledged to build the new territory upon a foundation of a set of principles known as Inuit Qaujimajatuqangit (IQ), "a body of accumulated knowledge of the environment and the Inuit interrelationship with the elements, animals, people and family."[7]

These principles of traditional knowledge are essentially an Inuit ethical framework for having a good life, summarized as follows:

- *Inuuqatigiitsiarniq*: Respecting others, relationships and caring for people.
- *Tunnganarniq*: Fostering good spirits by being open, welcoming, and inclusive.
- *Pijitsirniq*: Serving and providing for family and/or community.
- *Aajiiqatigiinniq*: Decision making through discussion and consensus.
- *Pilimmaksarniq/Pijariuqsarniq*: Development of skills through observation, mentoring, practice, and effort.
- *Piliriqatigiinniq/Ikajuqtigiinniq*: Working together for a common cause.
- *Qanuqtuurniq*: Being innovative and resourceful.
- *Avatittinnik Kamatsiarniq*: Respect and care for the land, animals, and the environment.

The government of Nunavut has attempted to incorporate these IQ principles into its governance structure, and you'll find everything from courts to child welfare organizations doing the same. While some critics argue these efforts are more lip service than the backbone of governance in Nunavut,[8] it is worthwhile to spend time not only understanding IQ but asking yourself how you can adapt your journalism practice to incorporate these values.

The government has produced a helpful "ally brochure" with ideas and suggestions for visitors to learn IQ,[9] which include learning to read/speak words and phrases in Inuktitut, participating in community celebrations, and, for the adventurous, trying *iqunag* (fermented walrus meat). Yum!

Brant's "Native Ethics and Rules of Behaviour"

When it comes to interacting and interviewing Indigenous people, should a journalist expect different behaviour and responses than when dealing with non-Indigenous people?

Yes, according to Dr. Clare Brant. Brant was a psychiatrist from the Mohawk community of Tyendinaga. He published an article in a journal of psychiatry two decades ago entitled "Native Ethics and Rules of Behaviour,"[10] in which he advocated for a more culturally appropriate approach to diagnosing and treating Indigenous mental health patients. The article remains widely quoted in psychiatry, anthropology, and sociology circles, both in Canada and internationally.

Brant argued that certain ethics, values, and rules of behaviour "persist in disguised form as carryovers from the Indigenous culture and which strongly influence Native thinking and action even today." He based his observations on "years of interactions with Iroquois people in Ontario and Crees in Northern Quebec and Ontario."[11]

Brant didn't pretend that the behaviour he described applied universally to all Indigenous Peoples. He recognized that Indigenous people grow up with a variety of cultural influences, and that there are likely variations among different Nations.

No question, there are dangers in generalizing about the psychology of any group of peoples. For every Indigenous person (such as myself) who finds truths in Brant's analysis, there will be another who feels their community acts in an opposite manner. Still, I hope my summary of the ethics set out by Brant serves as a useful starting point for journalists attempting to interpret the behaviour of the Indigenous people they meet and observe.

The Ethic of Non-Interference

The ethic of non-interference, says Brant, "is the principle that one Indian will never tell another Indian what to do."[12] Brant believed non-interference is an ethic based in pre-contact tribal society, which relied upon voluntary cooperation for the achievement of group goals. These days, the ethic of non-interference boils down to this: It's considered rude behaviour to give instructions or orders to an Indigenous person (or, for that matter, to pass any sort of judgment at all).

Journalists may encounter such behaviour when an Indigenous person expresses reluctance to go on the record to criticize another member of the community. The journalist may consider it necessary to get such a clip in order to build tension or conflict in a story, but to keep pushing for that on-the-record critique may be an exercise in frustration.

The ethic of non-interference may also come into play if a journalist is trying to advise or persuade an Indigenous person about what to do (for example, a cameraperson telling a grandmother to walk up to a gravestone and put flowers down, then telling her to repeat the action several times for cutaways). Indigenous people may consider such instructions or orders rude.

Conversely, an Indigenous person may be well aware that a journalist is doing something incorrectly (stepping haphazardly into a boat, for example, or interviewing the wrong person for a particular story), but won't say anything lest it be considered bad-mannered.

Anger Must Not Be Shown

Brant suggests that the notion that anger must not be shown—that is, anger must be suppressed—has its roots in Indigenous beliefs about the role of shamans and witches, whom one dare not offend or insult for fear of having their powers directed at you. In Indigenous societies, Brant argued, "angry behaviour is not merely unworthy and unwise, angry feelings are sinful."[13]

These days, many Indigenous people have lots to be angry about, and Brant observed that suppressed anger gives rise to repressed hostility and explosiveness under the influence of alcohol. He also noted that repressed hostility leads to a high incidence of grief reactions and cites statistics suggesting incidents of depression are twice as high among Indigenous populations as they are among white populations.

Journalists may encounter repressed anger from an Indigenous person when seeking a reaction to an emotional event. They may ignore an initial inquiry, or may avoid answering a question. Simply put, an Indigenous person who has experienced a tragic or sorrowful event may be reluctant to respond with anger or grief in public. If they do wind up expressing emotions, they may display an extreme response.

While an outburst of tears or an extremely angry reaction may look great on TV or social media, a journalist should be aware that an Indigenous person may be embarrassed afterwards. That journalist may also find themselves the object of hostility if they're perceived as being the one who provoked the reaction.

The Indian Concept of Sharing

Brant considered the concept of sharing to be a universal ethic among Indigenous groups, with its origin in the need to show hospitality to other groups of hunters, even when there was not much food in the village. "To take more than one's fair share or more than what one actually needs to survive is considered greedy and wasteful,"[14] says Brant. This custom of sharing manifests itself in the principle of equality. "Every Indian is just as good as everybody else," says Brant.

Sharing and equality may be at play when a journalist, seeking to simplify a story by reducing it to key characters, gets pushback from the people they're interviewing, along the lines of "You should interview so-and-so, and so-and-so, and so-and-so . . ." An

Indigenous person may be reluctant to be the main character or the focus of a news story if it's perceived that such a portrayal will elevate them over others in their community.

The Conservation/Withdrawal Reaction

When white people are placed in an anxiety-provoking situation, Brant observed, they are taught to react with a great deal of activity: they talk their heads off. But, according to Brant, Indigenous people have a completely different reaction: "an Indian will become less talkative, the more anxious he gets."[15]

He describes scenarios (such as a party or a psychiatric interview) where an Indigenous person who does not understand the rules or what behaviour is expected of them will simply slow down, becoming nearly catatonic, as if going into hibernation. "The more quiet the Indian becomes, the more frantic the White person becomes trying to get some sort of response out of him."[16]

For most people, an interaction with a journalist is uncommon, so it's not surprising that it may provoke anxiety. If you're interviewing an Indigenous person, you may find your subject is nervous and clams up, rather than sharing information.

If you want a productive interview, ensure the interviewee understands your expectations. Find a bit of time before the interview to establish rapport. Answer any questions the interviewee may have about the subject matter you intend to cover and how you plan to present their answers in your story. Hopefully, that will make everyone more comfortable and more open to dialogue.

EXERCISE 1   Journalism Ethics in Indigenous Communities

Break the class into three groups. Each group gets one of the following hypothetical scenarios. They have 10 minutes to discuss it and list possible responses. When the group reports back to the class as a whole, their response should identify both potential Indigenous cultural protocols (or how to find out about them) and standard ethical journalism approaches.

Scenario 1: You visit a First Nation community for a story on an oil pipeline. The Chief and Council offer you a traditional blanket as a gift of appreciation for your visit. What do you do?

Scenario 2: You are reporting on the case of a 22-year-old Nisga'a woman who went missing three months ago. After you finish an emotional interview with her mother, she wants to give you an eagle feather as "a sign of respect." What do you do?

Scenario 3: You're assigned a story on the opioid crisis. You find a healing circle for former drug users and want to interview the Indigenous Elder who is leading the circle. Her helper suggests you should offer her tobacco and $75 honorarium, which she "needs for groceries." What do you do?

Discussion Questions

1. Are there times you find it difficult, or inappropriate, to raise questions when talking about Indigenous customs and traditions? Why? How does this impact your work as a journalist?
2. Why do you think it's important for journalists to be aware of the cultural traditions of Indigenous Peoples? Why is cultural awareness of minorities in your community important?

Additional Readings and Resources

Bob and Cynthia Joseph, *Working Effectively with Indigenous Peoples* (Port Coquitlam, British Columbia: Indigenous Relations Press, 2017). https://www.ictinc.ca/

Aboriginal Worldviews and Education – Free online MOOC (massive open online course) taught by Anishinaabe educator J.P. Restoule that explores Indigenous ways of knowing and how they can benefit all students. https://www.coursera.org/learn/aboriginal-education

Robin Wall Kimmerer, *Braiding Sweetgrass* (Minneapolis: Milkweed Editions, 2013).

Endnotes

1. Christie Blatchford, "Canada's Native Reserves Deserve Foreign Correspondent," *Globe and Mail*, February 2, 2008. https://www.theglobeandmail.com/news/national/canadas-native-reserves-deserve-foreign-correspondent-treatment/article717978/
2. Cristina Azocar, "Native Americans," in Rachele Kanigel, *The Diversity Style Guide* (San Francisco: Wiley-Blackwell, 2018), 61–84.
3. NITV, "Indigenous Cultural Protocols: What Media Needs to Do when Depicting Deceased Persons," July 27, 2017. https://www.sbs.com.au/nitv/article/2017/07/27/indigenous-cultural-protocols-what-media-needs-do-when-depicting-deceased-persons
4. Australian Broadcasting Corporation Editorial Policies "ABC Indigenous Content," October 8, 2015. https://edpols.abc.net.au/guidance/abc-indigenous-content/
5. Rupert Ross, *Dancing with a Ghost* (Markham: Octopus Publishing, 1992), 4.
6. Laura Shin, "How Journalists Can Work Well with Interpreters When Reporting Stories," *Poynter*, November 12, 2012. https://www.poynter.org/newsletters/2012/how-journalists-work-well-with-interpretors-when-reporting-stories/
7. Government of Nunavut, "Iviqtippalliajut: In the Process of Falling into Place 2018–2023," https://www.gov.nu.ca/sites/default/files/ch_-_iviqtippalliajut_report_en_rev05.pdf
8. Lisa Gregoire, "Nunavut Must Move Beyond Paying Lip Service to Traditional Values, Says Glassco Fellow," *Nunatsiaq News*, May 19, 2020. https://nunatsiaq.com/stories/article/glassco-fellow-says-nunavut-must-move-beyond-iq-lip-service/
9. Government of Nunavut, Iviqtippalliajut Ally Brochure, https://www.gov.nu.ca/sites/default/files/ally_brochure_rev07_withedits.pdf
10. Dr. Clare Brant, "Native Ethics and Rules of Behaviour," *Canadian Journal of Psychiatry* 35 (1990): 534–539.
11. Ibid, 534.
12. Dr. Clare Brant, "Native Ethics and Principles." Lecture at Liscombe Lodge, Nova Scotia, 1982. https://www.cbu.ca/indigenous-affairs/mikmaq-resource-centre/mikmaq-resource-guide/essays/native-ethics-principles/.
13. Ibid.
14. Ibid.
15. Ibid.
16. Ibid.

✦ 2.3 ✦

Who Represents the "Indigenous Perspective"?

> In this chapter, students will learn to:
> - identify different Nations of Indigenous Peoples, and the difference between traditional versus elected band leadership; and
> - consider how to report on divisions within Indigenous communities.

It's tempting, when you have such little space in a news story, to get that *one quote* you need to represent "the Indigenous perspective." But think twice about letting that be the sum total of your research.

Just as there is no one spokesperson who represents all the "White" views in Canada, there is no one single voice that speaks for all Indigenous communities. If you rely on only one Indigenous source, you run the risk of presenting a story that's biased and inaccurate.

Not Homogenous

Indians are treated in Canadian legislation as if they are a homogenous group. But not all Indians are the same. Indigenous Peoples are a heterogenous bunch. A Cree is not a Haida; a Mi'kmaw is not a Dene. And you'd better believe an Indian is not a Métis nor an Inuk. Actually, the more you learn about First Nations, the more you discover an endless variety of differing perspectives. Off-reserve, on-reserve, status, non-status, treaty, "traditional," "progressive" . . . the list goes on and on. (I'll explain some of those categories in Chapter 3.1, Terminology and Lexicon.)

Don't let all the differences bewilder you. What's important is that you're aware they exist. For example, if you know something about Cree ceremonies in Alberta, don't assume that practice or custom will be the same when you're meeting with Cree folks in Manitoba or Quebec, and certainly not if you're reporting on the Tahltan Nation in northern British Columbia.

In the same way, if you are reporting on a story specific to an Indian reserve, don't assume that an urban Indigenous person is the correct person to speak to. Similarly, the media often rely heavily on Indigenous academics and politicians for comment because they're readily available in cities—but it's important to ask whether that privileges the view of a particular socio-economic class.

Traditional versus Elected Leadership

On any given story, your first call to a First Nation will often be to the band office, looking for a quote or a clip from the Chief. For a national story, you may ring up the Assembly of First Nations, looking for the press secretary to the National Chief. But don't make the mistake of letting one person, such as an elected Chief, be the sole Indigenous "spokesperson" on an issue.

Back in the 1880s, the Government of Canada introduced a system under the *Indian Act* where bands of Indians were expected to elect Chiefs and Councils as their leaders. Traditional forms of governance, such as hereditary chiefs selected by historical custom, were displaced. Some communities accepted the *Indian Act* electoral system; others were hostile to the changes. Governance structures continue to be matters of some debate.

Nowadays, according to the Ministry of Indigenous Affairs, less than half of the 600+ Indian bands in Canada are governed by Chiefs and Councils elected under the *Indian Act*. The rest operate under "customary" governance structures (which means pretty much whatever a community wants it to mean—leaders may be hereditary, or simply chosen using alternative electoral rules). In some communities, traditional and elected governments work side by side.

What does this mean for you? In some stories, the band office is a good point of entry, but, especially when it comes to issues of land or customs, you should also be asking whether there are traditional leaders or Elders whom you can consult.

Factions and Division

Like any group, community, or political body, Indigenous communities contain a full range of opinions on all manner of issues. Take resource development. Many First Nation, Métis, and Inuit communities engage in discussions about mining in their traditional territories. Some residents support such activities; others oppose it. Still others may not know what to think. That difference of opinion on a subject could be interpreted as a sign of mature debate, or it may indicate a schism in the community.

The Bottom Line on Perspectives

Recognize that there are many different perspectives within Indigenous communities. There's no easy way to determine who is most "appropriate" to include in your story. Ask questions, and do your research. When it comes time to get your story to air, make sure your viewers and listeners understand what perspective the subject(s) in your story are coming from.

Discussion Questions

1. What is the effect of various groups of Indigenous people being largely invisible in the media?

2. What might be some of the reasons that news reporters don't portray the diversity within and among Indigenous communities? How can those challenges be overcome?

3. In 2019, the National Inquiry into Missing and Murdered Indigenous Women and Girls found that Indigenous women and LGBTQ2S+ Indigenous people are underrepresented in the media, and often framed in ways that "[send] the message that Indigenous women, girls, and 2SLGBTQQIA people are not 'newsworthy' victims."[1] What stereotypes exist about Indigenous women or LGBTQ2S+ Indigenous people? What are the repercussions of these stereotypes?

Additional Readings and Resources

Understanding Indigenous Perspectives. This set of online learning modules from the Ontario Institute for Studies in Education (OISE) was created by Anishinaabe scholar Jean-Paul Restoule to inspire educators to gain a deeper understanding of Indigenous perspectives and an appreciation of Indigenous knowledge and worldviews. https://www.oise.utoronto.ca/abed101/

Lisa Charleyboy and Mary Beth Leatherdale (eds.), *Dreaming in Indian: Contemporary Native American Voices* (Toronto: Annick Press Ltd., 2014).

Lisa Charleyboy and Mary Beth Leatherdale (eds.), *Urban Tribes: Native Americans in the City* (Toronto: Annick Press Ltd., 2015).

Lisa Charleyboy and Mary Beth Leatherdale (eds.), *#NotYourPrincess: Voices of Native American Women* (Toronto: Annick Press Ltd., 2017).

Endnotes

1. National Inquiry into Missing and Murdered Indigenous Women and Girls. (2019). *Reclaiming Power and Place. The Final Report of the National Inquiry into Missing and Murdered Indigenous Women and Girls.* The National Inquiry. https://www.mmiwg-ffada.ca/wp-content/uploads/2019/06/Final_Report_Vol_1a-1.pdf

✦ 2.4 ✦
White Characters and Indigenous Agency

In this chapter, students will learn to:
- *identify narrative agency in an Indigenous context; and*
- *develop more representative journalism.*

> *Perhaps most destructive to the image of Indigenous people is the lack of character and personality afforded them by the media. Indigenous people are almost always cast in supporting roles or relegated to the background, and are rarely allowed to speak or display their complexity and richness as human beings. Whatever character they do have tends to reveal itself only in terms of their interactions with non-Indigenous people. Rarely is an Indigenous character portrayed as having personal strengths and weaknesses, or shown acting on their own values and judgements.*[1]
> – MediaSmarts

Hollywood was agog when Kevin Costner released his epic western *Dances With Wolves* in 1990. Real Indigenous actors! Speaking Lakota, with subtitles! Indigenous characters with differing opinions—some wanted to fight the white soldiers, some wanted peace!

But, much like the journals of the first European explorers and missionaries, *Dances With Wolves* revolves around a White guy's experience. "I've always wanted to see the frontier," says Costner's character, Lt. John J. Dunbar, "before it's gone." The movie purported to treat Indigenous people sympathetically; instead, it robbed Indigenous people of voice.

The Importance of Agency

Reporters would do well to remember *Dances With Wolves* (or other big Hollywood movies about Indigenous Peoples—*Little Big Man*, *Thunderheart*, or *Avatar*) when trying to sort out which interviews or characters to include in your story.

How often do we lead with a quote from a non-Indigenous expert, who offers a broad perspective on the issue at hand? How often do our news stories contain helpless Indigenous people, waiting for a government department to fix some dire problem?

Ask yourself: will Indigenous people have *agency* in my story?

In the fields of philosophy and sociology, "agency" refers to the power people have to think and act for themselves. Identifying who has agency in your story is important, because good news stories are more than a compendium of facts. Skillful news reporters use the same storytelling techniques as fiction writers or movie directors: dramatic arc, heroes and villains, denouement. Believe it or not, race and culture also play a role in our decisions on how to frame a story.

Reporters often treat Indigenous people differently than non-Indigenous people, according to one study of news coverage of Indigenous child welfare issues. Social work professor Robert Harding found Indigenous people are predominantly constructed as "victims" in news stories, while non-Indigenous people are typically portrayed as "heroes."[2]

Furthermore, reporters usually cast non-Indigenous people as active participants in news events, whereas Indigenous people are most likely to be assigned roles as passive recipients of events beyond their control. (For instance, in a story about a health crisis in an Inuit community, the reporter may build their story around a non-Inuit doctor who treats people at a clinic, then interview a non-Inuit government official to offer context to the crisis, without ever interviewing any Inuit.)

For Indigenous Peoples, being regularly portrayed in the media as lacking in agency has real consequences. Self-governance and self-determination are goals for many Indigenous communities, but other Canadians may view these aspirations in terms of the threat they pose to their lifestyle and standard of living. If Indigenous people are constructed in news reports as unable to exercise control over their own lives, the public is even less likely to show support for transfer of power or resources. In other words, your news story may unwittingly become an instrument to preserve the status quo in Canada, where Indigenous Peoples have little control over their own affairs.

How can you change that? By being conscious about race and culture when you frame your story. Your research may uncover a wide variety of non-Indigenous people with opinions about Indigenous issues. Academics and experts, politicians and bureaucrats. Or people hired by First Nations to speak for them: band managers or nurses or economic development officers. In some stories, you'll find non-Indigenous people impacted by Indigenous actions: neighbours, competitors, supporters.

Maybe these are all valid perspectives, but make sure you include Indigenous people in a *substantive* way in a story about Indigenous Peoples.

The reporter's tendency toward framing a story through non-Indigenous eyes is, perhaps, understandable. Non-Indigenous professionals may be more "accessible" to the media than Indigenous people because they're willing to play the media game. And academics, experts, and politicians often express their opinions in clear and concise sound bites. But is it necessary to build your story around that non-Indigenous person, or are you favouring that perspective because that person is easily available to you and delivers their message in a manner that you or your audience are more comfortable with?

Discussion Questions

1. Find three examples of news stories on cases of missing and murdered Indigenous women and girls. How do the media describe Indigenous victims or perpetrators compared to non-Indigenous victims or perpetrators? How would you improve upon these stories?
2. What is "agency" in a storytelling context? Can you think of a time when you have been powerless? Describe what it was like for you.
3. In your own words, explain how Indigenous Peoples may be impacted when they are deprived of agency in news stories.

Additional Readings and Resources

Looking for an Indigenous expert? The Yellowhead Institute is often a good starting point, as they have connections nationwide with their researchers. https://yellowheadinstitute.org/

Looking for Indigenous female voices? Try Informed Opinions, which has a database aiming to amplify perspectives of qualified women with diverse backgrounds. https://informedopinions.org/

John Kelly and Miranda Brady, *We Interrupt This Program: Indigenous Media Tactics in Canadian Culture* (Vancouver: UBC Press, 2016).

Jesse Thistle, *From the Ashes: My Story of Being Métis, Homeless, and Finding My Way* (Toronto: Simon & Schuster Canada, 2019).

Endnotes

1 ©2022 MediaSmarts, Ottawa, Canada, *Common Portrayals of Indigenous People*, http://www.mediasmarts.ca. Quoted with permission.

2 Robert Harding, "The Media, Aboriginal People and Common Sense." *The Canadian Journal of Native Studies*, XXV.1 (2005), 311–335.

✦ 2.5 ✦

Trauma-Informed Reporting

> In this chapter, students will learn to:
> - recognize the prevalence of trauma in Indigenous persons/communities;
> - practise trauma-informed journalism, an approach to reporting that respects the pain and psychic wounds of the traumatized;
> - show respect for and minimize pain to Indigenous subjects, while fulfilling essential journalistic needs for verification, detail, and information; and
> - understand the need for self-care.

I don't want to leave people in a worse situation. When you're dealing with Indigenous communities, trauma is interwoven into so many aspects of life. You have to be careful and respectful of how that impacts people.[1]

– Connie Walker

If I had to put a finger on why so many Indigenous people distrust the media, I'd highlight the ways journalists tend to treat victims and survivors of trauma.

How often have Indigenous communities experienced reporters who parachute in when tragedy strikes, thrust cameras and microphones into the faces of distressed community members, ask "how it feels," then pack up their gear and never return again?

Hint: it happens a lot.

So often, in fact, that Indigenous interviewees may be rightly wary of being retraumatized by unthinking or unwitting journalists.

This chapter aims to change that by encouraging you to be more attuned to the human beings at the centre of your stories—the ordinary Indigenous folks who have experienced something extraordinarily bad or difficult and choose to talk to journalists about it.

Of course, there's a long tradition of journalists risking their health and safety to bear witness to violence and destruction. Journalists around the world cover difficult and traumatic events every single day. "Trauma is at heart of news—and of the human condition," the Dart Centre for Journalism and Trauma has observed.[2]

Many journalists feel a sense of duty to undertake such reportage. Good journalism during times of crisis can help inform our audiences by making sense of chaos. It can spur citizens to action, encouraging them to help reduce or prevent suffering in the future.

Yes, trauma is innately newsworthy. But if you intend to report regularly on Indigenous communities, get ready to be exposed to an inordinate number of disasters and crises. House fires and catastrophic floods, severe illnesses, sexual assaults, gun violence, suicides, car crashes, and child abuse—Indigenous communities experience these miseries and more at disproportionately high rates.

With tragedy so unfortunately common in Indigenous communities, it goes without saying that many Indigenous people you meet have experienced trauma, "a horrific event beyond the scope of normal human experience."[3] To put a number on it, one study estimated Indigenous people have nearly four times the risk of severe trauma compared to the rest of the population in Canada.[4] That means odds are high that you will interview Indigenous people grappling with the fallout of accidents, injuries, or crime. Even if disasters aren't your beat—say, you cover arts or sports or business or politics—you *will* wind up sifting through layers upon layers of trauma if Indigenous folks are part of your story.

Because in addition to all the above, Indigenous Peoples also carry pains that are centuries old.

Historical Trauma

"Yes, apocalypse. We've had that over and over. But we always survived. We're still here,"[5] says noted Anishinaabe author Waubgeshig Rice's protagonist in his dystopian thriller *Moon of the Crusted Snow*.

It's been said by other Indigenous writers and thinkers, too: from biological warfare to cultural genocide, contemporary Indigenous societies have already experienced "the end of the world as we know it."

Unlike a car crash or a rape, the dispossession of Indigenous lands and destruction of Indigenous cultures didn't occur swiftly in Canada or the United States. Not at all. Colonialism has been a long, slow burn. But if you accept that *every* Indigenous person is a post-apocalyptic survivor, you will begin to understand why trauma is so much a part of every Indigenous story.

To be clear, the psychic wounds inflicted by colonialism are only *one* aspect of Indigenous life, and, as touched on in the previous chapter, being reduced to victimhood can be hurtful. For example, when Cree poet Billy-Ray Belcourt became a Rhodes Scholar in 2016, he stopped doing interviews after his accomplishment was inaccurately framed by a local paper. "Dear Media: I am more than just violence," he wrote in his blog. "Violence should not be your lede. Indigenous suffering should not be your angle."[6]

It's an important point. There are countless stories of success, achievement, and resilience in Indigenous communities. Pushing back against any notion of Indigenous Peoples as merely survivors, Anishinaabe cultural theorist Gerald Vizenor (once a journalist himself) used the term "survivance" to describe how present-day Indigenous Peoples transform oppression into resistance:

> Survivance is an active sense of presence, the continuance of Native stories, not a mere reaction, or a survivable name. Native survivance stories are renunciations of dominance, tragedy and victimry.[7]

Vizenor's concept of survivance helps remind journalists to actively seek narratives that point toward resilience, even when covering the bleakest of stories. They're there, if you look.

Nevertheless, our pasts haunt us still. We shouldn't pretend that stories of grief, anger, and loss don't often rise to the fore in Indigenous lives.

A growing body of work among psychologists and mental health experts suggests trauma as experienced by Indigenous Peoples ought to be considered through a wider lens, with an understanding that the disruption of pre-contact ways of life caused great shockwaves of stress that continue to reverberate and impact individuals today. What follows are some of the terms used to describe that trauma, and a brief description of each.

Historical Trauma

Lakota psychiatry professor Maria Brave Heart, who has conducted years of clinical practice in Indigenous communities, describes historical trauma as "a cumulative emotional and psychological wounding over the lifespan and across generations, emanating from a massive group trauma."[8] Drawing on Indigenous spirituality, psychologist Eduardo Duran describes historical trauma as a "soul wound." Here are but a few examples of the types of traumatic events Indigenous Peoples have endured:

- influenza and smallpox epidemics;
- famine and starvation;
- forced settlement of nomadic tribes;
- erasure of traditional Indigenous languages; and
- removal of children from their families into residential schools or foster homes.

Race-based Trauma

Race-based trauma is the mental and emotional injury caused by encounters with racial bias and ethnic discrimination, racism, and hate. Examples include:

- experiencing an emotionally painful and sudden racist encounter;
- witnessing videos of other people facing racism; and
- intergenerational transmission of historical acts of racism.[9]

Intergenerational Trauma

Intergenerational trauma is the idea that trauma from years ago can be transferred from generation to generation, and can continue to impact people today. Essentially, our parents' and grandparents' and great-grandparents' experiences affect us still.

The notion of historical trauma and intergenerational transmission began to be studied in earnest after the Holocaust. It's been suggested that the negative symptoms of historical trauma include:

- depression and mental illness, sometimes leading to suicide;
- feelings of hopelessness;

- addiction as a result of coping by drinking or doing drugs (substance abuse); and
- sexual and physical abuse, including domestic violence.[10]

While there are numerous studies examining the nature of historical trauma,[11] it's a relatively new concept in public health. Identifying symptoms remains an area of developing research and the source of some debate within the scientific community.

It's beyond the scope of this text to dive deeply into how experiences of colonialism manifest in the mental health of the colonized. Plus, as a general rule, no journalist should offer armchair pseudo-diagnosis of psychological disorders or mental illnesses without evidence and trained observation to back up the assertions.

However, it's essential for reporters to understand that interacting with people who have suffered immediate and/or long-term trauma is part and parcel of reporting in Indigenous communities.

Historical Trauma and Reporting

Covering pain and suffering doesn't come easily to many of us. Yet, each and every day, people invite journalists into their lives, often when they're at their most vulnerable.

Different people respond to trauma differently, but journalists hardly ever receive formal training on how to safely work with emotionally fragile people. Journalism professors rarely broach the subject with students. Working journalists don't typically feel comfortable discussing trauma, either. Instead, we learn through trial and error. Sometimes, we make mistakes and harm people in the process.

Thankfully, that's starting to change.

Just as health professionals have developed "trauma-informed care," which centres on the healing needs of patients suffering from trauma, awareness is growing among journalists about the importance of prioritizing the needs of interviewees who have experienced trauma.

There are excellent resources for journalists who want to learn more about this subject. The Dart Centre for Journalism and Trauma in the United States, for example, has published a guide called *Tragedies and Journalists: A Guide for More Effective Coverage*. Jo Healy of the BBC wrote a comprehensive book on the subject called *Trauma Reporting: A Journalist's Guide to Covering Sensitive Stories*. Both are full of tips and advice, which I've drawn upon to offer these suggestions for working with Indigenous communities in an ethical and responsible manner.

If you anticipate your assignment will delve into traumatic events, below are some tips on caring for interviewees (before, during, and after a story) and caring for yourself (before, during, and after a story).

Caring for Interviewees

If trauma reporting isn't approached with special care and attention, there's a real risk you may cause further trauma to the Indigenous people you interview. Caring for your interviewee is at the heart of trauma-informed journalism.

Before

Be human

When we prepare to interview someone who has experienced a traumatic event, some journalists steel themselves for the task by putting their game face on. It's understandable to want to protect yourself, but put yourself in the moccasins of the interviewee.

Remember that most people we interview don't have experience dealing with reporters. Ask yourself: How would I want to be treated in this moment? As best as possible under the circumstances, be kind and courteous and patient. Take the time to introduce yourself and the members of your team. In some cases, you may need to offer help or assistance. As the Dart Centre wisely advises, "You're a human being first, after all, a journalist second."[12]

Be humble

Known to the Lakota as *unsiiciyapi*, to the Anishinaabe as *dabaadendiziwin*, humility is a fundamental value in many Indigenous cultures. Essentially, to be humble is to think of others before yourself.

Journalists aren't typically good models of humility. We get wrapped up in ourselves, our deadlines, and our pursuit of truth. To be a good reporter takes persistence and a strong conviction that our work is in the public interest. But, as difficult as it is for some journalists to accept, not everyone who has experienced a traumatic event owes us their story.

It is a privilege to have a survivor of trauma share their experience with us. Treat that story and the person sharing it with care. Centring the needs of a survivor—not yourself—will show that you understand your place and go a long way toward creating an environment of trust.

Be transparent

An important way to avoid retraumatizing an interviewee is to give them as much control over their story as possible. This is especially true when working with Indigenous Peoples, who are well familiar with paternalism from outsiders. Most people don't know how news gets made, nor should we expect them to. So, take the time to explain your process. Tell them how you plan to use their interview, their photo, their words. Explain how long your story will be, and what kind of deadline you're facing.

All of this information helps an interviewee understand what you're up to. Knowing the ground rules give people an opportunity to decide whether or not they want to participate, rather than feeling they were taken advantage of.

Get informed consent

This goes without saying: Don't interview people about traumatic events without their consent. But consent is a bare minimum standard: Your responsibility goes beyond securing mere agreement. You need to offer more care and consideration when dealing with Indigenous Peoples, especially vulnerable or marginalized individuals.

When covering traumatic events, you should give interviewees as much information as you possibly can about possible impacts of their participation, to ensure their permission is fully and freely given.

In a Canadian Journalism Foundation forum on informed consent,[13] panellists referred to the approach taken by American columnist Neil Steinberg. When he was reporting for the *Chicago Sun-Times*, he routinely gave a warning—what he calls "The Speech"—to people he felt might not be fully aware of what it meant to talk with a journalist. Here is Steinberg's "speech":

> You understand I write for a newspaper. That I'm talking to you because I'm going to put what you say into an article, which will appear in the newspaper, which people will then read.[14]

While Steinberg's speech may be helpful to you in crafting your own version, note that he doesn't explore what good or bad things may result from media coverage.

Perhaps this is because it's difficult to predict the outcomes of publicity. People have lots of reasons for wanting to share their stories with journalists—to put pressure on the government, to educate the public, or simply to feel valued. However, in some cases, it is foreseeable that an interviewee could be retraumatized, shamed on social media, or face even more serious impacts when the content of an interview goes public.

That's a conversation you need to have, perhaps more than once, when dealing with vulnerable subjects such as trauma survivors. It's an extension of our journalistic responsibilities of fairness and minimizing harm.

Some journalists may ask: How will I ever win the trust of an Indigenous source if I'm obligated to discuss the potential risks they face by sharing their story with a journalist? But take that question further: If an Indigenous person feels unjustly treated by my journalism, how will it impact my long-term relationship with an Indigenous community?

On the flip side, seeking informed consent may build trust. When informed consent was imposed on the fields of anthropology and sociologists a few decades ago, research demonstrated that informed consent protocols to recruit subjects did not lead to a decline in participation rates.[15]

Furthermore, you'll find many Indigenous people are well versed in the notion of "free, prior and informed consent," often referred to as FPIC, as it forms a cornerstone of the United Nations Declaration on the Rights of Indigenous Peoples. FPIC is a principle intended to govern activity in the resource sector, but there's a growing expectation among Indigenous Peoples that the right extends to all manner of working relationships with outsiders.

During

Empower interviewees

Trauma turns a person's world upside down. You can help by doing your best to give interviewees a sense of control over this particular conversation. That may mean letting them choose the setting that is most comfortable for them to talk with you. This is not the time to worry about a perfect visual or someplace convenient for you—make do with whatever situation they choose.

Be patient

It may take time for an interviewee to open up when recalling a traumatic event. Give them that time. Allow for pauses and silences. If the person needs to take a break from the interview, let them. While you shouldn't try to provoke tears, tears may happen—be prepared with some tissues. And always turn your phone off and set aside as much uninterrupted time as you can.

Interview respectfully

It's okay to express sorrow for what happened, but resist the urge to over-empathize. A journalist's job is not to rescue anyone—we're there to listen, carefully. If you need to ask a tough question, advise the interviewee beforehand and make sure you've got consent to do so. Avoid that old cliché: "How does it feel?" Instead, ask simple, open-ended questions: "Tell me more" and "What happened next?"

Finally, respect an interviewee's right to say no. Don't retraumatize someone by pushing too hard. Nobody should be forced to provide every detail about a traumatic event they experienced.

Remember resilience

Resilience is a common theme in Indigenous healing programs. Look beyond your interviewee's trauma: A person is more than one single awful event in their life. Explore their strengths and successes during the interview, and do your best to fit those into your story.

Painting a holistic portrait of a survivor gives that person a measure of dignity. It's also a smart way to bring an interview to a close, allowing a person to end on a positive note, rather than an upsetting one.

After

Recheck facts

It's the golden rule of journalism: Getting the facts right always matters. But in difficult stories, facts matter more than ever. Misspelled names, distorted chronologies, and factual errors can break the trust survivors put in you, leaving them feeling victimized all over again. These are stories you need to tell with accuracy and understanding.

Stay in touch

It's not common practice for journalists to stay in touch with their sources once a story has been published. But, as mentioned in Chapter 1.1, Indigenous communities are familiar with outsiders who come to their communities to take precious things away. That's why it's so important to keep in contact with interviewees before and after a story is published. That continuing relationship signals that you care about getting the story right and that you're accountable for your work.

Community care

Journalists are not trained as therapists or healers or counsellors. We shouldn't pretend to be. In the majority of stories, we're part of an interviewee's world for an intense and short period of time, then we carry on. While you may not be able to offer ongoing support to an interviewee who has experienced or disclosed trauma, you can make an extra effort to ensure the person has someone in their life who is aware of the interview and can keep an eye on them in the hours, days, and months after you leave.

Consider a follow-up

Journalists tend to rush to the scene of a traumatic event and provide intense coverage for a short time. Then the news cycle moves on. Remote Indigenous communities, often visited by reporters only in times of crisis, are acutely aware of the media's penchant for tragedy.

If it is important to share a person's anger and grief and despair, it is equally important to share the aftermath of a traumatic event. It may be a story of recovery and healing, or it may be a story of ongoing distress. Either way, make the effort to reconnect with a community, a family, or an individual who made time for you once—follow-up reporting helps our audiences understand that coping with trauma is a long-lasting process.

Caring for Yourself

As much as it's critical for you to care for your Indigenous subjects who have suffered trauma, you will do them great disservice if you neglect to care for yourself.

The importance of self-care became clear to me while I was shooting a documentary about a Truth and Reconciliation Commission event in Vancouver. Hundreds of residential school survivors had gathered to speak their truths, both publicly and privately, about childhoods stolen. Mental health workers and traditional healers were everywhere, ready to offer support to those testifying and those witnessing. For three days, my cameraman and I raced around at a breakneck pace, recording one heartbreaking testimony after another.

At the end of the third day, we filmed Commissioner Marie Wilson as she met privately with her spiritual counsellor and a mental health worker. She had listened intently to survivors for several hours, and quietly shared how it was impacting her. When we turned the camera off, Commissioner Wilson asked me something I had not paused to ask myself.

"And how are *you* doing?"

My chest constricted and I had trouble speaking. Clearly, I was not doing so well.

The next morning, I told my cameraman to extend his coffee break. I walked into one of the small white tents that housed traditional healers. Two older Indigenous men sat there. They motioned for me to come in. We smudged. As the medicines wafted around me, they brushed me down, one with an eagle fan, another with a cedar bough. All of the hurt, pain, and anguish I had been analyzing in my head as clips and scenes for my documentary came rushing to me. My heart connected to my brain. I began to quietly sob. The men held me until I was ready to leave.

It was a powerful lesson. While journalists may "simply" be witnesses and conduits for others' stories, we can only absorb so much before it takes a toll on us, too.

In a raw and brave article in *Maisonneuve* magazine,[16] non-Indigenous reporter Jody Porter revealed the perils of a steady diet of covering tragedy during her long and respected career of reporting on Indigenous issues in northern Ontario.

> I plowed my emotions over one death into the story of another, and another and another. I couldn't see that I was blazing my own secret path, creating pity porn for a hungry audience. I ate up the clicks and likes and retweets from First Nations people I respected, mistaking my social media feed for something more nourishing.[17]

After years spent filing stories about preventable deaths, about children dying in homes without running water, in communities without mental health services, or far away from family in unsafe foster homes, Porter had her own personal health crisis. It gave her pause to reflect on her coverage.

> I thought my years of engaging on Indigenous issues had protected me from the white savior complex. (I'd been so good!) Instead, I was blindly galloping around on my white horse, not seeing the wholeness of Indigenous lives and experience. Not seeing my own brokenness. In focusing so much on the hurt in other people's lives, I'd missed the lessons they offered about healing.[18]

If you want your reporting to serve communities in a good way, and to continue to do so over the course of a long and fulfilling career, it's important to care for yourself. And much like the care you offer your story subjects, that means checking in before, during, and after a story.

Before

Stay healthy
Journalism is a difficult profession, and many journalists are accustomed to fuelling their adrenalin-filled days on little more than bottomless cups of coffee and potato chips. But lack of sleep and a lousy diet clouds your emotional and mental judgment, not to mention impairs your writing. Try to eat three square meals a day, make time for exercise, and get some sleep.

This can be especially hard when covering remote Indigenous communities, where lodgings may be haphazard and healthy food isn't always an option. Plan ahead: Bring plenty of protein-rich snacks, clean drinking water, and anything that acts as a sleep aid (don't be shy about packing your teddy bear, if that's what helps).

Develop a trauma plan
If you're heading to an Indigenous community where you're likely to be interviewing traumatized people, find time to sit down with your team (whether that's your senior editor, assignment editor, camera person, producer—anyone who is part of this story) and discuss what you may encounter. Reviewing the assignment—with the purpose of naming the emotional challenges ahead—helps everyone feel less alone, more connected, and better prepared.

During

Express yourself
Discussing painful experiences is difficult for everyone. While journalists are used to asking others to talk about their trauma, they often find it hard to discuss their own. Keeping a stiff upper lip has long been the norm in the profession. But talking helps. It helps make sense of the mess of emotions that swirl around traumatic events. Talking to

a person, especially someone who doesn't pass judgment, helps us feel connected to other human beings. If you don't have that someone, don't bottle it up—try writing in a journal or tell someone you need help.

Express gratitude
Journalism is hard work. Covering tragedies is especially hard. Make sure you acknowledge and express appreciation for everyone on your team—and everyone assisting you—for the good work they do. Feeling valued helps keep people balanced and emotionally well. In the same vein, when things don't go as planned, be careful with criticism. If emotions are running high, so are sensitivities. Your critical comments may also be observed closely in Indigenous communities, as noted in Chapter 2.2, "Indigenous Customs and Protocols," some Indigenous cultures have an ethic of non-interference. In a tense situation, you dishing out explicit criticism may be viewed negatively and impact your ongoing relationships.

Stay connected
Make time to stay in touch with your friends, family, and loved ones when you are navigating difficult emotional terrain. The people you love help keep you balanced and self-aware. When you're in a remote Indigenous community where you may have intermittent telecommunications, it's not a waste of time to ensure you have a place where you can have a few quiet moments to yourself with a steady internet connection, so that you can check in with folks back home.

Know your limits
If you have experienced trauma in your own life, or even if you have not, you need to be aware of how covering a tragedy may impact you. If you're feeling overwhelmed, despite your best efforts, it's important to say so. That can be difficult to do, however, if you're early in your career or you're worried it may impact future assignments.

But think of the long game. You may feel a calling to report difficult stories in Indigenous communities. You may be willing to experience some suffering to do so. But harming your emotional and mental health impairs your ability to do the work.

Journalists try different ways to deal with the difficult events they witness. You may compartmentalize such events in an attempt to stay at arm's length from the story. Dark humour, another coping mechanism, is common in newsrooms. In extreme cases, victims of trauma are known to disassociate, a situation where your brain disconnects from what you are experiencing to escape further harm. And newsrooms of old were strewn with grizzled, hard-drinking hacks who turned to drugs and alcohol to numb their pain.[19]

Whatever survival techniques people employ to cope with their feelings after traumatic experiences, attempting to bury them forever can interfere with healthy recovery.[20]

Instead, recognize and acknowledge your feelings. If that means taking a break from a story, whether short- or long-term, don't beat yourself up about it. Thankfully, the days are numbered for "macho culture" in the newsroom; knowing your limits is the mark of a professional who is trauma- and emotionally literate.

Table 2.1 Checklist for Evaluating Psychological Risk

Know your limits and understand your triggers. Here's a checklist of questions to ask yourself before scheduling an important interview, developed by the Global Investigative Journalism Network.[21]

	Yes	No
Do I feel ready to survive other people's high anxiety and distress?		
Have I recently had any emotional or psychological problems?		
Have I recently had personal losses?		
Do my relatives have health issues?		
Have any family difficulties, arguments, or illnesses forced me to change my plans?		
Do I feel more vulnerable than usual?		
Am I feeling physically healthy?		

After

Debrief

News is a hungry goat, as the saying goes. It's common for reporters to file a story and simply move on to the next. But after covering a tragedy or conducting a difficult interview, consider taking time to debrief with your team or a trusted colleague, perhaps your boss. A debrief can give you time to express your emotions, hopefully in a supportive environment.

Mind you, not every tough story or interview calls for professional traumatic-event debriefing. Studies suggest a one-time psychological debrief immediately after an event won't likely help prevent symptoms of post-traumatic stress disorder, and may even increase the risk of developing PTSD.[22] Take your time, and when you're ready to share, debrief in a way that's comfortable for you.

Seek support

"With social support and an understanding of what they have experienced, most people will recover naturally and on their own accord from exposure to traumatic stress," advises the Dart Centre reassuringly.[23] That said, there may be times when professional therapy or trauma counselling with a specialist is appropriate and necessary.

After covering a traumatic event, pay attention to signs that you're having a rough time: sleeplessness, irritability, or disinterest in work. Not every news organization offers counselling support to its staff or freelancers, but mental health is starting to get the attention and resources it deserves. Whether you have an employee assistance program or not, don't suffer in silence. It's okay to ask for help.

A Final Word on Trauma and Indigenous Communities

To wrap up, bringing awareness to human distress is important work. But when you ask Indigenous subjects to share their personal experience of trauma, you are walking a fine line.

Journalism that respectfully details and explains trauma can arouse empathy in audiences, hopefully leading to individual and collective healing. "Trauma porn," on the other hand, exploits someone's trauma for shock value, merely for the purpose of enticing audiences to consume the misfortune or suffering of others.

Most Indigenous people have suffered plenty of trauma in their lives. They don't need you, a journalist, adding more. Be part of a new generation of journalists that promotes resilience and healing by taking care of your interviewees and yourself.

Discussion Questions

1. What does it mean to be resilient in life? When explaining your answer, reference points in your life when you or your loved ones have experienced difficult times.
2. What harm may we do with our style of questioning and why? What phrases should we use or avoid when writing our stories?
3. What is historical trauma?
4. When covering a tragedy, how can we as journalists assure the Indigenous people we interview that we are trustworthy?

Additional Readings and Resources

Julian Brave NoiseCat, "Apocalypse Then and Now." *Columbia Journalism Review*, Winter 2020. https://www.cjr.org/special_report/apocalypse-then-and-now.php

Mark Brayne (ed.), *Trauma & Journalism: A Guide for Journalists, Editors & Managers* (Dart Centre for Journalism and Trauma, 2007). https://dartcenter.org/sites/default/files/DCE_JournoTraumaHandbook.pdf

Jo Healey, *Trauma Reporting: A Journalist's Guide to Covering Sensitive Stories* (London; New York: Routledge, 2019).

Eduardo Duran, *Healing the Soul Wound: Trauma-Informed Counselling for Indigenous Communities*, 2nd edition (New York: Teachers College Press, 2020).

Renee Linklater, *Decolonizing Trauma Work: Indigenous Stories and Strategies* (Halifax: Fernwood Press, 2020).

Canadian Resource Centre for Victims of Crime, "If the Media Calls: A Guide for Victims and Survivors." https://crcvc.ca/publications/if-the-media-calls/

Endnotes

1. Elon Green, "Using True Crime to Teach Indigenous History: Reporter Connie Walker on 'Finding Cleo,'" *Columbia Journalism Review*, July 5, 2008. https://www.cjr.org/q_and_a/finding-cleo.php

2. Mark Brayne (ed.), *Trauma & Journalism: A Guide for Journalists, Editors and Managers* (Dart Centre for Journalism and Trauma, 2007), 1. https://dartcenter.org/sites/default/files/DCE_JournoTraumaHandbook.pdf

3. Ricky Greenwald, *EMDR: Within a Phase Model of Trauma-Informed Treatment* (New York: Routledge, 2007), 7.
4. Shahzeer Karmali, Kevin Laupland, et al., "Epidemiology of Severe Trauma among Status Aboriginal Canadians: A Population-Based Study," *CMAJ*, 172.8 (2005), 1007–1011. https://www.cmaj.ca/content/172/8/1007#:~:text=The%20incidence%20of%20severe%20trauma%20among%20A boriginal%20Canadians%20(93%20patients,per%20100%20000%20population%20respectively.
5. Waubgeshig Rice, *Moon of the Crusted Snow: A Novel* (Toronto, ON: ECW Press, 2018), 149.
6. Billy-Ray Belcourt, "Dear Media: I Am More Than Just Violence." Personal blog, November 24, 2015. https://nakinisowin.wordpress.com/2015/11/24/dear-media-i-am-more-than-just-violence/
7. Gerald Vizenor, *Manifest Manners: Narratives on Postindian Survivance* (Lincoln: Nebraska, 1999), vii.
8. Maria Y.H. Brave Heart, "The Return to the Sacred Path: Healing the Historical Trauma Response among the Lakota," *Smith College Studies in Social Work* 68.3 (1998), 287–305.
9. Mental Health America, "Racial Trauma," https://www.mhanational.org/racial-trauma#:~:text=Racial%20trauma%2C%20or%20race%2Dbased,and%20hate%20crimes%20%5B1%5D.
10. Centre for Suicide Prevention, "Trauma and Suicide in Indigenous people," https://www.suicideinfo.ca/resource/trauma-and-suicide-in-indigenous-people/
11. Sarah E. Nelson and Kathi Wilson, "The Mental Health of Indigenous Peoples in Canada: A Critical Review of Research," *Social Science & Medicine* https://www.sciencedirect.com/science/journal/02779536/176/suppl/C 176 (2017), 93–112. http://drc.usask.ca/projects/legal_aid/file/resource407-2ce80424.pdf
12. Brayne, ibid, 3.
13. Canadian Association of Journalists, "On the Record: Is It Really Informed Consent without Discussion of Consequences?" February 10, 2014. https://caj.ca/blog/informed-consent
14. Neil Steinberg, *You Were Never in Chicago* (Chicago: University of Chicago Press, 2013), as cited by Canadian Association of Journalists, ibid.
15. Ibid.
16. Jody Porter, "Pathfinding," *Maisonneuve*, October 20, 2020. https://maisonneuve.org/article/2020/10/20/pathfinding/
17. Ibid.
18. Ibid.
19. Michelle Presse, "Last Call Is Over for the Hard-Drinking Journalist," *The Signal*, December 11, 2015, https://signalhfx.ca/why-todays-journalists-are-kicking-liquor-to-the-curb/. A 2017 study of British journalists (with an admittedly small sample size) found that over 40% of journalists consumed more than 18 alcoholic drinks per week. https://www.taraswart.com/mental-resilience-of-journalists/
20. Hannah Storm, "My Mental Health Journey: How PTSD Gave Me the Strength to Share My Story," *Poynter*, July 24, 2020. https://www.poynter.org/business-work/2020/my-mental-health-journey-how-ptsd-gave-me-the-strength-to-share-my-story/
21. Olga Simanovych, "How Journalists Can Deal with Trauma While Reporting On COVID-19," Global Investigative Journalism Network, March 24, 2020. https://gijn.org/2020/03/24/how-journalists-can-deal-with-trauma-while-reporting-on-covid-19/
22. Jonathan Bisson, Suzanna Rose, Rachel Churchill, and Simon Wessely, "Psychological Debriefing for Preventing Post-Traumatic Stress Disorder (PTSD)," *Cochrane Database of Systematic Reviews* 2 (2002), 1–38. https://pubmed.ncbi.nlm.nih.gov/12076399/
23. Brayne, ibid, 17.

✦ 2.6 ✦

Story-Takers: How to Deal With 500+ Years of Rage

> *In this chapter, students will learn to:*
> - *interpret cultural clashes when they arise; and*
> - *develop skills to respond to conflicts in a way that maintains relationships.*

The clash of media and Aboriginal cultures—operating on such different timelines, values and worldviews—creates endless potential for miscommunication, misunderstanding, and mistrust.[1]

–Melissa Sweet

Story-Takers

Journalists sometimes encounter frustrated, angry people who don't want us around. After all, we often arrive on the scene during times of conflict and crisis, poking around, asking tough questions. It's never easy to cope with the wrath of a grieving relative or someone who feels their privacy has been violated. But, we tell ourselves, it's the nature of the beast.

Still, you may find a different kind of frustration when you head out to report in Indigenous communities. You may run into an Indigenous person who unleashes on you a seething anger that comes from a deep, dark place, centuries of colonialism in the making—let's call it "500+ Years of Rage." How you deal with this may make or break a story.

Perhaps it happens unintentionally. Maybe, determined to act with respect, you've brought tobacco and familiarized yourself with local customs. Or, maybe you're acting like an ignoramus. No matter your intentions, all you've done is made a simple request. You're just asking for an interview. You want to tell someone's story.

That's when it happens. Some Indigenous person explodes, directing their rage at you. "Hey, $%@# you Reporter!!!!!! Take your *%$ing microphone off this rez, back to the $%#&ing city, and don't come back!!!!!"

Suddenly, you represent every colonizing, raping, pillaging outsider who has ever stolen children, land, or sacred artifacts away. You are the living embodiment of Christopher Columbus, the Minister of Indigenous Affairs, and the Pope.

You are a story-taker.

How to Respond

Before you respond, take a deep breath, stay calm, and remember a few things:

- Some Indigenous people you interview may have attended residential schools, or been taken away from their families, where they experienced abuse and trauma. It's not surprising, then, that they have feelings of bitterness or rage toward authority figures. In a news-reporting scenario, you may represent a person of authority.
- Unless you're offering your interview subjects the power to veto or edit your final story (and that's unlikely, isn't it?[2]), then you *are* a story-taker. This Indigenous person has probably had a lot of experience with people who keep looking to tell Indigenous stories, whether it's the missionaries and anthropologists of old, or, more recently, a steady barrage of administrators and bureaucrats looking for statistics, data, or "consultation."
- The mainstream media have done a lousy job of representing Indigenous Peoples over the years—you can't blame an Indigenous person for wanting to vent about that. You've got your colleagues and predecessors to thank for your current chilly reception.
- And, finally, not all Indigenous people are angry. Rest assured, this hypothetical scenario happens rarely.

Good. Now that you've remembered all that, it's time for a response.

In a dignified way, you may try to clarify the person's concerns and explain your objectives. Ask what you can do to make things right, and remember that saying sorry may help mend the relationship. In some cases, though, you may conclude you can't make headway with someone who views you as a story-taker and decide to beat a hasty retreat.

What you do *not* want to do is respond with anger. Why not? Because you may say something you regret. That statement will spread like wildfire around this Indigenous community and others—which could ruin any chance you have at this story or the next one you're assigned.

Don't fear. The fallout from the 500+ Years of Rage won't be directed at you often, if you conduct yourself with respect. Still, recognize that it will happen from time to time. Don't beat yourself up about it. Just move on. There are plenty of fish in the sea (at least there used to be), and there are lots of Indigenous folks to interview.

Better yet, don't be a story-taker! Start incorporating the Indigenous practice of reciprocity into your journalism, something I'll discuss further in Chapter 3.3.

Discussion Questions

1. Recall an incident where you had to deal with someone in your personal life who was angry with you. How did you handle it? Were you able to defuse the situation? Would that approach be helpful when dealing with someone in the field who is frustrated with you? Why or why not?

2. If editorial independence is what turns you into a story-taker, how might you operate differently? Consider *Turning Points*, a documentary short series that explores alcohol use, addiction, resilience, and healing in Yellowknife, NWT, the premise of which is described by the UBC Global Reporting Centre:

   > Stories about alcohol use among Indigenous people are often overlooked or misrepresented by the media. By sharing editorial control with the featured storytellers, *Turning Points* aimed to alter typical power dynamics that can perpetuate harmful stereotypes and misinformation. Participants not only chose what they spoke about, but also assisted with aspects of production like selecting locations and editing the final pieces. They were the writers and directors of their own films. Participants also retain control over all material produced—raw footage was returned to each storyteller after filming, and they keep copyright of the stories.[3]

   Watch the documentaries in *Turning Points* (https://globalreportingcentre.org/turning-points/). What lessons does this collaborative approach teach you about your journalism?

Additional Readings and Resources

Alicia Elliott, *A Mind Spread Out on the Ground* (Toronto: Doubleday Canada, 2019).
Lee Maracle, *My Conversations with Canadians* (Toronto: BookHug Press, 2017).
Colonization Road. https://www.cbc.ca/firsthand/episodes/colonization-road
Angry Inuk. https://www.cbc.ca/cbcdocspov/episodes/angry-inuk
Tim Giago, "If You Come Out to Indian Country to Write About Us, Do Your Damned Homework." *Nieman Reports*, July 2, 2019. https://niemanreports.org/articles/if-you-come-out-to-indian-country-to-write-about-us-do-your-damned-homework/

Endnotes

1. Melissa Sweet, "Is the Media Part of the Aboriginal Health Problem, and Part of the Solution?" *Inside Story*, March 3, 2009. https://insidestory.org.au/is-the-media-part-of-the-aboriginal-health-problem-and-part-of-the-solution/

2. Because editorial independence is a key journalistic principle, you're unlikely to offer pre-publication review or story approval to a source. However, anyone working with Indigenous Peoples should be aware of a set of guidelines designed to decolonize Indigenous–Western research relationships. These are known as OCAP, which stands for "ownership, control, access, and possession." These four ethical principles were developed by the First Nations Information Governance Centre in 1998 to govern data collection. In a nutshell, OCAP acknowledges the importance of First Nations people possessing their own data and aims to prevent non-Indigenous researchers from exploiting Indigenous communities. Ownership assumes that a community owns cultural knowledge or data collectively, in the same manner that an individual owns

personal information, so the community's consent is required to use its knowledge. The principle of <u>control</u> asserts that Indigenous Peoples have a right to control various aspects of the research on them, including the formulation of research frameworks, data management, and dissemination. <u>Access</u> is the ability for Indigenous people to retrieve and examine data that concerns them and their communities. The principle of <u>possession</u> refers to the actual possession of data. Many First Nations now expect academics to incorporate OCAP into their proposals. Research ethics of journalists and academics sometimes clash, but Indigenous community members may not appreciate or understand the differences. That's why all journalists should be aware of Indigenous Peoples' historical grievances surrounding outside researchers and be ready to navigate discussions about the intellectual property rights of Indigenous Peoples. [See Appendix 3 for a more detailed articulation of OCAP guidelines.]

3. Peter Klein, Britney Dennison, et al., "Turning Points." Global Reporting Centre. https://globalreportingcentre.org/turning-points/about/

✦ 2.7 ✦

Breaking News: Indians Are Funny!

> *In this chapter, students will learn to:*
> - *recognize the importance of humour in Indigenous cultures;*
> - *identify when humour is helpful to use in a news story; and*
> - *judge when it's appropriate to use humour in relationships with Indigenous subjects.*

There were a lot of adjectives attributed to Native people. Lacking among them was funny. Savage irony and morbid humour did sometimes enter the picture as a kind of self-flagellation device for whites, but on the whole, Natives were treated by almost everyone with the utmost gravity, as if they were either too awe-inspiring as blood-curdling savages or too sacrosanct in their status of holy victim to allow any comic reactions either of them or by them.[1]

– Margaret Atwood

I know a lot of you white people have never seen an Indian do stand-up comedy before. Like, for so long you probably thought that Indians never had a sense of humor. We never thought you were too funny either.[2]

– Charlie Hill

Substance abuse, suicide, ill health, poor housing conditions, historical grievances. When assigned an Indigenous news story, it's not surprising some reporters want to hide under their desk. It's all so . . . dreary.

To read our newspapers or watch our news programs, one might get the impression there's little more to Indigenous life than desolation and misery. When Indigenous people come on the news, who can blame a reader for turning the page or a viewer for switching the channel?

Indeed, the image of Indians as tragic and stoic is so well entrenched that the title of this chapter may strike you as odd. What's so funny about Indians?[3]

Actually, humour is an intrinsic part of life in Indigenous communities. You'll find your stories will improve if you employ humour in the field. Heck—go crazy! Maybe even include some humour in your story!

Humour in the News

Before discussing Indigenous humour, a quick word to journalists who consider it sacrilege to use humour in news stories.

Canadians flock in great numbers to political satire shows—*The Rick Mercer Report* or *This Hour Has 22 Minutes*, or American programs such as *The Colbert Show* and *The Daily Show with Trevor Noah*—and that should be an indication to every journalist that we need to lighten up. Reporters or anchors don't need to start cracking one-liners, but we ought to consider how our audience is increasingly looking to satire and drama as a way to engage in political debate. Furthermore, if we're going to use mediums such as television to their fullest, humour is but one more powerful arrow in a storyteller's quiver.

When it comes to using humour in stories on Indigenous issues, news outlets don't need to go so far as the comedic observations of *Walking Eagle News*, an Indigenous news satire website run by former journalist Tim Fontaine. (See Teachings, Section 4.7 for an interview with Tim.) But how hard is it to include an Indigenous person smiling or laughing in a news story every once in a while?

Understanding Indian Humour and Using it in the Field

In one of our discussions on Native humour, Thomas King and I considered that Heisenberg's uncertainty principle might apply here. It was Heisenberg's belief that the art of observing alters the reality being observed. Maybe putting Native humour under the microscope changes its effects or impact. I don't know. I was always weak in physics.[4]

– Drew Hayden Taylor

Let's not second-guess authors Drew Hayden Taylor and Thomas King, who have funny down to a fine art, and let's not try to define Indigenous humour. If you haven't experienced it, you'll have to take it for granted: Indians, Inuit, Métis—they all love to laugh. Different Nations have different humour, but there are a couple of universal factors in Indigenous humour: teasing and self-deprecation.

Theories abound on why Indigenous folks take such pleasure in taking each other down a notch. As discussed in Chapter 2.2, Mohawk psychiatrist Dr. Clare Brant related it to efforts of small, family-based groups to maintain social harmony. Back in the day, keeping good humour was a way to defuse tensions, which was critical to group survival in a harsh environment.

Thomas Anguti Johnston, a cast member of the Inuktitut-language TV comedy show *Qanurli*, attributed the source of Inuit humour to the close relationships between Inuit on the land. "Under hard living conditions, it helps to go with the flow," Johnson has said.

Canada to present full-grown Indigenous man to Royal Couple as engagement gift

NOVEMBER 27, 2017

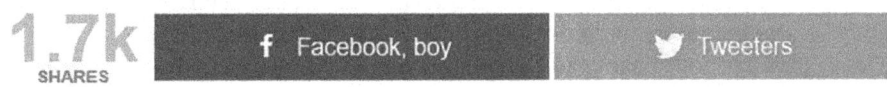

Canada has announced that it will present a full-grown Cree man as an engagement gift to Prince Harry and Meghan Markle, continuing a little-known custom that has existed since treaties were first signed between the Crown and First Nations.

Walking Eagle News Royal Family Headline.
A much-shared headline from the Indigenous news satire website Walking Eagle News. Former CBC/APTN journalist Tim Fontaine, a member of the Sagkeeng First Nation in Manitoba, started Walking Eagle after he left his journalism career behind in 2017.

Source: Used with permission of Walking Eagle News https://walkingeaglenews.com/Photo: Anwar Hussein/Alamy Stock Photo.

Qanurli captures Inuit humour in a contemporary context by taking a lighthearted look at life across the north, using advertisement parodies and fake newscasts. Vinnie Karektak, one of the creators of the program, described it this way: "Inuit humour tends to be a lot of self-deprecating work that we do; we make fun of ourselves."[5]

Sioux author and philosopher Vine Deloria Jr. had his own take on the importance of teasing in Indigenous communities, in *Custer Died for Your Sins*:

> Rather than embarrass members of the tribe publicly, people used to tease individuals they considered out of step with the consensus of tribal opinion. In this way, egos were preserved and disputes within the tribe . . . were held to a minimum.[6]

If someone in an Indigenous community teases you, even if it seems harsh, it may be intended as a sign of acceptance. If you can laugh at yourself—even better, make fun of yourself—Indigenous people will warm to you more quickly. This is especially true if you're white—Indigenous people love white people jokes (like the one about the John Wayne toilet paper). (If you don't know the one about the John Wayne toilet paper, I'm sorry. Really. I am. But I'm not going to tell it here. Ask an Indian.)

If the news you're covering is serious or tragic, it's still worth quietly observing the community to see whether humour may be able to play a part in your story. A funny quote or a scene of a character laughing in the face of grave circumstances speaks volumes to an audience, helping to illustrate how Indigenous people use humour as a coping strategy or perhaps as a subversive survival tactic.

Indian Humour in Your Story

If you list your probation officer as a reference, you might just be a redskin.[7]
– Don Burnstick

Do be careful, though, about your use of Indian humour in news stories. If you read the fine print on Indian jokes, it says: "Humour may cause offence if not used wisely."

Journalists are not comedians, and our audiences don't expect the news to be a yuk-fest. Being funny, or even mildly amusing, is not a skill easily learned. It may take time for a storyteller's personality and voice to evolve before they're able to successfully incorporate humour into a piece.

Furthermore, if you head to the rez hunting for a story that plays like a stand-up comic routine, you're unlikely to find it. Some Indigenous people joke more than others. In some situations, humour isn't appropriate.

Still, any observant reporter visiting an Indigenous community will find themselves surrounded by Indian humour. Here are two tips on how to escape that dreadfully stereotypical image of the stoic and tragic Indian.

- **Look for humour to help illustrate a point about the Indigenous community.** A character's joke or chuckle may break up the dreariness of a serious story, and help audiences identify and empathize with the humanity of an Indigenous character.
- **Include photos, video, or descriptions of Indigenous characters smiling and laughing.** Surprise and intrigue your audience by turning that stereotype of the angry, weeping Indian on its head.

Discussion Questions

1. Why might humour be an important storytelling tool in a news story involving Indigenous people? How might it help your audience connect with your story?
2. Can laughter be subversive? Can it be used as a weapon? In what situations?
3. Does satire make you laugh? Take a historical account of an Indigenous issue and turn it into social commentary. Develop your argument using a blend of basic essay structure and a humorous take on the historical account to "retell" the story. Be sure to use satire and irony to add humour. Also consider puns and a "tongue-in-cheek" approach.
4. Do people of different cultures find different things humorous? Are there things that are universally funny? Provide examples to illustrate your answer.

Additional Readings and Resources

Walking Eagle News. http://walkingeaglenews.com/
Drew Hayden Taylor, *Me Funny* (Vancouver: Douglas & McIntyre, 2006).
Drew Hayden Taylor (dir.), *Redskins, Tricksters and Puppy Stew* (Canada: National Film Board, 2000). https://www.nfb.ca/film/redskins_tricksters_puppy_stew/
Drew Hayden Taylor, "Narrating Indigenous Stories with a Pinch of Humour Isn't Odd. It's a Part of Healing." *Globe and Mail*, January 7, 2021. https://www.theglobeandmail.com/arts/books/article-narrating-indigenous-stories-with-a-pinch-of-humour-isnt-odd-its-a/
Sima Sahar Zerehi, "*Qanurli*, Nunavut's Inuktitut TV Show, Travels to Other Inuit Regions." *CBC North*, February 20, 2016. https://www.cbc.ca/news/canada/north/qanurli-nunavut-s-inuktitut-tv-show-travels-to-other-inuit-regions-1.3455962
Mark Sandiford (dir.), *Qallunaat! Why White People Are Funny* (Canada: National Film Board, 2007). https://www.nfb.ca/film/qallunaat_why_white_people_are_funny/
Paul Seesequasis, *Blanket Toss Under Midnight Sun: Portraits of Everyday Life in Eight Indigenous Communities* (Toronto: Alfred A. Knopf, 2019).

Endnotes

1. Margaret Atwood, "A Double-Bladed Knife: Subversive Laughter in Two Stories by Thomas King." *Canadian Literature* 124–25 (1990) 243.
2. Oneida comedian Charlie Hill, from his debut on "The Richard Pryor Show" in 1977. Hill was the first Indigenous comedian to perform on American national television. See: https://www.youtube.com/watch?v=UWaDJvSYusM
3. As mentioned in Chapter 1.2, I use the term "Indian" throughout this textbook, in a variety of contexts. In this instance, it is used conversationally, as Indigenous people often do amongst themselves in a humourous situation. I offer some specific advice in the Terminology and Lexicon chapter on how and when the term "Indian" should be used by journalists. Once again, be aware that some Indigenous people may be offended if the word is used inappropriately by non-Indigenous people.
4. Drew Hayden Taylor, *Me Funny* (Vancouver, BC: Douglas & McIntyre, 2006), 2.
5. CBC Radio, "*Qanurli*: TV Show Part Inuktitut Language Preservation, Part Laughter as Medicine," *CBC Unreserved*, June 6, 2019. https://www.cbc.ca/radio/unreserved/art-in-iqaluit-how-creativity-fosters-healing-1.5153402/qanurli-tv-show-

part-inuktitut-language-preservation-part-laughter-as-medicine-1.5160626

6 Vine Deloria Jr., *Custer Died for Your Sins: An Indian Manifesto* (Norman: University of Oklahoma Press, 1988), 147.

7 ICT Staff, "10 Hilarious 'You Might Be an Indian' Lines from Don Burnstick," *Indian Country Today*, September 13, 2018. https://indiancountrytoday.com/archive/10-hilarious-you-might-be-an-indian-if-lines-from-don-burnstick

Part 3

On the Air

✦ 3.1 ✦

Terminology and Lexicon

> In this chapter, students will learn to:
> - consider how journalists' word choices are shaped by colonialism;
> - recognize how the terms used to describe Indigenous Peoples are continually evolving, and how best to use them; and
> - use accepted and up-to-date terminology about Indigenous Peoples in their stories.

Our word choice and what we see to be appropriate is entrenched in colonial narratives.[1]

– Tara Campbell

It's time to sit down and write your story, and you probably find yourself facing the NAFNIP question. Otherwise known as, the "Native-Aboriginal-First Nations-Indigenous Person" question (Indian head nod to Anishinaabe author Drew Hayden Taylor for coining this fabulous acronym). What term should a journalist use to describe a NAFNIP?

Your news organization likely has a style guide. That may offer some guidance, but the terms used to describe Indigenous Peoples are continually evolving. Reporters may find it a challenge to understand the distinctions among these words and to whom they apply.

Terminology

Ultimately, there is no sole agreed-upon name for the original peoples that inhabited North America before European settlers arrived. In Canada and at the United Nations, "Indigenous Peoples" is often used. In the United States, "Native American" is still a common phrase.

If you are unsure about names and terms, *ask the Indigenous people you're reporting on which term they prefer.*

Why does terminology matter? Throughout Canadian history, words have been employed in colonial and ethnocentric ways. Indigenous people, who typically refer to themselves by the traditional name of their specific group, rarely had a say in how they were described. Use of proper terminology, then, is not just a matter of being "politically correct." For journalists, use of proper terminology is a matter of accuracy, fairness, and respect.

If you write regularly about Indigenous Peoples, I highly recommend having a copy of *Elements of Indigenous Style* by Gregory Younging at your side. It's an essential Indigenous style guide that offers not only suggestions when searching for the right word, but also guidance on the importance of relationships and trust.

What follows here is not intended to be a definitive or exhaustive style guide—consider it more a style touchstone that serves as a quick reference.[2]

Affiliation by Nation

Many diverse and autonomous peoples lived in the territory now known as Canada for thousands of years. Each community or culture had distinct languages, religious beliefs, and political systems, as well as its own name for its people and names for the peoples around them.

Whenever possible, characterize Indigenous people using the identities of their specific tribe or Nation (e.g., a Métis painter, a Huron-Wendat school, a Blackfoot radio station).

Note that many Indigenous people are using English transliterations of terms from their own languages to identify themselves. For example, the Mohawk call themselves "Kanien'kehá:ka"; the Blackfoot, "Siksiká"; Ojibways, "Anishinaabeg"; and the Swampy Cree, "Mushkegowuk."

For broadcasters, it's always good practice to ask interviewees to spell and pronounce their Nation on tape, for future reference.

Indigenous

You'll most often find the term "Indigenous" used in United Nations documents, such as the *UN Declaration on the Rights of Indigenous Peoples* (UNDRIP), and "Indigenous" is often the preferred term in an international, academic, or activist context. It is increasingly the preferred term in Canada. The adjective "indigenous" has the common meaning of "from" or "of the original origin." The United Nations has yet to define "Indigenous Peoples," as the concept has been subject of much debate.

Apache/Purépecha legal scholar James Anaya offers this definition. "Today, the term *indigenous* refers broadly to the living descendants of pre-invasion inhabitants of lands now dominated by others. Indigenous Peoples, nations, or communities are culturally distinctive groups that find themselves engulfed by settler societies born of the forces of empire and conquest."[3]

According to UNDRIP, Indigenous Peoples have a right to cultural sovereignty and self-determination.

Reporters should be careful using this term, however, because "Indigenous Peoples" generally applies to First Nations, Inuit, and Métis. If you are describing a particular government program that is only for First Nations or Status Indians, such as band funding, avoid using "Indigenous Peoples," as it may cause misunderstanding.

Suggested usage
Avoid describing Indigenous Peoples as "belonging" to Canada. The inference is that Canada owns Indigenous Peoples. Use less possessive terms instead.

- Improper: Canada's Indigenous people have traditions and cultures that go back thousands of years.
- Improper: Our Indigenous people have traditions and cultures that go back thousands of years.
- Proper: Indigenous Peoples in Canada have traditions and cultures that go back thousands of years.

Avoid the term "Indigenous Canadians." Not all Indigenous people consider themselves Canadian.

- Improper: More than 4,000 Indigenous Canadians served in uniform during the First World War.
- Proper: More than 4,000 Indigenous people served in Canadian uniform during the First World War.

First Nations

This term came into common usage in the 1970s to replace the word "Indian," which some found offensive. Many people today prefer to be called "First Nations" or "First Nations people" instead of "Indians." Although the term First Nation is widely used, no legal definition of it exists.

Generally, "First Nations people" is used to describe both Status and non-Status Indians. Reporters should also take care in using this term. If describing a program that is for only registered Status Indian youth, for example, they should avoid using "First Nations youth," which may cause misunderstanding. Many communities have also adopted the term "First Nation" to replace the word "Indian band."

The term shouldn't be used as a synonym for "Indigenous Peoples" because it doesn't include Inuit or Métis people.

Suggested usage
Generally, include a definite article ("the") before the proper noun.

- Example: They found the artifact on the Sioux Valley Dakota First Nation, west of Brandon.

Use as a noun and a modifier. The term "First Nation" is acceptable as both. When using the term as a modifier, the question becomes whether to use "First Nation" or "First Nations." There is no clear right or wrong in this area, provided that reporters are consistent about the way they choose to use modifiers. Note the different uses in the following examples.

- (plural modifier, plural noun): The number of First Nations students enrolled at Canadian universities and colleges has soared over the past twenty years.

- (singular modifier, plural noun): The association assists female First Nation entrepreneurs interested in starting home businesses.
- (plural modifier, singular noun): Containing recipes from across the country, the First Nations cookbook became an instant hit at church bazaars.
- (singular modifier, singular noun): Many people have said that *North of 60* and *The Rez* were the only shows on television that depicted life in a First Nation community with any realism.

Métis

Métis is a nation-specific term connected to an Indigenous people in western Canada.[4] Métis people evolved from the intermarriage of First Nations people and European settlers beginning in the eighteenth century and arose with their own specific identity, unique culture, traditions, language, and way of life.

Today, Métis people are represented by the Métis National Council (MNC), which defines Métis as "a person who self-identifies as Métis, is distinct from other Aboriginal peoples, is of historic Métis Nation ancestry and who is accepted by the Métis Nation." This historic Métis Nation emerged in the Northwest during the course of the eighteenth and nineteenth centuries, according to the MNC. This area is known as the historic Métis Homeland, which includes Saskatchewan, Alberta, and Manitoba, and extends into Ontario, British Columbia, the Northwest Territories, and the northern United States.

Métis should only be used in circumstances where individuals and communities use the term "Métis" themselves. Do not use Métis to refer to mixed-descent individuals, as there are many First Nations people who have some non-First Nations ancestry, but are members of First Nations communities. Use Métis to refer to those who identify as Métis and belong to Métis communities as described above. Métis is best understood as a communal identity, and not for describing mixed-descent individuals.

The term can be used accented or unaccented, but the accented "Métis" is the most common usage among Métis themselves. In certain formal agreements, like the Sahtu Dene and Metis Comprehensive Land Claim, the term is unaccented.

"Indigenous and Métis" or "Aboriginal and Métis" should never be used, as Métis are definitionally Indigenous and Aboriginal.

Be aware that the Métis are often at the centre of disputes over Indigenous identity. While self-identification is an important principle of Indigenous identity, so is acceptance of this identification by the specified Indigenous group. A journalist should not be an arbiter of whether an individual or a group have a right to call themselves Métis. However, where an individual's or group's Métis identity is in dispute, make sure to present relevant facts or background, including opposition or concerns about claimed Indigeneity.

Inuit

Inuit is an Indigenous group comprised of circumpolar maritime people. They are also found in Greenland, Alaska, and Russia.[5]

Inuit means "people" in Inuktut languages, while Inuk means "person." Do not use "Inuit people" as it is redundant.

As an adjective, use Inuk when describing a person (i.e., "an Inuk doctor") but use Inuit if describing more than one (i.e., "three Inuit doctors"). Inuit can be used as an adjective for everything else (e.g., "Inuit drum," "Inuit community").

Three-quarters of Inuit in Canada live in 53 communities across the northern regions of Canada in Inuit Nunangat, which means "the place where Inuit live." Inuit Nunangat is comprised of four regions: Inuvialuit (NWT and Yukon), Nunavut, Nunavik (Northern Quebec), and Nunatsiavut (Labrador). About 43,455 Inuit live in these regions. There is a fifth Inuit group called Nunatukavut, the Southern Inuit of Labrador. They are not yet recognized by all the other groups and their land claim is being negotiated.

Inuktut refers to Inuit languages as a whole, both Inuktitut (spoken largely in the Baffin Island regions of Nunavut) and Inuinnaqtun (generally spoken in the Western Arctic). There are many dialects of Inuktut that vary from region to region, along with spellings and pronunciation. Use what the subject prefers. Inuit from Nunatsiavut are called Nunatsiavummiut (sometimes Labradorimiut but this is an older term), Inuit from Nunavik are called Nunavimmiut, Inuit from Nunavut are called Nunavummiut, and Inuit from the Inuvialuit Settlement Region are called Inuvialuit.

Do not use Eskimo. It is a Cree word that means "eater of raw meat" and is considered offensive.

Inuit communities are often confused with First Nations, but they have different terminology and governmental systems. Inuit do not have chiefs but rather community leaders, though in some communities they have a mayor. Inuit do not live on reserves. Never use Native to refer to Inuit. Also, many Inuit prefer to be called Inuit instead of Indigenous.

Inuit are represented nationally by the Inuit Tapiriit Kanatami (translates as "Inuit United in Canada"), which is led by a president.

Do not describe Inuit as being Arctic people, as Nunavik and Nunatsiavut are located south of 60 latitude in the subarctic.

Inuit are not to be confused with Innu, a First Nations people who reside in Eastern Quebec/Labrador.

Aboriginal

The Constitution of Canada identifies Aboriginal as Indians, Métis, and Inuit peoples. When you are referring to "Aboriginal People," you are either referring to all the Indigenous people in Canada collectively, without regard to their separate origins and identities, or you are simply referring to more than one Indigenous person.

Aboriginal was a preferred term in Canada from the 1980s to early 2000s. However, many Indigenous people now object to the connotation of the "Ab" prefix, which has been interpreted by some to mean "away from" or "not."

For that reason, the term should be avoided, unless referred to in a proper name ("Aboriginal Peoples Television Network") or in a legal context (Indigenous interests in land are described by Canadian courts as "Aboriginal rights and title," in reference to section 35 of the *Constitution*).

Suggested usage

Use as an adjective. The use of "Aboriginal" as a proper noun, in stories or headlines, is grammatically incorrect.

- Improper: The government's new strategy will support increased business with Aboriginals.
- Proper: The government's new strategy will support increased business with Aboriginal Peoples.

Indian

Ever since Columbus sent a letter back home in 1493, identifying the folks he met as *los Indios*, the term "Indian" has been applied to the first occupants of the Americas.

The term "Indian" is laden with history and associations, and some argue the whole notion of "Indian" is purely a white man's construction. Some find the term offensive, akin to the n-word used to describe African Americans.

That said, some Indigenous folks themselves, particularly in the Prairies, use the term "Indian" regularly in conversation. Does that give you the licence to use it? Probably not.

Still, for the sake of accuracy, there are times you should use the term "Indian":

- in discussions of history where necessary for clarity and accuracy;
- in discussions of some legal/constitutional matters requiring precision in terminology;
- in discussions of rights and benefits provided on the basis of "Indian Status"; and
- in statistical information collected using these categories (e.g., the Census).

Indians are one of three Peoples recognized as Aboriginal in the *Constitution Act, 1982*. Specifically, that means "Status Indians." However, you may also encounter the terms "non-Status Indians" and "Treaty Indians." You should use "Indian" when referring to the *Indian Act* or Indian reserves.

Status Indians

Status Indians are people who are entitled to have their names included on the Indian Register, an official list maintained by the federal government. Certain criteria determine who can be registered as a Status Indian. Only Status Indians are recognized as Indians under the *Indian Act*. Status Indians are entitled to certain rights and benefits under the law.

Non-Status Indians

Non-Status Indians are people who consider themselves Indians or members of a First Nation, but whom the Government of Canada does not recognize as Indians under the *Indian Act*, either because they are unable to prove their status or have lost their status rights. Many Indian people in Canada, especially women, lost their Indian status through discriminatory practices in the past. Non-Status Indians are not entitled to the same rights and benefits available to Status Indians.

Treaty Indian

A Status Indian who belongs to a First Nation that signed a Treaty with the Crown.

Indian Act
The principal federal statute dealing with Registered Status Indians and/or Treaty Indians. The *Act* was created in 1876 in an attempt by the federal government to assimilate First Nations people into Euro-Canadian society and assume First Nations land for European settlement, development, and agricultural purposes.

Indian Reserve
Defined in the *Indian Act* as a tract of land set aside for the use and benefit of an Indian band. The federal government has assumed jurisdiction over reserve lands and the First Nation people living on them.

Indian Country
A multi-faceted term that has been used historically in the U.S. as a geographical designation, a legal term, and a cultural concept. The term first appeared in the *Royal Proclamation of 1763*. It embodies the idea that there is a "place" for Indians. "Indian Country" is a specific legal category in the U.S. that includes "all land within the limits of any Indian reservation," "all dependent Indian communities within the borders of the United States," and "all Indian allotments, the Indian titles to which have not been extinguished." However, it also has popular usage, describing reservations and areas with American Indian populations. The term is also used colloquially in parts of Canada.

Native

The word "Native," derived from Latin *natus* meaning "born," is used to mean a group who lived in some place before the arrival of Europeans.

Like "First Nations," the term "Native" evolved to replace the word "Indian." It has no legal definition in Canada, and generally describes Indians, not Inuit or Métis.

However, because "native" also has a specific meaning of "born in," the term "native Canadian" could also legitimately apply to anyone born in Canada. For this reason, though "Native" is often used in common speech, it's being used with less and less frequency.

Reporters should note "Native American" is used in a legal context in the United States, and can be used interchangeably with "American Indian."

People versus Peoples

Most of the time, "people" is the correct plural for "person."

However, in international law, the concept of "peoples" has been much debated. Generally, "peoples" have more rights than "populations" or "groups." Peoples have the civil and political rights accorded to individuals, but also collective rights such as self-determination. That "s" was a stumbling block for years during UNDRIP negotiations. Eventually, Indigenous negotiators successfully advocated for the term "peoples" rather than "people," as the former (being a collective of distinct groups) have the right of self-determination, whereas the latter (in reference to individuals) do not. While the UN has yet to define "Indigenous Peoples," the term has become gradually accepted.

In some contexts, then, "Indigenous people" may seem homogenizing, or seem to refer simply to a collection of individuals. Use of the plural "Peoples" acknowledges the Indigenous population of Canada is made up of more than one distinct society.

Capitalization

To capitalize or not to capitalize? This can be a thorny debate—some style guides capitalize terms such as "Indigenous," and others do not.

In *Elements of Indigenous Style*, Gregory Younging makes the case that certain terms should always be capitalized when writing about Indigenous identity, institutions, or rights.

Here are a few examples of frequently capitalized terms:

- Elder
- Indigenous
- Indigenous Peoples
- Survivor
- Aboriginal
- First Nations
- Métis
- Chief
- Creator; Creation
- Inuit/Inuk

Younging puts forth three reasons for capitalization. First, the terms being used are proper noun modifiers, which describe people, language, and culture. Second, the capitalization of terms is a sign of respect for those people to whom the term refers. Third, capitalization of terms "redresses mainstream society's history of regarding Indigenous Peoples as having no legitimate national identities; governmental, social, spiritual or religious institutions; or collective rights."[6]

He also makes the following suggestions regarding the term "Indigenous":

- An *Indigenous person* is an individual who identifies as First Nations, Inuit, or Métis.
- *Indigenous Peoples* are the distinct societies of First Nations, Inuit, and Métis peoples in Canada.
- An *Indigenous People* is a single one of the distinct societies of First Nations, Inuit, and Métis peoples in Canada. For example, the Nisga'a are an Indigenous People.
- *Indigenous people* refers to people who identify as First Nations, Inuit, or Métis in a context where their specific identity is not at issue.

This is merely a sampling of instances when capitalization should be considered. If you're not sure whether to capitalize a term or not, consider whether it relates to Indigenous identity, institutions, or rights—in which case, capitalization is probably in order.

Discussion Questions

1. Why is it important to ask the Indigenous people you're reporting on how they self-identify?
2. In her article on Indigenous style (see below for reference), copy editor Tara Campbell argues journalists' word choices are shaped by colonialism. Do you agree? Why or why not?
3. In 2017, Canadian Press announced an update to its go-to reference book for journalists, the *CP Stylebook*. It now states both Aboriginal and Indigenous are to be capitalized in all stories. Why does capitalization of certain terms relating to Indigenous Peoples matter?
4. Have you ever been afraid of using a "wrong" word in a discussion with or about Indigenous Peoples? Why or why not? What are ways to become more confident about terminology?

Additional Readings and Resources

Gregory Younging, *Elements of Indigenous Style: A Guide for Writing By and About Indigenous Peoples* (Edmonton, Alta: Brush Education, 2018).

Tara Campbell. "A Copy Editor's Education in Indigenous Style." *The Tyee*, January 17, 2020. https://thetyee.ca/News/2020/01/17/Copy-Editor-Indigenous-Style/

Christine Weeber. "Why Capitalize Indigenous?" *SAPIENS*, May 19, 2020 https://www.sapiens.org/language/capitalize-indigenous/

Lenny Carpenter et al. "Style Guide for Reporting on Indigenous People." Toronto: Journalism for Human Rights, 2017. https://jhr.ca/wp-content/uploads/2017/12/JHR2017-Style-Book-Indigenous-People.pdf

Native American Journalist Association. "Reporting and Indigenous Terminology," 2017. https://najanewsroom.com/wp-content/uploads/2018/11/NAJA_Reporting_and_Indigenous_Terminology_Guide.pdf

UBC Brand/UBC First Nations House of Learning. *Indigenous Peoples: Language Guidelines* (Vancouver: University of British Columbia, 2018). https://indigenous.ubc.ca/indigenous-engagement/featured-initiatives/indigenous-peoples-language-guideline/

"Words First: An Evolving Terminology Relating to Aboriginal Peoples in Canada." Indian and Northern Affairs Canada Communications Branch (October 2002). http://publications.gc.ca/collections/Collection/R2-236-2002E.pdf

Endnotes

1. Tara Campbell, "A Copy Editor's Education in Indigenous Style," *The Tyee*, January 17, 2020.
2. Some of this material is based on the terminology guide developed by the Strategic Alliance of Broadcasters for Aboriginal Reflection (SABAR), a group of national broadcasters founded in 2003 to increase participation of Indigenous people in Canadian media. Some examples of usage are drawn from a communications briefing developed by Indian and Northern Affairs Canada in 2002, entitled "Words First: An Evolving Terminology Relating to Aboriginal Peoples in Canada."

3. S. James Anaya, *Indigenous Peoples in International Law* (New York: Oxford University Press, 1996), 3.
4. This definition is adapted from the "Style Guide for Reporting on Indigenous People," published by Journalism for Human Rights in 2017. See full reference in Suggested Readings.
5. Ibid.
6. Gregory Younging, *Elements of Indigenous Style: A Guide for Writing By and About Indigenous Peoples* (Edmonton, Alberta: Brush Education, 2018), 77–78.

✦ 3.2 ✦

Context and Colonial Amnesia

> In this chapter, students will learn to:
> - recognize why context is critical to news stories involving Indigenous Peoples; and
> - use graphics, sidebars, or online extras to ensure context is added to abbreviated news copy.

A feature of contemporary journalistic writing is its tendency to fixate on the extreme socio-economic conditions of colonized peoples, while simultaneously exhibiting a general amnesia about colonial history and its connection to the current state of affairs.[1]

– Robert Harding

Pity the poor reporter, who has but two or three sentences at their disposal to explain centuries of colonialism or the complicated political-legal jurisdiction governing Indigenous Peoples.

"Wow. Big residential school lawsuit. Get on this!" (And, make sure it doesn't run a second over a buck fifteen.) "Hey. What's this presser on this new land claims tribunal thing?" (Try explaining *that* in 450 words.)

Indigenous issues aren't unique in this regard. Over and over, our producers and editors send us out to tackle complicated news issues, and give us precious little space to tell the backstory.

But, putting aside debate over the shrinking attention spans of news consumers, the lack of context in news coverage of Indigenous issues is one of the most recurring criticisms of our work—and it may actually be causing a great deal of harm. Here's why.

The Importance of the Backstory

Without the "backstory," our audiences are hampered in their ability to interpret and make sense of news events and images, especially those who have limited access to a broad source of information about Indigenous people. Thus, a decontextualized Indigenous person becomes a "problem" Indian: the incompetent manager of a child welfare agency, the homeless drunk on the city street, the needy victim of residential school sexual abuse.

How can you "walk a mile in another's moccasins" if a reporter never offers you the opportunity to put those moccasins on? It's easier to understand why audience members have little sympathy or empathy for Indigenous people, when the nuances of racism or the history of colonialism are left unexplained. One news story at a time, we further entrench the communication gap between Indigenous Peoples and the rest of Canada.

So, how do you get context into your story?

"Life is a game of inches," growled Al Pacino in his role as a coach in the 1999 football film *Any Given Sunday*. Forgive the sports metaphor. But, like a running back fighting for that inch on the gridiron, you need to do battle with your editors for those precious extra words or seconds/minutes. Claw. With. Your. Fingernails. For. That. Inch.

Maybe your publication or program really, really doesn't have more space for you to squeeze that context into your story. If so, it's up to you to get creative in how you present that background material. Strategize how you'll pitch it to your boss. Here are a few tips on how you might fit in that all-important context.

Graphic journalism

Your colleagues in the graphics department are your friends when it comes to reporting on Indigenous issues. A historical timeline, a visual portrayal of a complex piece of legislation, a summary of a legal case, an explainer on cultural traditions—all of these are perfect examples of how you can use images and graphics to complement your story and put it in context. Here are the keys to helping them make good graphics:

- be on the lookout, while you're doing your research, for material that cries out for a graphic presentation, and
- bring the graphics folks into the loop early in your news gathering process.

Sidebars

Sometimes, our news stories hone in on the dramatic, which can inadvertently misrepresent a situation. Shorter, sidebar stories help balance the presentation of an issue, without clogging up the body of the main story.

For example, for every elementary school dropout sniffing glue in a community, there's likely another kid doing well in school, who says, "I don't want to have anything to do with that." Alternatively, a sidebar talk with a professor or an expert can offer historical context to the main players.

Online extras

In your race to get the story to air, you will come across all kinds of resources and material that help you put an issue in context. Court decisions, historical essays, statistical reports. While you can't include all that information in the body of your story, direct your audience to your website, where you can share links, scanned documents, and such. That allows them to do their own research and learning, if they're so inclined.

The "2-for-1" Deal

Argue that this story demands context, and that the best way to provide that is to assign two or more different reporters to a news event: one reporter to cover the "news of the day," and others who can focus on history and background.

If your assignment editor balks at tying up their precious resources in one subject, try pitching the one- or two-reporter tag-team as a package treatment, further supplemented with graphics—heck, you could even promote it as an "in-depth" feature!

Discussion Questions

1. How did settlers in Canada and the U.S. benefit from the attempt to erase the histories of peoples whose lands were taken?
2. During a speech in 2016, Marie Wilson, commissioner of Canada's Truth and Reconciliation Commission, posed the following question: "If some sides of a story are never told . . . can truth exist?" What do you make of her question?
3. Have you ever had to leave important background information out of a news story because of space considerations? How did you resolve that problem? How could that strategy assist when it comes to reporting on Indigenous issues?
4. Why does context matter when it comes to reporting in Indigenous communities?

Additional Readings and Resources

Robert Joseph, *21 Things You May Not Know about the Indian Act* (Port Coquitlam, BC: Indigenous Relations Press, 2018).
Native American Journalists Association, *100 Questions, 500 Nations: A Guide to Native America* (Front Edge Publishing, LLC, 2014).
Dee Brown, *Bury My Heart at Wounded Knee: An Indian History of the American West* (New York: Holt, Rinehart & Winston, 1970).
Chelsea Vowel, *Indigenous Writes: A Guide to First Nations, Métis & Inuit Issues in Canada*. (Winnipeg, MB: High Water Press, 2016).
Jean Teillet, *The North-West Is Our Mother: The Story of Louis Riel's People, the Métis Nation* (Toronto: Harper Collins, 2019).

Endnotes

1. Robert Harding, "Historical Representations of Aboriginal People in the Canadian News Media," *Discourse and Society*, 17.2 (2006), 229.

✦ 3.3 ✦

Accountability, Reciprocity, and Criticism

> In this chapter, students will learn to:
> - illustrate why reciprocity is such an essential aspect of Indigenous cultures;
> - modify their journalistic practice to incorporate "giving back"; and
> - operate in an accountable manner in order to enhance a trust relationship with Indigenous subjects and communities.

> *Giving back is not a difficult concept, yet one of the most egregious actions of Western research into the lives of Indigenous peoples is the negligence of this ethic. Giving back does not only mean dissemination of findings; it means creating a relationship throughout the entirety of the research.*[1]
>
> – Margaret Kovach

OK, your story is finished. It's out there. You've done the best you can, with the resources you've got, in the time allowed. Tomorrow is a new day, new story, right?

Not if you want to do a good job covering Indigenous communities.

Success on any beat revolves around building strong, reliable relationships. This goes doubly so for reporting in Indigenous communities, given the historic concerns Indigenous communities have about theft and appropriation of culture. Recognize that your story will have consequences—sometimes good, sometimes bad—for the people you've reported on, and for Indigenous Peoples across the country. By staying in touch with your subjects, you signal your willingness to be accountable for your work (plus you may find fodder for follow-up stories!).

Giving Back

A journalist's pursuit of a story is often a one-way street. We assume that publishing someone's point of view is payment enough for granting us that interview. Rarely do we consider requests that conflict with our prime directive: editorial independence.

Furthermore, if someone consents to an interview, that material typically becomes the property of the reporter's news organization, governed by the ethics policy of their newsroom.

Indigenous Peoples, on the other hand, generally distrust anyone who refuses to share. Selfishness contradicts a fundamental value of Indigenous societies: reciprocity. A hunter asking permission from an animal before a kill, a healer placing tobacco on the earth before picking a plant—these are simple expressions of reciprocity.

This clash of values can be overcome by acknowledging you have reciprocal obligations once a story is shared with you (aside from pledging that your reportage will be truthful and balanced). Make sure the people you've interviewed and the people who assisted you along the way get to see, read, or hear the story. Perhaps it's as simple as sending them an email with a weblink to your story and inviting feedback. But don't assume all Indigenous people have access to computers. They might want something more old-school, so get an address where you can mail them a newspaper, CD, or DVD.

Once the story is published or broadcast, you could offer your story subjects JPEGs of the photos you took. After all, how many people get a professional photographer to take pictures of them? Or, you could ask if they'd like a transcript of an interview or copies of raw video footage. Many Indigenous communities lack time or capacity to gather information from community members—your work may serve as valuable information long after you've moved on to a different story.

A note of caution: It may be unwise to share such content if you are reporting on a sensitive or controversial story, as releasing raw material could invite scrutiny and critique of your editorial choices and decisions. Furthermore, most media outlets have policies about ownership of their audiovisual archival material—you may need permission from a senior producer/editor before releasing your work free of charge.

Further down the road, if you ever get a call from that Indigenous person who gave you the interview you so desperately needed, and they have a story idea of their own, remember the importance of reciprocity. If you can't make a news story out of the tip, try to help that person find a reporter who can.

Taking an even longer view of reciprocity, newsrooms often find ways to build social capital in the town or city they report on, whether by offering ad space to local charities, raising money for a food bank, or participating in Pride Day celebrations. Think about how you can forge ongoing relationships with the Indigenous community you're reporting on. What skills and assets do you have that you can give back?

Perhaps, on an individual level, you could volunteer your time to assist with a community event—for example, contributing or preparing food, or transporting Elders during a special gathering. Maybe you could organize a media skills workshop for Indigenous youth or provide interview training to a cultural department seeking to gather stories from community members. The possibilities are endless.

To be clear, such contributions should never be offered as a bargaining chip in exchange for a story. Our journalism should not be tainted with suspicions of quid pro quo. Rather, think of informal and friendly ways to foster trust that help build capacity in a community and show you're serious about not being a story-taker (see discussion in Chapter 2.6, "Story-Takers: How to Deal With 500+ Years of Rage").

Shake It Off

Perhaps your story is not well received, either by the people in it or by other members of the Indigenous community, or both. Perhaps you get nasty emails and phone calls to that effect.

Don't blow them off.

You'll be amazed how quickly your run-in with someone will come back to haunt you, thanks to that remarkably efficient and informal word-of-mouth network known as the "Moccasin Telegraph" (see more about that in the next chapter).

Instead, it's wise to hear someone out. Not only does it show respect for the person you've upset, but it also gives you an opportunity to reflect upon your own biases and decision-making process. Maybe you'll become more determined that your approach is the right one. Or, maybe you'll do things differently next time. Either way, you learn.

But it's also important to not take criticism from your Indigenous audience personally (as noted in the Story-Takers chapter, Chapter 2.6). Recognize that anger and frustration will sometimes be directed your way, conduct yourself with respect, and move on.

Discussion Questions

1. Why is reciprocity important to journalism when you are reporting in Indigenous communities?
2. What are ways that you could give back to the Indigenous people you are interviewing or the community you are working in?
3. What are some of the challenges of building a reciprocal relationship with someone?

Additional Readings and Resources

Margaret Kovach, *Indigenous Methodologies: Characteristics, Conversations, and Contexts* (Toronto: University of Toronto Press, 2000).

Deborah McGregor, J.-P. Restoule, and Rochelle Johnston (eds.), *Indigenous Research: Theories, Practices, and Relationships* (Toronto: Canadian Scholars, 2018).

R.D.K. Herman (ed.), *Giving Back: Research and Reciprocity in Indigenous Settings* (Baltimore, MD: Project Muse, 2018).

Maya Lefkowich, Britney Dennison, and Peter Klein, "Empowerment Journalism." *Journalism Studies* 20.12 (September 10, 2019), 1803–9.

Seth C. Lewis, Avery E. Holton, and Mark Coddington, "Reciprocal Journalism." *Journalism Practice* 8.2 (March 4, 2014), 229–41.

Endnotes

1. Margaret Kovach, *Indigenous Methodologies: Characteristics, Conversations, and Contexts* (Toronto: University of Toronto Press, 2000), 149.

✦ 3.4 ✦
Social Media: The New Moccasin Telegraph

> In this chapter, students will learn to:
> - understand that Indigenous Peoples use social media for a myriad of uses, such as staying connected, sharing Indigenous culture, and asserting power;
> - use social media as a way to source stories in Indigenous communities, and to grow Indigenous audiences for news content; and
> - operate in an online environment in a way that stays accountable to Indigenous communities and minimizes harm to Indigenous people.

For Indigenous social media users, to have control of how oneself and one's social group are represented is to challenge forces that define them in terms of what they lack, and to make possible other futures.[1]

–Bronwyn Carlson and Ryan Frazer

Long before the invention of Morse code, the telephone, and radio waves, European settlers had noted the seemingly remarkable ability of Indigenous Peoples to spread stories, news, and information far and wide across the North American landscape.

"It has defied both scientific analysis and the metaphysical gropings of whites," waxed author Hal G. Evarts in his 1927 novel *The Moccasin Telegraph*, set in 1840s Yukon. "Yet the fact remains that weird rumours, later proven to be founded . . . are circulated by some mysterious agency [among] isolated native camps that are separated by vast distances. And those who have lived long in the North do not disregard the mutterings of the Moccasin Telegraph."[2]

To native folks, it ain't no thing.

Lots of important stuff travels by word-of-mouth amongst Indigenous Peoples. There's a long history of that. First Nations and Métis people themselves have co-opted the term "moccasin telegraph" to describe this ancient information sharing network and, in many ways, social media simply functions as an upgrade of the moccasin telegraph for this digital age.

It's important to recognize that the digital divide remains a real problem for Indigenous communities in North America. Many reserves in Canada and tribal lands in the U.S. still lag far behind national rates of broadband access.[3] Yet, even in areas where wealth is scarce and connectivity poor, Indigenous folks are posting smiling selfies on Facebook and busting moves on TikTok like nobody's business.

Benefits of Social Media to Indigenous Peoples

Indigenous social media users are no different than human beings worldwide: They make use of social media to stay connected to kith and kin, or as a source of news and entertainment. Still, it's helpful for journalists to keep in mind that Indigenous people turn to social media for some uniquely Indigenous activities, namely culture, control, and connection. In fact, observing how Indigenous people use social media can offer important insights into how journalists might represent Indigenous voices in their own stories.

Culture

Given the ways mainstream media commonly distort or stereotype Indigenous Peoples, it should come as no surprise that social media gives Indigenous people a sense of power over their own identities, which is why these platforms have become significant tools of cultural resurgence.

Bronwyn Carlson's surveys of Aboriginal social media users in Australia suggest that not only do Indigenous social media users often express and display their Indigeneity online, sharing of culture is a also regular activity on Indigenous social media channels.[4] Virtual communities are allowing for a safe space for Indigenous people to pass on cultural knowledge, whether it be language, stories, traditional knowledge, or song. The multimedia nature of the digital world also makes for a good cultural fit with the oral traditions of Indigenous Peoples.

Control

While Indigenous Peoples have skilfully embraced social media as a means to control and broadcast their own stories to the world, Indigenous people are also responding rapidly to mainstream media coverage. They are holding newsrooms to account by offering critique when journalism is done poorly and rewarding news outlets that take Indigenous issues seriously by sharing widely stories that matter.

For example, when missing and murdered Indigenous women became the most covered Indigenous issue in Canadian media in 2014–15,[5] it wasn't because the issue itself was new — Indigenous women and girls had been going missing for decades with little notice by mainstream media outlets. What changed was that Indigenous activists and community members had the means to broadcast stories that mattered to them, and that influenced mainstream political agendas, which in turn forced news media to listen.

Connection

Kinship and familial ties, so crucial to Indigenous identities, sometimes get weaker when Indigenous people leave their home communities or homelands for urban centres. Thus, the most popular feature of social media amongst Indigenous users may be the ability to affordably and instantly connect with geographically distant family and friends.

In her research into the pervasive use of Facebook amongst First Nations, Tahltan journalism professor Candis Callison suggests social media is not only rekindling those community connections, it's creating new ways to pass knowledge between urban and reserve residents. "There remains an incredible flow of ideas and all kinds of capital between the reserve and the city, forming 'communities in motion.'"[6]

Similarly, Indigenous communities worldwide are forging relationships and building coalitions like never before, sharing knowledge, resources, and lobbying efforts on everything from land rights to language revitalization.

The Upside of Social Media for Journalists

For plenty of different reasons, social media has become a useful—some say essential—tool for journalists. Here's a few ways social media can help connect you with Indigenous communities.

Great Source of Stories

Finding information is one of the main functions of a journalist. On that front, social media is manna from heaven. While there's still a place for good ol'-fashioned gumshoe journalism, it's hard to beat social media as a starting point for Indigenous story ideas and contacts.

Be aware that different social media platforms attract different segments of the Indigenous community. Facebook is the most widely used of all social media platforms, attracting all demographics, but it is a favourite of reserve and northern residents. Instagram is popular amongst Indigenous creatives. Twitter tends to attract professionals and those with higher education, such as Indigenous academics, politicians, and activists who seek to influence the news. TikTok has emerged as a preferred social platform for youth and meme-makers. Pretty much everyone, from powwow singers to Indigenous language students, watches YouTube.

Whether you're serious about covering the Indigenous beat, or want to diversify your newsfeed, you should follow Indigenous influencers on a variety of platforms (you'll find ideas in the Additional Readings and Resources at the end of this chapter).

Of course, there's no keeping up with the speed of social media trends. No doubt, by the time this is published, the kids will be using a new platform in new ways that make this discussion seem archaic.

Spread the Word

Social media has disrupted how people get their news. If you're intent on reaching Indigenous Peoples, you need to be adept at promoting your work to Indigenous social networks. Tagging Indigenous people in your post will get your stories in front of more people. Try reaching out to Indigenous social media influencers. They share Indigenous content they care about with their vast numbers of followers, which helps build your Indigenous audience base.

Social media posts with hashtags receive more reach than those that don't. Try adding #Indigenous or #NativeAmerican to your posts, but also consider piggybacking on other Indigenous-related hashtags, such as #idlenomore, #waterislife, or #MMIWG. Similarly, Indigenous land defenders have used hashtag activism such as #WetsuwetenSolidarity or #NoDAPL to mobilize support for their actions and amplify their message.

Expand Story Formats

Different social media platforms operate differently. To maximize your reach on a particular platform, you need to do more than just drop links to articles—inject some storytelling creativity into your posts! For example, if you're travelling to an Indigenous community, take your followers behind the scenes of your journey so they can learn a little more about life in the community. If you're covering a breaking news story, consider going live with an update or a brief interview. Maybe experiment with an online poll.

Social media is driven by the power of visuals—even print or online journalists should always be on the lookout for a great picture or video. That said, remember the discussion in Chapter 2.2 about Indigenous customs and protocols: You should always request permission to film or photograph a ceremony, and in this scenario, ask whether it's okay to post it on social media. If you're asked *not* to record a ceremony, it's unwise to ignore that request.

The Downsides of Social Media for Journalists

Social media also has disadvantages, as far as reporting in Indigenous communities is concerned.

Verifying Information

In the era of fake news, journalists can never become complacent about verifying the information they report. Fighting disinformation has always been a challenge, but social media has made it exponentially more difficult.

Indigenous communities are not immune from the spread of gossip, rumours, and falsehoods on social media. In fact, social media has amplified the well-documented phenomenon of "lateral violence"—Indigenous people who have endured oppression or discrimination directing anger, bullying, and abuse toward their own communities.[7]

If you are following an online news story from an Indigenous community—whether it be eyewitness reports from the front lines of a protest, allegations of sexual abuse, outing of "pretendians," disturbing reports of racist attacks, the list goes on—you simply *must* ensure you get your facts right before you publish a story or amplify a post by sharing it. As newsworthy as a social media post or video may seem, resist the urge to be first or chase likes and retweets until you've verified the information through multiple sources.

Of course, verification is a fundamental tenet of good journalism. But if you are going to build credibility and trust in Indigenous communities, you cannot afford to inadvertently victimize Indigenous people or damage your reputation by using your platform to spread mistruths.

Racism/Online Bullying

As much as Indigenous people enjoy social media, the digital age has a dark side: the amplification of abuse, hate, and discrimination. Racism thrives online, in disturbing ways. While social media companies clearly have a responsibility to do better at weeding out trolls, bullies, and white supremacists, journalists also need to be aware of the risks social media poses to Indigenous people.

In a 2018 survey of Indigenous social media users in Australia, Bronwyn Carlson and Ryan Frazer found that over half of respondents were "selective" about what they posted online for fear of attracting racist or violent responses. Of the respondents, 88 per cent reported they had seen examples of racism toward Indigenous people on social media. The comments sections of news articles about Indigenous people were highlighted as being particularly harmful.[8]

Journalists can manage the unsavoury aspects of the internet in a couple of different ways.

First, news organizations should be aware that stories on Indigenous subjects often attract hateful comments. The problem can be mitigated by careful curation of comments sections. That takes resources—assigning a member of a digital team to weed out hate speech and personal attacks. But it may also require more drastic measures. In 2015, CBC closed comments on stories about Indigenous Peoples, because a disproportionate number violated submission guidelines.[9] "Some comments are clearly hateful and vitriolic, some are simply ignorant. And some appear to be hate disguised as ignorance (i.e., racist sentiments expressed in benign language).... We don't want violations of our guidelines by a small minority of our commenters to derail our good work or alienate our audience," wrote CBC's acting director of digital news Brodie Fenlon.[10]

Second, journalists owe it to their Indigenous sources and story subjects to make sure they understand the potential impacts of sharing their story online. This means clearly explaining that their words and/or pictures will be on social media. Indigenous people may be eager to share their story with you, but they may not be prepared for how widely it could travel, or the kinds of comments the story may attract. It's important you prepare them for the possibility of negative comments online, so that they can make an informed choice about what to share with you.

You may not be the cause of online racism and harassment, but you are responsible for minimizing harm to the best of your ability.

Managing Online Relationships

Indigenous people are keenly aware of the capacity of social media to hold power brokers accountable, including journalists. Indigenous social media users can be helpful in spreading your stories, but you can bet they'll also respond in force to stories they find objectionable.

You likely have your own approaches to responding to online audiences—some journalists are more interactive than others. But if you use social media regularly, take special care in responding to negative comments from Indigenous social media users.

Accountability is an essential aspect of building trust and relationships with Indigenous communities, as discussed in the previous chapter. If Indigenous social media users are upset or frustrated with your story, you should pay attention and consider a reply. You'll never satisfy everyone (and shouldn't try), but if you respond in a friendly way to legitimate critiques of your journalism, it shows you're listening and willing to learn. Responsiveness may even build respect. On the other hand, if you sweep negative feedback under the carpet, you may damage your reputation in the Indigenous online community. It doesn't take long for outrage to go viral on social media.

When crafting your online responses, be careful about directing angry or sarcastic social media comments at an Indigenous person (or any person, really)—they can spread like wildfire. As discussed in Chapter 2.6, "Story-Takers," an ill-considered outburst could ruin your chances at building relationships with other Indigenous people, either in the online sphere or in real life.

Discussion Questions

1. Who do you follow on social media, and what motivates you to follow someone? Are there Indigenous people in your social media sphere? If you are looking for more Indigenous people to follow, see articles below about Indigenous Instagram and TikTok influencers. Plus, to start diversifying your online news sources, read through the list of Indigenous media compiled for the #Next150Challenge. Choose 5–10 Indigenous media makers you don't know and follow them on your social media.

    https://next150.indianhorse.ca/challenges/diversify-your-news

2. Find a meme on social media made by an Indigenous content creator. Share it with the rest of the class. How are these memes expressing humour? Teaching? Resisting?

3. Have you had personal experience of online abuse? What impact did this abuse have on you? What strategies do you feel were most helpful to you? How does this experience inform the way you work with Indigenous people in a news context?

Additional Readings and Resources

Bronwyn Carlson and Ryan Frazer, "'They Got Filters': Indigenous Social Media, the Settler Gaze, and a Politics of Hope." *Social Media + Society* 6.2 (2020), 1–11.

Bronwyn Carlson and Ryan Frazer, *Social Media Mob: Being Indigenous Online* (Sydney, Australia: Macquarie University, 2018).

Bronwyn Carlson, "The 'New Frontier': Emergent Indigenous Identities and Social Media." In Michelle Harris, Martin Nakata, and Bronwyn Carlson (eds.), *The Politics of Identity: Emerging Indigeneity* (Sydney: University of Technology Sydney E-Press, 2013), 147–168.

Candis Callison and Alfred Hermida, "Dissent and Resonance: #Idlenomore as an Emergent Middle Ground." *Canadian Journal of Communication* 40 (2015), 695–716.

Rohina Katoch Sehra, "26 Indigenous Instagram Accounts to Follow Right Away." *HuffPost*, November 10, 2020. https://www.huffpost.com/entry/indigenous-instagram-accounts-to-follow_l_5f9b17e5c5b65a0efac98867

Andreas Krebs, "'Number One Tool' for First Nations? Facebook." *The Tyee*, May 30, 2011. https://thetyee.ca/Mediacheck/2011/05/30/FNFacebook/

Jessie Loyer, "Indigenous TikTok Is Transforming Cultural Knowledge." *Canadian Art*, April 23, 2020. https://canadianart.ca/essays/indigenous-tiktok-is-transforming-cultural-knowledge/

Dakshana Bascaramurty, "Power at Their Fingertips: Indigenous People Turn to Social Media to Expose Injustice." *Globe and Mail*, November 7, 2020. https://www.theglobeandmail.com/canada/article-power-at-their-fingertips-indigenous-people-turn-to-social-media-to/

Lenard Monkman, "Indigenous Meme Creators Point out Harsh Truths with Dark Humour." *CBC Indigenous*, September 19, 2018. https://www.cbc.ca/news/indigenous/indigenous-meme-creators-instagram-1.4828555

Endnotes

1. Bronwyn Carlson and Ryan Frazer, "'They Got Filters': Indigenous Social Media, the Settler Gaze, and a Politics of Hope." *Social Media + Society* 6.2 (2020), 4.
2. Hal G. Evarts, *The Moccasin Telegraph* (Boston, Mass: Little, Brown, and Company, 1927), as cited by Kay Vandell in *Telegraphies: Indigeneity, Identity, and Nation in America's Nineteenth-Century Virtual Realm* (New York: Oxford University Press, 2020), 19.
3. In the United States, approximately 60% of people have high-speed internet access on tribal lands, compared to 97% of Americans in urban areas, according to a 2020 report by the Federal Communications Commission. In Canada, a 2017 survey by the Canadian Radio-television and Telecommunications Commission found that 97% of Canadians have internet access at home, while only 24% of households in Indigenous communities have access to quality, high-speed internet.
4. Bronwyn Carlson and Ryan Frazer, *Social Media Mob: Being Indigenous Online* (Sydney, Australia: Macquarie University, 2018).
5. See JHR's 2019 report *Buried Voices: Changing Tones*: https://jhr.ca/wp-content/uploads/2019/10/JHR-IRP-Report-v3online.pdf
6. Andreas Krebs, "'Number One Tool' for First Nations? Facebook." *The Tyee*, May 30, 2011. https://thetyee.ca/Mediacheck/2011/05/30/FNFacebook/
7. Native Women's Association of Canada, "Aboriginal Lateral Violence." Factsheet, 2011. https://www.nwac.ca/wp-content/uploads/2015/05/2011-Aboriginal-Lateral-Violence.pdf
8. Bronwyn Carlson and Ryan Frazer, *Social Media Mob: Being Indigenous Online* (Sydney, Australia: Macquarie University, 2018), 12.
9. Full disclosure—in 2015, I was part of the small group of Indigenous staff at CBC who reviewed online comments and advised shutting down the comments section. This recommendation was implemented by *CBC News*.
10. Brodie Fenlon, "Uncivil Dialogue: Commenting and Stories about Indigenous People." *CBC News*, November 13, 2015. https://www.cbc.ca/newsblogs/community/editorsblog/2015/11/uncivil-dialogue-commenting-and-stories-about-indigenous-people.html

✦ 3.5 ✦

Reconciliation and Journalism

> In this chapter, students will learn to:
> - recognize the media's contribution to public misconceptions about Indigenous issues; and
> - understand the responsibilities of reconciliation include encouraging media organizations to develop Indigenous action plans, hire more Indigenous journalists, and build ongoing relationships with Indigenous communities.

Journalism is not a reconciliation-free zone.[1]

– Karyn Pugliese

On Monday, November 30, 2020, New Zealanders awoke to a surprise mea culpa from *Stuff*, one of that country's oldest and largest media outlets: a front-page apology for its portrayal of Māori over the past 163 years, presented in both English and the Māori language.

"Nō mātou te hē"—"We are sorry," read the massive headline on *Stuff*'s homepage and the front pages of its regional papers across the country.

The Colonial Press

The apology was the result of a three-month investigation by 20 *Stuff* journalists into a century's worth of its own coverage. Combing through their archives, it wasn't hard for them to find openly racist front pages and characterizations of Māori as an "inferior race" in nineteenth-century print editions. But analysis of contemporary *Stuff* stories also revealed one-sided coverage that often ignored Māori perspectives in favour of Pākehā (the Māori term for a white person/non-Māori New Zealanders), from bile-filled letters to the editor to a tendency to over-report Māori child abuse cases.

"Our coverage of Māori issues over the last 160 years ranged from racist to blinkered. Seldom was it fair or balanced in terms of representing Māori," wrote editorial

***Stuff* front cover.**
The November 30, 2020, front cover of *Stuff* states, "We've been racist, contributing to stigma, marginalisation, and stereotypes against Māori."

director Mark Stevens.² *Stuff* is not the only media outlet to examine its representation of Indigenous Peoples and find it lacking. In 2018, the venerable American magazine *National Geographic* apologized for what it called decades of racist coverage—particularly, its famed photography—and the role the magazine had played in reinforcing prejudice.

"[U]ntil the 1970s *National Geographic* all but ignored people of color who lived in the United States, rarely acknowledging them beyond laborers or domestic workers," wrote editor-in-chief Sally Goldberg. "Meanwhile it pictured 'natives' elsewhere as exotics, famously and frequently unclothed, happy hunters, noble savages—every type of cliché."³

Apologies are nice. But an apology alone isn't enough.

As Mark Stevens of *Stuff* observed, "apologies are hollow without a commitment to do better in the future." In addition to saying sorry, *Stuff* released a new charter, intended to address historic wrongs and foster more trust, by building deeper relationships with Māori communities.⁴

In Canada, the media's relationship with Indigenous Peoples has faced increased scrutiny since the Truth and Reconciliation Commission (TRC) released its 94 Calls to Action in 2015, three of which highlighted media and reconciliation. The TRC called on the federal government to invest in CBC, for APTN to continue its work, and for journalism schools to teach students everything from treaties to Indigenous-Crown relations.

Reviewing Canadian media's long history of perpetuating negative stereotypes and underreporting issues of importance to Indigenous communities, the TRC urged media outlets to engage in their own acts of reconciliation "to ensure that the colonial press truly becomes a thing of the past in twenty-first-century Canada."⁵

Perhaps not surprisingly, the media didn't rush to report on the call for media to reconcile with Indigenous Peoples. One could almost see thought-bubbles popping up in newsrooms from coast-to-coast-to-coast. "Colonial press? Huh?"

However, as historians Mark Anderson and Carmen Robertson so vividly illustrate in *Seeing Red* (see discussion in Chapter 1.2, "Historical News Stereotypes of Indigenous Peoples"), Canadian journalists have a well-documented pattern of taking a stand on Indigenous issues, whether consciously or unconsciously. By continually focusing on stories of conflict and by underreporting Indigenous issues in Canada,⁶ journalists have aided and abetted the colonial project for well over a century, reinforcing the very policies that prevent reconciliation.

Certainly, many individual journalists in Canada strive to provide news coverage that includes Indigenous Peoples' perspectives. The fact that you've made it this far in this book suggests you are one of those individual journalists committed to personal action: you want to get to know Indigenous people and learn to speak with them respectfully, and you seek to be knowledgeable about the history of this country (though I recognize it may also mean you are a student and your professor is quizzing you on the full contents of the book).

Still, journalists with good will and good intentions can't do it alone. Media creates narratives that shift culture, but no single news story or series is going to be the magic bullet that decolonizes journalism. If newsrooms, media organizations, and journalism schools don't undertake systemic change, reconciliation will only be empty platitudes. Here's a three-point test to see if your organization is walking the talk.

1. Develop an Action Plan

It is all fine and good for newsrooms to pledge to do better when it comes to Indigenous news coverage. But systemic change requires more than a hodgepodge of well-meaning efforts that may or may not be hitting the mark. As author Antoine de Saint-Exupéry once wrote, "A goal without a plan is just a wish."[7]

If your newsroom is serious about addressing gaps in Indigenous coverage or hiring, it needs an action plan.

Consider, as an example, the national Reconciliation Action Plan (RAP) program launched in Australia in 2006. RAPs are essentially business plans that an organization uses to document the actions they're taking toward reconciliation. The plans set realistic targets and timelines for improving the relationship between Indigenous people and other Australians, both within the organization and more widely. Since the launch of the program, over a thousand Australian businesses, community organizations, and schools have developed RAPs. That includes the Australian Broadcasting Corporation (ABC), whose "demonstrable actions" tackle everything from Indigenous programming and employment, to cross-cultural training and changes to the style guide incorporating Indigenous languages. "As the national broadcaster, it is incumbent on the ABC to show leadership in advancing reconciliation," declared the broadcaster in its 2019–22 RAP.[8]

Canadian newsrooms have long seemed allergic to collecting data about diversity, but the importance of tracking numbers must be baked into any commitment to a long-term Indigenous strategy. You can't manage what you can't measure, as the maxim goes.

How many Indigenous staff do you have? How many Indigenous sources were quoted this week? How many Indigenous stories did you run this year?

If you can't answer those questions, how will your newsroom know if it's improving?

2. Hire More Indigenous People

As discussed in Chapter 1.7, what data exists on the diversity of Canadian newsrooms shows Indigenous journalists are consistently underrepresented. Likewise, journalism schools have a paucity of Indigenous instructors and professors.

Put bluntly, Canadian media have a whiteness problem.

I won't dwell on why that's a problem. In this day and age, the moral and business case for diverse newsrooms should be self-evident. "We cover a diverse world," *National Geographic* editor-in-chief Sally Goldberg has said. "If we want to do so accurately and with authority, we need a diverse staff to cover it."

If your newsroom is going to serve Indigenous communities properly, it can't be done without having some Indigenous journalists in the mix. Indigenous journalists bring important skillsets to covering Indigenous communities, whether by having an ear to the ground on the latest happenings or offering their lived experience to news coverage.

So, is your newsroom serious about Indigenous hiring?

Are they actively recruiting Indigenous journalists by offering Indigenous internships or creating Indigenous reporting positions? Is there a mentorship and/or training program for younger Indigenous journalists? Are there resources dedicated to ensuring proper Indigenous news coverage? Are you building an inclusive newsroom, where

Indigenous and other diverse journalists feel culturally safe? Can Indigenous journalists access traditional healers through your organization's benefit plan, if they so choose, or take time off to attend ceremonies or cultural events? Are there Indigenous people in senior editorial and management roles? If not, is there a strategy or training program to develop Indigenous leaders in your newsroom?

These are all signals to Indigenous employees that their workplace satisfaction and perspectives are taken seriously. Without such actions and initiatives, no one should act surprised when Indigenous hires seem difficult to attract and harder to keep.

3. Build Relationships with Indigenous Communities

"Reconciliation is about forging and maintaining respectful relationships," the Honourable Murray Sinclair, chair of the TRC, said. "There are no shortcuts."[9]

If media outlets are serious about reconciliation, they must begin the hard work of building relationships with Indigenous communities. That means listening—and acting.

It can start with actively engaging your Indigenous audience. Try asking targeted questions on social media or publishing guest columns by community members. But engagement goes much further than seeking input or feedback on reportage.

Newsrooms should take an active role in the Indigenous communities they report on. As discussed in Chapter 3.2, the possibilities for building social capital are endless. Host Indigenous-specific workshops or open houses. Hold a "roadshow" at a First Nation to talk about the impacts of coverage or deliver community stories. Offer volunteer support at Indigenous cultural celebrations.

Journalism schools, too, need to seek Indigenous partnerships. Community input not only helps develop curriculum more deeply responsive to Indigenous needs, it will also potentially enrich non-Indigenous students' exposure to the Indigenous communities that surround them. These relationships can take many different forms: partnering with other Indigenous programs on a school campus, reaching out to urban Indigenous organizations, or developing connections to more remote Indigenous communities.

Relationships can be complex and messy—anyone who has ever been in love knows that. Relationships between news organizations and Indigenous communities are no different. There will be missteps and miscommunication. But, it's all about building trust. Over time, the benefits will be apparent. Journalists will report that sources trust them more, which in turn leads to better access and better stories. It all translates to a more loyal audience—and ensures that our journalism matters.

Can Journalism Be Decolonized?

Since the release of the TRC report in 2015, there are promising signs that the media landscape when it comes to Indigenous people is finally changing in Canada.

There's an award for journalists who broaden the understanding of the relationship between Indigenous and non-Indigenous Peoples. There are a growing number of fellowships and internships for Indigenous journalists. More journalism schools are embedding Indigenous content in their curricula.

But there is still much work to be done.

If newsrooms, media organizations, and journalism schools don't devote proper resources to hiring and retaining Indigenous staff, building relationships with Indigenous communities, and developing strategic, long-term plans, there's a danger of simply paying lip service to reconciliation, when there's an urgent need for change.

Exercise 1 Create a Reconciliation Event

Looking for small, everyday acts of reconciliation that everyday Canadians can undertake?
Check out this blog post: "150 Acts of Reconciliation for the Last 150 Days of Canada's 150," by Crystal Fraser and Dr. Sara Komarnisky.
http://activehistory.ca/2017/08/150-acts-of-reconciliation-for-the-last-150-days-of-canadas-150/

Discuss how your class could create a reconciliation event. It could be held in your classroom, or be a school-based event or an ongoing, community-engaged project. Who would be invited to this event? Over what period of time? How can you verify that your call to action is meaningful and will not cause more harm? What do you need to support your action?

Discussion Questions

1. In 1998, as part of its response to the Report of the Royal Commission on Aboriginal Peoples, the Government of Canada delivered a Statement of Reconciliation to Aboriginal Peoples. The churches also apologized for the role they played in Indian Residential Schools. In 2007, the Indian Residential Schools Settlement Agreement came into effect. This was followed by the 2008 federal government's apology to survivors (see Appendix 4) and the creation of the Truth and Reconciliation Commission in 2009. Do you believe apologies are important? Why?
2. What is truth? What role does truth play in the process of reconciliation?
3. What do you believe needs to be done to reconcile the relationship between Indigenous and non-Indigenous people? Do you think reconciliation can be achieved?
4. What actions can you take as a journalist to improve relationships between Indigenous and non-Indigenous people?
5. Why do you think the TRC's Calls to Action are not merely recommendations?

Additional Readings and Resources

Truth and Reconciliation Commission of Canada, *Final Report of the Truth and Reconciliation Commission of Canada: Summary: Honouring the Truth, Reconciling for the Future* (McGill-Queen's University Press, 2015). http://www.trc.ca/about-us/trc-findings.html

"Beyond 94: Truth and Reconciliation in Canada." *CBC Indigenous*, March 19, 2018. https://newsinteractives.cbc.ca/longform-single/beyond-94

Wawmeesh Hamilton, "How Can Journalism Support Reconciliation with Indigenous Peoples?" *The Discourse*, June 17, 2016. https://thediscourse.ca/urban-nation/journalism-reconciliation-indigenous-peoples https://www.sciencedirect.com/science/journal/02779536

Meagan Gilmore, "Long Journey of Reconciliation Ahead at Canada's Journalism Schools." *J-source*, April 20, 2018. https://j-source.ca/article/long-journey-of-reconciliation/

Patricia Elliot, *Decolonizing the Media: Challenges and Obstacles on the Road to Reconciliation*. Canadian Centre for Policy Alternatives (Saskatchewan Office), October 2016. https://www.policyalternatives.ca/sites/default/files/uploads/publications/Saskatchewan%20Office/2016/11/Decolonizing%20the%20Media%20%28final%29.pdf

Abigail Plener, "How Discourse Media Is Addressing Reconciliation." *Ryerson Review of Journalism*, December 19, 2016. https://rrj.ca/how-discourse-media-is-addressing-reconciliation/

Tanya Talaga, "Reconciliation Isn't Dead. It Never Truly Existed." *Globe and Mail*, February 29, 2020. https://www.theglobeandmail.com/opinion/article-reconciliation-isnt-dead-it-never-truly-existed/

Alexandria Neason, "On Atonement." *Columbia Journalism Review*, January 28, 2021. https://www.cjr.org/special_report/apologies-news-racism-atonement.php

Endnotes

1. Karyn Pugliese, "Reconciliation" in Royal Canadian Geographical Society. *Indigenous Peoples Atlas of Canada: Atlas des peuples autochtones du Canada*, 2018. https://indigenouspeoplesatlasofcanada.ca/article/reconciliation/
2. Mark Stevens, "Stuff's Apology to Māori—Our Truth, Tā Mātou Pono," *Stuff*, November 30, 2020.
3. Sally Goldberg, "For Decades Our Coverage Was Racist. To Rise Above Our Past, We Must Acknowledge It," *National Geographic*, March 13, 2018.
4. "*Stuff*'s Charter: A Brave New Era for NZ's Largest Media Company," *Stuff*, November 30, 2020. https://www.stuff.co.nz/pou-tiaki/our-truth/300168692/stuffs-charter-a-brave-new-era-for-nzs-largest-media-company
5. Truth and Reconciliation Commission of Canada, *Canada's Residential Schools: Reconciliation: The Final Report of the Truth and Reconciliation Commission of Canada, Volume 6* (McGill-Queen's University Press, 2015), 294.
6. Journalism for Human Rights (JHR) surveyed Indigenous coverage in Ontario's print/online media between 2010 and 2016. During that six-year period, Indigenous issues occupied less than 0.5 per cent of media space, while Indigenous Peoples represent approximately 2.8 per cent of the province's population. JHR also examined story tone and concluded negative coverage outweighed positive. For more, see JHR's *Buried Voices: Changing Tones* report: https://jhr.ca/wp-content/uploads/2019/10/JHR-IRP-Report-v3online.pdf
7. Antoine de Saint-Exupéry, *Le Petit Prince* (New York: Harcourt, Brace & World, 1943).
8. Australian Broadcasting Corporation, *Elevate: Reconciliation Action Plan, July 2019–June 2022*. See: https://about.abc.net.au/wp-content/uploads/2019/11/ABCElevateRAP201922.pdf
9. Murray Sinclair, "If you thought the Truth was hard, Reconciliation will be harder," Knight Lecture, University of Manitoba, October 30, 2014. See: https://news.umanitoba.ca/if-you-thought-the-truth-was-hard-reconciliation-will-be-harder/

Part 4
Teachings

4.1

Becoming Trauma-Informed: A Conversation with Connie Walker

Connie Walker is an award-winning investigative reporter, podcast host, and producer of the podcast *Stolen: The Search for Jermain* for Gimlet Media.

Prior to joining Gimlet, Connie Walker worked for CBC, hosting the acclaimed podcast series *Missing & Murdered*, which focuses on missing and murdered Indigenous women and girls. In 2018, *Missing & Murdered: Finding Cleo* won the inaugural Best Serialized Story award at the Third Coast International Audio festival. The podcast was also featured in the *Columbia Journalism Review*, *Rolling Stone*, *Vulture*, *Teen Vogue*, and *Chatelaine* and was named one of the Best Podcasts of 2018 by Apple Canada.

Highlights from her career include acting as the lead reporter for CBC Indigenous, a producer for the acclaimed *8th Fire* documentary series on contemporary issues for First Nations people, and as a reporter for the flagship CBC news show, *The National*.

Connie Walker.

Source: Photo courtesy of Connie Walker.

Walker, who was honoured as one of the YWCA's "Women of Distinction" in 2017, is from the Okanese First Nation in Saskatchewan. She currently lives with her family in Toronto, Ontario.

Preparing Interviewees

DM: You have done some very difficult stories about missing and murdered women, the Sixties Scoop, sexual abuse. When you're interviewing Indigenous subjects about their trauma, how do you prepare them for those discussions?

CW: The preparation starts from the very initial conversation, the initial reach out. I try to be as transparent as I can be about what it is I'm doing, what it is I would like to do, and really try to give them the agency and control over deciding if they want to participate or not. I used to joke with Marnie;[1] I would be like "Would you talk to us? No pressure at all.

Don't feel you have to say yes." (laugh) Not warning people, but really trying to have them feel that this is their decision.

Because I think that's incredibly important, especially in Indigenous communities: this idea of what it means to have informed consent.

Particularly important because the way our stories have been told in the past is people dropping in. People who are not from the community, dropping into a community, asking in a way that implicitly they have some kind of authority that people need to respond to or need to comply with. I have felt that at times, that people feel like, "Oh, you're here talking to me. So, I should talk to you." I'm really trying to unpack that and have people realize that this is your choice. This is something that you can choose to do.

It sounds so basic, but it's really important for anyone who goes into an Indigenous community to understand the history of what our contact has been like in the past with journalists and media in general. And be aware of that, even just asking for an interview.

When Trauma Is Disclosed

DM: You joked about the challenges of being transparent, but there must be times when you fully disclose everything you're hoping to accomplish, that people say, "No, I don't want to share about my sexual abuse or whatever trauma I may have experienced." What do you do then?

CW: With a story that I'm reporting right now, it's about a woman who has gone missing. And most of my interviews have been with her family. Her grandmother, aunts, cousins. I haven't yet spoken to her mother. I've spoken to people in her family about why that's a difficult conversation, obviously, for her mother. I've totally tried to be understanding about all of the reasons why she might not want to talk to me for the podcasts that we're doing.

But also, I have approached her now three or four times to say, "If you ever feel like you want to, feel free to reach out. I can make myself available. If you even just want to have a conversation off the record, or if you have any questions." Because I feel some unease about reporting on a story about her daughter without including her. I know that that's obviously such an important person in her life and an important person in her daughter's life. I would be concerned that she would feel—once it is out there—excluded or disrespected. But I also feel if she talked to me, I certainly wouldn't anticipate that I could ask her about her trauma in that conversation right away.

I don't feel like I go into an interview with an expectation that people are going to share terrible things. If it feels like that's happening, that they are going to be talking about trauma, then I want to give them the space. These interviews I'm talking about are sometimes one hour, two hours, three hours long.

I did an interview with this woman, where it was the first time that she had ever disclosed, not only to a journalist, but I think to anyone, some of the abuse that she had experienced. We sat together for three hours that afternoon and I wanted to give her the space to have that conversation. I didn't know that was going to come up. It was an interview that was actually about something completely different. But it was disclosed in that interview.

I always try to end the interview by focusing more on the resiliency aspect—which is <u>always</u> present when there is trauma, especially with Indigenous women, which is the community that I mostly am talking to. Then I always check in with the person. A couple of days after we did that interview, she reached out and she was like, "I am still unpacking everything that we talked about. I'm concerned about some of the stuff that I shared and I'm not sure if I want my interview to be included."

My reaction to that is, "I totally understand. I want to have another conversation with you and whatever you are comfortable with. But I certainly don't want to publish anything that you are not comfortable with." I know that's a different approach than we sometimes have as journalists.

Revisiting Consent

DM: How do you help people after you've had that interview? Because the typical approach, which we're both familiar with, is that this interview is now the journalist's property.

CW: Yeah, and in some newsrooms, consent is something you get at the beginning of the interview and it's implied throughout the process. We really need to reconsider that, especially when we're talking about marginalized communities that have been so misrepresented or who have this mistrust of media, about what it means to actually have consent.

DM: That puts a burden on you, though, after you've invested all that time in that interview. What if she says, three days afterwards, "I'm not sure about whether I want that to go public"?

CW: It's so tricky. I mean, we have a JSP,[2] which is very black and white. This is allowed and this is not allowed. And if you want to do this, you have to do this, this and this, and the other thing. What I learned coming up through that system is all of the rules.

When I started reporting on violence against Indigenous women or girls, doing more in-depth investigative reporting and Indigenous communities, then started being mindful of the trauma and the impacts of that trauma on the people whose lives you're diving deep into and the impacts of your journalism on their health and their lives . . . it made me realize how that [JSP] is a starting point, maybe, but it can't be the end of the conversation.

> For a discussion about consent when interviewing survivors, see Chapter 2.5, "Trauma-Informed Reporting."

DM: What you're suggesting is it's really important in terms of the relationship and the person's health to continue to revisit consent, if that's necessary. And to continue to revisit transparency.

CW: When we started reporting on violence against Indigenous women and girls, the first project that we did was the database project.[3] It was trying to come up with the database of as many unsolved cases as we could possibly find. It was a very small team that was working on this, mostly Indigenous journalists. They had the very difficult job of reaching out to families. They contacted over 100 families through that project, asking them about their loved one who was either missing or who had been murdered.

For a lot of those families, this was the first time any journalist had ever come to call them to ask about their loved one. These are all unsolved cases. This was a particular kind of experience that these families had had with law enforcement or the justice system, and our focus as journalists was to try to tell the story behind the statistics. Trying to not only focus on the violence that resulted in their deaths or disappearance, but also try to—it sounds so basic and almost terrible, but . . . humanize the statistics and the women behind the stories. Because so much of the reporting that has been done in the past about violence against Indigenous women or girls was dehumanizing.

These researchers spoke to families and had these conversations that were hours long. Sometimes they talked about their favourite anecdotes about their mother, their sister, their auntie, their daughter. I wasn't doing that part of the process. My role in that project was helping to lead the editorial vision but also to do the reporting once the project came out. But I was working closely with some of those researchers and they were talking about the impacts these interviews were having on the families and they were feeling this responsibility to the families and were also dealing with the impacts of hearing those stories. Because they were Indigenous themselves. We are Indigenous women and we have personal experience with some of the traumas that we're reporting on.

It's really terrible and unfortunate to state, but I think going through that experience and realizing how we weren't prepared for the impacts we were going to be having on families and communities, or on the journalists who are doing this work, *that* has informed the kind of care I try to take now. That's something not written in the JSP. It's not a best practice at CBC, but because we had those experiences, I'm trying to do what I can to minimize the harm.

After the Interview

DM: We're not counsellors or psychologists. Are there any other things that you do, in terms of after-care with your story subjects?

CW: The biggest thing is: these are not transactional kinds of relationships. I'm still in touch with several, if not all, of the families that I've done this kind of reporting with. Johnny and I message at least once every couple weeks. I'm in touch with Christine probably about once a month.[4] I'm friends with Leah Anderson's sister on Facebook.[5] When she became an auntie, just the other day, I was like, "Congratulations!"

I feel like we have these relationships that are lasting. It's a unique kind of relationship because it is still very much one-sided, right? I was with Johnny and Christine over several months when they were learning—not just what happened to their sister—what happened to them as children. It was unpacking a lot of childhood trauma that they had experienced and not disclosed. It was through that process that we had very close contact for a really long period of time. So I have come to care about them very deeply, and they feel like I'm an important part of that journey and that part of their life. That doesn't end just because the story is over.

I feel a huge level of responsibility to the families who open up and share. That makes the process of being a journalist infinitely more complicated and tricky.

DM: Does it make you wary to be considered a friend?

CW: Like I said, it's kind of a one-sided friendship. Obviously, I am a huge part of their lives. But we don't talk about me.

DM: Okay, I understand now what you mean about one-sided.

The Importance of Self-Care

DM: You mentioned the impact that journalists themselves experience—let's call it vicarious trauma. How important is self-care to you when it comes to telling these really difficult stories?

CW: I think it's hugely important. There isn't enough awareness about how important self-care is, and there isn't enough of an understanding that these are things that actually need to be built into the conversations that are happening in newsrooms. Obviously, the understanding of trauma has changed a lot in the last few years, but still, so much of it is focused on conflict reporting or people who visit crisis zones in the world. There's less of an understanding about how people who are doing reporting in our communities are impacted by trauma. Those are conversations that are starting to happen, but when we were starting to do that work, there was very little conversation about that at all (laugh). . . .

Because I'm an Indigenous woman, because I have the lived experience that I have—it's especially important that if you're doing work that could be potentially triggering for you that that's something that you're aware of and that the people that you're working with are aware of.

But that's also not a typical conversation that you have in newsrooms, with producers or editors.

See Chapter 2.5, "Trauma-Informed Reporting," for more advice on taking care of yourself while reporting on traumatic events.

Sharing with Your Team

DM: You're saying it's important to build conversations into the process, when you may be talking about traumatic stuff with your team. How do you balance the fact that you are just a conduit to share that story with the impacts that it may be having on you? How do you let it go?

CW: It's a really individual thing. I do specific things for myself that might not necessarily be helpful for somebody else. But I think that having some kind of intention around understanding what self-care is and why it's important when you're doing work that coincides with trauma and maybe triggering for yourself.

Also, for me, what has been integral to taking on this kind of work is having the trust within your team. I worked with my producer Marnie Luke from the very first story all the way through the podcast. Our senior producer was Heather Evans. Through that reporting, we developed a shared understanding of the sensitivity of the kind of work that we were doing, but also trust. You need that. That's implicit in being open about trauma and being open about self-care; there's a fear that if you are open about those things, you could be seen in a certain way within the newsroom.

DM: Being weak, for example.

CW: Being weak, or a fear that you would lose out on certain assignments or that you would be considered biased or you'd have some kind of objectivity issue. There are lots of misconceptions around what it means to be impacted by trauma and how that could affect your job as a journalist, so having people who have that kind of understanding in leadership positions in newsrooms is really important. I've been very lucky.

DM: Have you seen the negative impacts of reporting on these difficult stories on journalists you know?

CW: Absolutely yes. Serious negative impacts, absolutely. I've experienced that, personally. Some of the reporting that I've done has definitely impacted my own mental health and has led me to feel like I need to better understand how this is impacting me, why it's impacting me, and what can I do to help myself. But also help protect myself, because I'm committed to doing this kind of reporting. I feel like it's incredibly important.

But I've seen that it's impacted people that I've worked with. As somebody who has been part of those teams and projects, we all need to be aware of the potential harm that this kind of work can have. Not just on the people who we're reporting on, but also the people who we are working with.

Be Open and Transparent

DM: You've talked about investigative journalism and your consent-seeking process. But I'm struck by something. You don't stop being persistent. It seems to me you're saying that being empathetic and trauma-informed doesn't mean you put aside that doggedness that's required for investigative journalism?

CW: There are things that we can do at the outset, like try to be transparent about your process. Try to make sure that you're creating a space that feels safe for the person to talk in, so you don't have time constraints. You're not like, "I need to get in and out of here in an hour."

The way that I generally approach interviews—giving people space in the interviews and really trying to allow them to warm up and become comfortable—is a very important part of it. Trying to leave them in a place where you focus more on the resilience aspect.

DM: I think all investigative journalists have to build a rapport with their sources. But you're describing it as a continuum of a long-term relationship. That makes that investigative journalism fraught, potentially . . .

CW: Taking those preparations and checking in with people . . . Hopefully [that] then helps put you in a position where you have been open and transparent and trying to establish a good relationship that is not one of exploitation, or transactional, or taking from people for your own benefit and then saying, "Thank you. See you later."

It makes the work a lot more complicated, and there are definitely drawbacks, for sure.

DM: It's a drawback in terms of resources. It just takes longer.

CW: For sure. It requires way more of an investment.

There are situations, obviously, where I don't think it would ever be appropriate for somebody to withdraw their consent. Like, if you're an elected official and you've done the interview and then at the end of the interview: "Like, actually, can I take that back?" (laugh) . . .

There would be lots of journalists who would say, "If you agree to this interview, I can use it how I would like to now." That just becomes tricky when you are trying to be sensitive to some of the historical impacts that are affecting the work that you're doing right now.

Don't Skip the Context

DM: So many people have praised your *Missing and Murdered* podcasts as being so much more than just true crime. You have explored the history of the residential schools or the Sixties Scoop. What recommendations would you have for journalists about how to fit the context of this complicated history—like the *Indian Act* or residential schools—into their stories, if they don't have a 10-part podcast? If they only have 1000 words or two minutes on the radio?

CW: The way that we were able to do it successfully in the podcast was to show where it was relevant to the story. So, not trying to shoehorn it in. Whether the story is two minutes or 10 minutes or two hours, there's an arc. You're trying to have it happen naturally within the story. It is really important but very difficult. I worked at CBC for 19 years in news and current affairs—it is very difficult to do that in a compelling and thoughtful way when you have so many limitations placed on it.

When we were doing the first season of the podcast and very much focused on the mystery around Alberta Williams and her unsolved murder,[6] I went to this conference in Saskatchewan called "Reconciliation in the Media," put together after the death of Colton Boushie in Saskatchewan[7] . . . One of the keynote speakers was Dr. Marie Wilson, who was one of the Commissioners of the Truth and Reconciliation Commission and who herself had been a journalist. I was, at that point, writing episode four of the podcast. She gave a keynote about how important context is and how it's part of our job as journalists to make sure that we include it and that we need to be connecting the dots for Canadians. And if you can't do it in this story, do it in the next one. But don't skip the context.

You need to ask the question to yourself about whatever story it is that you're undertaking: when did this story actually begin? I thought about that as I was listening in the audience. When did Alberta William's story actually begin? It didn't begin with her murder in 1989. It didn't even necessarily begin with her birth. She was part of a bigger story about her family and her community and how that was connected to Canadian history in residential schools and to this relationship between the RCMP and Indigenous communities. Whatever size your story is, big or small, you can think about: When did it actually begin? Is there a single piece of context that is important to understand, that's important for me to bring in? That's a lot easier said than done.

For more tips on fitting in the context, see Chapter 3.2, "Context and Colonial Amnesia."

DM: It *is* easier said than done, but you're also pointing toward something really key, which is not to think of it as a chunk of history that I have to give you but figure out how to weave it in, in a way that is informative but also engaging.

CW: And hopefully relevant. It should be relevant to your story. Fitting it in is very difficult. That's also why I'm so committed to wanting to tell these stories through podcasting, because the traditional forms of broadcast seem like they're shrinking in a lot of ways, and [it's becoming] harder and harder to include that context when you're fighting for 30 extra seconds in a news story on TV or radio. The context is so important to understanding not just the true crime mystery but Indigenous lives. . . .

I feel like it's way easier to *not* report in Indigenous communities because the challenge is that we did it poorly for so long. The media got it wrong for so long and caused so much harm in terms of the kinds of stories and the way that we were represented in media. It's meant that we not only need to get things right and be accurate and truthful in our stories, but we also are trying to undo harm in our reporting.

That's a big responsibility and a big burden. And it's hard to do.

"We Are More than Violence"

DM: Are there things that journalists should be mindful of when they're telling stories about Indigenous women?

CW: Most of the reporting around Indigenous women and girls, including my own, has been focused on the violence. Because it's a horrifying crisis that has been ignored for so long. That seems to be the subject matter that seems to be the entry point into understanding Indigenous life and the realities Indigenous people live. What I'm trying to do with my work is use the interest and the popularity and insatiable appetite for true crime to tell this bigger story about Indigenous women and girls. And they're centred in the podcast.

But I think that in reporting and focusing on that violence, there's a tendency to forget that we are more than that violence. We need to be mindful of the incredible strength and resilience that exists within Indigenous women and girls and within our communities.

> See Chapter 1.4, "Positive versus Negative Stories," for more discussion about expanding the lens of Indigenous news coverage.

In unpacking a trauma, there's almost always a flip side to it... There's so many Indigenous women who experienced these traumas in their personal lives... and then carry that forward to try to create some kind of conversation and change. That strength and resilience is equally important in understanding the realities and the bigger picture context.

Discussion Questions

1. What are the challenges of being open with your journalistic colleagues about your own experiences when you are reporting on a difficult story?
2. How does Walker approach interviewees who may disclose trauma?
3. What concerns does Walker express about the representation of Indigenous women in the media?

Suggested Works by Connie Walker

Stolen: The Search for Jermain. https://gimletmedia.com/shows/stolen
Missing and Murdered: Finding Cleo. https://www.cbc.ca/radio/findingcleo
Missing and Murdered: Who Killed Alberta Williams? https://www.cbc.ca/missingandmurdered/podcast

Endnotes

1. Marnie Luke works in the investigative unit at CBC, and produced the *Missing and Murdered* podcast.
2. "JSP" refers to Journalistic Standards and Practices policy.
3. The CBC Missing and Murdered database, launched in 2015, explores the unsolved cases of over 300 Indigenous women in Canada. https://www.cbc.ca/missingandmurdered/
4. Johnny Semaganis and Christine Cameron appeared in Connie's podcast *Finding Cleo* about a 13-year-old Cree girl who died in 1978. Cleo was their sibling.
5. In 2013, the body of 15-year-old Leah Anderson was found in Gods Lake Narrows, Manitoba. Her killer has yet to be found. Connie reported on her story for CBC's *The National*.
6. In 1989, 24-year-old Alberta Williams from the Gitanyow Band was found dead along the Highway of Tears near Prince Rupert, B.C. Police never caught her killer. Her death was the subject of the first season of the *Missing and Murdered* podcast.
7. Colten Boushie was a 22-year-old from the Cree Red Pheasant First Nation who was fatally shot on a rural Saskatchewan farm in 2016. The farmer, Gerald Stanley, stood trial for second-degree murder and for a lesser charge of manslaughter. A jury found him not guilty.

✦ 4.2 ✦

Lessons in Humility: A Conversation with Waubgeshig Rice

Waubgeshig Rice is an author and journalist from Wasauksing First Nation on Georgian Bay.

His journalism experience began as an exchange student in northern Germany, writing articles about being an Anishinaabe youth in a foreign country for newspapers in Canada. He graduated from Toronto Metropolitan University's journalism program.

He spent most of his journalism career with the Canadian Broadcasting Corporation (CBC) as a video journalist, web writer, and producer. He received the Anishinabek Nation's Debwewin Citation for excellence in First Nation Storytelling. His final role with CBC was hosting northern Ontario's afternoon radio program, *Up North*.

His first short story collection, *Midnight Sweatlodge*, won an Independent Publishers Book Award. His debut novel, *Legacy*, followed. His latest novel, *Moon of the Crusted Snow*, was a national bestseller and received widespread critical acclaim, including the Evergreen Award.

He currently lives in Sudbury, Ontario, with his wife and two sons.

Waubgeshig Rice.

Source: Photo courtesy of Waubgeshig Rice.

Being a Video Journalist

DM: Everybody now knows you as an author and writer, but for a lot of your career, you were a video journalist. Are there specific challenges about bringing a camera into an Indigenous community that you were conscious of as a VJ?

WR: Oh, absolutely. It always changed the dynamic of the setting just by carrying a camera into the room or into the ceremonial grounds, even if I always had prior consent to bring a camera into whatever sort of situation it was, because there was an agreement that I would be covering this event for CBC. But at the same time, a camera is a big, intimidating machine. It represents a lot of different things. Of course, it's a conduit to tell stories, but it hasn't always necessarily served Indigenous people properly or respectfully.

We know that from a young age. The only time I saw a TV camera was when something bad happened. When crews would come into my community, from either Barrie or Toronto, to cover a bad story. There is that imagery or that symbolism attached to a camera that you really have to be mindful of. You really have to be careful and considerate of the people around you when you bring a camera into a particular environment.

DM: Can you describe how you would navigate getting consent from an Indigenous person, to explain to them that you're a VJ and you're bringing a camera and you'd like to record stuff?

WR: Any time that I set something up with a community or organization, or even a family, I always first and foremost would mention that I work primarily for TV. I have a TV camera and I'm going to be editing the imagery and the sounds together to do a story that's going to be broadcast to thousands of people later.

I was always forthright with that. It's kind of a heavy thing to bring to a conversation, especially if you're covering something really sensitive or personal, so I always made sure I spent enough time on the phone beforehand. Just laying out the whole process, explaining exactly what would happen, how I would spend X amount of time doing the interview on camera, then I would spend X amount of time getting the visuals afterwards, then how I would write things. I would usually spend that time laying out my process, how it works for me as a video journalist.

Then there were times where I came to events or a scene where there wasn't an opportunity to have that previous conversation. I always left my camera in the van and never brought it out immediately. I'd go in, assess the situation, and talk to people who appeared to be in charge or at the centre of an event or story.

I would talk to them and say, "I work for CBC. There's my van." It was helpful having a big white van with the CBC logo on it, because it was clear what that vehicle and I were there for. I would explain that I work for TV and I have a camera. If we're able to do a story, here's what I'm going to shoot. If there's anything you don't want me to shoot, I won't do that. If there's anything you don't want me to ask about, I won't ask about those things. It was about creating that foundation of mutual respect, and that comfortable and safe environment that we were all inhabiting at that particular moment.

There'd also be times where we would have those previous conversations to come in there and I'd set up my camera and put it on the tripod. But if there was something happening that I didn't think was appropriate to shoot or portray or represent in a story, I'd tilt my camera up or down, and make it clear that I wasn't shooting. That was for the safety and comfort of all the people there. As a VJ, your camera really is an extension of yourself. In many ways, it's a journalistic tool and you spend a lot of time carefully shooting and editing. But there's just so much other thought that needs to go into that, whether that's tilting the camera up or down or just leaving it on the ground and pointing the lens away from the action.

Those are some of the principles I tried to adhere to as a video journalist. To make sure that people knew I was there, not necessarily as their ally or friend, but as somebody who could help them get their story out there. I wasn't this sort of stereotypical media figure coming to exploit them or their story because I never wanted to behave that way. I never wanted to be perceived as that by Indigenous communities, and understanding the power of the camera and my relationship with it and how I used it was a really key part of that.

To Roll or Not to Roll

DM: You said if there were events you felt perhaps you shouldn't be filming, you would turn the camera away. How would you assess that?

WR: Part of that comes from my own ceremonial knowledge that I acquired in my upbringing. I grew up in my community going to various kinds of ceremonies of various intensity and seriousness. I knew from an early age what could be shared and what couldn't. What needed to remain in the private ceremonial realm and what could be shared outside. That's not to say those rules from each individual community apply right across the board. They don't at all. Different Elders in different communities have different protocols about what can be shared.

But I tried to go by that baseline of, "Okay, this seems like something very intense or spiritual. I probably shouldn't shoot this. This seems like a private moment among the people who are at the centre of this particular event or story. Maybe I should just hold off."

On the occasions that I wasn't able to establish an understanding beforehand, I just wanted to err on the side of caution. I didn't want to upset anybody at all, so I would stop shooting and then ask later if there was something related to that, that maybe I'd be able to shoot.

Generally, if there's a song going or people are standing up, I would stop shooting. In our culture, traditionally, that's a serious moment. That's something that is maybe a little more spiritual than just sharing for the public domain. So, I would look for cues like that, but as I said, if I wasn't able to establish that baseline beforehand, I just wouldn't shoot. Then I'd figure out something that I could maybe shoot afterwards.

DM: You have knowledge about Anishinaabeg customs. What if you're amongst the Haida or Mi'kmaq or Inuit, where you don't necessarily know the customs? How would you conduct yourself?

WR: When I worked in Winnipeg, there were Cree and Lakota people and Métis people. And in Ottawa, there were Algonquin people, and a lot of Métis people and Inuit. If I knew I was going to be involved in a story with a community I wasn't necessarily familiar with, I took the extra time to do that research and maybe spend a few more minutes talking to the organizer, or the person who invited me in there … Just triggering that empathy within myself, understanding that there are some things I wouldn't want to see on TV for my culture and these other cultures likely feel the same way about certain elements of this situation that I'm coming into with them. It was about having those conversations ahead of time and making sure I knew what was appropriate and what wasn't.

> More tips on navigating Indigenous customs are offered in Chapter 2.2, "Indigenous Customs and Protocols."

"We Need to Respect Each Other"

DM: You mentioned earlier how important it is to make the people that you're working with feel safe and treat them with respect. Why is that so important when you're reporting on Indigenous people?

WR: There is a foundational principle of respect in Anishinaabeg culture that we all try to abide by. It's deeply ingrained in our teachings: we need to respect each other. We need to respect the culture. We need to respect the land and the world around us. I think applying that to journalism, and to storytelling, is crucial. It's essential to have that fundamental belief at the core of your practice as a journalist.

DM: But you're coming into a community sometimes asking difficult questions. How do you balance those two things?

WR: Part of respect is being as transparent as possible. There's this debate amongst journalists about sharing questions ahead of time or showing your journalistic hand. Allowing an interview subject to finesse their response or how they're going to behave in a particular situation. But there's a way to work around that, too. Really be respectful of those people you're coming to question, even if there are controversial elements around that particular story. It can simply come down to, "Okay, you likely know what I'm calling you about. You likely know why I want to come out. I'm going to be asking you about this. This is your opportunity to clear the air or present your side."

There's the whole ambush thing that a lot of journalists really like. But I don't think that necessarily is effective when you're covering Indigenous communities because there's already guardedness and reservations about the media. It's only going to close the door more tightly if you take that approach.

That didn't always necessarily work for me. I didn't always get access if I was coming into one of those difficult stories, but for me, that was more important than misrepresenting myself.

Transparency and Humility

DM: You're talking about being transparent in *every* conversation you're having with *all* of these people. It takes a lot of time, but it seems the process of transparency and explaining who you are is very important to you.

WR: It's how I was raised. Being genuine and being respectful are at the core of what I believe to be Anishinaabe. My parents, my grandparents, aunts, and uncles would be disappointed or even ashamed of me if I misrepresented myself in any way or pretended to be somebody who I wasn't. Or if I lied or fibbed my way into a particular situation. I don't feel comfortable doing that. I never did.

Perhaps that was one of my shortcomings as a journalist, if you look at it through the perspective of mainstream journalism. There is that idea that you are a saviour or a freedom fighter for information or the truth. There's a stereotype of "being a journalist" that I think props journalists up and really inflates egos. Part of that approach is not being transparent, not being as forthcoming about your intentions as a storyteller. It's a game, right? It's all about manipulation and getting certain bits of information.

I never felt comfortable doing that, especially if it related to Indigenous stories. There were moments where I would say to an assignment editor, "I have a personal connection, not directly to this particular community or story, but this could come around to me in a personal way. So, I don't feel comfortable and I'm not going to do that."

DM: What you're talking about is an expression of an important Anishinaabe value: humility. You've written that there's an inherent sense of humility required when you're doing journalism in Indigenous communities. What do you mean by that?

WR: The nature of the industry of Canadian journalism really promotes a sense of ego and even a saviour complex. It goes back to how journalism schools are created. There is an intense competition to get into journalism schools, especially at the university level. You're reminded of that once you're in the fold, as if to imbue some sense of prestige—that you made it into this program, you're somebody special, you deserve this position and you deserve the stories that will be coming to you. These are *your* stories.

It becomes a very individualized process, which I believe strays from the collective beliefs that we have as Anishinaabeg that we all work together. We are trying to expose truths and make people aware, for the greater good. But you have an industry of lone wolves who want to be heroes, who are in it mostly for themselves. They try to acquire stories for that reason. That's the opposite of being humble. There's no humility there at all. . . .

It's not just about your status or stature as a journalist. That's my personal belief, and a lot of people may disagree with that. But for me, staying humble was key to getting a better sense of inclusion, a better spirit of storytelling, by just coming into a situation on a level playing field. Not coming in as "the journalist" who's coming to take your story away.

"The Archaic Fallacy of Neutrality"

DM: I have to ask you about your wonderful article "Letters to a Young Indigenous Journalist" (https://thewalrus.ca/terra-cognita-letter-to-a-young-indigenous-journalist/), where you tackled the idea of objectivity and the need for a paradigm shift. You talk about "the archaic fallacy of neutrality" in that piece. When you were a journalist, how did you navigate being fair and balanced in your relationship with your Indigenous subjects?

WR: That was probably the hardest thing to do in my whole career. I care deeply about Indigenous communities, even if I'm not a part of them. Because I know what the history of journalism in this country is: at best, a disservice to Indigenous people and at worst, violence. It has perpetuated colonialism. It's been harmful . . .

What you want is a fair representation for these Indigenous people that are being covered, even if you're not connected to them personally. So, what is neutrality? What is objectivity? There is this white baseline that has been applied to the industry as a whole. I don't even know really what it means anymore. What does "being neutral" actually mean? Does it mean becoming white? Does it mean abandoning my identity, my background as an Indigenous person, and looking at everything through white eyes? Putting all my past knowledge and personal experience on the shelf to try to cover something, to explain to just white people?

> See more about objectivity in Chapter 1.7, "'Where Are You From?' Rethinking Objectivity."

DM: Can you think of an example where that was a challenge for you?

WR: When I worked in Ottawa, there was a junior football team called the "R-word," much like the NFL Washington team used to be called. I was assigned that story one day. I said, "I consider that a slur, so I don't want to have to voice that in my TV story."

DM: To say the "R-word."

WR: Yeah. I don't want to say the "R-word" because I consider that a slur. I was called that as a kid and the intent was strictly malicious. So, before my bosses could make any sort of decision, I said, "Well, I can't cover the story then because I consider that offensive." I guess maybe the objective view, at that point in our history, was that it wasn't a slur. That this was a word that could be said over the CBC airwaves, which is really harmful and hurtful. I had a really tough time with that, but there was nothing I could do about that other than saying, "I'm not saying it myself. So, remove me from the story."

That shouldn't be the baseline of objectivity. There should be a baseline of decency and common sense. If some people consider something to be a slur, then maybe we shouldn't be saying it on the CBC airwaves.

Navigating "Indian Time"

DM: Most of your career, you were a daily assignment reporter with daily deadlines. How do you navigate the really strict deadlines that we have and Indian Time?

WR: If a story wasn't a news-of-the-day, agenda item, if it was something that could benefit from taking a little more time to do, I would—as early as possible—mention that to my assignment desk and say, "Okay, this is happening, but it may not come together in a day's turnaround. We may need to wait until tomorrow's show to get this out there." A lot of my senior producers were really accommodating because they knew it was important to do things right and to go at the pace of what the subjects wanted it to be, and they saw the value in that.

But this didn't happen early on in my career . . .

DM: Those are not easy conversations to have when you're a young journalist.

WR: No, no. They didn't happen at all. In my first few years as a daily journalist, I was too scared to even ask. Because it's such an intense process to be in a daily TV newsroom. Everybody's on edge. No matter what the stories of the day are. There are many pressures. I didn't want to rock the boat. Initially I was like, "Okay, I'm taking the story that is assigned to me and I'm busting my ass to turn it around and to do it by deadline."

It took a little bit of confidence and a lot of experience to know what I was capable of, in terms of production and being able to pitch something to the desk that wasn't going to be on that night's *CBC News*.

DM: What you're saying is that the quality of the piece would improve greatly if you could work within these cultural confines of doing it in a good way.

WR: Absolutely, because it would allow for the time to have a more natural conversation. There would be no rushing in and out. That was the toughest thing for me in those early years, whenever there were those stories that had to go that night, like having an interview that lasted only five minutes with an Elder. I'd come away from those situations feeling really bad. I would feel like I disrespected that Elder. Then when I would be writing and editing that story later on, I'd only be taking 10 or 15 seconds of what he or she said.

CBC is so much better equipped to allow those conversations to live in other areas, like current affairs radio. It takes a while to learn that. "Okay, I only used 10 seconds in a clip . . . afternoon show, here you go. Take the whole five-minute interview and run the whole thing." CBC is well suited to accommodate those kinds of situations, but it takes a while to learn.

> Other suggestions for navigating Indian Time are covered in Chapter 2.1, "Indian Time."

DM: That's a smart workaround. Even outside of the CBC, if you work for an independent website, you could post the full interview with the Elder online, if you're not using it in your story, as a way to honour the Elder.

WR: Yeah. When you're talking about respectfully and properly doing a story, it does take that time. We need to let those subjects of the stories dictate that. We have to accommodate in that way. That means our assignment desks and bosses putting their egos aside, thinking about stories in different ways, thinking outside the box. Not being confined to these rigid structures and formats of TV and radio news as we've come to know them.

It's not like they're traditional storytelling methods that are enshrined in any sort of edicts or laws. They should be able to evolve, and they should be able to accommodate different cultures and different ways of telling stories.

DM: You mentioned being under the pressure of having to edit something quickly as well. In Indigenous stories, were there things you were conscious of in the video editing process?

WR: We have to really think about what our approaches to different situations are. Do we absolutely need to have the crying clip . . .

DM: Or show the sacred fire . . .

WR: . . . or the drum sound up? How much do we perpetuate stereotypes, just by showing those typical expected visuals or [playing those] sounds? It's just a matter of people in the newsroom opening their minds to different ways of doing things.

Using Social Media

DM: You are extremely active on social media. In terms of accountability, are there things you think journalists should be mindful of when it comes to social media and Indigenous communities?

WR: Journalists should approach social media as another tool in their tool kit, and apply those same standards and principles. We talked earlier about what you shouldn't shoot or information that you shouldn't share. You should apply that to social media too.

Journalists often get caught up in the moment, if they're in a particular situation where something is happening. They want to tweet it out or put it on Instagram or Facebook right away because it could get some eyeballs. But again, you have to consider the long game and the benefit of putting something particularly sensitive out there immediately for potentially even more people to see or hear.

DM: The long game being, having a relationship with the community. But there may be some journalists who listen to you and say, "How am I ever going to get any challenging stories on the air if I'm conscious of that?"

WR: There's patience that needs to be applied to the overall practice, and that applies to the humility components of it as well. As a journalist, you're not owed anything. People you come up to don't owe you their story. You really have to remember that in every single situation. You could potentially burn your whole organization and your reputation going forward within a particular community . . .

If you're a journalist that's not aware of what a sacred fire is, you don't just go up and shoot a picture of it and tweet it right away, right?

> See Chapter 3.4, "Social Media: The New Moccasin Telegraph," for more discussion about social media use.

Coping with Covering Trauma

DM: Has there been a challenge that you faced in your career reporting in Indigenous communities? And how did you overcome it?

WR: There's the emotional challenge that is huge to overcome. I think a lot of Indigenous people, especially Indigenous people who grow up in First Nations, are very familiar with tragedy and trauma. Even if you grow up in a balanced, positive, healthy household, those tragedies and traumas are part of your family story. Those things happen. Maybe not necessarily in your lifetime, but before you're born. Your family members carry that with them.

You see that regularly when you're out covering Indigenous communities, whether it's a family grieving a missing or murdered sister or cousin or daughter, or whether it's a residential school survivor recounting the horror that they endured.

It's triggering. That word is thrown around a lot these days, but I would say Indigenous journalists are probably triggered on a regular basis. Even if it's just that the big story of the day has to do with Indigenous issues, like a blockade or a pipeline protest. The language that arises as a result of the racism that bubbles to the surface—it just never gets easier to deal with. It's a lifelong thing.

So, we have that to deal with regularly, more so than any white journalists, for sure. For me, regulating and accepting and working through those emotions was probably the biggest challenge. Because I have an aunt who was murdered. My grandfather died tragically due to alcohol. My community went through waves and waves of tragedy and trauma, up until I was born. And it continued. I have lost relatives too many tragic ways, even as recently as five, six years ago.

You're triggered a lot. It's hard to find that balance or healing. Because we work such intense jobs and such long hours. Often, when we're on a big story, we work nine, ten, eleven hours a day. Where do you work in the time to recalibrate or really heal? That's not always necessarily there.

DM: What were your strategies for recalibrating?

WR: I would try to talk to family. I've been with my partner now for almost a decade. She's always been hugely supportive. I've been able to go home to her and talk about some of these things and work through them. Also, talking to my Elder relatives—who've gone through worse things than I have—and confiding in them.

It's not always necessarily talking about the thing that I'm working through; it's just talking to them. It's having them in my life and knowing that I can talk to these people. Maybe even most important is talking to fellow Indigenous journalists. . . .

Even though I'm out of the industry, I still believe in it. I still support Indigenous journalists who are out there working really hard. I believe in them and I respect them. I look forward to seeing them changing the world.

Discussion Questions

1. Rice discusses various approaches to make subjects more comfortable with a camera. How could you adapt the way you take pictures or video when reporting in Indigenous communities?
2. What do you think of the importance Rice places on humility in his journalism?
3. If you are "triggered" while reporting on a story, what are ways you find balance or healing?

Suggested Work by Waubgeshig Rice

"Letter to a Young Indigenous Journalist." *The Walrus*, August 31, 2020. https://thewalrus.ca/terra-cognita-letter-to-a-young-indigenous-journalist/
"Why It's Important not to Lose Oral Storytelling." *Globe and Mail*, October 16, 2020. https://www.theglobeandmail.com/arts/books/article-why-its-important-not-to-lose-oral-storytelling/
"Living Languages Looks at How Indigenous Languages are Being Revitalized in Northern Ontario." *CBC Sudbury*, March 5, 2020. https://www.cbc.ca/news/canada/sudbury/up-north-living-languages-celebrates-united-nations-international-year-of-indigenous-languages-1.5485087

✦ 4.3 ✦

"In Love with My People": A Conversation with Mark Trahant

Mark Trahant is editor of *Indian Country Today* (*ICT*). Under Trahant's leadership, *ICT* launched the first national daily newscast available through stations in the PBS network.

Trahant is known for his election reporting in Indian Country, developing the first comprehensive database of American Indians and Alaska Natives running for office. His research has been cited in publications ranging from *The New York Times* to *The Economist*, and most recently, *Teen Vogue*.

Trahant has been a reporter for PBS's *Frontline* series. His most recent *Frontline* piece, "The Silence," was about sexual abuse by priests in an Alaska Native village. He was the editorial page editor of the *Seattle Post-Intelligencer* and has worked for *The Arizona Republic*, *Salt Lake Tribune*, *The Seattle Times*, *The Navajo Times Today*, and the *Sho-Ban News*.

Mark Trahant.

Source: Photo taken by Tomas Karmelo Amaya and used with permission of Mark Trahant.

Trahant is a member of the American Academy of Arts and Sciences and has held an endowed chair at the University of North Dakota and the University of Alaska Anchorage.

He is a member of the Shoshone-Bannock Tribes.

Reporting Across the Medicine Line

DM: What have you observed about the differences between reporting in Native American communities versus Indigenous communities in Canada?

MT: The biggest difference to me is that Canadian viewers and readers are so much better informed about the States. That bugs the hell out of me. I wish we were more clued in. One of the greatest reporting nights in my life was in Canada. It's a story I love to tell, often because Americans just don't get it. That's the night after the Meech Lake Accord was voted down. Of all places, I ended up in Kettle Point, Ontario, and the guest speaker was Elijah Harper.[1]

DM: Oh wow.

MT: When he walked into the room, in this little reserve, the place erupted as if a conquering hero just walked in the door. I still get chills thinking about the sounds I heard that night. When you tell Americans, even really well-informed people, a few of them will know who Elijah Harper was, but not the way it would be in Canada. I've wondered why is that? I mean, the border is so *not* ours to deal with. And yet that still is a deal. Yet seven per cent of our audience at *Indian Country Today* are Canadians. They're reading everything we're doing. I've wondered a lot why it doesn't go back and forth, the way it perhaps should.

DM: Which is a really important point about audience reach and how the border is non-existent when covering Indian Country. That material is important to people all over Turtle Island.

MT: I'm Shoshone-Bannock. If you look at Shoshone trade routes, pre-contact, they went all the way from Mexico City well into northern Canada. That trade route was vibrant and active and really remarkable. If we could do the same thing again today, what opportunities that would create!

Reporting in the North

DM: I want to ask about your time in Alaska. You're not from the North, but you spent a long time there. Did you face challenges as a reporter working up there that you weren't expecting?

MT: Not really. Because the first bit of my Alaska experience was basically spot news—covering the oil spill.[2] One of the things I determined early on, in that story—I was working for *The Arizona Republic* at the time—I didn't want to do what everyone else was doing. So, when everyone else went to the actual spill site, I went way off and started talking to fishermen. I really worked hard to find a different path. The nice thing about that is I was the only one there. Whenever you're the only one there, you can spend time with people and look at it differently than if you're trying to do everything in the pack. That would be my main message: stay away from everybody else.

DM: What kinds of mistakes have you seen reporters making in the North?

MT: Not understanding history. Alaska has such a unique history. Things that happened 100 years ago are extraordinarily significant. If you try to write a story based on what you know right now, you're not going to get it.

A great example of that is the pandemic. Alaska was so impacted by the flu a century ago. It changed everything. To be able to put that into context today—I mean, the way communities are handling this pandemic—we talk about the high death rates, which is certainly true. But, the other side of it is that Native communities largely have been saying, "We're going to do whatever it takes." If that means shutting down for a year, it means shutting down for a year. You don't have that same false bravado that you're seeing in non-Native communities about, "We can do what we want. We don't need to worry about this." It's because people have been through this before and they know what happens.

DM: So, it's important for reporters to have that sense of history and context.

MT: Absolutely. It's essential.

> See Chapter 3.2, "Context and Colonial Amnesia," for ideas on how to include more historical context in your work.

Delving into Sexual Abuse

DM: One of the incredible pieces you worked on was about childhood sexual abuse in Alaska. When you're approaching a really big and difficult subject like that, what was your thinking in terms of the narrative lens of covering that kind of tragedy?

MT: The first thought was I didn't want to do the story.

DM: Why?

MT: The way my mind works, I'm much more drawn to good public policy stories and big-picture stuff. I was really afraid of spending time with survivors. It was scary to me. When *Frontline* first called, I told them no at first. At the time, I was working on healthcare policy and I had a fellowship that I loved, and I was really excited by writing about really very detailed things about how to change healthcare perceptions, so I was busy. Then, the more I thought about it, I thought, "If you don't do the story, someone else is going to do it. Will they give it the attention it deserves?"

The way I approached that particular story was to spend a lot of time reading court cases. All of the pleadings involved. There were over 100 lawsuits filed by individuals against predators. I probably read at least half of them. I read the whole files, not just the cases, and some of the detailed interviews, and everything I could. That gave me a sense going into it how deeply affected people were.

The surprise for me, and the main reason I'm glad I did it, was I never expected the resilience. That was the part of the story I'll take away from it because it was so inspiring... Just people figuring out ways to survive. People figuring out ways to deal with it and build on that chapter in their lives. Some of it isn't stuff you think about. For example, there's a young woman in St Michael's, Alaska—to this day, when a priest walks into the room, she turns around and she will never look at them again. The mechanics of doing that every time is really remarkable but that's her way of being resilient, of saying "I will never give them my eyes again. They can never look at me and take that from me." She goes to great lengths to do that.

DM: You said you were scared at first about getting deep into that trauma. In terms of the old tropes of tragic and pitiful Indians, how did you balance that?

MT: I just tried to listen as much as I could, to stay away from the story that's always been told. About how, basically, this ruined everybody's lives and "move on." I mean, it was devastating, but there's another side of the story that was more complex. Trying to pay attention and listen to that... I was really lucky that people in the community were so open and welcoming...

The Catholic bishop, who gave us unprecedented access, was really hard to interview. I interviewed him five times on camera, which is just an amazing number of times. But it's because his reactions were just so—nothing. I kept trying to press, to get something. I remember... writing down on a piece of paper, "What would Jesus do if he went to this community?" I threw that line out to the bishop. Nothing! Just nothing. He gave an answer, but there was no emotion there. Just nothing.

I carried that notepad back into another interview with one of the survivors. She saw it and, for her, that became everything. It became a major part of the film because she saw this notepad with a question for the bishop, not for her. But that question connected to her immediately and she wanted to talk about it.

> How to interview survivors and victims of trauma is covered in more detail in Chapter 2.5, "Trauma-Informed Reporting."

DM: Were there ways that you prepared for dealing with survivors and the stories they were going to be sharing with you?

MT: Basically, I tried to think how I would want to talk about something like this and tried to be tepid. It's not something you wanted to charge into and be all-knowing. But be completely open and listen to anything they say and follow their lead. To me, the interviews that work best are when you start off somewhere and end up in a place that you don't expect to go. Because the person you're interviewing tells you where they want to go.

The Native American Political Beat

DM: You mentioned you're more of a policy geek. A political geek, in particular. You've made your reputation for covering Native American politics in ways other outlets weren't paying attention to. What makes for a good pitch when it comes to covering Native politics?

MT: History is really important. We are so much thinking about policy being unique, rather than seeing the waves of how things happened in the forties and fifties and sixties. The thing about things like that is, you always build on something. You may not get everything at once, but over fifty years, to see that arc is really important, to see how things change or don't change over that long period of time.

DM: All journalists face constraints in terms of space. How do you—either personally or with your reporters—work at getting that historical context in?

MT: People that work with me know that when they ask, "How long should the story be?" my answer is always, "What do you need to tell the story?" We're in an age where space is different. When I first started in the business, it was newspapers. We had to fight like hell to get 100 inches for something we were talking about. Now, really, we have no constraints. It really is, "What do you need to tell the story?"

Then it becomes a question of—can you be compelling? Can you tell the story in a way that's going to keep people engaged? One of the great things about the digital age is, we can measure how people read. We know what works and what doesn't.

We had this story a year ago—if you don't know treaties, you don't know history. That story was over 10,000 words. We know people read the whole thing for the most part because of the metrics. What's really remarkable is 80 per cent of our readership is on a mobile device. So, you think—"Wow. Long story. It'll never work on a mobile device." But it does. Because it's a mobile device, people can read for 10 minutes at their bus stop, another 10 minutes when they get there, and they can do it over time. So, then it becomes, "Can you tell the story in a way that will keep people going through that whole period?"

Politics really comes down to profiles of people, and people are inherently interesting. It's figuring out what makes that story worth doing. I like lots of different ways to do that. A book I did on Forrest Gerard was about 70,000 words, on someone [most people] would consider a bureaucrat.[3] That was someone who wrote really substantial pieces of legislation. I wanted to go back and look at the whole picture. To me, that length was really required to tell that story.

DM: Using that example of a 10,000-word piece, you said it needs to be compelling. When you're dealing with complex Native American history or lots of data, what are ways you advise your reporters to try to make that compelling?

MT: That's where good editing comes in. When you start off as a reporter, you think everything is perfect and important. (laugh)

DM: It's *all* important. (laugh)

MT: You really need to say: does that really move the story? Then you get into really very terribly narrow questions like, "Is this moving the piece forward or can we get rid of it?" That gets into the whole idea of "killing your babies" and the tough, tough work of editing a piece.

I'm a big believer in shitty first drafts and starting with everything you can think of, then going through and just being ruthless. Then look to shape the story as tough as you can, to make it compelling.

Tribal Sovereignty

DM: There are differences between tribal sovereignty in the United States and the situation in Canada. Are there essential things journalists need to know about tribal sovereignty in the U.S. before they head into Indian Country?

MT: Probably the crazy history. So much of sovereignty comes out of a 10,000-year history. One of the things I just love with that long history is Shoshones used to hunt mastodon. Which means, we've gone through a few transitions. (laugh) Even the idea of climate change gets into those transitions.

To me, the first premise of sovereignty is that we were here before the United States and we're going to be here after the United States. This last 200 years is still a very narrow period of time. . . .

In the United States, it took all kinds of crazy twists and turns, with the courts and primarily the Marshall trilogy and how that limited sovereignty in many ways.[4] [Now] we're in a new era with how the United States and Canada look at sovereignty in a global context, with the UN Declaration on Rights of Indigenous Peoples . . .

DM: What about operating principles for a journalist who goes into a tribal territory or reservation? Does sovereignty require a different approach?

MT: To start with, [there's] the idea that you're a guest and that you're going to be reporting like you would in any kind of international body. It means sometimes you might be told that this is not going to happen. This is not going to be covered. You're going to have to go away and say to your editor, "I don't have a story to tell you."

The number of times that that happens, though—and it's kind of the big fear of a lot of journalists—is almost never. It's certainly the principle, but in practice, I've never experienced it. Because every community I've been in is so glad to see you, and so welcoming, that the *other* side is true. You get more than you'll ever need. . . .

I've been covering Indigenous communities from the very southern tip of Nicaragua all the way up to the Arctic Circle. Every community I've been to has just been amazing and saying, "We're so glad you're here."

Independent Indigenous Media

DM: On the other hand, there are tribal media who face challenges about reporting on their own communities. You've said that independent press is a pain in the ass, especially for tribal leaders—but you've argued that having an independent press makes our Nations stronger. What are the challenges for tribal press?

MT: The toughest thing to do is to cover your own community. There's nothing tougher than that. The biggest part of that is, in an urban area, say the size of Phoenix, if you write a really nasty story about the city of Phoenix, they'll take it and accept it and that'll be the end of it.

In a tribal community, that same story, you're going to have to have coffee with people you wrote about. They're going to come in and say, "I want to talk to you about that story, dammit." Your reasoning is going to have to be solid enough to be able to defend yourself.

On top of that, not every leader is going to be particularly well-educated or thoughtful about the process. They're just going to want to do whatever they can to stop it. I think the world of the people who followed me at the *Sho-Ban News*, my tribal paper. Because, day in and day out, not only do they have to defend what they do as journalists, but they have to then ask that same tribal government for money to keep going. That may be the toughest job in the entire world. . . .

Covering Internal Conflicts

DM: Do you have hesitations at all about covering Native American politics when the community is so small? You may not be filling up at the same gas station as people you're covering, but you're going to bump into them. It is a small community. How do you balance being a Native American journalist with being a Native American community member?

MT: The smaller the community, the tougher that is. I have been really lucky my whole career. For the most part, even in my own community, people wanted a voice. They're willing to give you the benefit of the doubt because of wanting a voice. . . .

Except for my experience with *Navajo Times*, which was unique—Navajo Nation is pretty divided, and the *Navajo Times* is right in the middle of it. I was editor [in the early 1980s] . . . Several years later, when I was at *The Arizona Republic*, Navajo had a very short civil war. I don't think civil war is too strong a term, because it was pretty intense. They had an incident very similar to that on Capitol Hill here a few weeks ago,[5] where a group tried to take back the tribal government. They had a group with clubs and they attacked a couple of police officers. Two people were killed in this incident.[6]

I was in Phoenix at the time, and someone called me up and said, "You got to get over here right now. They're having this Navajo riot." I remember getting a photographer, leaving *Arizona Republic* at two o'clock, and we found a flight to Gallup, New Mexico. We took a cab from Gallup to Window Rock, which is about 30 miles. Got out of the cab, and I was dressed in a suit and tie. Phoenix-type stuff. The photographer and I walked over to this riot and these people had big bats they were carrying. They were carved but they were basically bats. Somebody shouts, "There's the guy that started the Senate investigation."[7] And they're getting their bats up. And the photographer says, "I don't want to be around you right now." (laugh)

But the thing was, even then, as they surrounded me, they wanted to talk. And there is nothing as disarming as pulling out a notebook. I remember reaching in my back pocket, pulling out my notebook, and starting to write down what they were saying. They started out pretty hostile, but within 20 minutes, they were like old friends. Because, if they know you're there to give them a voice—even when it's intense—there's an opportunity to defuse it.

> For more advice on how to defuse a tense situation, see Chapter 2.6, "Story-Takers: How to Deal With 500+ Years of Rage."

The Impact of Social Media

DM: Let's talk about Standing Rock. It's not the first protest where Native Americans have taken a stand, but it seems the biggest in many ways, and you've observed that the only reason for that was social media. How has social media impacted reporting on Indian Country?

MT: One good comparison would be Standing Rock[8] and Alcatraz.[9] At Alcatraz, there was no social media. But what's interesting is how the media changes. At Alcatraz, the media were doing things like bringing truckloads of food. They were very much supportive, in a way that the media wouldn't be 20 or 30 years later.

Both Standing Rock and Idle No More came at about the same time.[10] Idle No More was first, and what people saw was the impact of social media and how it really expanded the reach. All of the lessons from that go into Standing Rock. They were able to be very sophisticated about it. Folks at Standing Rock didn't need the media anymore. They could go directly on Facebook live, every night, give an update, do their own media, and would have incredible audiences.

But I used to tease them because I said, "There's something you're missing by doing that." This idea of a journalist, even a Native journalist, gives you something different. You need both. I think their direct media was brilliant—I don't want to take away from that. But I also think the advantage of a journalist is they can go to both sides—or many sides, because there's always more than two sides—and start questioning people. You can't do that if you're an activist. You're really committed. I think you need both.

With social media, we really see the good and the bad. I don't think we're writing enough about the bad, actually. But social media just expands your reach in a way that we never could have imagined, even a year ago.

There are two things that are different about social media: 1) the reach, and 2) we're now in a generation, for the first time maybe ever, where somebody who goes to a place like Standing Rock, or even a conference or just a casual encounter, will then know those people for the rest of their lives. When I was young, you would meet somebody, and you might not see them again for 20 years. You might talk to them on the phone once, 10 years from then. Now, they're saying what they're doing every day. That's really different. That part of it is really encouraging.

The flip side is—and I saw this at home—I've always kind of been a contrarian and we have a general council form of government. Really, one of the only roles for general council is to vote on big settlements and per capita.[11] I used to go when we had a proposed per capita and vote against it. I was probably in a 300 to 5 minority. (laugh) Voting "no" when everyone said, "Dammit, we want the money." Now that social media is out—and I've seen this at Colville, I've seen this in my tribe—social media works people up into almost a frenzy, where not only do they vote *for* per capita, but they attack anyone who is *against* and villainize them. The danger of vilifying people you disagree with on social media is as great as anything we've ever faced and, in a tribal community, really tough.

> See Chapter 3.4, "Social Media: The New Moccasin Telegraph," for more discussion about uses of social media in Indian Country.

DM: Is there a lesson for journalists in that?

MT: Be really careful . . . What voices do you amplify? Be careful about how you amplify those voices. Maybe we don't have a say, because social media takes care of itself, but be really careful of giving voice to destructive forces.

DM: Just because they're loud on social media.

MT: And Twitter is not the world.

DM: Have you seen examples of negative forces within Native American communities being amplified by the press?

MT: Two stories come to mind. One is this per capita phenomenon and how social media just becomes relentless. In Colville, they recalled several tribal council members, just because they posted on social media.[12] [The other] is identity. . . . On one hand, there are people who deservedly should be called out for a variety of reasons, but then there's also times when it goes too far. It looks at people that *have* ties, but they may not be perceived as legitimate by some, and it gets really ugly.

DM: From a journalistic perspective, you're urging caution.

MT: And being very careful about what you report—to back it up, not just factually but contextually.

"There Are So Many Great Stories"

DM: Any last thoughts for journalism students or reporters about covering Indian Country?

MT: There are so many great stories. I'm in love with my own people. I really *like* hanging around them, listening to them. The stories I'm told, I could listen to for days and days and days because I'm so enamoured with them.

To me, the rest of the world misses out on them. Because if you're only writing about the things that everyone else is writing about, you're not getting to that. That's where you want to be.

Discussion Questions

1. Trahant discusses a tense situation he faced while reporting on the Navajo Nation. What lessons do you take away from his response to that situation?
2. Why is "history so important" to Trahant in Native American coverage?
3. What are some of the pros and cons of how social media is used in Indian Country?

Suggested Works by Mark Trahant

"Better Than This? That's Not U.S. History." *Indian Country Today*, January 11, 2021. https://indiancountrytoday.com/news/better-than-this-that-s-not-u-s-history-Dmv5lhGMBkumsi3wxI5UpQ

"A Tribute to Those Who Always Imagined Native Women in the Congress." *Indian Country Today*, January 21, 2019. https://www.indiancountrynews.com/index.php/columnists/mark-trahant/14675-a-tribute-to-those-who-always-imagined-Native-women-in-the-congress

"Coins Grandmother Had Saved Now Add Up to a Treasure." *Seattle Times*, December 19, 1999. https://archive.seattletimes.com/archive/?date=19991219&slug=A19991221083518

Endnotes

1. Elijah Harper was a Cree MLA in Manitoba who achieved national fame in 1990 for his refusal to accept the Meech Lake Accord, a constitutional amendment package negotiated to gain Quebec's acceptance of Canada's Constitution.

2. On March 24, 1989, the *Exxon Valdez*, an oil tanker owned by the Exxon Shipping Company, spilled 11 million gallons of crude oil onto Alaska's coastline, killing hundreds of thousands of seabirds, otters, seals, and whales.

3. Forrest Gerard of the Blackfeet Tribe of Montana was a civil servant and the key architect of self-determination policies that have defined Native American affairs for more than 40 years. In various government postings in the 1960s and 70s, Gerard helped develop the *Indian Self-Determination and Education Assistance Act*, the *Indian Financing Act*, the *Menominee Restoration Act*, the *Indian Health Care Improvement Act*, and legislation establishing the American Indian Policy Review Commission.

4. The Marshall Trilogy is a set of three U.S. Supreme Court decisions in the early nineteenth century that established federal primacy in Indian affairs, excluded state law from Indian country, and recognized tribal governance authority. Justice John Marshall described tribes as "domestic dependent nations," meaning that although tribes were "distinct independent political communities," they remained subject to the paternalistic powers of the U.S.

5. The 2021 storming of the U.S. Capitol was a riot and a violent attack against the United States Congress on January 6, 2021, led by a mob of supporters of President Donald Trump who were attempting to overturn his defeat.

6. Peter MacDonald, a former Navajo Code Talker who led the Navajo Nation in the 1970s and 80s, was suspended in 1989 by his own tribal council, which accused him of taking kickbacks and bribes. MacDonald refused to step down. In July 1989, in Window Rock, Arizona, two men were shot to death and 10 people were injured in a clash at Navajo headquarters between MacDonald's supporters and tribal police.

7. Writing for *The Arizona Republic*, Trahant investigated the allegations of corruption at Navajo Nation. Ultimately, a special Senate investigation was launched. In 1993, ousted tribal chairman Peter MacDonald was convicted on federal fraud, racketeering, and conspiracy charges. He was also convicted of inciting the riot at tribal headquarters in 1989.

8. The Standing Rock protests were a grassroots movement that began in early 2016 in reaction to the approved construction of the Dakota Access Pipeline in the northern United States. While the Standing Rock Sioux and other tribes fought the pipeline in court, thousands of people occupied protest camps near the Missouri River. There were multiple clashes with police and private security forces, and hundreds of people were arrested.

9. From 1934 to 1963, Alcatraz Island in San Francisco Bay was home to a notorious U.S. prison. In late 1969, a small group of Native American students and activists announced they were taking over the island. The occupation lasted 19 months, attracted widespread attention for Native American rights, and inspired further direct action by the American Indian Movement (AIM) in the 1970s.

10. Idle No More began in November 2012 as a protest against the introduction of a bill by Stephen Harper's Conservative government designed to weaken environmental protection laws. The movement gained supporters from across Canada and abroad, and grew to broadly encompass environmental concerns and Indigenous rights.

11. When U.S. tribes or Nations generate discretionary revenue, either through land settlements, income from natural resource activities, or other businesses such as casinos, some opt to redistribute a portion or all of the revenues to their citizens. This process is known as "per capita distribution" and often requires a referendum.

12. In 1992, the Confederated Tribes of the Colville Reservation in Washington State accepted a $193-million settlement offer from the U.S. government for decades of mismanagement of tribal trust funds. The settlement prompted months and years of fighting amongst members over how much should be distributed per capita.

4.4

Northern Reflections: A Conversation with Juanita Taylor

Juanita Taylor is originally from Arviat, Nunavut, and has also lived in Saskatchewan, Iqaluit, and Rankin Inlet. She worked for Inuit organizations and the Nunavut government before completing the TV & Radio Broadcasting program at the Academy of Broadcasting in Winnipeg.

Juanita got her start as a journalist at APTN in Nunavut, where she became co-host of *APTN National News* in Winnipeg, before moving to CBC North in Yellowknife. In her 12-year CBC career, Juanita has been a reporter, news reader, current affairs producer, radio host, and host of the North's supper-hour TV news show, *Northbeat*. Now, Juanita is a senior reporter and national correspondent for the North with CBC News Network. Her passion is to tell stories from her people and her culture.

Juanita Taylor.

Source: Photo courtesy of Juanita Taylor.

Advice for Southern Journalists

DM: A lot of younger journalists come from the South to get reporting experience in the North. As an Inuk, what are some common mistakes you've seen journalists make when they come to the North?

JT: It's a very different lifestyle. It's a very different culture. It's a very different perception. A lot of these southerners who come into the North have a very excited and eager personality. They want to absorb everything they can in such a short amount of time.

When it comes to reporting on stories from the North, they tend to lean a lot on the Indigenous broadcasters, the Inuit broadcasters, which is great because how else are they going to learn? It's great they reach out to them, but it can get frustrating sometimes because you do want northerners to [also] be the journalists in the regions. . . .

Learning to be able to connect with the communities is very different from how a reporter in Toronto connects with politicians or characters of a certain story. We do it a little bit differently in the North.

If we want to get into a community, for example, we call the mayor or the chief and we say, "This is a story that we're going to be working on. We'd like to come into your community and be able to talk to residents in your community." That's lesson number one that we like to offer to southern journalists: how to approach these smaller communities.

Another piece of advice we like to give: show respect to the community. Some communities in the Northwest Territories, they appreciate reporters who come in without that "southern attitude."

DM: You're putting "southern attitude" in quotation marks. Can you describe what you mean? You're being kind, I think.

JT: (laugh) It's okay to smile at somebody walking down the street! Or, if you're passing somebody, it's okay to say hello! It's not weird. They're not going to think you're strange for doing that. It's okay to shake hands with Elders. It's okay to start up a conversation with kids. You become part of the community, even if you're only there for a couple of days.

DM: That's huge. What you're saying is, you may be a journalist, but you're still a member of the community.

JT: One hundred per cent. You need to immerse yourself into the community. If you're being told not to speak to a certain person, you have to respect that. You don't be that hard-nosed journalist who says, "No. I need to. I'm going to." If you really need that character, you figure out a [different] way to get to a [similar] character.

Some northerners might not like to share or open up to a southerner because you've got to build that trust first. How do you do that? Like I said, you say hello, you shake a hand, you smile. You nod at the person in front of you. You respect their culture, you respect their traditions, you respect their community. That means just relax, be comfortable, and get to know the people in the community.

Avoiding "Southern Attitude"

DM: You said that it's helpful for southern journalists to approach Indigenous staff and journalists to get assistance. But there are frustrating things about that, too. Are there good ways for southern journalists to ask for assistance from their colleagues?

JT: Be open-minded and admit that you don't know what to expect. Ask your Indigenous colleague, "What can I expect? What is something that the community would appreciate from me going into their community, to ask these questions and to talk to their people and to tell a story?" The end result is telling a story—good or bad—from the community. So what is good to know?

Every culture has different expectations. What it's like to go into a Nunavut community is totally different than what it's like to go into an Northwest Territories community or a Yukon community. I'm an Indigenous person. I'm an Inuk but I'm not too sure what it's like going into Yukon communities, so I want to ask the chief, "What's the best way to go about getting my characters? Are there any signs of respect that I can show that would help open up my characters to tell me their story?" Because the biggest appreciation that we as journalists have is having somebody tell us their story.

You want your characters to be comfortable with you. You want your characters to open up to you, so you have to understand how to be able to sit down and speak with somebody that is not going to turn them away.

DM: I know that northerners get concerned, because southern journalists often focus on bad news in the North, whether it is suicide or climate crisis or housing shortage. What should journalists be mindful of when they're tackling those tough stories?

JT: There is always another side of the story to tell. There's always a perspective from somebody in the community . . . What can be told from their point of view? Because it's not just a "crisis." For example, let's take suicide. In Nunavut, the suicide rate is seven times higher than the national average. What does that mean? Talk to an Indigenous person in the community to find out what that means. It's not just because of the residential school experience or drugs and alcohol. Find out why young people are hurting themselves.

Don't just talk to the RCMP. They've been there maybe two, three years max. Talk to the Elders in the community. Talk to home-grown people that are in the community. Teachers as well, because they're with the children every day. They know, the ones that have been there for a while.

Just realize there's more voices that should be heard when it comes to tackling these issues. Climate change—don't just talk to the scientists. Talk to the Elders. Realize there's traditional knowledge when it comes to each of these hard issues. Because you're right—they [southern journalists] talk about these issues so much and the real stories come from the people in the communities.

> For more discussion about broadening the range of Indigenous voices in your work, refer to Chapter 2.4, "White Characters and Indigenous Agency."

Another point—something that I find southern journalists do a lot of times when reporting on Inuit names or Inuit community names—they try to pronounce Inuktitut names and words. It's great but it's also annoying. Like, they'll go 'ee-*kha*-loo-eet' [dramatically overemphasizes "kha" sound] because they can't say "Iqaluit." That's fine, because they don't have the vocals to be able to say Inuktitut words and names.

Don't try too hard to be who you're not! You're not Inuk, so don't try to say "Qikiqtarjuaq" and butcher it! Just say "Ki-kick-tar-joo-whack." You know?! (laugh)

Working in Indigenous Languages

DM: (laugh) That's a good tip! What advice would you give journalists about working with translators?

JT: Try to find a reputable translator. If your words are going to be translated into another language, or, vice versa, from English into an Indigenous language, that's a really important job for the translator. They don't want to get any of the information incorrect, because that reflects badly on them, too.

Find the right translator who wants to do the job and who can do the job. Because people who speak the language and are not translators, that kind of gets annoying to them. They get interrupted to do a job that they're not paid to do. Some like to help out and some don't. My advice would be to ask a translator if they're willing to help out.

DM: That's such a good point about budgeting for translation and making sure you pay someone properly. It's a job. Just because someone is Indigenous, and they happen to speak the language, doesn't mean they're necessarily able to provide you with translation services.

JT: Exactly. The CBC has money to pay people for their skills and their expertise. So, if you want to have some stories translated, make sure that you respect the translator's time and abilities and pay them for it.

DM: Are there instances when you will choose to use a translator when you're out in the field?

JT: Yes. For example, I want to get into Arviat. That's my home community. They went through over 100 days of isolation because of the COVID-19 outbreak in the community. I want to go in and hear some of the stories that people have about their experience of isolation, especially for that long.

But because I know it's an Inuktitut-speaking community, mostly, I don't want to go in there and interview somebody and expect them to talk to me in English.[1] Because that's not their first language. So, I want to bring a translator with me, to be able to do that job of translating. Get their responses in Inuktitut and translate it back to me in English. Because they're more comfortable.

I've had a lot of experiences with people whose first language is Inuktitut and they don't want to do the interview unless they can speak back in Inuktitut because their English isn't as good. They get worried. They get nervous. They get a little self-conscious that they can't speak English that well. They don't want the people listening to your story to get the impression that they don't have good English.

The language they speak the best is the language you should get your interviews in. Because that is going to be the strongest interview that you can ever get from somebody.

> See Chapter 2.2, "Indigenous Customs and Protocols," for more tips on working with Indigenous languages.

Interviewing Inuit Elders

DM: You've mentioned Elders. Are there things journalists should keep in mind when interviewing Elders?

JT: You *never* cut off an Elder. No matter how long they're going on. And Elders speak slowly a lot of the time, and they have a lot to say. You never cut off an Elder. You let them speak their mind.

DM: How do you deal with that if you only have a three-minute story on *The National*?

JT: Well, you let them talk. What I can do is, when I'm asking the question, I'll say, "We only have a few minutes, but I would like to really know from you what was the biggest impact this had on you?" So, in your question, let them know you only have a few minutes. Then, when they start talking, don't interrupt them. Do not interrupt them, even if they didn't listen to you and they want to go on for five or ten minutes. You are just going to have to go through that tape, paraphrase, and cut to edit.

DM: Will you talk to them afterwards, so they don't get upset about you not having the whole 15-minute answer on the TV?

JT: Oh, yeah—either before or after the interview. Just letting them know I only have three minutes to tell this story, and I have a couple other voices, but I really want to hear from you. And if you can tell me as briefly as you can why this is important to you, that would be great.

> Interviewing Elders is further discussed in Chapter 2.2, "Indigenous Customs and Protocols."

DM: I've gone into communities in the North where there is an expectation that Elders will be paid honorariums. Have you had that experience, and if so, how do you deal with it?

JT: That's a tough one, yeah. I just have to explain that we don't pay anybody for their story. As much as I know it's important to them and they would like to get an honorarium, it's just beyond my control. It's not something I can authorize.

If they really, really want to get an honorarium, then I can ask and then get back to them. That's something I would do, in case it's somebody that's really adamant about it. Then I would go back to them and say, "I'm sorry but I was told by my supervisors that we can't pay you. So I'm sorry for that, and thank you for considering." Then you have to just look for another character.

DM: Have you lost interviews that way?

JT: No.

DM: Have you ever received approval for giving an honorarium to an Elder?

JT: No. I can't say it happens all the time—I think it's happened one or two times. It would set a precedent, and I understand that. I've got my supervisors and I've got our policies and procedures at the CBC that I abide by. . . .

DM: Amongst Anishinaabe, bringing tobacco is often considered a sign of respect for an Elder. Are there ways amongst Inuit for doing the same?

JT: Showing gratitude. The handshaking, saying thank you, and giving them tea. Getting them a chair. Anything that would make them more comfortable for the interview is showing a sign of respect. But we don't give gifts. We don't pay. It's just showing respect.

"A Little Glimpse of Our History"

DM: When you're trying to fit Northern or Inuit history into your very short stories, how do you do that?

JT: Just as a piece of conversation. For example, when I was doing a story about housing in the North, I was speaking with the chief of a Dene community. Based on our backgrounds and our knowledge about housing in the North, we were able to plug into our conversation that when the white people started coming up North, they brought houses with them . . . because we were nomadic people back then. It was just a few sentences talking about how matchbox houses were built for Inuit to live in. That opened up a whole new vision of what the North was like way back then, because people don't think about that.

When you're talking about housing, it's hard to get a house in the North. Because it's something that's just come along over the last 50 years or so. We're still learning, I guess, how to live in a [contemporary] society. A lot of people in the North don't think about buying a house or they don't think about building a house. They're thinking about getting on the waitlist for a public housing unit because that's just how it is.

DM: It's important to not just focus on the present but to take audiences back through history.

JT: Yes. To be honest, I didn't think that was going to be very prominent in the story. But it turned out to be … Southern people got a little glimpse of our history and it helped them understand why the shortage of housing is such an issue in the North.

DM: Are there challenges you've faced as an Indigenous person doing journalism in your community, and how did you overcome them?

JT: One of the biggest challenges is being able to tell a story in such a short amount of time when there's so much more to tell in a story. You want to give context to what you're talking about, you want to explain why this is important, and that was always my biggest challenge. Condensing my story, shortening it. It's like, "I don't want to take this out!" But you have to because of timing. So it's important, but maybe you can put it in a few words. You know, paraphrase and paint a picture in those few words that you're trying to tell. A couple of paragraphs. Which is the hardest, hardest thing because I don't like cutting anything out. So, I rely heavily on my producers to help me find the right words, to be able to tell it in as few words as possible. That is just the reality.

As journalists, we're not telling documentaries. We're telling a story that's going to catch somebody's attention in the shortest amount of time but have the biggest impact. The challenge is being able to do that.

DM: But you're also saying that context is important—you need to try to fit it in.

JT: Oh, very much.

Voices of Inuit Women

DM: From your perspective as an Inuk woman, what should journalists be aware of when they're pitching stories in the North, in terms of including women's voices?

JT: It's growing now, the number of women that could be a character. But when you're talking about past leaders or current leaders or the history of Nunavut or even things that happened five or ten years ago, in a lot of those stories, the characters are Inuit men. Because the culture back then was male-dominated.

I'm finding nowadays, there's more female leaders, more female journalists, which is wonderful. Because they open up their minds and are able to include more Indigenous and Inuit women voices in their stories. This generation is amazing when it comes to outspoken youth! There are a lot of youth these days who are just go-getters. There are even politicians in Nunavut who are younger than me. Youth are really stepping up to the plate when it comes to getting into politics or getting those jobs that make them a character in a story.

Things are shifting right now. You still have the "old boys' club," but you also have this movement happening where the youth are taking charge, wanting to be heard, being more vocal. I would say it's thanks to social media that messages are getting out a lot easier and more freely these days.

I would say to future journalists or southern journalists, don't limit yourself on who to contact. Contact them all and get that wide range of opinions and voices.

Social Media in the North

DM: You brought up social media. It's my experience that Facebook is now the primary means of communication in the North. Everybody is on Facebook. How do you use Facebook as a journalist?

JT: A good chunk of my time, I use it to fish for stories. I found great stories using Facebook and I use it a lot to make contact with people. That's one of the easiest ways to reach out to people—using Facebook Messenger. It is the way to connect right now. Instagram is slowly creeping in there, but it's more the younger generation that's using Instagram. Facebook is used by almost everybody. If you're not on Facebook, you're missing out.

DM: It's a great way to connect with people across the vast distances of the North, but are there downsides to the way social media is used in Inuit communities that journalists need to understand?

JT: There are the people who use it to their advantage, when it comes to being overly opinionated. Because it's easier to speak publicly from a computer desk or from your phone. It's way easier to give your opinions or share information that way rather than face to face. So, I would say, check your sources before using Facebook as a source. . . .

The most recent example is the rant that Mumilaaq Qaqqaq posted on her social media.[2] That was shared so many times and used to either support her or not support her. There were a lot of accusations going around on social media that she was intoxicated at the time that she posted that. There were a lot of people supporting her, too, saying, "It's great that you're going for help again," because her post ultimately led her to another two weeks of leave from her work. Because she says the doctor instructed her to take some time off work.

Facebook is used as a way to voice your opinion, whether you have accurate information or not, so I would suggest to any journalist to double-check your sources and your facts if you're going to be using somebody's comment or want to chase somebody who's on Facebook as a character. Follow your gut—if this person doesn't sound credible or is ranting and raving, just double-check.

Check out Chapter 3.4, "Social Media: The New Moccasin Telegraph," for more advice on Indigenous communities and social media.

DM: What often used to be our own dirty laundry ends up on social media and can be amplified in ways that may not be accurate. Is that what you're getting at?

JT: For example, you don't want to use somebody in your story that's got a bad reputation as somebody who's always ranting and raving on Facebook and not getting the right information. Unless you know the person personally, I would always suggest double-checking your sources.

DM: One of the differences of being an Indigenous journalist is that our communities are small. We will see everybody, at the grocery store or the community event, after our stories. Particularly after a difficult story, are there ways you stay in touch with people?

JT: I just did a story about Wren Acorn. She's Yellowknife speed skater who's training for the Olympics. When you have such a close connection with somebody that you're doing a story about, I made sure I kept in touch with her, to let her know when it was going to air and on which show, just to keep that close connection and keep that bond. In ways like that, Facebook is great.

DM: Miigwech! Any last words of advice?

JT: Respecting the culture, understanding where you are and why you're there, is always good to keep in the back of your mind. Just be truthful with your stories. That's one of the most important things you can do.

Discussion Questions

1. Taylor suggests journalists need to avoid a "southern attitude" when working in the North. What do you think she means by this? Is there anything you would change about your approach if you were reporting in the North?
2. Taylor recommends using a translator if an interviewee is more comfortable speaking an Indigenous language. How would you prepare for an interview when using a translator?
3. When you hear the word "Inuit," what images come to your mind? List the words, either individually or as a group. What are some of the problematic ways Inuit have been covered by the press and portrayed in popular media?

Suggested Works by Juanita Taylor

Audio: "The North Rising." CBC Radio's *The House*, November 28, 2020. https://www.cbc.ca/listen/live-radio/1-64-cbc-news-the-house/clip/15811409-the-north-rising or https://www.cbc.ca/radio/thehouse/cbc-radio-s-the-house-special-the-north-rising-airs-nov-28-1.5812898

"'This Is So Powerful:' Kitikmeot Women Revive Traditional Inuit Tattoos." *CBC North*, May 3, 2016. https://www.cbc.ca/news/canada/north/inuit-women-traditional-tattoos-kugluktuk-1.3563446

"Love, Northern Style: Yellowknife Husband Drives 1,400 Km to Pick Up KFC Meal for Wife." *CBC North*, April 23, 2016. https://www.cbc.ca/news/canada/north/yellowknife-kfc-wedding-anniversary-1.3547659

Endnotes

1. Juanita grew up in Saskatchewan before moving to Nunavut. Though she doesn't consider herself fluent in Inuktitut, she says she has "simple" conversations in the language, can read syllabics, and properly pronounce Inuktitut words and names.

2. In 2019, Nunavut MP Mumilaaq Qaqqaq took to Twitter to challenge the ancestry of Labrador MP Yvonne Jones, who describes herself as a "descendent of Inuit and settlers in Labrador" with ties to the NunatuKavut people (previously known as the Labrador Métis Nation). NunatuKavut land claims have been disputed by both the Innu Nation and Inuit organizations in Canada. In April 2021, Qaqqaq posted a 33-minute video on Twitter calling on Jones to "validate" her Inuk identity. Qaqqaq subsequently deleted the post and apologized.

✦ 4.5 ✦

Respect and Relationships: A Conversation with Tanya Talaga

Tanya Talaga is an Anishinaabe journalist. Talaga's mother's family is from Fort William First Nation, and her father was Polish-Canadian.

For more than 20 years, she was a journalist at the *Toronto Star*, covering everything from health to education, investigations, and Queen's Park. She's been nominated five times for the Michener Award in public service journalism and been part of teams that won two National Newspaper Awards for Project of the Year. She is now a regular columnist at the *Globe and Mail*.

She is the award-winning author of two national bestsellers, *Seven Fallen Feathers* and *All Our Relations: Finding the Path Forward*. Talaga was the 2017–18 Atkinson Fellow in Public Policy and the 2018 CBC Massey Lecturer, the first Anishinaabe woman to be so.

Talaga heads up Makwa Creative Inc., a production company focused on amplifying Indigenous voices through documentary films, TV, and podcasts. She holds honorary doctorates from Lakehead University in Thunder Bay, Toronto Metropolitan University in Toronto, and Ontario Tech University in Oshawa.

Tanya Talaga.

Source: Nadya Kwandibens/Red Works Photography. Used with permission of Tanya Talaga.

Building Trust

DM: You haven't shied away from tough stories: *Seven Fallen Feathers*, the Massey Lectures—dealing with the children who died in Thunder Bay and suicides. With those difficult subjects, how do you go about building trust with your interviewees?

TT: It's difficult. As a newspaper reporter, which is what I have been for over 20 years, you have deadlines. You have a crush of a story and you're working with time sensitive materials and it's tough, you need to get families to react to what's happened. Whatever tragedy you're reporting on, whatever good story or awful story, you have to reach out to family. That's difficult to do, especially when an event has just happened that shocks you, let alone family.

The one thing that I've learned is that we can't put our presumptions as to how we're feeling on to everyone else. Sometimes there are members of the family that you contact that *want* to talk. That's an integral part of their grieving process, and somebody wants to say and share things with you.

Approach is a lot of the issue. We as journalists have to be very careful and respectful of the people we're talking to and the people we're reaching out to. We can't go in with guns blazing and screaming, "I've got a deadline!!!" You don't get anything that way.

Another thing I've learned is about building relationships with people and how important that is. Being kind and considerate and respectful; that's the only way really to handle a situation that is very difficult. Also, sometimes, don't approach the family right off the bat directly. Don't call a mom or dad that's just lost a child. There are ways to call around.

If we're looking at a community, I'll often go and speak to somebody in a band council, to try and get somebody that way. Try and speak to an Elder, and then work my way in, I find is a good way to do it. Always state your intentions: who you are, what you're doing, and also . . . that you won't be the only person writing the story. There'll be other people out there, and if that person wants the correct version told or the version told sensitively, suggest that you can do that. You can do that by showing them some of your previous work.

When Interviewing about Trauma

DM: When you talk about being kind and considerate and sensitive, are there specific things that you do for your Indigenous interviewees when you know you're going to be touching on trauma, whether it's residential schools or suicides or family violence?

TT: I like to think that I treat everyone with the same amount of respect and consideration. We always have to be aware of the trauma that people in our communities live with. We as Indigenous journalists know that intimately. We have family members that have been affected by the trauma. We've been affected by that trauma. We all live in it; we know what that means.

Having that knowledge is such a help because we write in a different way. We see things in a different way. Lee Maracle once said to me, "You write seeing backwards and forwards, at the same time."[1] I totally agree that to be true. It's like we're in a circular motion. We see things in circles. Circles are important parts of who we are. The continuum of life and knowing that all of your actions affect the past, the present, and the future.

That all plays into it when you speak to somebody from our community. You just know that it's going to be difficult. Some things might be more difficult than others. You know when to back off, you know when not to be hard.

Beyond being an Indigenous journalist, you should have that sense as a journalist anyway. If you don't have that empathetic sense, I think you're in the wrong field.

DM: Empathy is one thing. Do you worry when you're starting to prod around into someone's psyche about how prepared you are to do that?

TT: For sure. You have to be responsible. I hope I wouldn't write something that's taken from somebody that [spoke to] me in a moment of weakness; [I'd be] exploiting it by using that quote out of context. I hope I have enough sense in myself to know not to do that and to put the brakes on that.

Some people say it's editing yourself, but you know when you've stepped over the line, right? You know when you're talking to somebody and if you've made them feel uncomfortable and if they don't want that used. I don't think there's any shame in reviewing an interview with somebody after you've written. I'm a columnist now, but before, when I was a journalist, I would often call back, and I would read—you're not supposed to (laugh)—I would read what I wrote and I said, "I want you to hear this. Are you okay with this?" Before I would file.

> For more tips on covering historical trauma, see Chapter 2.5, "Trauma-Informed Reporting."

Do No Harm

DM: You acknowledge that isn't necessarily common practice, but you're saying that the impact of a disclosure, for example, weighs on you more than the rules we're supposed to play by?

TT: I guess it does, but I was always very conscious of that. Especially when you're dealing with losses and when you're dealing with people who are traumatized. So many in our communities are traumatized. It's the responsible thing to do. When I wrote *Seven Fallen Feathers*, which is a non-fiction book based on investigative journalism, we were in contact with all the families of the seven and we sent them each of the chapters, so they could review [the chapter on] their own child.

We did this for a number of reasons. There's a "do no harm"—I didn't want a book to come out and them to read something and just be devastated. I wanted them to read it, and also see if it's right. See if we honoured their child, which is the point of the book: to honour each of the lives and to show that each life lost is a loss to so many.

That was really important. That was a book, so it's different. You've got a longer lead time but still, with investigative writing, long-form writing, you still have the time to do that. You can still call them. If you're an investigative journalist and you're looking into these things, and you're writing about trauma, you develop a relationship with the people that you're writing about so it's not unheard of. Because you're spending time with that person, that person trusts you. I know you've said this before and so well—don't be a story-taker. It's a relationship.

> See Chapter 1.1, "First Contact," and Chapter 2.6, "Story-Takers: How to Deal with 500+ Years of Rage," for discussions of story-takers.

DM: You mentioned "don't be a story-taker." The extractive nature of our business has long concerned me. How do you balance that—editorial independence versus respecting the person's right to their own story?

TT: We don't have the right to go in and be the arbiter of good and decide whose story should be told in a certain way and whose shouldn't be. As a journalist, you have to be fair. You have to have two sides of the story. . . .

You know when you're going over the line. You know when something's too far. You can say something to your editor if you don't like the headline, if you don't like what you see online. I just finished doing a podcast that was also non-fiction. It's journalism as well, and you have to take care of those stories. If you have time, make sure you're getting it right. Don't be pressured by others who tell you, "Could we just juice up a little bit? Change the wording here? Can we just add this here?" Just say no.

I am lucky, I am in a position in my career where I can do that. But when you're starting off, it's not as easy. You often have to do what you're told. You often don't get to choose your stories. You're told what to do.

Take Care of Yourself

DM: It's personal for a lot of Indigenous journalists when you're dealing with this difficult subject matter. How do you take care of yourself?

TT: Thanks for the question. Ceremony. Smudging. Keeping in contact with certain people in my life. I talk a lot about Sam Achneepineskum, who is someone I consider to be almost "my Elder." I speak to him every day, and he helps me a lot. Just like, debrief. Little things. He keeps me feeling on the straight and narrow.

I'm also very blessed to be really close to people in my community in the north. We speak almost every day and without that, it would be hard. It's a reminder that I'm not the only one doing this work. There are others . . .

This is a pet peeve of mine: how, when we talk about trauma for reporters, reporters having PTSD, we never talk about how Indigenous journalists are. Their mental health. You asked me how I handle it? I'm always mindful to ask others about it, but you see these seminars in newsrooms for covering wars or accidents or trauma.

This is a war. You don't hear news organizations say, "How are you doing? Would you like to take a trauma-informed class?" It's always about the foreign war, the old-fashioned foreign correspondents.

DM: You mentioned that when you're doing deep-dive investigations, you form relationships with your interviewees. Are there other ways you try to take care of them after your interview and in the follow-up to a story?

TT: I keep in touch. I really try to keep in touch with everyone, over time. So, it's not just calling them up after the story has run. For example, Dora Morris, Jethro Anderson's aunt in Thunder Bay—I still talk to her frequently. One of Jethro's cousins, Haley—I speak to her.[2] Reggie Bushie's family; for a while there, I was in contact with them all the time.[3] It just ebbs and flows, because these are relationships you have over the years. It's like friends—sometimes you see them a while, and then they go away and then they come back.

I keep in contact with a lot of the families through Facebook and [with] a lot of people that I write about that way. It's really nice, getting a "Happy New Year!" message from the parent of a child who took her life when she was 12 years old, and I'm still in contact with. There's something lovely about that.

"You're Part of a Community"

DM: Does it ever feel like a burden?

TT: No, never. You know that family, that person, has let you into their life. You are part of their story now too, because you have told their most intimate details, most tragic details and you shared them with the world. You're part of it now. You're not a casual observer. So it's never a burden to me.

It's hard, though. It's really hard . . . I mean, I had a hard time last year.

I was in Thunder Bay, shooting a documentary. We got in late, and I was staying at a local hotel. It was around midnight and I went outside to have a cigarette. I didn't have a light, and I'm like, "Oh gosh. Well, I'll just stand here for a moment. I know a neechie is gonna come around."[4]

I see this man walking towards me, smaller than me, very slight. I asked him for a light and he gave me the light and then he said to me, "Are you the journalist, the speaker that I've seen?" I said "Yes, my name is Tanya." So, then we got to talking and he told me that he was in Thunder Bay to pick up his son. He said his son had just died, and I said, "I'm so very sorry for your loss." I could tell he was still in shock and he said, "I'm here to pick up my son's body."

I said, "Can I ask what happened?" And he said he didn't know. He's still trying to get answers out of the police. All he knows is that his son went to the hospital. He was having a mental health breakdown. Paramedics were in the hospital and the next thing he knew his son had been found hanging in the tree across the street from the hospital.

This is honestly around 12:30 in the morning. I'm talking to Troy. His son is Craig, and I was devastated.[5] And I could tell he is. He was from Mishkeegogomang so I knew he was with a Nishnawbe Aski Nation [NAN] community, and I said, "Are you getting any help?" He said no. Him and his family were there, and you could tell they just didn't really know what to do. So I called NAN, texted right away, at midnight. (laugh) I woke up Alvin Fiddler[6] (laugh), just saying, "There's a family here that needs your help. This is what's happened."

Over the next few days, NAN stepped in and Alvin started to help the family, to be a go-between. They're a political territorial organization, but sadly, this is something we now do in Thunder Bay, in our communities. We have to do this. So, they started to help him. Then I started to talk to Troy. At that point, I was a columnist for the *Star* and I couldn't write about it right away. I left it and I didn't feel comfortable. I felt like I was too close to the story.

We left it for several months, but Troy and I would always keep in contact. He wanted to get justice and find out what happened to his son. Eventually, I did write about it, and turns out that his son basically spent five, six minutes in hospital and was escorted out the door. He wasn't even seen by a doctor. It was security staff that took him to Lakehead University, where he was found hanging in a tree.

It turns out there's more stories like this. This is before Joyce Echaquan.[7] I just finished writing a book [called *All Our Relations*], on racism in the healthcare system throughout Canada. Especially in Thunder Bay, we know how bad the hospitals are. They have not treated our people well, in many respects.

It's a very long story, but it shows you the depth of how you can become entwined with people. I wrote about Craig and I wrote about Troy and his pursuit of justice. It turned out to be bigger. He retained a lawyer. He and Alvin met with the hospital staff to try and figure out, "Why is this hospital so racist to our people in Thunder Bay?" (small laugh)

Sadly, last summer, Troy took his life. The father took his life. That was a shock. Alvin called me and said, "This is what's happened." Because the grief was so huge, with the loss of his son, that he took his life. That's what we're dealing with. You have relationships. You're not just on the outside of the story looking in. Because when you are part of a community, that's just who you are. It's your responsibility to tell these stories and to treat them with care.

DM: Thank you for sharing that story. Because so often we're criticized for parachuting in. And, the truth of the matter is, you and I, we don't just work on one family's story for our entire career. We do lots of different stories. We're in and out of people's lives. But what you're speaking to is the long-term commitment you have, if families want to have an ongoing relationship with you.

TT: For sure.

Resilience and Love

DM: You've written about the importance of resiliency and love in telling these stories. Can you explain that?

TT: Every child that we lose is an opportunity lost. Every child that has gone, for no reason of their own, is such a sorrowful shame. For so long in this country, people have looked away. People have not cared. How many times have we gone back and seen a newspaper article written about a murdered or missing teenage girl that was badly done and called her "a party girl," if she's found dead at 12 or 13. Or little tiny stories. Our people have not been valued. They have not been cared for by the media.

I wanted to change that. Reporting on love and resiliency and showing people that we're actually the same inside. We care about our children. We love our children. We love our communities. We are resilient. Colonial laws and racism haven't killed us all. A lot of us, but not all of us. We're still here and we're getting stronger. We're fighting. It's important that everybody knows that we're not an extinct race or dying out. We're here.

DM: How important is it to you, when you're casting about in this potentially discouraging and depressing subject matter, to ask questions that will bring out those positive aspects of people's lives?

TT: I hope I'm asking those questions. I hope I'm showing that side of people. I know that honouring our children is really important, and showing the world how talented and important our kids are. Also pointing out that a lot of bad stuff has gone on in this country and no one has talked about it. They haven't confronted the truths, and children do not ask for the circumstances in which they are born. That's important to know.

The Fight for Context

DM: How do you propose that journalists get that context into their work, given the constraints that we have?

TT: It starts with curriculum reform. It starts with teaching our children the truth about what's happened in this country. That means we've got to go back to the drawing board.

I don't think that any of us start off, as Indigenous journalists, to become activists and teachers and to be doing all of these things. Educators. But that's what we end up doing. . . .

Our history was not an elective. We did not get to choose it. It happened. It's a truth; it needs to be told. Kids need to understand that. We have to look at education reform all across the board. What do we do now, as we're waiting for that generational change? I would hope that journalism schools would have a history course or a course on how to deal with BIPOC communities.

DM: But when you have a word limit for your *Globe and Mail* column, for example, how do you try to fit that history and context into a relatively short piece?

TT: It's not easy. Seven hundred words. It's a little bit easier in a column; I have a lot more control as to what words are used. It's me that's controlling the column. Editors don't make massive changes to column writing, so it's easier that way. As a journalist it's harder.

That was something I always found difficult, when I was a reporter at the *Star*—trying to get all of that context in. I'm not saying you've got to write volumes on the history of residential schools and the *Indian Act* and what it means, but you do have to know how to weave it in. And weave it in so it's not taken out by the desk or by copy editors. That's always a huge problem, because that's the thing they would want to chop. They want to keep it short and move on.

> Find more discussion on why context is important in Chapter 3.2, "Context and Colonial Amnesia."

DM: Do you feel a tension between narrative and context when you're trying to weave that tapestry?

TT: It was hard because it was like you're butting up against editors who are saying, "You gotta put that in? I don't have room for this. It's the same old story. I hear this all the time from you." And I'd say, "But it's important to put it in because you actually don't really understand why this is important, by you and I having this conversation." That's difficult. I did that for years. You probably did too.

For example, missing and murdered women. Having to say, "Well, it's not just a crime story. It's not just a story of a girl or a woman that's gone missing or is found dead." You've got to look at the vulnerabilities around this woman and [find out] why this is so. Maybe her mom went to residential school; maybe her mom didn't raise her; maybe there's Sixties Scoop. All that context is important in telling that story. . . .

DM: What you're saying is that internal newsroom management is as much a part of the struggle as anything else.

TT: Absolutely. When you're working in the mainstream, it is 100 per cent. It's like you have two jobs in a newsroom. You're not just doing your job; you're also doing the other job of educating. When you and I started, we would be the only Indigenous people within a newsroom. So, you would get all the requests for phone numbers, because, you know, we all know each other, right? (laugh) And there's no difference between Métis, Inuit, and First Nations, right? (laugh)

And to explain things. I would be like, "I don't know! I can explain maybe a little bit about northern Ontario, but I'm still learning. I don't know what the heck's going on with the Coast Salish people over there. I don't know about that!" (laugh) It's a lot of education, and that's why I was saying earlier that when we signed up to be journalists, we didn't think we'd be doing this too.

Through a White Lens

DM: Could you talk about the habit that many journalists have of privileging non-Indigenous experts? Is that something that you've observed, and are there ways to work around it?

TT: The white historian who is an expert on the *Indian Act*? That's hard. When I started at the *Star* in 1995 . . . it was all white journalists. There were no Indigenous journalists. So, then you have all these non-Indigenous journalists looking for comments. They don't know. So they call Carleton [University]. They speak to some guy who's a professor there and who's non-Indigenous, but he's giving a perspective because that's the person who's filling that academic seat. It's like a trickle-down effect.

There are non-Indigenous journalists looking for help and they don't know what to do, so they call who they know. For a long time, there's been a lot of non-Indigenous people in those roles. Is it getting better that way? I think so, but there's still so few academics and people in power, in positions of authority, that we're still looking at the same people.

> The importance of seeking out Indigenous voices is discussed in Chapter 2.4, "White Characters and Indigenous Agency."

DM: That just takes time. It takes longer to find those sources.

TT: It does, but you just have to go farther afield. A lot of working journalists become lifers. They're in this for a very long time and they just do things how they've always done them. Not every journalist is like that, but some are.

DM: Is it an issue for you to have non-Indigenous journalists telling the story?

TT: There's space for non-Indigenous journalists to tell the stories. There's space to do so responsibly. A reality is that non-Indigenous journalists will be telling the stories because we don't have a lot of Indigenous journalists in mainstream media.

It's worthy for people to want to tell our stories and to write them down. It's a great joy and responsibility, but I would urge our kids to do it. I want space made for our people as well.

Discussion Questions

1. What are some of the ways Talaga recommends building trust with Indigenous communities?
2. Have you ever formed long-term relationships with news sources? What were the challenges and benefits of that approach?
3. Why does Talaga emphasize the importance of "resilience and love" in Indigenous stories?

Suggested Works by Tanya Talaga

"Brayden Bushby's Guilty Verdict Was a Relief for Indigenous Women, But It Was Also Deeply Imperfect." *Globe and Mail*, December 14, 2020. https://www.theglobeandmail.com/opinion/article-guilty-verdict-in-thunder-bay-trial-ultimately-about-race-but-what/

"There Have Always Been Two Canadas. In This Reckoning on Racism, Both Must Stand Together for Indigenous People Now." *Globe and Mail*, June 16, 2020. https://www.theglobeandmail.com/opinion/article-there-have-always-been-two-canadas-in-this-reckoning-on-racism-both/

"Friends to the End: How the Suicides of Seven Indigenous Girls Revealed a Community Undone," *Toronto Star*, April 27 2018. https://www.thestar.com/news/atkinsonseries/2018/04/27/friends-to-the-end-how-the-deaths-of-seven-Indigenous-girls-revealed-a-community-undone.html?rf

Endnotes

1. Lee Maracle was a Sto:lo author and poet who often spoke out as a critic of the treatment of Indigenous Peoples by the Canadian state, and on issues relating to Indigenous women.
2. Jethro Anderson, a 15-year-old from Kasabonika Lake First Nation, was found dead in Thunder Bay, Ontario, on Nov. 11, 2000. He was a student at Dennis Franklin Cromarty High School. Police determined his death not suspicious, but a 2018 independent police review into the deaths of Indigenous Peoples in Thunder Bay found deficiencies in the police investigation of Anderson's case.
3. Reggie Bushie, a 15-year-old from Poplar Hill First Nation, was found dead in Thunder Bay, Ontario, in 2007. He was attending Dennis Franklin Cromarty High School. A 2016 coroner's inquest later determined his death was accidental.
4. "Neechie" comes from the Anishinaabemowin word "*niijii*," which means friend/brother and is often used as slang for a First Nations person.
5. Craig Neekan, 21, was found dead, hanging in a tree on the Lakehead University campus in September 2019, not long after he had been discharged from a hospital in Thunder Bay, Ontario.
6. Alvin Fiddler is Grand Chief of the Nishnawbe Aski Nation (NAN).
7. Joyce Echaquan was a 37-year-old Atikamekw woman who died in 2020 in the Centre hospitalier de Lanaudière in Saint-Charles-Borromée, Quebec. Before her death, she recorded a Facebook Live video that showed her screaming in distress and healthcare workers abusing her.

4.6

In Pursuit of Truth: A Conversation with Karyn Pugliese

Karyn Pugliese, aka Pabàmàdiz, is best known for her work as a Parliament Hill reporter and as the Executive Director of News and Current Affairs at APTN (Aboriginal Peoples Television Network), where she ran the news department for seven years. She joined Toronto Metropolitan University's School of Journalism as a professor in 2020 while completing a Nieman Fellowship at Harvard University. Karyn has worked in both daily news and on long-form investigations at a variety of outlets including iChannel, VisionTV, CBC, and CTV. In 2022, she became the editor-in-chief of the *National Observer*.

Karyn is the past president of the Canadian Association of Journalists (CAJ), and an ambassador with Journalists for Human Rights. Her journalism has been recognized by the CAJ, the Canadian Screen Awards, the Native American Journalists Association, and the Public Policy Forum. She holds degrees in Journalism and History.

Karyn Pugliese.

Source: Photo courtesy of Karyn Pugliese.

A citizen of the Pikwàkanagàn First Nation in Ontario, Karyn is of mixed Algonquin and Italian descent.

Good Pitches and Bad Pitches

DM: You ran a newsroom for APTN for several years. Do you have any advice on what makes for a good pitch when it comes to covering Indigenous communities?

KP: I'm thinking of when we used to interview people [for a reporter position]. Part of the interview process was we asked them: "What story do you think is not getting covered right now that needs to be covered?" A lot of people would say, "Missing and murdered Indigenous women." Which is a topic, not a story. Too often stories about Indigenous people are pitched that way, as issues rather than human stories. Also, it's a mistake to pitch stories that are already being covered by the newsroom you're pitching to. We're always looking for what we're *not* covering, people whose stories we're missing, so we can fill that gap.

Something I look for in a story is impact. When writing for an Indigenous audience, you want to have a story where you feel like you have your finger on the pulse of the community. What are people talking about? Thinking about? Worried about? Happy about? Right now. And what matters to them? I think differently when I'm writing for a non-Indigenous audience. Then the story has to be crafted to explain what's happening in the Indigenous community to this other audience.

Pitches should also include the person who is most affected. Who is most impacted by the story? Who's the person who's going to be able to speak to the importance of it and be able to carry it through? What is the landing point of the story? Sometimes it's an open question. Sometimes it's a plea for help. Sometimes it's a solution, that if other people saw it, they could say, "Oh, I could do that too."

So, the story pitch would also have a landing point to it. That can change. Sometimes you go into the field and the landing point is not what you thought it was. That's fine, but at least, initially, you know where you're going with it.

> See Chapter 1.6, "How to Pitch a Story Successfully," for more tips and advice on pitching stories.

DM: You mentioned having a solutions-oriented focus to the pitch. Why is that so important?

KP: When we're really focused on Indigenous audiences, the idea is that if you go into one community that solves the problem, then you take us through the steps of how they did it. Other communities could look at that as a roadmap and say, "Hey, maybe we can do that too." Sometimes that would happen. We had one community that declared a state of emergency because of mould in their community. After we covered that, we were actually getting calls saying, "How do you declare a state of emergency? We want to do that, too." I was like, "I don't know. Talk to the chief." (laugh) But we got a lot of calls about it. Then it became a thing in First Nations communities because it actually was effective at getting responses from the government, or seemed to be.

I think about it differently in terms of mainstream media. I think it's really important to show Indigenous people have agency and have the knowledge and the skills to solve their own problems. The gaps that I notice often in writing about Indigenous communities are that journalists will find the person most affected . . . but they skip over all the things that might have been tried [by the community]. Then it just becomes "Well, the government should do something about this." So you have an Indigenous person who's got a problem. And somehow, the uncaring government—who is actually never going to solve it—should solve the problem. And that's kind of a template for the story. It's the trope of the "Indian as a helpless victim," without agency. It leaves out all the knowledge of the Indigenous people along the way who are working to solve the problem.

DM: What's the impact when the Indigenous subject is so often the problem, but Indigenous people aren't necessarily part of the solution in a story?

KP: You know, when government goes to invest money and education for non-Native people, that's an "investment." But when it's Indigenous people, it's "spending." There's different language that gets used. So, there's that bias that comes in: that Indigenous people are a problem, the communities don't work, everything is broken, it cannot possibly be fixed. There are no solutions coming anywhere.

> Solutions journalism is addressed in more detail in Chapter 1.5, "Searching for Solutions."

Context Is Key

DM: Are there times that the importance of getting the news on that day outweighs either cultural protocols or best practices when we're covering Indigenous communities?

KP: No, never. Especially at APTN, we knew that we would very rarely be first with the story. Because, for years, the internet was only part of APTN's story, right? There was a time when news did not go up on the internet, but there were 24-hour news channels. For years, we always knew: if something's breaking, somebody else is going to have the story first, so it's important that we have the story best. And that we give the context. So our stories were always longer, more time, more information, more of why it matters. Because that's what we could offer that you weren't going to get in that [news] hit.

But when things did get more competitive, and we started turning stories around for the web, and we did want to get it first, one of the things that we would do is: if we had somebody out in the community and there was something breaking, we'd just say, "Okay, don't worry about filing a full pak. Give us a one-minute hit and at least we have it on the news that night. You can spend all night working on the context story and we'll run it tomorrow." But probably in that one minute, we have the same amount that they're going to have anywhere else. . . .

DM: But, even at APTN, you're still limited to a 1500-word web piece or a two- to four-minute TV news story. That's just the convention of news. So, how did you suggest to your reporters that they squeeze that context in that is so important?

KP: We would have stories that were a minute-and-a-half. There's nothing wrong with that. Some stories are perfectly great at one-minute-and-a-half. But we also did deep dives. We'd call them three-part series. Those might be a three- to five-minute piece, and we do more than one of them. So we'd break it up, run Part 1 on Monday, Part 2 on Tuesday, and Part 3 on Wednesday. If you post them on the web, you can watch them back to back, like a little mini-doc series.

Famously, I once filed a 15-minute piece and they ran it all in one newscast. Half the newscast was this one piece about a community with a combination of a water problem and a third-party management problem. So, there was always that flexibility with the show template that we had at APTN.

DM: For mainstream, would you recommend that when covering Indigenous communities, context is so important that they need to be flexible with their programming models?

KP: I would love to see that happen. I think mainstream takes formulas way too seriously. I mean, sometimes even the formula gets to be really boring.

DM: But what advice would you give journalists about how they can make treaties or Aboriginal title palatable to Canadians, without their eyes glazing over during a 15-minute history lesson?

KP: You have to write to be interesting. You can do one-minute-30 and make it boring. You know, we always talk about how long something *felt*. Sometimes my reporter would file something that was five minutes and I'd be like, "That didn't feel like five minutes." There's a talent to writing in an interesting way. You just need to know what to cut. I do a lot of editing on my writing. I'm actually terrible for doing a first draft that's 5000 words when they asked for 750. It's a process of cutting it down and cutting it down. Then going through it again and making sure that it's interesting. Because there's a craft to doing this well.

> See Chapter 3.2, "Context and Colonial Amnesia," for more ideas on fitting history into your story.

Covering Blockades and Land Defenders

DM: Talking about covering daily news, what tips would you have for reporters who get sent out to cover Indigenous protests?

KP: The first thing that I always noticed is that people wait for it to become a hotspot. Normally, a lot of these things that become hotspots have really been going on for six months to a year beforehand. So they're really stories that you should be covering or following beforehand. You can look at any of the hotspots that we've had. Wet'suwet'en—that was going on for six years before it became a conflict.[1] Caledonia rises and falls, the conflict. But it's been going on forever. Since the Haldimand Treaty.[2]

I think a lot of journalists rush in when the blockades go up. I remember at Rexton,³ it had been a peaceful protest for months, then there was video that went out when the police went to arrest the chief. Somebody pushed the police officer and there was a big crowd. And I thought "Oh, all the reporters will be there now." Because it just got dramatic. Somebody pushed somebody. (laugh) The problem with that is the story becomes about the officer being pushed, and is framed as violent. It becomes about the standoff.

"Are there weapons? Is somebody going to get hurt?" Those are valid questions to ask, but it's not actually the story of what's happening and why, which deserves more coverage. Even though I know the photos are really exciting for reporters, of people in warrior dress along the blockades. But it's not the story. . . .

DM: I was covering a blockade at the Cheam First Nation, many, many moons ago.⁴ I spent several days there. I remember we had this one scene where my line was, "The biggest rush by these warriors was on a passing ice cream truck." It was true. This ice cream truck drove by and all these warriors ran up and they were all ordering Dilly Bars. (laugh)

KP: (laugh) One of the first ones I covered was a blockade—it was a split-off community from Barriere Lake called Kokumville.⁵ Mary Whiteduck was the Elder there. So, they blocked the road, but their roadblock was really just one rock and a guy standing beside it. You know, they hadn't really blocked the road, but the trucks stopped.

Then Mary comes out and she's got one of those big cauldrons, and she makes this big stew. She's like, "Okay, everybody come and eat. Go get those police and we'll feed them." So, everybody's eating this moose stew—even the truckers who they had "blocked." (laughs) I remember we had a non-Native executive producer and when he saw the tape I shot he asked me, "Well, where's the blockade? You didn't get photos of it." I was like, "That's it. The rock is the blockade." Often the images that make the news are not the whole picture. There can be a lot of sitting around, talking—sometimes even friendly interactions at blockades.

DM: Anyone who's spent time at blockades understands it's as much about community spirit building as it is about land rights. What do journalists need to be mindful of when they decide to "embed" with land defenders?

KP: It's important to be there, because it's important to be an eyewitness. I always use Ipperwash and Dudley George—when there were no media there the night that the police moved in—as an example.⁶ All the reporting that happened subsequently was wrong. The police lied and said Dudley had a gun, and there was nobody there to be an independent witness. The journalists defaulted to believing the authorities over the Indians, because white people sometimes have implicit bias telling them police don't lie. They're good guys. But if you're a BIPOC person, you have a different perspective on this sometimes, based on lived experience. And in this case, the police were lying. We found that out later. So, it's important to be there because the force that is used is often an overkill on what's needed.

One protest that I missed being at, people had taken their own video on smartphones. It was another protest at Kokumville; the signs were in French and said things like "Non baton," meaning "No clubs" and "No tear gas" and "We're peaceful." The land defenders were there with their kids. So, they're holding the signs, then, sure enough, you just see police come in with the pepper spray and start just spraying them, right? The land defenders weren't doing anything but standing there. The police were all in riot gear and everything. It's so often overkill, when police move in on Indigenous land actions. So being an independent eyewitness is important.

DM: Being there.

KP: To be there. But the other thing that's really important is to remember that you're not on anybody's side. You are not there to tell one side of the story over another. You're not there to be an advocate or to advocate for anything. You may feel in your heart sympathetic to one side or the other. But that's not what you're going to do. As a reporter, I think you should amplify the voices of others, and never elevate your voice over the people you cover. You're going to do the fairest job that you can reporting, and you are not going to get involved in any way. In Indigenous communities, there are many sides to a story. You've done a good job when the community feels like you fairly represented all sides.

There will be times—especially as an Indigenous person there . . . [For me], there were times where people were saying, "Karyn. What should we do?" Because they feel like you know something. "You're out at a lot of these blockades. You probably know some tricks or something." And maybe I even do. But I can't direct. I can't tell them. I just say, "I'm a reporter. It's not my role here. My role is just to write down what happens and what people say."

We did have people up with the Wet'suwet'en—the camp there was very concerned with how they're being portrayed and how their message was getting out. APTN was banned from the camp, because we dared to speak to others in the community who supported the pipeline. After doing that, a couple of the hereditary chiefs were so upset that we had reported a different point of view that disagreed with them, they wouldn't let the reporters back into the camp again.

DM: Why was that an important choice for you?

KP: Because everybody gets a voice. There is no Indigenous tradition of telling your people to shut up. That is not an Indigenous right. (laugh) It is not an Indigenous way. Silencing people is a learned behaviour from colonization. Everybody should be able to express their opinion.

"You Cannot Do Anything that Crosses that Line of Fairness"

DM: You said it's important not to get involved. Where is that line of involvement—when you are often spending days with people in difficult circumstances—with regard to participating in a ceremony or sharing in a feast?

KP: We had the general rule at APTN. When I was still a cub reporter, I visited the Gull Bay First Nation to do a story about toxic mould in their homes. I was going around to all the different houses. And people are saying, "The chief wants to see you at the school.' I'm like, 'Yeah, yeah, yeah, I'll go see him at three o'clock. I'll be there." They're like, "No, he wants to see you now." Eventually, the chief sent the police to come and get me. (laugh) I said, "What's going on? I better go down to the school!"

It turns out, they had arranged a welcome feast at the school, because I was a visitor to the community and I was coming to do a story that was important to them. Apparently, all these kids had been waiting for us to come, because they're not allowed to eat until the guests eat first. They were so hungry! I felt terrible I'd kept them waiting. But I had another problem. According to my journalism training that I got from my Western-based university, I couldn't eat the food. It could be perceived as a "gift." Journalists do not accept gifts from sources—it's a conflict of interest. But I'm an Indigenous person and they were honouring me and they weren't going to understand if I refused the feast. It would be insulting.

So, I ate the food. Then I called my news director and said, "I don't know what to tell you. I don't know if I can file the story now. What do you think?" That was Rita Deverell at the time, who is a Black woman from Texas and not Indigenous to my knowledge.[7] She was trying to navigate this. So, she asked a series of questions. Ultimately, she rewrote the APTN journalistic policy to state that, if a community had a custom of offering gifts or a feast—it could be accepted. This is similar to the custom of "swag" in the Western community. If someone is giving out free pens to everyone, that type of gift is okay for a reporter to accept, because it's clearly not a bribe meant to influence the outcome of the story. So, even though most newsrooms say free meals are not allowed, in APTN's policy it was okay so long as this was how they would normally treat any Indigenous person coming into their community. But it can't be in exchange for a story or influence the independence of your reporting.

It served us pretty well. But there are those times where it blurs the line. Very purposely, when Paul Barnsley was reporting on a story—and people love-hated Paul, you know. He's a tough reporter. He's not an Indigenous guy. Still, he was the most respected non-Indigenous reporter in Indian Country and probably more respected as a reporter than I am.[8] One time Paul was covering a chief's meeting and they were doing this money giveaway—I guess it's a tradition out West. We don't have that in our community. They knew as a journalist he could not accept money. But they also knew that he had good character and he would never want to disrespect the culture. So, they kept sending money his way; they knew it was a conflict of interest for him. They were all just enjoying how awkward it made him feel. (laugh)

More seriously, though, there are lines that haven't been well-defined yet. I think of the Karl Dockstader arrest.[9] He was covering the land action at Six Nations over housing development on unceded land. Police arrested him, and the only reason they ever gave was that he was not behaving like a journalist. Karl believed, because of the timing of the arrest, it was because he had played a game of lacrosse with the land defenders. I believe the police were purposely trying to make a test case, implying there is a limit to what journalists can and can't do when reporting. The judge threw the case out, which is great. The courts have already drawn a line that journalists cannot participate in a protest, or aid and abet protestors. But this, a game of lacrosse, was new. The police should not be the ones to decide where the lines are—whether it's playing lacrosse or having a coffee with a source.

Karl's case raised a really important question. As journalists we may need to think about what crosses a line when we interact with Indigenous communities, especially in ceremonies while covering stories. What is your obligation to somebody after you've done a pipe ceremony? What if you are covering a story where the community is divided on development? You have to be *seen* as being able to be fair to everyone. Will you be trusted by one side if you engage in ceremony with the other? Some ceremonies can lead people to believe you made a promise. You need to be very clear that the promise is only to have an open heart and an open mind.

The Challenge of Being a Female Journalist

DM: Is there any time that you've faced a challenge in your career when it comes to reporting in Indigenous communities? And how did you end up dealing with it?

KP: The sexism in the male political leaders. That can be frustrating. (rolls eyes) Some of them do like to get in your face. I'm a small woman. Some of them will come and hulk over you and lean into you and try to be physically intimidating. I imagine I look like a little Chihuahua going, "YIP, YIP, YIP, YIP!" back up to them. You just gotta push back and make your space and say, "You are not going to physically intimidate me." I worked with female journalists who have been grabbed, pushed, and one had her car run off the road. My last year as news director at APTN, we had three incidents in a week, and our CEO, Jean La Rose, put chiefs on notice that the next time they or a member of their staff laid a hand on one of our female reporters, he'd press charges. It is not all of them, of course, but a few bad actors who offend repeatedly can make the job very frustrating.

Sometimes, there's really rough stuff—the rape threats and the death threats.

DM: You have received rape threats and death threats?

KP: Oh, yeah.

DM: That's tough.

KP: Yeah. It's unpleasant. The first couple ones that you get, it is kind of freaky. Especially back in the day, when we had phone books, right? You didn't need to be doxxed—everybody knew where you lived. (laugh)

But then, you know, these things come in anonymously by email. After a while, you just kind of blow it off because you just realize nothing's going to happen.

DM: I'm an Indigenous journalist, but I have male privilege. I have not had a rape threat, most certainly.

KP: You must have been threatened to be beaten up?

DM: I think that's a different ballgame than a female journalist facing a rape threat, or a death threat, for that matter. And you've done such an amazing job exposing some of that, when you talked with all of the female Indigenous journalists. I really hope students and news managers do read that work because it's important.[10]

Media and Reconciliation

DM: OK. You've said, "Journalism is not a reconciliation-free zone." What are some of the missteps news organizations are making when it comes to reconciliation?

KP: The TRC said that journalism had the power to influence whether or not reconciliation would happen. I believe that. Because the media has the power to educate and build a common understanding of the true history of Canada, and how it led to inequities today, and build an understanding of Treaty and Indigenous rights . . .

The challenge for journalism is to recognize systemic racism did not end with residential schools. It still influences other institutions—the lack of schools in First Nations communities, the disproportionately high numbers of Indigenous kids in foster care, or the gaps in health care, for example.

Here's another problem. There are not enough people in newsrooms making decisions about what gets covered, who actually understand what's happening in our communities. In as much as newsrooms even hire Indigenous people, a lack of understanding or empathy means they often dismiss Indigenous stories as uninteresting, or unlikely to get ratings.

You know, those who choose and frame the stories often imagine news as a conversation between someone like themselves. That's natural. We default to our own lived experiences. The issue is the people making the decisions about what gets covered are still mostly Caucasian. That's where the problem of "the white gaze" and "implicit bias" arise.

It works like this. You've got this boomer, grey-haired Caucasian man who's imagining his audience being a group of boomer, Caucasian men. They're going to have a conversation amongst themselves about the events of the day. They choose stories that matter to them, and tell the news in ways that are useful to their lives. If it doesn't feel relevant, the story doesn't make it to air. . . .

Making newsrooms more diverse and making a conscious effort to think about how we choose and construct stories emphatically and [become] conscious of our own biases will be key to building a media equipped for reconciliation.

It's also important to understand: News is a service, not a product. We have become far too concerned with how many clicks or views we get. I worry that, too often, important human rights stories impacting minority populations are overlooked because they will not get as many clicks, views, or likes as a story serving a larger population.

> For more discussion about reconciliation, see Chapter 3.5, "Reconciliation and Journalism."

DM: That's a really important systemic change that you're recommending. What about for individual journalists who feel it's important to be part of reconciliation, who ask, "What can I do?"

KP: The most important thing is to have the context. Twenty-five per cent of the staff at *APTN News* are not Indigenous, and they have proven you do not have to be Indigenous to do a fabulous job covering and serving Indigenous communities. To a certain point, because they're working for APTN, the brand helps them get access to communities, because it is trusted. But they have learned to work in an Indigenous newsroom culture. I don't know what that's like for them. (laugh) But I think there's a point where they walk in, and it all feels very strange and then slowly it gets to be normal. Because the culture is different. It tends to be a lot more humour and a lot more laughing and a lot more teasing and there's no hierarchy.

When I was a news boss there, I didn't walk around going, [British accent] "I'm the news boss." (laugh) They would have kicked my ass. (laugh) You don't act like that. So, it's a different dynamic.

I talked quite a bit to Kenneth Jackson about this.[11] He did talk about coming in and feeling very shy, following the other reporters around and just trying to see how they behaved or how they did things or how they handled things, how they spoke to people.

Your best bet is to talk to a lot of Indigenous people and ask them questions. Or find people who are experts in the community who can tell you what might be unique. What might be sensitive for that particular community and what kind of things are easy to talk about. They're all very different.

I remember, one of our reporters had worked out West. He'd go up to Ojibway communities, where people tend to be very quiet. And he moved out East, to the Algonquin communities, where I'm from. (laugh) And he's like, "Oh my God, the Ojibways, you can't get them to talk, and the Algonquins, you can't get them to shut up!" (laugh)

It's not just me, it's my culture. (laugh)

Discussion Questions

1. What benefits does Pugliese see in a solutions journalism approach?
2. How does Pugliese recommend navigating the challenges of Indigenous cultural protocols and journalism ethics?
3. What criteria does Pugliese use for evaluating a pitch on an Indigenous news story?

Suggested Works by Karyn Pugliese

"If Indigenous People Exercise Their Right to Say No . . . Then What?" *National Observer*, December 8, 2020. https://www.nationalobserver.com/2020/12/08/opinion/un-declaration-rights-indigenous-people-right-to-say-no-then-what

"Racism, Discrimination and Trauma Are Driving Indigenous Women Out of Media—We Must Do Better." *National Observer*, November 25, 2020. https://www.nationalobserver.com/2020/11/25/opinion/racism-discrimination-trauma-indigenous-women-media

"Media and Reconciliation." *Indigenous Peoples Atlas of Canada* (Toronto: Canadian Geographic, 2018). https://indigenouspeoplesatlasofcanada.ca/article/reconciliation/

Endnotes

1. In early 2020, solidarity actions took place across Canada in support of hereditary chiefs of the Wet'suwet'en Nation opposed to the Coastal GasLink pipeline crossing their traditional territory in northwestern B.C.
2. In autumn 2020, police clashed with protesters at a land reclamation camp, which centred on a parcel of land in Caledonia, Ontario, slated for a housing development. The land was part of the Haldimand Tract, which was granted to the Six Nations of the Grand River in 1784 for allying with the British during the American Revolution.
3. In October 2013, RCMP officers fired "sock rounds" and used tear gas to break up an anti-shale gas protest organized by the Elsipogtog First Nation in eastern New Brunswick.
4. In spring 2010, B.C.'s Cheam First Nation blocked access to a highway running through their reserve during a dispute over land and fishing rights.
5. In fall 2010, members of the Algonquin community of Kokumville in Quebec blockaded a logging road in La Verendrye Park in an attempt to keep a forestry company out of old-growth forest.
6. The Ipperwash Crisis was a dispute over Anishinaabe land that took place in Ipperwash Provincial Park, Ont., in 1995. Several members of the Chippewas of Kettle and Stoney Point First Nation occupied the park to assert claim to nearby land that had been expropriated from them during World War II. During a violent confrontation, the Ontario Provincial Police killed unarmed Anishinaabe protester Dudley George.
7. From 2002 to 2005, Canadian artist and broadcaster Rita Deverell was Director of News and Current Affairs at APTN.
8. The Review of Journalism described Paul Barnsley as "one of Canada's best Aboriginal affairs investigative reporters." Prior to becoming APTN's senior producer of investigative news in 2007, he wrote for *Windspeaker* and the Six Nations weekly newspaper *Tekawennake*.
9. In 2020, Oneida journalist Karl Dockstader was charged with mischief and failure to comply with a court-ordered injunction. Dockstader had spent half the summer reporting on the reclamation movement dubbed 1492 LandBack Lane. Dockstader's charges were later withdrawn.

10   Karyn Pugliese, "Silent No More: What Indigenous Women Journalists in Canada Face, and What Can Be Done to Help Them," in *Half the Story Is Never Enough: Threats Facing Women* (Canadian Commission for UNESCO, World Press Freedom Canada and Journalists for Human Rights, 2020).

11   Kenneth Jackson is a non-Indigenous journalist with nearly two decades of reporting experience who focuses on crime and social issues, including child welfare and wrongful convictions. He began working with APTN in 2012.

✦ 4.7 ✦

Punching Up: A Conversation with Tim Fontaine

Tim Fontaine is a journalist-turned-satirist who founded *Walking Eagle News*, a website that parodies Canadian and Indigenous news, in 2017.

Before becoming a pretend journalist, he was a real-life journalist for almost two decades, working for CBC and APTN. Since turning to comedy, he has written for CBC's *Because News* and contributed to and appeared on CTV's *The Beaverton*.

Tim is a member of the Sagkeeng First Nation, an Anishinaabe community in Manitoba. He now lives in Winnipeg with his family.

Tim Fontaine.

A Humorous Approach

DM: Let's talk first about how you use humour when you're approaching Indigenous subjects and going to ask them to be part of a story.

TF: Indigenous people use humour when dealing with hard things. A lot of us do. In real life, there was that approach to very serious things. It's kind of become cliché now, but there's a lot of laughter at Indigenous funerals, let's put it that way....

When I became a professional mainstream journalist, I realized that a lot of journalists had gallows humour. Especially because of the work that we do. It's not making light of whatever it is that you're dealing with. That's how people cope: grim, dark, gallows humour. So, that carried over really easily....

Journalists and Indigenous people were both funny, so when I made that switch to do *Walking Eagle News*, a lot of what I was doing was expanding on jokes that I had already told on Twitter. Jokes that I had made when I was a journalist. It was a humorous look at things that are very serious.

> For more on Indigenous humour and the news, see Chapter 2.7, "Breaking News: Indians Are Funny!"

Being Teased

DM: As far as being in the community, I've heard you say being teased is important. That if you're *not* being teased, then maybe you should think about the way you're operating.

TF: Yeah. That's a very important thing you should learn when you go into Indigenous communities—that they might tease you. If they don't tease you or if they are being very, very cold with you, then there's something wrong. (laugh) You might have to change your approach. That's not always true, but that's a good indication—if you're going in and people are joking around, then there's that rapport, no matter how serious it is. . . .

There is a fine line between you coming in and initiating the joking and being disrespectful, as opposed to going in, immediately being teased, and knowing basically that this community is taking a liking to you.

DM: Rapport is part of the trust-building process, really. It's okay to be teased, and it's actually important.

TF: Yeah, but it's tough. The business has changed. I was listening to a British TV presenter named Ray Mears.[1] He did a lot of documentaries on Indigenous communities and he was talking about the importance of time and how much time he used to have to go into these Australian Indigenous communities. They would spend a week there beforehand, just letting themselves warm up with the community. Forming little bonds. It's very rare to get that anymore. . . .

Your time in the community is [brief]. The amount of material you put out is very often very short. Everything is just so condensed now that it is tough to make those relationships. I understand that, but that's one of the problems—we don't have enough time.

DM: Taking that time ends up improving the quality of the piece.

TF: If you're in an area where there are Indigenous people, there's nothing stopping you from forming those bonds beforehand. I knew some reporters in Manitoba that were just constantly calling communities. Even if they weren't going to do a story, they're just constantly calling and letting them know that they're there and they're interested in what they're doing. They've done very good work.

I don't think you should be a stranger to those communities. You should know that there's stuff going on there and it's a good idea to get to know who some of the people are. It only takes a couple of minutes.

Using Humour in News Stories

DM: News is, for the most part, serious business. How did you approach incorporating humour into a news story? It's one thing to do a satire piece, but in a straight-up news piece, is there a place for humour?

TF: It depends on the story. When I was out on the East Coast, you just try to put some of the colour of the community in and how they have a sense of humour. I think that's the way to do it. But it's a tough line for you as a journalist to try to be funny and make a joke about something that's going on. It's very easy for that to be misconstrued as disrespect. You don't want to seem like you're being flippant. You have to be very careful about that. But there's been times where I've shown the humorous colour of things that are happening in the community. It just shows who we are. . . .

DM: You talk about adding colour to a story and to a community. What you're saying is that it's important to give your audience a more holistic picture of the place?

TF: I often think of coverage of Oka. I'm not saying that there were lots of moments to laugh because I wasn't there. I don't know for sure. It's one of the stories that got lost in history now, but I absolutely remember, they had a water balloon fight.[2] Right in the middle of this, it was just this moment. Some of the photos and things that people on the Warrior side were saying, and the way they were behaving, was very humorous. It was very rezzy, funny, Indigenous humour. That absolutely came through. That sort of colour is important to show. A lot of it has to do with busting that image of stoicism . . . It's nice to show us being contemporary and funny and balanced people.

DM: You mentioned rezzy humour at a really serious time at Oka. Some of our humour is quite dark. How should a journalist interpret that?

TF: You have to be careful. You have to know what it is that you're dealing with, and you have to be able to read it. That's why it is very important to have Indigenous people in your newsroom. Especially if you're going to be covering Indigenous stories.

At one of the roadblocks in Saskatchewan, there was a guy who said his name was Chisk Dieter.[3] (laugh) There was another guy—and there are Indigenous people in CBC Manitoba's newsroom—but when they [CBC] went up north to cover the two young guys that had gone on a killing spree. Very serious story. And there's an Indigenous guy who said his name was Tugguy Lawrenchuk, another situation where he used Indigenous slang to say that's what his name was[4] . . . (laugh)

DM: For the super . . . (laugh)

TF: Plude Choochman was another, which is so specific to Manitoba.[5] Some producer in Toronto is not going to know what that means. The guy is being interviewed by CTV and he had given his name. . . .

DM: Plude Choochman?

TF: That's a very, very specific Manitoba reference. So "plude" means "penis." "Chooching" is slang for masturbation. (laugh) So the guy said his name is Plude Choochman. And there's this very serious interview with him, right? (laugh)

DM: (laughing)

TF: You read the article, it says, "Choochman, an organizer of the protest, says they're going to be coming . . . " (laugh)

DM: (laughing)

TF: Indigenous people on Twitter after that said, "This is why you need Indigenous journalists." (laugh) That's the thing about joking, how to interpret joking and the mood of a community. That's why it's important to know Indigenous people and it's also important to have Indigenous people in your newsroom.

Punching Up

DM: You've said Indigenous humour rarely punches down. Can you explain that?

TF: You're making fun of the people that are above you. You're making fun of leaders. You're making fun of the people that have "power" over you. Good Indigenous humour, that's the way they do it. But they also punch sideways. So, you tease your friends, you tease your family, you tease the people you like. That's good Indigenous humour to me. When it starts punching down and you start making fun of the people below you, that's where it becomes a problem.

DM: It's a very complex way of keeping people humble.

TF: It's a fine line—you've heard of the Indian crabs saying, where they pull you down?

DM: For the sake of our readers, tell me the Indian crab story.

TF: There's two guys fishing, an Indigenous guy and a white guy. White guy has a bucket full of crabs; his crabs keep crawling out. He looks over at the Indigenous guy. His crabs are staying politely in the bucket. He says, "How do you do that?" Guy says "Well, they're Indigenous crabs. Anytime one tries to get up, the others pull him down."

That's an example of a sort of bad humour, where you're getting too big—we're going to tease you in a way that brings you down. That's not usually what it is.

Sometimes they tease you because they're proud of you. Think of Ernest Moonias. (laugh) Ernest Moonias—for people who don't know—is a very famous singer from northern Manitoba who is the subject of thousands and thousands of memes. We tease the people that we love and care about. It's a good thing to be teased.

Humour as Reconciliation

DM: You're as concerned as I am about the way news focuses on tragedy and conflict so often. Do you think if assignment editors and newsrooms become more conscious of Indigenous humour, they can shift the narrative?

TF: We're seeing it now. We're seeing where our humour, the things that we laugh at, are making news now. It shows that we're a very diverse group of people and also that we're humans. We laugh. There's joy in our communities.

I think about Indigenous people adopting Baby Yoda. Just a silly thing that actually became a fairly big news story. That's strictly born out of our sense of humour and our cultural adoptions. Because everybody watched *The Mandalorian* and looked at that thing and said, "That baby is Indigenous!" It just became this thing.

It shows that newsrooms are trying to get their finger on the pulse of what's happening.

> See Chapter 1.4, "Positive versus Negative Stories," for more discussion about expanding Indigenous news coverage.

DM: You've also said there's a role for humour and reconciliation. I use the term *reconciliation* with you guardedly (laugh), but what are your thoughts on that?

TF: That Baby Yoda is an example there, where we could all have a good laugh at this thing. That can't be bad. Our humour was a way of opening up a window into our world that was not like the other stuff. That wasn't the Four Ds, like you've talked about. We have joy, we have creativity. Yeah, we have all of these bad things in our communities. Sometimes it's nice to just look at it and say, "You know what? They've got a pretty good sense of humour or they're very creative to be able to do this."

You see a lot of really cool stories now about how this economy is being built on things like Instagram, Facebook, Twitter. Beadwork or all of these things that communities do to connect with other communities. They're often very humorous and very joyful. That's why it's important [that] newsrooms cover those things, because our communities tend to really like when that happens. Finally, a news story where it's not people dying . . . People get joy from that, and that's an important thing.

There is a reconciliation that needs to happen between journalism and Indigenous communities. That's a big part of it, where it's trust that's being built between these two cultures.

Explain the Rules

DM: You say there's a reconciliation that needs to happen. What needs to happen?

TF: Trust is a big one. Journalists tend to have rules that have been created by them and that communities don't understand. One of the biggest things that I was asked when I was a journalist was, "What are you going to ask me? What are the questions? Can you send the questions?"

That's a huge no-no in journalism, and yet we rarely tell them why. We rarely explain to them why we do things the way we do them. Why they *can't* see the story before it's published. Why they *can't* approve things that are being said before they hit the air.

If they're not told clearly why journalists do that, there's always going to be mistrust. Some of the rules don't make sense to Indigenous communities. The way a journalist behaves, and the rules that journalists follow, often are mysterious to people and frustrating.

Political reporters especially live—or should live—by a very rigid code. We have to talk to this person, we have to talk to that person. For somebody who's in a community, they don't understand why. You can't just get frustrated and say "Balance." It has to be explained to people.

That's also the problem with the speed of journalism these days. The relationship that newsrooms have with Indigenous communities is often parachuting in when something really bad happens. There's no long-term relationship. When the story is done, they're gone.

It's all about building relationships. . . . If you're in an area where there's Indigenous people, there's nothing stopping you from having ongoing relationships with those people. It's not going to mess up your bias; it's just good to have contacts.

"Transparency Is a Huge Thing"

DM: You mentioned sharing questions or offering editorial approval over a story before it airs. You're not suggesting that when you were a working journalist, you changed that practice?

TF: No, no, no. But my point was that we rarely had time to explain to people why that was.

Transparency is a huge thing. When you go in with this set of rules, the people you're talking to don't understand. They don't even know that you have a set of rules. So, if you're expecting someone to trust you enough to tell you something very terrible, then they need to know that these are the set of rules that you have.

That information sharing has to go both ways. That often doesn't happen. Part of that is media literacy, but communities are dealing with other things. They don't always have time to learn the rules of journalism. The rules journalists live by are not that transparent and they're not that understandable.

DM: You're also expressing some pretty fundamental values, in terms of respect and consent. Are there times that you lost interviews because you were so transparent?

TF: No, but it was tough because there's been times when people that I've talked to felt burned by the story. The big thing they would say, "You come in here, you talk to me for an hour and then you show two clips." Or, "I was only on there for 15 seconds." They don't understand the constraints that journalists are under. They don't understand that there's not a lot of time to do this. They don't understand that.

The other thing that's tough for them to understand is that the story is not entirely about them. Very rarely is a story entirely about one person. Or the cutting room floor—that's another thing. You go in and talk to somebody and you get calls or emails from somebody later, "You talked to me. Why wasn't I in the story?" You have to take the time to explain, "Somebody else said the same thing you said." Or whatever reason you had for not including every voice that you talked to.

We take for granted the length of stories, the way journalism articles work. All of those things that we take for granted and we live by, communities don't often understand them. . . .

That simple thing of telling a community and giving them a heads up and saying, "Look, we're publishing a story about this. You should know." Or, "Remember when I talked to you a couple days ago? That story is going to be published right away." Because especially with MMIWG communities, there's been a lot of times where people have said they felt blindsided by it, even though they had talked to them. It is a difficult thing to suddenly see—you know, you're going about your day and all of a sudden, you see one of your deepest traumas publicly shared all over the place.

Every step of the way there, there has to be some sort of communication with that community.

You don't have to give approval for the story, but I just think you have to be open with them and say, "This is how it's going to work. I'm going to talk to you. I'm going to formulate a story. I'm going to talk to a couple of other people. You may not agree with them, but I have to talk to these other people. The story is going to come out probably around this time. I'll probably give you an email or give you a shout and let you know this is going to be published tomorrow."

And you remind them, "I'm sorry, but you cannot see the story before. That's not how it works. But I want you to know when it's coming out."

> More tips on building relationships are offered in Chapter 3.3, "Accountability, Reciprocity, and Criticism."

Cultivating Sources

DM: What you're talking about is accountability. That takes time and relationship-building. It seems like that's really important to your approach.

TF: But I also find that, for some journalists, it seems almost foreign. But then, when you really think about people that cover politics, people behind the scenes are always in touch with so-and-so. They have a process. They have what's called "contacts." It's called creating relationships and not friendships. It's important that we say that it's often not a friendship, but it is a relationship.

There is a give-and-take that needs to happen. You see that that happens, especially with political reporters. Politicians and their offices get way more back-and-forth for a story than other people do. That's something that we need to apply to—I hate to say it—to real people that we talk to. Why do they not get the same consideration as a politician or business leader?

I've lived in Ottawa. I've covered politics. I've seen the way those relationships are, with your sources and your contacts. It should be just as respectful as that. Maybe even more respectful because you're dealing with somebody who doesn't understand what you're doing.

Making Mistakes

DM: Let's talk a little bit about *Walking Eagle*. You have no problems finding material to satirize almost daily. What does that say about the state of news media.

TF: It's got a long way to go. What happens is, there's high turnover, newsrooms are shrinking—we're in the middle of a major transformation of journalism, and particularly mainstream news, but also Indigenous media. Because while mainstream newsrooms are shrinking and evolving and changing, Indigenous journalism is growing. There are probably more Indigenous journalists now than there have ever been.

Mistakes happen when that happens. There's room for mistakes when we're learning how to cover stories differently and we're learning how to try and do something in hours that used to take a lot more time. Because I remember, there'd be days where something breaks and you've got not a hell of a lot of time to try to pull a story together. The age of beats is dying. Every newsroom is not going to have a specialist. Every single day you're an expert in something else. I understand what's happening—I just don't agree with it all. Because the stakes are so high. Because oftentimes, the mistakes you make affect real people.

It's also why I don't miss being a real journalist (laugh), because I hated that pressure of knowing the night before a big story publishes, feeling that fear and dread that you've done something wrong—not on purpose, obviously—and it's going to have a very real effect on a human being. I don't miss that at all.

DM: That feeling never goes away your whole career.

TF: Oh yeah! I've made very big mistakes with *Walking Eagle News* as well. It's usually that punching up thing. At least if you're punching up and you swing and miss (laugh), it's often a lot better than trying to punch down and really messing up and hurting someone.

News through an Indigenous Lens

DM: To get back to your journalism career, you spent a lot of time at APTN. Is there something that mainstream should take away from the way Indigenous broadcasters approach news?

TF: It's all about perspective. I found that APTN and CBC Indigenous were quite good at taking news from *our* perspective. The way a story lands for us and the way that feels and that sensibility when crafting a story is important to learn. There's nothing wrong with doing that. You're seeing the world through a (different) lens.

That's the thing with news. When you see a story and the things that shock them and the things that surprised them or the things they're talking about are often from *their* perspective. If you want people to consume your news—it's not about bias; it's just about understanding that there's another worldview that's existing right here in Canada. . . .

DM: You said thinking about an Indigenous perspective and how this story is going to land is not a question of bias. What do you mean?

TF: It has to do with the [fact that the] way Indigenous people are going to consume or react to that story is probably going to be much different than if it was about a small town or if it was about a certain area of Winnipeg. It's easy for a community to feel attacked by a story.

That's true of any community, I'm sure. But there is this feeling, especially when it has to do with health or things that are out of a community's control . . . there's a tendency for communities to feel like Canada is pointing at them and saying, "Look at all the wrong stuff that's happening there. Aren't those people bad?" You need to have respect for stories like that. Often in smaller local markets, you'll see a very, very, very brief story about a car crash in an Indigenous community and it'll say, "Alcohol not suspected." For Indigenous communities to see that, it feels like it was very important for somebody to write that in there. There's a tendency to feel like you're being ostracized or judged. Whereas oftentimes you'll see the same story about some small farming community and they'll name the person and have photos of the person. They get to be humanized in stories.

Mainstream media are so big on balance; make sure that's balanced too. I do see it happening now. Unfortunately, we do cover tragedy. They're often going out there, trying to talk to who these people are, they try to find out who the neighbours are and get a rounder picture of who these people are.

Whereas before, it was "Brown person dead, alcohol suspected." (laugh) That's often how we felt about the news. It's changing, and a lot of it has to do with the fact that there are people in newsrooms who do have connections to the communities.

Expanding Indigenous Voices

DM: Has there ever been a big challenge that you faced when you were covering the Indigenous beat? And how did you overcome it?

TF: Not being able to find someone. We often ended up using the same voices over and over again, because those people answered their phones. I still grappled with that, right till the end. There's a reason why we see Indigenous politicians or Indigenous academics in stories. Because they're immediately available.

> See Chapter 2.3, "Who Represents the 'Indigenous Perspective'?" for more on diversifying sources.

The one thing I tried to do, the thing that I criticize the media about, I tried to find out who these other people were. I tried to keep track of whoever was talking about whatever it was, so that when the time came to talk to someone, I could call them and hopefully coax them into talking to me.

That was a big thing, the importance of cultivating a relationship and understanding that not everybody is going to be the pundit. They're not going to give you those sound bites that you want often. But they'll give you something. That's something I tried to do as much as I could—try to bring new voices.

Discussion Questions

1. What are some of the dangers of using Indigenous humour inappropriately?
2. Why does Fontaine emphasize the importance of journalists being transparent with Indigenous people?
3. Have you ever been teased while reporting in Indigenous communities? How did you respond?

Suggested Works by Tim Fontaine

"Canada Discriminates against Children on Reserves, Tribunal Rules." *CBC Indigenous*, January 26, 2016. https://www.cbc.ca/news/indigenous/canada-discriminates-against-children-on-reserves-tribunal-rules-1.3419480

"'How Are My Indians?' Queen Asks Trudeau." *Walking Eagle News*, April 18, 2018. https://walkingeaglenews.com/2018/04/18/how-are-my-indians-queen-asks-trudeau/

"Reporter Bursts into Flames After Word Racism Published without Quotes." *Walking Eagle News*, March 1, 2018. https://walkingeaglenews.com/2018/03/01/reporter-bursts-into-flames-after-word-racism-published-without-quotes/

Endnotes

1. Ray Mears is a British woodsman, author, and TV presenter. His TV appearances cover bush craft and survival techniques. He hosted a BBC show called *Ray Mears Goes Walkabout*, based in Australia, in 2008.
2. On September 25, 1990, in the final days of the standoff at Oka, Canadian soldiers turned a water hose on an individual Mohawk Warrior behind the barricades. Other Mohawk Warriors responded by taunting the soldiers and launching water balloons at them. The incident did not escalate further.
3. On February 8, 2020, CTV Regina News ran a story about a road blockade that included clips from "Chisk Dieter." "Chisk" in Cree translates to "ass." https://twitter.com/anishinaboy/status/1226147250637811717
4. On July 25, 2019, CBC Newsnet ran a story about a manhunt that included clips from a gentleman identified as "Tugguy Lawrenchuk." "Tugguy" is a Cree word for "penis." https://twitter.com/lenardmonkman1/status/1154488630355857409?lang=en
5. On February 12, 2020, CTV News Winnipeg ran a story about a pipeline protest that included a quote from a man identified as "Plude Choochman." "Plude" in some dialects of Anishinaabemowin means "penis." https://twitter.com/lenardmonkman1/status/1227728280675061762?lang=en

✦ 4.8 ✦

The Need for Knowledge-based Journalism: A Conversation with Merelda Fiddler-Potter

Merelda Fiddler-Potter is a proud Métis woman, whose ancestors fought in both the 1869–70 Red River Resistance and the 1885 Battle of Batoche. She was born and raised in Meadow Lake, Saskatchewan—a town founded by her Métis ancestors—and was recently awarded a Vanier Canada Graduate Scholarship

Merelda's research explores the media's role in helping Canadians learn the truth of past and present colonial policies and the impact on Indigenous Peoples. She is a sessional lecturer at First Nations University of Canada and the University of Regina. She was also the Dallas W. Smythe Chair at the University of Regina School of Journalism.

Prior to entering academia, Fiddler-Potter was an award-winning current affairs producer and reporter for CBC Saskatchewan, recognized by the Radio Television Digital News Association of Canada for her work with Saskatchewan's murdered and missing Indigenous women.

Merelda Fiddler-Potter.

Source: Photo courtesy of Merelda Fiddler-Potter.

She is currently a PhD candidate at the Johnson Shoyama Graduate School of Public Policy in Regina, and lives in Regina with her husband, two children, and two goofy Labradors.

On Métis Coverage

DM: You're a proud Métis woman. What's your observation about how the Métis have been covered by the mainstream media?

MFP: There are two kinds of stories that I see right now. There's either the stories of division, amongst who is Métis and what does it mean to be Métis and how do you know who you are, and then there's the stories of people who claim to be Métis who've made a lot of money being Métis, whatever their version of it is. . . .

People seem to think that Métis means a little mix of any Indigenous group there is, but it's not quite where we come from. . . . The real issue is there are Indigenous people out there who are not status, maybe not connected to their communities in any way. The only other place they can think to look for some sort of belonging is in the Métis community.

Journalists get quite focused on the Métis community being mixed. They don't really understand our history or where we come from or why certain groups are Métis. That idea of being mixed doesn't make you Métis. You need to be part of the community.

Probably the best way I've heard it described was by the Indigenous Screen Institute in regards to Michelle Latimer.[1] Ancestry is not identity. I'm working on a policy paper right now talking about this—because all of these grants and scholarships and other things that are meant to bridge the gaps between Indigenous people and non-Indigenous people—to bring those ideas in to make sure that the communities are connecting. Reconciliation is about us having these really difficult conversations. How can we do that when the people involved in selecting the winners of these scholarships—tens of thousands of dollars in grants for arts and other things where our stories are being told—are not even aware of what it means to be part of a community, or to have to do the work to be part of that community? There's a lot of work. So that idea of who is Indigenous and who is not—if you don't have people in the newsroom who can say to you, "I don't know who that is," or "I don't know what this means." Or someone around a hiring table or a scholarship granting organization. It's very easy to say "Oh, I'm Métis. I'm mixed." But that means you're part of a group. But it might not be my group.

DM: We've heard concerns from the Métis community about the claims of Eastern Métis or Woodland Métis. What should the process be for a journalist, in terms of trying to verify the ancestry claims of people they're interviewing?

MFP: Those communities have to have a conversation about what their ancestry is. If it doesn't fit the current definition of Métis, it might be that this is something else. [I'm not saying] their identities are not legit. They are. I'm not trying to be a purist because Métis people can't really be purist about almost anything. (laugh) We are mixed, but we come from very specific communities.

For journalists, you need to know who different groups of people are. When I first started journalism school, people would say "I think she's Mohawk." I'm like, "What? The Mohawk people live in the East. I'm from Saskatchewan." It's bizarre to me.

There's a real fear for journalists in trying to understand who is who because it's not defined the same in every space. Métis people are particularly difficult. One of the things that I like to remind people [of] is that there were a lot of people who were removed from their communities and their families. Who are residential school survivors, who are the kids of residential school survivors, who were never allowed to return to their communities. Who are Sixties Scoop kids. Who are inner-city. Who don't have a connection to community. That identity is still theirs, and no one else can be part of taking away [that identity] or giving that identity to them. There is a certain amount of work that needs to be done by an individual person to come into your own in your community.

I know because even though I grew up in my community, my dad left when I was two. I wasn't as connected to his family. It's probably hard to believe now, but I was a really shy kid. And I really struggled with identity. Thankfully, when I came to Regina, I ended up at

First Nations University by accident. And Mervin Brass brought me in.[2] It was him who kind of saved me and helped me understand who I was. Then there were all these other people who helped me understand, but who also were very clear that to be Métis, you really had to do the work to figure out where your community was. What your history is. Who are the other people that you need to have conversations with? You know, go to ceremony, be part of things and really know your place. Not your place in a pecking order, [but] your place in being involved in supporting community.

Journalists are very stuck on the ancestry piece of this. The ancestry piece is what people are looking at. That's not our identity. For example, I have some German ancestry. My grandma's grandpa was German. But I don't like sausage and I'm allergic to chocolate. (laugh) . . . I'm not German but I have some German ancestry. That's where people are getting stuck. They see ancestry but not identity. For Indigenous people, ancestry is included in identity, but it's in all of the actions that you take. It's in the intentions you have when you do things. It's deeply personal. It's taken me a really long time to get here, so I understand how that can be confusing to other people, but the idea that somebody's ancestry is the only thing that ties them to community is why a lot of non-Indigenous people might be able to say things like "I'm Irish."

But what makes you Irish?

Indigenous Identity Politics

DM: Because of that disconnection from community that's happened to so many Indigenous people, self-identification is often seen as a gold standard. Do you think that journalists should be doing more than just asking people how they identify?

MFP: We have to start there, but I think the other piece of all of this is they have to ask themselves, "What is that connection to community, and what are people in the community saying?"

When I read the Michelle Latimer stories, the answers that have been given have never been, "This is my community." The answers are, "I'm going to hire a geological company to prove that I have some ancestry." Well, that's not good enough.

Journalists should start keying off that. The other thing is, we like talking to Indigenous people when they're kind of outside of community because there's real fear still that journalists have about going into Indigenous communities. If you're actually in an Indigenous community—if you're on a reserve, if you're in one of those urban spaces where people gather—you're not going to run the same risks that you will run when you're not in the community. So, telling stories in the context of the community will really help you. Because the Elders in the room know who is giving you a bill of goods or who's been using this as a crutch. They'll tell you. They'll tell you, sort of a little side-eye. (laugh) But you need to start getting comfortable in communities. Those communities will give you all the information that you need because you're in their community.

> The importance of having a diverse range of Indigenous voices is discussed in Chapter 2.3, "Who Represents the 'Indigenous Perspective'?"

The other part of it might be adding a couple of disclaimers in there, which is what we're really good at. Which is, "She *says* she's Mohawk, she *says* she's Métis." Then finally, if we're going to talk about the groups outside of what the Métis National Council represents, I don't think we can be too cavalier about the fights that Métis people on the Prairies had to have in order to be recognized and still have to have.

Métis people who aren't recognized by the Sixties Scoop settlements. Entire residential school communities shut out because they were day schools for Métis people, but yet they experienced the same things. Resettlement communities like Green Lake, which is near Meadow Lake, where Métis people were shoved and moved and ripped out of their communities, which they burned down and then put them on trains and made them walk to Green Lake. There's some real history there, so when Métis people on the Prairies get frustrated about everybody using a term that they have had to live, that's lived experience.

That's kind of the third piece of this I would say to journalists. There's ancestry—identity in the community as you stand today—and then there's the lived experience that people have. When you talk to them, maybe they can't get reconnected to their community, because they are a Sixties Scoop kid. That's the lived experience piece. People like Joseph Boyden and Latimer and others, they're going to be missing these things[3] . . . and that's really what a journalist has to ask themselves.

DM: That's where the red flag should be going off.

MFP: That's when you should say to yourself, "Damn, something's not right."

Journalists as Teachers of History

DM: In the research work you've been doing, you're looking into the media's role in terms of helping Canadians learn about past and present colonial policies. What *is* the media's role?

MFP: The first thing is mainstream media needs to look probably more specifically at language than they ever have before.

> See Chapter 3.1, "Terminology and Lexicon," on why terminology and lexicon matter.

I'll give you an example. I was at CBC, and they asked if we could talk about MMIWG. I said, "I'll give you an example of something that I started to realize when we talk about governing narratives, how we view Indigenous people." There are a lot of people who really want to avoid language, like in this case, "prostitute" or "hooker." They want to sort of watch how they use the language around where an individual comes from.

But when you think about what a governing narrative is, it's the way we describe an issue. Instead, what I started to read over and over and over again was the phrase "at risk." It's not politically correct, but it's descriptive. But it means the exact same thing. It means a hooker or a prostitute or somebody who uses drugs, or a combination of all of those things. That's what that means. That phrase hasn't changed the way we view Indigenous women. It's just a new way of saying it without using a word that almost everybody finds offensive. . . .

DM: How do journalists go about tackling colonial history within the mediums that we're working in?

MFP: That's the institution of how something is made, right? That's kind of the unwritten rule that radio has to be short. We may not see a big change in how radio and TV stories are done in the near future, but I think journalistic institutions are going to have to start asking themselves what it is they want to do.

I'll give you an example. A lot of times when people explain the Sixties Scoop and they try to explain what that means for identity, they're not able to do it. Because they haven't actually explained a lot about it. Just they're a "Sixties Scoop survivor." If anyone doesn't know what that is, they just rely on them to go look it up. So, they'll tell a story [like] "so and so is here and this is what they're asking for from the government." These stories eventually get put online, because most of them do now . . . just kind of like a dressed-up version of whatever hit the radio. Super short. That's the only place you have now where you could have explained things. But, instead, it remains a mystery that people have to go look up. Or there'll be so many embedded links in a story—I counted once, like, 14 embeds! Have you ever tried to click through the CBC site on 14 embeds?! Like, ads pop up now . . . (laugh)

I think you have to start saying to yourself, "If all I'm doing is confirming for most Canadians that what we have is a problem, then I'm not part of the solution.". . .

Our job is to connect and communicate. It's to tell stories that matter. I can't even think about the number of times we had conversations about what is the goal of journalism? It's to tell stories. Sometimes what I'm hearing is not a story. It's disjointed history and contemporary complaints or concerns. But it's not a story. So, if truly at the heart of what you want to do is tell these effective stories, you may have to start doing that differently. . . .

> For more advice on how to fit in the context, refer to Chapter 3.2, "Context and Colonial Amnesia."

How Journalism Can Be Part of Reconciliation

DM: The TRC has said journalists are not arm's length from reconciliation and that they play a role in reconciliation. What do you see as the role for an individual journalist who says, "I want to do the right thing. I want to be part of reconciliation"?

MFP: Let's take one step back from that journalist and let's ask what the journalism schools themselves are doing in terms of preparing journalists to work not only in Indigenous communities, but in culturally diverse communities. Every other academic unit—education, justice, policing, social work—they're all light years ahead of where journalism institutions are in terms of preparing people to go and work in Indigenous communities. They have reconciliation classes. They have basic Indigenous studies so you know the history of your country. A lot of these places are doing self-reflection work, [encouraging students to ask,] "How do I fit into this story?"

What are we doing to prepare new journalists? Some of that is definitely the schools asking, "What are your requirements to be here?" If your requirements to be here are a couple of history classes, some English, maybe an extra language, and then get that math out of the way that journalists hate doing, then how does that make you a well-rounded person at all to be able to go out into the field?

You don't know the communities that you're going to be in. You're lacking some of your history and now we're going to go out there and we're gonna give them hell. Well, you know what? Here's what's going to happen. You're going to go out to a place where people know you don't know the history and they're either going to talk circles around you or you're going to be the kind of journalist who says, "I don't know about that," and you're gonna have to take longer to figure it out. . . .

The next thing that's going to have to happen for journalists is they're going to have to admit that they have some bias walking into every situation. Because we do. And even though we can tell very balanced stories and we'll try to get a range of opinions put on there, you are going to have to admit that you thought something before you walked into the story, and you didn't think it after. You don't know what you don't know.

Take Treaty Land Entitlement [TLE].[4] [It was formally recognized in] 1992 here, but they started working on it in 1976. So, when I first told stories about TLE, I didn't know all the history of 1976. I wasn't born when it started. So, I had to actually learn. I was fortunate, in that some of the Chiefs that I was talking to at the time were more than willing to explain that process to me. There were other places we could get that information too and figure it all out. But I heard somebody recently describe TLE to me as a "modern-day treaty."

Well, if you're living in B.C., you know that a modern-day treaty is not TLE.[5] Because TLE is a framework agreement that's meant to address the inequities of the first round of treaties. If you don't know that and you're living in Saskatchewan and you're trying to tell these stories and you're talking about urban reserves and why we have more urban reserves and how that's connected to TLE—when you go on and you explain that a newer urban reserve is being developed, you and I both know what the comments look like under that story on social media. There's no context for people. Or there'll be one line that says, "There was a shortfall, and now we fixed it." (laugh) No idea why, no nothing.

So, I wasn't always the most popular journalist, because I was always trying to add more details. I'm standing at a desk arguing, "We have to say that because people won't know that." (laugh)

DM: You're saying those internal newsroom arguments are important to have. You gotta fight for that space.

MFP: You gotta fight for that space, and you've got to fight to actually inform people, because if you tell the story without that information then you're *not* doing the only thing that you've set out to do, which is inform the Canadian conversation.

> See Chapter 3.5, "Reconciliation and Journalism," for more discussion about the role of a journalist and reconciliation.

"What Did You Do to Inform That Conversation?"

DM: You talk about understanding your biases. You're talking about objectivity. Have you seen any examples of reporters who have done a good job when they're working with Indigenous communities of broadcasting to their audience their biases and where they're coming from?

MFP: In Indigenous methods of research, in my academic world, which is a little easier, part of what we do is self-location. It's really setting up who you are, where you come from, what you're using. It's so much easier to do in academia than it is in journalism. . . .

A good example would be, in Saskatchewan, we had a young First Nations girl who wore a shirt to school that said "Got Land? Thank an Indian." The conversation in the newsroom about what that meant informed everything that happened after.[6] I think a non-Indigenous person ended up covering that story, but the conversation we had in the newsroom about this girl was everything. Because they said, "Imagine being from Treaty 4 territory where the school that you're attending is off-reserve." Most of the other people in that area own land that you no longer have any access to. And your reserve, like some of the reserves, they're broken up into these little pieces, like all over that territory. So, imagine you're 15 and you start really learning some of this history and you're like, "I'm gonna make a statement. I'm going to show people I know what is up here." But that *initial* conversation—about who gets offended and why—very quickly shifted because we had Indigenous people in the newsroom who were able to say, "Wait a second. Before we just talk about people having an argument over a sweatshirt that this girl wore and her being told to go home and change, what if we had a *better* conversation about why would she be motivated?"

DM: What her point was!

MFP: Exactly. She's got a decent point, and she gets to say it. Because *that* is the way of hosting that conversation. She came out and said, "This is why I'm wearing this shirt; this is what I'm trying to say here." She has every right to add that to the conversation, and we have a responsibility to effectively say, "I didn't know this." I don't actually often hear a lot of journalists saying—and this would be very actually easy, in all of the live hits that get done now—it would be a very easy spot for a journalist to acknowledge what they actually learned. "Did you know this? Because I didn't know this, and this is why it's in my story." That sends a kind of message that you can't really get from just trying to insert facts here and there. . . .

In the end, a journalist can and will have a role in reconciliation, whether we want to or not, and it will really be [a case of], "What did you do to inform that conversation?" But before you can even ask yourself about that conversation, you have to ask yourself what you bring to the table in terms of knowledge to be able to even *participate* in that conversation. Because, not everybody has the knowledge to participate in every conversation. I'm not going to be very good at quantum physics conversations, I can tell you that much. It takes a lot of reading for me to be able to understand a minuscule part of that. But we treat history and geography and all these things like you can just pick it up that day and become an expert. If we stop that, if we say, "Actually, I'm not an expert in that. What are we trying to get here?" it would change the way we talk about doing stories.

Why Knowledge-Based Journalism Is Needed

DM: If journalists don't start to rethink our modes of sharing stories, what kind of harms are we committing?

MFP: More people are checking out of that national conversation. You have a whole group of people who will disengage. . . . Then we're not creating that space where everyone can talk about these things. That's the hardest part, [that] people need the information about what has happened to understand the contemporary context of a situation. It is just essential. As Canada becomes more diverse and we have more people move here who have no basis in any Canadian history, really, until they get here and start learning it, they're going to miss this piece. And this piece informs how you vote. This piece informs how you participate in the system. This piece informs the people who run our education systems, the people who run the justice system, the people who get elected to government. . . .

So, the role that journalism really plays is really just explaining how we got here, because nothing will change until we understand how we got here.

That's why, when people say things like, "Well, money won't fix things," when we're talking about residential school survivors or Sixties Scoop, you're right. This is meant to bridge some gaps or to meet the legal needs that our country has, but that won't be enough. We have to understand how we got here, so we can try to move forward together.

DM: I'm putting on my best *Star Trek* voice here, but how would you respond to a journalist who said, "Dammit Jim, I'm a journalist, not a teacher!" What would you say to that?

MFP: Until our knowledge and our story . . . are part of the elite knowledge, people will never understand why we're trying to walk down this road of reconciliation and what it is that we need reconciled.

It's not just, "Read this book about what happened in residential schools." That's such a small part of what reconciliation is, when you look at all the [TRC] Calls to Action. Specifically, in journalism, we're asking people to understand the role they play in either a) shaping this conversation, so that we have a better future together, or b) perpetuating the same conversation, which means we will change nothing. Journalists are so key. I cannot overstate how key they are, but I know that there are a lot of people who are getting frustrated by the medium. . . .

We're problematizing people over and over and over again, and we're *not* problems. We are people who have been affected by history, the way many groups have been affected by history. In this country, until we figure out what that means and how we can work together and just acknowledge that, it's just so hard to have faith that somebody else can tell your story.

If we keep saying, "Dammit Jim, I'm a journalist, I don't do history lessons. I tell you what's happening right now." Well, if you can't tell people *why* this is happening right now, who's going to care? If you can't tell them how we got here, why would anyone care about that? Why would I bother tuning in? I'll just go learn about it myself. And not everyone is going to do the work. . . .

If mainstream organizations want to keep Indigenous people engaged with them, they have to start asking themselves what it is that they want from their Indigenous journalists. They have to start asking themselves, "If we've told stories like this since the beginning of journalism, is this what we want to keep doing? Or can we make actual spaces that Indigenous journalists want to be a part of?" And I think there are a lot of non-Indigenous journalists who are trying to create space to tell bigger stories. This is not an individual effort—it's going to be a group effort. But organizations themselves know they're struggling with ratings, know they're struggling to keep newsrooms afloat. If we lose journalism, we run the very, very real risk of losing probably one of the most important pieces of our democracy.

Discussion Questions

1. What are some of the problematic ways Métis have been covered by the media?
2. What is an essential aspect of the media's role in reconciliation from Fiddler-Potter's perspective?
3. Why is it important for journalism schools to teach Indigenous content?

Suggested Works by Merelda Fiddler-Potter

"Melanie Dawn Geddes Case Remains Unsolved." *CBC News Saskatchewan*, April 6, 2015. https://www.cbc.ca/news/canada/saskatchewan/melanie-dawn-geddes-case-remains-unsolved-1.3011242

"Tracing the Story of Missing Delores Whiteman of Saskatchewan." *CBC News Saskatchewan*, April 6, 2015. https://www.cbc.ca/news/canada/saskatchewan/tracing-the-story-of-missing-delores-whiteman-of-saskatchewan-1.3016237

Video: *Fiddler's Map*. Regina: Non-Inferno Media Productions, 2003. https://vimeo.com/96463496

Endnotes

1. Michelle Latimer is a Canadian actress and filmmaker who claimed, through much of her career, to have Algonquin and Métis heritage, based on family oral history. In December 2020, her Indigenous identity was questioned after the release of her NFB film *Inconvenient Indian* stated her connection to the Kitigan Zibi First Nation in Quebec, which the community denies. Latimer subsequently apologized for claiming connection to Kitigan Zibi, and resigned from the production of her CBC-TV series *Trickster*. In May 2021, she stated that two experts, commissioned by her, backed her claims. "I am a non-status Algonquin of mixed blood, Métis, French Canadian heritage," she maintained.

2. Mervin Brass is an Anishinaabe/Cree journalist from Key First Nation in Saskatchewan who attended First Nations University of Canada. In 2020, he was named senior managing director of CBC North.

3. Joseph Boyden is an award-winning Canadian author of Irish and Scottish descent, best known for writing about First Nations culture. Throughout his career, Boyden identified as Indigenous, but in 2016, Boyden's past claims of Mi'kmaq, Métis, Nipmuc, and Ojibway descent were called into question. Boyden admitted he erroneously claimed to be Mi'kmaq, but continued to identify as a "White kid with native roots."

4. In Saskatchewan, many First Nations received their entire land allocations under their treaties. However, some First Nations did not. Treaty Land Entitlement (TLE) agreements fulfill federal obligations to set apart the promised amount of reserve land as part of those treaties.

5. Modern treaties, also known as comprehensive land claim agreements, are generally signed with Indigenous groups/Nations where Indigenous title and rights have not been settled i.e., unceded lands.

6. In 2014, 13-year-old Tenelle Starr was told by administrators at her high school in Balcarres, Saskatchewan, that she could not wear at school a sweatshirt with the words, "Got Land? Thank An Indian" on it. After meetings with Starr's family and her Cree community, school officials reversed their decision.

4.9

Asking Hard Questions: A Conversation with Tristan Ahtone

Tristan Ahtone is a member of the Kiowa Tribe and is editor-in-chief at the *Texas Observer*.

He has reported for multiple outlets including *PBS NewsHour*, *National Native News*, *NPR*, *Al Jazeera America*, and *High Country News*, where he served as Indigenous Affairs editor.

Tristan's stories have won multiple honours, including investigative awards from Public Radio News Directors Incorporated and the Gannett Foundation. He additionally was awarded a Nieman Fellowship to study at Harvard University in 2017.

Tristan is a director of the Muckrock Foundation and is a former president of the Native American Journalists Association (NAJA).

Tristan Ahtone.

Source: Photo by Katri Heinämäki and used by permission of Tristan Ahtone.

Invisibility of Native Americans in Mainstream Media

DM: I was researching Canadian coverage compared to the United States and this jumped out at me: Until recently, NPR didn't even track coverage of Native Americans because the numbers were so low. Is there a reason for the invisibility of Native Americans in mainstream press in the U.S.?

TA: The answer to that question is probably a PhD thesis, but having been a former public radio reporter, one of the issues that I always saw, and is being debated today, is that there's just no hiring of Indigenous people. That's an overly simple explanation, but there's just nobody there that knows, "Oh, this is a story." This is especially so with the big outlets—from the *LA Times* to the *New York Times*, the coverage has been generally terrible.

Most of this stems [from] the idea that there's probably not anything worth covering in Indian Country because there's not a lot of people there and nothing is happening anymore and these folks have been on the way out for decades. Outlets have been reporting that for years now, and I'd argue they generally don't feel the need to put resources there because nothing happens there.

I started covering in Indian Country in 2008 when I was working for the *NewsHour*. I would pitch a story. And they were like, "Well, do we want another Native story? We did one last year." (laugh)

I don't see that anymore. Nowadays it's a different take, like "Well, maybe that's not a story" or "Maybe that's not important."

DM: The Native American Journalists Association is working with media organizations to try to quash very basic stereotypes that keep recurring about Indigenous people in the news. Why do you think that persists in U.S. media?

TA: Some of it is just to do with how people have encountered Indigenous communities through media. Popular portrayals of Indian Country have persisted from the thirties, forties, fifties, and on. People are just not aware of those hard-wired cultural biases, like what you see in a John Ford film.[1] Those narratives continue and they resurface in coverage.

To be blunt about it, a lot of these reporters just aren't doing the research. White people invented Google and don't use it. (laugh) I just don't understand. We have had to actually put a bingo card together so reporters can tack it up in their offices because they refuse to Google *anything* about coverage in Indian Country, of which there's a *massive* amount from all over the world. It's not hard: Googling it, finding it, taking 10 minutes to read through existing guides. It doesn't take a lot of time and, for some reason, reporters just don't do it.

> See Chapter 1.3, "Beyond Victims and Warriors: Choosing Indigenous News Stories," for the bingo card created by NAJA plus tips on how to avoid Indigenous stereotypes.

DM: When you visit newsrooms, what kinds of reactions do you get from reporters about why those stereotypes persist in their coverage?

TA: In terms of training situations, usually, you've got 45 minutes. So, you kind of have to throw the kitchen sink at it. We haven't really been able to have conversations with a lot of these reporters at major news outlets, primarily because, in the past, they just didn't answer emails when we asked them about it. There's this level of disconnect. Even being able to write and say, "Hey, this is a really big problem. Can we talk it through?" Generally, we have not seen a response.

The last time we had an in-depth conversation with anybody about coverage was the *New York Times*. It was after the "Drawn from Poverty" piece about Nunavut.[2] Essentially, they deferred to the story's author. "Our reporter knows best. We trust our reporter." So, I put that responsibility back on the reporter and said, "Well, can we talk to the reporter? No, no, no, we cannot." So, there are a number of systems in place to prevent any sort of accountability.

Some systems make a lot of sense for an investigative story, for instance. But in terms of coverage of Indigenous communities, we haven't seen a lot of accountability.

Avoiding Ahistorical Analysis

DM: In that particular case, the *NYT* [*New York Times*] fell back on the facts in the story. They said, "We've gone back to check them and they're all verifiable." But the point you're raising is how that reporter framed the story. Can you explain a bit more?

TA: It's how you *use* the facts. You're right, the facts weren't incorrect. But how you use them is a completely different story. There are a number of different ways you can come at any story. So, the *New York Times* comes at it as if this is art that's drawn from poverty. That the only thing all the facts point to is that these people are absolutely impoverished and have no hope at all ever of not being impoverished. That's what the facts say.

Those analyses are ahistorical. The facts are the facts. But there are *reasons* those facts are what they are.

A decent reporter, or somebody at least with deep familiarity of the community, is going to say those facts actually speak to larger systemic issues. That often requires a lot more context, history, and understanding of the law. All of the context that brings those facts together is something that is not being considered.

One of the examples I like to use is reporting on violence on reservations in the U.S. A lot of times it's throwing up the Department of Justice statistics, saying "These are the horrifying statistics about the violence happening in Indian Country." Saying, all of those facts only point to one fact: reservations are incredibly violent places.

But take a step back and say, "Okay, why is that?" There are no police out there because the federal government has taken that ability away from tribes to have an effective police force. More than half of prosecutions that are referred to authorities are declined. Also, you forgot to throw in the fact that about 60 per cent of crimes committed against Native people and reservation communities are committed by White people.[3]

These are all *really* important bits of information that shed light on those facts in a lot of different ways. If you take that out—sure, it's a violent scary place. But if you look at *why* that is, you've got a lot of different bits of information that help you put it in context.

"Wrapping the Vegetables in Bacon"

DM: Context is so often key in reporting on Indigenous communities because our audiences often don't know that history. Within the space limitations we face, how do you encourage reporters to include that historical colonial context that is so essential?

TA: Most of the folks I work with covering these areas are really good at knowing that and popping it in, because everything needs that context. Basically, it's word craft. There are some really effective ways to get a lot of history into an explanation really quickly. Sometimes it just needs to say, "Yes, this reservation has some pretty high rates of violence. It's important to note that four different federal laws prohibit that tribe from actually doing any sort of policing." Then, moving on with the story. I hate to put it down to just wordcraft, but obviously when we're talking about space, we just have to be creative about it. . . .

It also comes from a deep understanding and knowledge. Somebody who just walks up and wants to do some Indigenous Affairs reporting, they've got a long way to go with that. They have a lot of research that they have to do to be able to get to that point. It's all about expertise.

DM: You've also experimented, as an editor, with assigning different modes of presenting that information—whether it's graphics journalism or comics journalism—in a way that's still going to reach your audience, without them feeling they're being lectured to.

TA: Yes. Part of it is just advocating for and really putting your foot down and saying "We have to have this in here because it changes the story. It's the ethical thing to do."

The other thing is placement. A lot of the feature stories we work on, we really work to—for lack of a word—bury that context so that it doesn't feel like you're getting it. Part of that is just craft, of where that goes. In our feature writing, we do a lot of work in trying to mimic screenplay structures, which are usually very good about burying the context and the exposition. That's something we try to do as well.

DM: Education by stealth!

TA: It's wrapping the vegetables in bacon. (laugh)

Elements of a Good Pitch

DM: From your perspective as someone who assigns stories, what makes for a good pitch when it comes to Indian Country?

TA: I need character. I need stakes. I have a log line that I work with reporters on. I need a specific character, with a specific goal or objective. If they are not able to fulfill that objective, what are the stakes? Those are some of the things that I look for.

I'm looking for place and I'm looking for stories that hint toward more accountability or positivity. I don't usually like to use that word, but I'm looking for things that are also going to inform readers. The readers I am thinking of when I'm assigning stories are other Native readers. . . .

> For more tips on pitching stories, refer to Chapter 1.6, "How to Pitch a Story Successfully."

DM: I can understand your hesitancy with using "positivity," but why is that an important consideration when it comes to Native news?

TA: There is so much negative coverage of Indian Country. That's the majority of stuff you see from most mainstream outlets. I don't think any of the stuff I've assigned is strictly on the positivity or solutions journalism side. I'm not really looking for solutions, but I'm looking for something that you walk away from with a feeling that isn't inherently (deep sigh) . . .

DM: Despairing? You're looking for hope.

TA: To some degree. One example of a really good story that I would like to see more of in the U.S. is by Graham Brewer. It was about the stickball tournaments in Oklahoma. Pretty straightforward sports story and I love a good sports story. They're fun. They're loud. They're really great to do.

But there was something really particular about it. It was just following a team and explaining the game. Are they gonna win or lose? All your basic storytelling stuff. But one of the things I realized about it afterwards: there were no non-Natives in the story. Not a single mention of anything that was essentially non-Native. There was no reference to Trail of Tears or federal laws.

It really stood as a moment that I want to be working for all the time. This was something that was specific to this community and had no outside influences on it at all. I have not found another story in a non-Native news outlet, at least in the U.S., that has accomplished that.

DM: I love it when there's a full story with stakes, characters, accountability—all the things that make for a good story—but no non-Indigenous people. It becomes about the community.

TA: Yeah! Those are the kind of things I'm thinking about with this audience, I'm trying to bring something new to it.

For example, MMIWG here in the U.S. Last year [2020], there was an explosion of coverage on the topic, and rightfully important coverage. At *High Country News*, we didn't step into it until we knew we could add something new to the conversation. Because Indigenous communities have known about this for decades, there wasn't value for readers to say this thing is happening. We already know that. So, what can we do with that story?

Eventually, when we stepped into it, we realized we just needed to really re-focus on all of the federal laws and policies that created the gaps for this to be happening, without any sort of punishment or any sort of accountability. Looking at how the system is set up to essentially allow for this to happen. That's where we felt we could lean in on that.

That's how I'm thinking about it with assigning stuff. I have conversations with a lot of young reporters about this too, who say, "I don't want to write stories for white audiences. I don't need to have that context because we already know." My pushback is usually, "You're also writing for other Native readers. There are a lot of people who don't understand the context in your community. Somebody in upstate New York doesn't have the same context that you do for what's going on right here, right now."

It's something to keep in mind. Context is always key. It just depends on how you handle it.

Holding Tribes Accountable

DM: You mentioned something else that's important in a pitch: accountability. You've had an incredible career as an investigative journalist. How do you navigate or manage to hold tribes accountable and still get access?

TA: It's just being really, really thorough. Being really, really fair. I'm always going back to folks, really following up, to make sure I can get interviews. I want to make sure that everybody knows what I'm up to, and make sure that they feel like they have had an opportunity to respond.

Any sort of investigative reporting is going to put somebody on the spot. You're going to piss somebody off. That's where that fairness and thoroughness comes in, being able to say, "I asked you four different times to call me back about this. I gave you the opportunity on this date and this date. I told you what I was working on. There were no 'gotchas' here. You didn't respond. And now you're upset about it?" I'm sorry. I'm happy to do some follow up with you. I do leave that door open too, because maybe there is an opportunity to do even more reporting. . . .

The other thing is thoroughness. I don't work on investigative pieces by relying on rumours. You say that happened? I need you to help me find a way to prove that. Do you have an email? Do you have a text message? Do you have a memo? Do you have a recording? How can we corroborate what you're saying is happening?

You're still going to piss people off. But if you're doing accountability stuff, you're working in service of a community that's going to benefit from having that information revealed. So you're still going to have good relations with the folks that you're ostensibly working for.

DM: Investigative journalism is about digging deeply, it's about public interest, but it seems you're describing an additional layer, in terms of maintaining relationships when you're covering Indian Country and doing investigative work?

TA: With any reporting, it's all about relationships. With investigative work, somebody needs to know they can trust you. A lot of the investigative work that I've done in Indian Country has been with small groups of individuals or just individuals. They need to know that they can trust you with something that could get them in a lot of trouble.

There's a lot of care that goes into that. Everything from scrubbing of digital tracks to encrypted communications, all the way to establishing rules right from the get-go.

In almost all the stories that I do, or my teams do, we almost always go back and try to get critique from folks afterwards. How do they feel about it? What did we do right? What did we do wrong? We really try to check in with folks not only a) because it's just good practice to get better, but b) there might be more stories down the line.

Just keeping in touch with people can make for great relationships and good sources. You know, I want more stories. I want to work more with different communities and people. It's important to have those good relations with folks.

Also, you see people again in Indian Country. This is the difference, in terms of the ethics that we employ as reporters. We don't have the opportunity to go in, screw it up, and then never see that person again. I've seen most of my sources in some social form or another afterwards, in the years since I've reported on it. It's very rare that I don't see somebody again or see them pop up on social media. You have to be able to interact with them again.

Maintaining Relationships

DM: Are there times you have let a story go, because of those connections—whether it's kin, or friends—because Indian Country is so small?

TA: I don't think so. I let a lot of stories go when they focus on areas of cultural coverage. Anything that feels like it could be perceived as anthropology, it's not my thing. I don't touch it. . . .

Say, somebody recently discovered that a particular tribe does puberty ceremonies. That's not news. That's anthropology. There are all kinds of things I encounter that are of cultural importance, but I don't really see those as news stories.

DM: You're cautious about ceremony in particular?

TA: Yeah. It's nobody's business but our own, as far as I'm concerned. It can be taken out of context or written poorly. . . .

DM: Are there particular ways you negotiate relationships with Indigenous sources, when you're starting out a story?

TA: I'm sure it's the same with you. "Who's your family? Where are you from?" That comes up almost all the time. You're always trying to triangulate, "How do you know this person?" because everybody sort of knows each other on some level. Even if it's through four different sources, it's not hard to do a "six degrees of Kevin Bacon" situation.[4] (laugh)

People are always, "Oh yeah, I know that guy! We went to school together." You're looking for connection. We kind of do that with other stories or sources, like "Oh you're from Colorado. Cool. I've been to Denver. It's nice." You're looking for a connection, but it's not really the same. (laugh)

DM: Absolutely the same thing happens for me, even, I imagine, if I was reporting in the United States. Is it equally important for non-Indigenous journalists to share who they are and where they're from?

TA: I think it's important for them to share what kind of work they've done in this area before. It's not "Show up with your resume!" It's like, "What do you know? What is your understanding of this? Do you have a Native editor?"

Somebody can show up, say, "Look, I don't have a Native editor. I'm not working at a Native organization. I've never done any sort of Indian Country reporting before. This is my goal in terms of doing this story." There's an option there that allows people to negotiate and think about, "Do I want to talk to this person?" I do think all of that's relevant.

What works for a lot of non-Native reporters that do this kind of work is being able to point to the kind of stories they've done before. It's really helpful.

> The importance of locating yourself and your journalism is discussed in Chapter 1.7, "'Where Are You From?' Rethinking Objectivity."

Asking the Tough Questions

DM: I'm thinking of the story you did on the National Congress of American Indians and sexual abuse allegations there [see citation in Suggested Works by Tristan Ahtone at end of this piece]. Do you have advice for journalists about the importance of pushing hard and covering stories that may raise difficult issues for Native communities?

TA: I do believe in journalism as a public service. That's one of the reasons that I got into journalism in the first place, knowing that it can make a difference in people's lives when done correctly.

In terms of that hard pushing, it's part of the job. That's part of the thing that makes our roles different from anybody else's, is asking those hard questions and finding ways to reveal what people don't want revealed.

That story was a six-month investigation. It relied almost entirely on speaking with whistleblowers who could also provide the evidence that we needed to be able to make the claims that we did. Every line, every factual assertion in that story was backed up by documentation. It takes a long time.

But the Executive Director stepped down afterwards, after 20 years. It opened up a whole new conversation with folks there, and also helps us to be able to do more investigative work in the future when folks are in situations that they want to do that kind of whistleblowing with reporters.

I just think that's the goal of journalism.

> See Chapter 1.4, "Positive versus Negative Stories," on why it's so necessary for a news outlet to publish a wide range of stories about the Indigenous community.

DM: It makes me think how difficult it is for whistleblowers in Native American communities because they are small communities. The stakes are much higher. You can't just escape into the big city.

TA: Exactly. We worked really hard in that case to make sure that people's identities weren't revealed or revealing documents that would very obviously link to particular peoples. There's a lot of talking, negotiation, that kind of thing.

On Data Journalism in Indian Country

DM: You're also known, as part of your investigative work, for data journalism. Just going through incredibly large amounts of data and making sense of it. Are there particular challenges when it comes to trying to get accurate data from Native American communities?

TA: There's a Five D Rule we use a lot [disparity, deprivation, disadvantage, dysfunction, and differences], which came out of the Indigenous data sovereignty book I read a while back...[5]

For example, Googling Indigenous statistics, those statistics are usually going to fall into that Five D rule. So, if those are the only statistics that you have in Indian Country, does that represent all of Indian Country and what's happening in Indigenous communities? Or is this just a particular slice?

Generally, the problem is that the data that's generated about Indian Country is usually not good. It's usually being created for particular purposes, to look at issues of deprivation or disparities or to look at negative issues in Indigenous communities. The reason why it's created is something we have to look at.

But also, there's just not a lot out there. So, the trick in the future is going to be creating our own data sets that can be used for more investigative work. Because relying on government data sets or studies, for instance, depends on why it was created in the first place.

DM: So, understand who was creating those data sets and what their purposes may have been because they may be skewed?

TA: You got it.

DM: What about when it comes to collecting data from tribes?

TA: We're not very good at that, mainly because, as sovereign governments, they usually don't let that stuff out. At least here in the U.S., the only way we can do investigative work is finding ways *into* tribal governments, because you can't get public records *from* tribal governments. They're not subject to the same laws.

So, we're always having to find ways. Who are they interacting with? Thinking about the immense amount of bureaucratic paperwork that's been created. They might have talked to the Bureau of Prisons about a contract they had. Let's go after that. They might have talked to the Army Corps of Engineers. That's the way we're going about doing it. It's very rare to get stuff internally. . . .

DM: Because most tribal governments don't have freedom of information laws. So, you try to find out where they may connect with state governments or federal departments?

TA: Yeah.

Decolonizing Journalism

DM: My last question. You wondered about the title of this book, *Decolonizing Journalism*. What does decolonizing journalism mean to you?

TA: If the idea is, can you decolonize the industry as it exists? To me, the short answer is, no. It can't happen. In terms of the reckoning that media is having at the moment, decolonization is not on the table. It's a movement of reform, not revolution.

We're looking at some trickle-down reforms, where maybe you get a couple of people hired, maybe there's a little bit more pay equity. These kinds of little things that are cosmetic to the industry . . .

But, if it's a matter of building a practice based on those histories, traditions, and ideas of what journalism *can* be—or record keeping, storytelling, whatever we're calling it in Indigenous communities—that's a different conversation. And maybe even lends itself more to Indigenous journalism, rather than decolonizing, if it's a *methodology* that we're thinking about.

I just don't feel like you can change the journalism industry. It's a massive revolution you have to have, if you're going to make any sort of changes, and there are too many people invested in the system as it is, that, at the end of the day, don't actually want change. They just want window-dressing.

Discussion Questions

1. What are Ahtone's concerns about journalism with "ahistorical" analysis?
2. How does Ahtone practice accountability to his sources and his community?
3. What are the challenges of finding and relying on data in Indigenous communities?

Suggested Works by Tristan Ahtone

"Land-Grab Universities: Expropriated Indigenous Land Is the Foundation of the Land-Grant University System." *High Country News*, March 30, 2020. https://www.hcn.org/issues/52.4/indigenous-affairs-education-land-grab-universities

"National Congress of American Indians Roiled by Claims of Harassment and Misconduct." *High Country News*, October 18, 2018. https://www.hcn.org/articles/tribal-affairs-national-congress-of-american-indians-roiled-by-claims-of-harassment-and-misconduct

"Telling Indigenous Stories." *Nieman Reports*, June 7, 2017. https://niemanreports.org/articles/telling-indigenous-stories/

Endnotes

1. John Ford is an American film director renowned for his Westerns, a genre he is often credited with creating. His films, from the 1920s to the 60s, have been critiqued for invoking deep anti-Indian sentiment and leaning heavily on racist portrayals of Indigenous Peoples as uncivilized and violent.

2. An October 2019 article by the *New York Times* Canada bureau chief, Catherine Porter, about Inuit art in Cape Dorset, Nunavut, drew widespread criticism from Inuit for perpetuating stereotypes about poverty and violence, without exploring the history of colonialism in the North. https://www.nationalobserver.com/2019/11/09/news/inuit-reporters-call-out-new-york-times-trauma-porn

3. According to U.S. Bureau of Justice statistics gathered in 2004, at least 66 per cent of the violent crimes experienced by Native American victims are committed by persons not of the same race, and 9 per cent of offenders were described by the victim as Black. https://www.courts.ca.gov/documents/Tribal-NAmericanStatsAbstract.pdf

4. Inspired by "six degrees of separation," the theory that nobody is more than six relationships away from any other person in the world, "six degrees of Kevin Bacon" is a game that requires players to link celebrities to the movie star Kevin Bacon, in as few steps as possible, via the movies they have in common.

5. Tahu Kukutai et al., *Indigenous Data Sovereignty and Policy* (New York: Routledge, 2020).

✦ Conclusion ✦

The Last Word

In this chapter, students will learn to:
- *recognize that learning is an eternal journey.*

> *For once a story is told, it cannot be called back. Once told, it is loose in the world. So you have to be careful with the stories you tell. And you have to watch out for the stories you are told.*[1]
>
> – Thomas King

I hope you found this guide useful. If any of the information or advice within helps you tell a more complete, balanced, truthful news story, then it has served its purpose.

As you set out to research and report in Indigenous communities, let one principle guide you: respect.

Respect is deeply embedded within traditional Indigenous teachings, and it's a fundamental value not always appreciated by outsiders or extended to Indigenous people.

Cynical reporters may scoff at this, bearing witness as we often do to the many forms of violence Indigenous people inflict upon each other, or the bitter internal political disputes that sometimes threaten to tear Indigenous communities apart. So much for "traditional teachings," you may rightly say. But good things will happen if you follow these guidelines:

- respect people's customs and traditions;
- show a genuine interest in learning;
- recognize there is no "one-size-fits-all" approach to Indigenous Peoples; and
- nurture relationships.

You will discover a goldmine of news stories, you'll be treated to inside scoops, and your belly will be bursting from a steady diet of rubber chicken at all those journalism award dinners.

Much, much more importantly, you'll find your understanding of the world enriched. And the seeds of trust you've sown may even grow into relationships outside the narrow confines of a newsroom.

You, your stories, and your audience will be better for it.

Exercise: What I've Learned about Reporting in Indigenous Communities

Take five minutes to reflect on your journey to learn more about reporting in Indigenous communities, then answer these five questions.

1. What's the most important thing I learned about reporting in Indigenous communities?
2. What still confuses me about reporting in Indigenous communities?
3. What should I do with what I learned about reporting in Indigenous communities?
4. What could I learn next about reporting in Indigenous communities?
5. What's different about me as a journalist after reading this book? Is there something new that I know? Something new that I can do? Is this a small change or a new way of seeing things?

Endnotes

1. King, Thomas, *The Truth about Stories: A Native Narrative* (Toronto: Anansi, 2003), 10.

Appendix 1

UNDRIP Articles Relating to Media

Article 16

1. Indigenous peoples have the right to establish their own media in their own languages and to have access to all forms of non-indigenous media without discrimination.
2. States shall take effective measures to ensure that State-owned media duly reflect indigenous cultural diversity. States, without prejudice to ensuring full freedom of expression, should encourage privately owned media to adequately reflect indigenous cultural diversity

Article 31

1. Indigenous peoples have the right to maintain, control, protect and develop their cultural heritage, traditional knowledge and traditional cultural expressions, as well as the manifestations of their sciences, technologies and cultures, including human and genetic resources, seeds, medicines, knowledge of the properties of fauna and flora, oral traditions, literatures, designs, sports and traditional games and visual and performing arts. They also have the right to maintain, control, protect and develop their intellectual property over such cultural heritage, traditional knowledge, and traditional cultural expressions.
2. In conjunction with indigenous peoples, States shall take effective measures to recognize and protect the exercise of these rights.

✦ Appendix 2 ✦

TRC Calls to Action Relating to Media

Call to Action #84

We call upon the federal government to restore and increase funding to the CBC/Radio-Canada, to enable Canada's national public broadcaster to support reconciliation, and be properly reflective of the diverse cultures, languages, and perspectives of Aboriginal peoples, including, but not limited to:

   i. Increasing Aboriginal programming, including Aboriginal-language speakers.
   ii. Increasing equitable access for Aboriginal peoples to jobs, leadership positions, and professional development opportunities within the organization.
   iii. Continuing to provide dedicated news coverage and online public information resources on issues of concern to Aboriginal peoples and all Canadians, including the history and legacy of residential schools and the reconciliation process.

Call to Action #85

We call upon the Aboriginal Peoples Television Network, as an independent non-profit broadcaster with programming by, for, and about Aboriginal peoples, to support reconciliation, including but not limited to:

   i. Continuing to provide leadership in programming and organizational culture that reflects the diverse cultures, languages, and perspectives of Aboriginal peoples.
   ii. Continuing to develop media initiatives that inform and educate the Canadian public, and connect Aboriginal and non-Aboriginal Canadians.

Call to Action #86

We call upon Canadian journalism programs and media schools to require education for all students on the history of Aboriginal peoples, including the history and legacy of residential schools, the United Nations Declaration on the Rights of Indigenous Peoples, Treaties and Aboriginal rights, Indigenous law, and Aboriginal–Crown relations.

Appendix 3

OCAP® Principles for Indigenous Research and Data Collection

In 1998, the First Nations Information Governance Centre developed a set of guidelines intended to govern data collection in Indigenous communities and decolonize Indigenous-Western research relationships. These four ethical principles are known as The First Nations Principles of OCAP®, which stands for "ownership, control, access, and possession."

This backgrounder from the Assembly of First Nations briefly explains OCAP® principles.

What is OCAP®?

The First Nations Principles of OCAP® (ownership, control, access, and possession) means that First Nations control data collection processes in their communities. First Nations own, protect, and control how their information is used. Access to First Nations data is important, and First Nations determine, under appropriate mandates and protocols, how access by external researchers is facilitated and respected. The right of First Nations communities to own, control, access, and possess information about their peoples is fundamentally tied to self-determination and to the preservation and development of their culture. OCAP® allows a community to make decisions regarding why, how, and by whom information is collected, used, or shared.

The Components of OCAP®:

- **Ownership**: Ownership refers to the relationship of First Nations to their cultural knowledge, data, and information. This principle states that a community or group owns information collectively in the same way that an individual owns his or her personal information.
- **Control**: The principle of control affirms that First Nations, their communities and representative bodies are within their rights in seeking to control over all aspects of research and information management processes that impact them. First Nations control of research can include all stages of a particular research

project-from start to finish. The principle extends to the control of resources and review processes, the planning process, management of the information and so on.
- **Access**: First Nations must have access to information and data about themselves and their communities, regardless of where it is currently held. The principle also refers to the right of First Nations communities and organizations to manage and make decisions regarding access to their collective information. This may be achieved, in practice, through standardized, formal protocols.
- **Possession**: While ownership identifies the relationship between a people and their information in principle, possession or stewardship is more concrete. It refers to the physical control of data. Possession is a mechanism by which ownership can be asserted and protected.

Source: https://www.afn.ca/uploads/files/nihbforum/info_and_privacy_doc-ocap.pdf

✦ Appendix 4 ✦

Residential School Apology

On June 11, 2008, the prime minister of Canada, Stephen Harper, made a Statement of Apology to survivors and former students of Indian Residential Schools, on behalf of the Government of Canada. The text is as follows:

> The treatment of children in Indian Residential Schools is a sad chapter in our history.
>
> For more than a century, Indian Residential Schools separated over 150,000 Aboriginal children from their families and communities. In the 1870's, the federal government, partly in order to meet its obligation to educate Aboriginal children, began to play a role in the development and administration of these schools. Two primary objectives of the Residential Schools system were to remove and isolate children from the influence of their homes, families, traditions and cultures, and to assimilate them into the dominant culture. These objectives were based on the assumption Aboriginal cultures and spiritual beliefs were inferior and unequal. Indeed, some sought, as it was infamously said, "to kill the Indian in the child". Today, we recognize that this policy of assimilation was wrong, has caused great harm, and has no place in our country.
>
> One hundred and thirty-two federally-supported schools were located in every province and territory, except Newfoundland, New Brunswick and Prince Edward Island. Most schools were operated as "joint ventures" with Anglican, Catholic, Presbyterian or United Churches. The Government of Canada built an educational system in which very young children were often forcibly removed from their homes, often taken far from their communities. Many were inadequately fed, clothed and housed. All were deprived of the care and nurturing of their parents, grandparents and communities. First Nations, Inuit and Métis languages and cultural practices were prohibited in these schools. Tragically, some of these children died while attending residential schools and others never returned home.

The government now recognizes that the consequences of the Indian Residential Schools policy were profoundly negative and that this policy has had a lasting and damaging impact on Aboriginal culture, heritage and language. While some former students have spoken positively about their experiences at residential schools, these stories are far overshadowed by tragic accounts of the emotional, physical and sexual abuse and neglect of helpless children, and their separation from powerless families and communities.

The legacy of Indian Residential Schools has contributed to social problems that continue to exist in many communities today.

It has taken extraordinary courage for the thousands of survivors that have come forward to speak publicly about the abuse they suffered. It is a testament to their resilience as individuals and to the strength of their cultures. Regrettably, many former students are not with us today and died never having received a full apology from the Government of Canada.

The government recognizes that the absence of an apology has been an impediment to healing and reconciliation. Therefore, on behalf of the Government of Canada and all Canadians, I stand before you, in this Chamber so central to our life as a country, to apologize to Aboriginal peoples for Canada's role in the Indian Residential Schools system.

To the approximately 80,000 living former students, and all family members and communities, the Government of Canada now recognizes that it was wrong to forcibly remove children from their homes and we apologize for having done this. We now recognize that it was wrong to separate children from rich and vibrant cultures and traditions that it created a void in many lives and communities, and we apologize for having done this. We now recognize that, in separating children from their families, we undermined the ability of many to adequately parent their own children and sowed the seeds for generations to follow, and we apologize for having done this. We now recognize that, far too often, these institutions gave rise to abuse or neglect and were inadequately controlled, and we apologize for failing to protect you. Not only did you suffer these abuses as children, but as you became parents, you were powerless to protect your own children from suffering the same experience, and for this we are sorry.

The burden of this experience has been on your shoulders for far too long. The burden is properly ours as a Government, and as a country. There is no place in Canada for the attitudes that inspired the Indian Residential Schools system to ever prevail again. You have been working on recovering from this experience for a long time and in a very real sense, we are now joining you on this journey. The Government of Canada sincerely apologizes and asks the forgiveness of the Aboriginal peoples of this country for failing them so profoundly.

Nous le regrettons

We are sorry

Nimitataynan

Niminchinowesamin

Mamiattugut

In moving towards healing, reconciliation and resolution of the sad legacy of Indian Residential Schools, implementation of the Indian Residential Schools Settlement Agreement began on September 19, 2007. Years of work by survivors, communities, and Aboriginal organizations culminated in an agreement that gives us a new beginning and an opportunity to move forward together in partnership.

A cornerstone of the Settlement Agreement is the Indian Residential Schools Truth and Reconciliation Commission. This Commission presents a unique opportunity to educate all Canadians on the Indian Residential Schools system. It will be a positive step in forging a new relationship between Aboriginal peoples and other Canadians, a relationship based on the knowledge of our shared history, a respect for each other and a desire to move forward together with a renewed understanding that strong families, strong communities and vibrant cultures and traditions will contribute to a stronger Canada for all of us.

Additional Resources

This is a brief compendium of websites and resources for journalists seeking Indigenous content.

Historical Overview

Crown–Indigenous Relations and Northern Affairs Canada (CIRNAC) – The official website of CIRNAC presents a cultural overview, spanning historical treaties to present-day rights. https://www.canada.ca/en/crown-indigenous-relations-northern-affairs.html

First Peoples of Canada – Canada's Museum of Civilization has a virtual exhibition looking at some of the facets of the history of Indigenous Peoples. https://www.historymuseum.ca/cmc/exhibitions/aborig/fp/fpint01e.html

Indigenous Canada MOOC – Indigenous Canada is a 12-lesson Massive Open Online Course (MOOC) from the University of Alberta's Faculty of Native Studies that explores Indigenous histories and contemporary issues in Canada. https://www.coursera.org/learn/indigenous-canada

Indigenous Peoples Atlas of Canada – Indigenous perspectives, much older than the nation itself, shared through maps, artwork, history, and culture. https://indigenouspeoplesatlasofcanada.ca/

Indigenous Services Canada (ISC) – This site is categorized into several sections, including "Indigenous Health," "Education," "Water in First Nations Communities," "Social Programs," "First Nations Housing," and "Governance." https://www.canada.ca/en/indigenous-services-canada.html

Métis History – A brief history documenting significant dates in the development of the Métis nation. https://www2.Métisnation.ca/about/

Reconciliation through Indigenous Education MOOC – Free, online, open-access course through UBC and edX that offers lessons on Indigenous histories, perspectives, worldviews, and approaches to learning. https://www.edx.org/course/reconciliation-through-indigenous-education

Royal Commission on Aboriginal Peoples (RCAP) – The RCAP report was completed in 1996. It is a broad survey of historical and contemporary relations between Indigenous (Aboriginal) and non-Indigenous peoples in Canada, and includes 444 recommendations for the future. https://www.bac-lac.gc.ca/eng/discover/aboriginal-heritage/royal-commission-aboriginal-peoples/Pages/introduction.aspx

Virtual Museum of Métis History and Culture – The Gabriel Dumont Institute's online chronicle of traditional Métis history and culture contains a wealth of primary documents—oral history interviews, photographs, and archival documents—in visual, audio, and video files. http://www.metismuseum.ca/index.php

Maps

First Nation Profiles in Canada – Profiles of the individual First Nation communities across Canada. Includes links to interactive maps of the communities, with census and community statistics. https://fnp-ppn.aadnc-aandc.gc.ca/fnp/Main/index.aspx?lang=eng

Indigenous Map Room – Comprehensive thematic maps covering Indigenous Peoples, communities, and initiatives undertaken by Crown–Indigenous Relations and Northern Affairs Canada (CIRNAC). Themes include "Indigenous Peoples," "Community Development," "Education," "Health and Social Services," "The North," and "Treaties, Claims and Agreements." https://www.rcaanc-cirnac.gc.ca/eng/1605796363328/1605796417543#h4

Ontario First Nations Map – Map locating all First Nation reserves in Ontario. Includes a list of all the communities, with links to their respective addresses and websites, providing information regarding the Chief in charge, the Treaty land it sits on, band number, and Tribal council. http://firstnation.ca/

Government Acts and Land Claims

Canadian Encyclopedia: Land Claims – Brief exploration of the history of land claims in Canada, with progress of claims divided by region. https://www.thecanadianencyclopedia.ca/en/article/land-claims

Ontario Land Claims – List and general overview of current land claims in Ontario. Includes link to information on the land claim negotiation process. https://www.ontario.ca/page/current-land-claims

Treaty Background from Canadian Government – Covers the different Acts, agreements, and land claims that have transpired between the government and Indigenous Peoples in Canada. Divided by topic: "Treaties and Agreements," "Self-government," "Nation Rebuilding," and "Ongoing Negotiations." https://www.rcaanc-cirnac.gc.ca/eng/1100100028568/1529354090684

Treaties

Treaties in Canada Education Portal – An educational guide to treaties prepared by Historica Canada. http://education.historicacanada.ca/en/tools/260

Treaty Research Reports – Historical interpretations of treaties the Crown has signed with Indigenous Peoples since the eighteenth century. https://www.rcaanc-cirnac.gc.ca/eng/1100100028653/1564411361775

Indigenous Languages

B.C. First Nations Languages Map – A comprehensive map of First Peoples' languages in British Columbia. http://maps.fphlcc.ca

First Voices – A suite of web-based tools and services designed to support Indigenous Peoples in B.C. engaged in language archiving, language teaching, and culture revitalization. https://www.firstvoices.com/home

Original Voices – An immersive and extensive exploration of Indigenous languages in Canada, created by CBC Indigenous. https://www.cbc.ca/originalvoices/

Residential Schools

Beyond 94 – A website maintained by CBC Indigenous that monitors governments, communities, and faith groups in their progress toward meeting the TRC's 94 Calls to Action. https://newsinteractives.cbc.ca/longform-single/beyond-94

Brief History of Residential Schools – Brief overview of the history of residential schools and subsequent compensation in Canada. http://www.cbc.ca/news/canada/story/2008/05/16/f-faqs-residential-schools.html

Google Earth: Residential Schools – The aim of this Google Earth Voyager story is to encourage all Canadians to learn more about residential schools. Includes maps, photographs, and video links with firsthand accounts from residential school survivors. https://www.canadiangeographic.ca/article/mapping-canadas-history-residential-schools-google-earth

The National Centre for Truth and Reconciliation (NCTR) – The NCTR was created to preserve the memory of Canada's residential school system and its legacy. Its website contains excellent resources for educators and others. https://nctr.ca/

Truth and Reconciliation Commission (TRC) Findings – Contains links to the text of the full report of the TRC in 2015. http://www.trc.ca/about-us/trc-findings.html

MMIWG

Canada's Response to MMIWG Inquiry – Resources about the national inquiry as described by the Government of Canada. https://www.rcaanc-cirnac.gc.ca/eng/1448633299414/1534526479029

Honouring Indigenous Women Toolkit – The Native Women's Association of Canada created this educational resource for children to raise awareness on the perspectives of Indigenous women, girls, and gender-diverse people. https://www.nwac.ca/wp-content/uploads/2018/05/Honouring-Women-Booklet-PrintReady-20PTFont.pdf

National Inquiry into Missing and Murdered Indigenous Women and Girls – Text of the final report of the National Inquiry into Missing and Murdered Indigenous Women and Girls. https://www.mmiwg-ffada.ca/final-report/

Indigenous Rights

Canadian Government/Status Indian Rights – Covers the benefits and rights accorded to Indigenous Peoples in Canada. Divided by topic: "Band Moneys," "Estates," "Human Rights," "Indian Status," and "Matrimonial Real Property on Reserves." http://www.aadnc-aandc.gc.ca/eng/1100100032329/1100100032333

Indigenous Foundations – Information resource developed by First Nations Studies program at UBC on key topics relating to the histories, politics, rights, and cultures of the Indigenous Peoples of Canada. https://indigenousfoundations.arts.ubc.ca/home/

United Nations Declaration on the Rights of Indigenous Peoples (UNDRIP) – A concise and accessible version of UNDRIP. https://www.un.org/development/desa/indigenouspeoples/wpcontent/uploads/sites/19/2018/11/UNDRIP_E_web.pdf

UNDRIP Comprehensive – Full version of the United Nations Declaration on the Rights of Indigenous Peoples. http://www.un.org/esa/socdev/unpfii/documents/DRIPS_en.pdf

Terminology

Journalism for Human Rights (JHR) Style Guide for Reporting on Indigenous People – An overview of general definitions of terms relating to Indigenous Peoples in Canada from JHR. https://jhr.ca/wp-content/uploads/2017/12/JHR2017-Style-Book-Indigenous-People.pdf

Strategic Alliance of Broadcasters for Aboriginal Reflection (SABAR) Key Terminology Guide – Provides a comprehensive glossary of terminology and definitions, indicating the appropriate contexts to use each of them. Additionally lists high-profile legal cases spanning the last 50 years affecting all Indigenous Peoples in Canada, and describes pertinent government legislature. Appendices include links to national non-political and political organizations. Categorized by theme: "Identity & Citizenship"; "Culture & Traditions"; "Rights, Policy & Politics"; and "Governance." https://www.oise.utoronto.ca/deepeningknowledge/UserFiles/File/SABAR-Glossary-English-Final.pdf

Reporting in Indigenous Communities

Interviewing Elders – A general overview of protocols to be observed when dealing with or interviewing Elders in a community. https://icwrn.uvic.ca/wp-content/uploads/2013/10/InterviewingElders-FINAL.pdf

On-screen Protocols and Pathways – A media production guide by the imagineNATIVE Institute for working with Indigenous communities, cultures, concepts, and stories. https://drive.google.com/file/d/1Pda2O918udFqVFK31scXm9HXPfmKlu2p/view

Reporting in Indigenous Communities (RIIC) – A look at the basics of reporting in Indigenous communities. Includes a "Reporter's Checklist" and a guide leading users through the reporting process from the desk to the field to the final product. http://www.riic.ca/the-guide/

Indigenous Media/Blogs

Aboriginal Peoples Television Network (APTN) National News – http://aptn.ca/news/
CBC Indigenous – http://www.cbc.ca/news/indigenous
First Nations Forward – https://www.nationalobserver.com/special-reports/first-nations-forward
imagineNATIVE – The imagineNATIVE Film + Media Arts Festival celebrates the latest works by Indigenous Peoples leading the way in radio, video, film, and new media. http://www.imagineNative.org/home/
Indian Country Today – https://indiancountrytoday.com/
IsumaTV – IsumaTV is the world's first website for Indigenous media art now showing over 7,000 films and videos in 84 languages. http://www.isuma.tv/
Media Indigena – A podcast dedicated to Indigenous views and news. http://www.mediaindigena.com
National Film Board of Canada (NFB) – The National Film Board of Canada has a large catalogue of free films related to Indigenous issues. https://www.nfb.ca/indigenous-cinema/
Native Appropriations – A blog discussing how Native peoples are represented. Topics include stereotypes, media representations, activism, news, and cultural appropriation. A thought-provoking forum. http://Nativeappropriations.com
Walking Eagle News – http://walkingeaglenews.com/
Windspeaker – windspeaker.com

Contact Sources

National

Assembly of First Nations, Ottawa, ON www.afn.ca/index.php/en
Inuit Tapiriit Kanatami, Ottawa, ON www.itk.ca/
Métis National Council, Ottawa, ON www.metisnation.ca/

Atlantic

Atlantic Policy Congress of First Nations Chiefs, Dartmouth, NS www.apcfnc.ca

Newfoundland/Labrador

Innu Nation, Sheshatsiu, Newfoundland www.innu.ca
Newfoundland Council of Conne River Micmacs, Conne River, NL www.mfngov.ca

Nova Scotia

Confederacy of Mainland Micmacs, Truro, NS www.cmmns.com
Union of Nova Scotia Indians, Membertou, NS www.unsi.ns.ca

Prince Edward Island

Mi'kmaq Confederacy of PEI, Lennox Island, PE www.mcpei.ca

New Brunswick

Union of New Brunswick Indians, Fredericton, NB www.unbi.org

Quebec

Assembly of First Nations of Quebec and Labrador https://apnql.com
Grand Council of the Crees (Quebec), Nemaska, QC www.gcc.ca

Ontario

Anishinabek Nation, Union of Ontario Indians, North Bay, ON www.anishinabek.ca
Association of Iroquois & Allied Indians, London, ON www.aiai.on.ca
Chiefs of Ontario, Toronto, ON www.chiefs-of-ontario.org
Grand Council Treaty No. 3, Kenora, ON www.gct3.net/
Nishnawbe-Aski Nation, Thunder Bay, ON www.nan.on.ca

Manitoba

Assembly of Manitoba Chiefs, Winnipeg, MB www.manitobachiefs.com
Manitoba Keewatinowi Okimakanak, Thompson, MB www.mkonorth.com
Southern Chiefs Organization, Winnipeg, MB www.scoinc.mb.ca

Saskatchewan

Federation of Saskatchewan Indian Nations, Saskatoon, SK www.fsin.com

Alberta

Confederacy of Treaty No. 6 First Nations, Edmonton, AB www.treaty6.ca
Treaty No. 7 Management Corporation, Tsuu T'ina, AB www.treaty7.org
Treaty 8 First Nations of Alberta, Edmonton, AB www.treaty8.ca

British Columbia

Union of BC Indian Chiefs, Vancouver, BC www.ubcic.bc.ca
First Nations Summit (BC), West Vancouver, BC www.fns.bc.ca

Yukon

Council of Yukon First Nations, Whitehorse, YK www.cyfn.ca

Northwest Territories

Dene Nation, Yellowknife, NWT https://denenation.com/

Nunavut

Nunavut Tunngavik Incorporated https://www.tunngavik.com/inuit-associations-and-affiliated-organizations/

Additional

Idle No More http://www.idlenomore.ca/
National Centre for Truth and Reconciliation http://nctr.ca/about.php
Native Women's Association of Canada (NWAC) nwac.ca/contact/
Pauktuutit—Inuit Women of Canada https://www.pauktuutit.ca/

Bibliography

Books

Alia, Valerie. *The New Media Nation: Indigenous Peoples and Global Communication* (New York and Oxford: Bergahn Books, 2010).

Alia, Valerie. *Un/Covering the North: News, Media and Aboriginal People* (Vancouver: UBC Press, 1999).

Anaya, S. James. *Indigenous Peoples in International Law* (New York: Oxford University Press, 2004).

Anderson, Mark, and Carmen Robertson. *Seeing Red: A History of Natives in Canadian Newspapers* (Winnipeg: University of Manitoba Press, 2011).

Archibald, Jo-Ann. *Indigenous Storywork: Educating the Heart, Mind, Body and Spirit* (Vancouver and Toronto: UBC Press, 2008).

Brayne, Mark (ed.). *Trauma and Journalism: A Guide for Journalists, Editors and Managers* (Dart Centre for Journalism and Trauma, 2007).

Brown, Dee. *Bury My Heart at Wounded Knee: An Indian History of the American West* (New York: Holt, Rinehart and Winston, 1970).

Browne, Donald R. *Electronic Media and Indigenous Peoples: A Voice of Our Own?* (Ames: Iowa University Press, 1996).

Callison, Candis, and Mary-Lynn Young. *Reckoning: Journalism's Limits and Possibilities* (New York: Oxford University Press, 2020).

Canada, Georges Erasmus, and René Dussault. *Report of the Royal Commission on Aboriginal Peoples: Volume 3– Gathering Strength* (Ottawa: The Commission, 1996).

Charleyboy, Lisa, and Mary Beth Leatherdale (eds.). *Dreaming in Indian: Contemporary Native American Voices* (Toronto: Annick Press Ltd., 2014).

Charleyboy, Lisa, and Mary Beth Leatherdale (eds.). *Urban Tribes: Native Americans in the City* (Toronto: Annick Press Ltd., 2015).

Charleyboy, Lisa, and Mary Beth Leatherdale (eds.). *#NotYourPrincess: Voices of Native American Women* (Toronto: Annick Press Ltd., 2017).

Churchill, Ward. *Fantasies of the Master Race: Literature, Cinema and the Colonization of American Indians* (San Francisco: City Lights Books, 1998).

Deloria Jr., Vine. *Custer Died for Your Sins: An Indian Manifesto* (Norman: University of Oklahoma Press, 1988).

Duran, Eduardo. *Healing the Soul Wound: Trauma-Informed Counselling for Indigenous Communities*, 2nd edition (New York: Teachers College Press, 2020).

Elliott, Alicia. *A Mind Spread Out on the Ground* (Toronto: Doubleday Canada, 2019).

Fleras, Augie. *Social Problems in Canada: Conditions, Constructions, and Challenges* (Toronto: Pearson Prentice Hall, 2005).

Francis, Daniel. *The Imaginary Indian: The Image of the Indian in Canadian Culture* (Vancouver: Arsenal Pulp Press, 1992).

Francis, Daniel. *Copying People: Photographing British Columbia's First Nations* (Calgary and Saskatoon: Fifth House Ltd, 1996).

Greenwald, Ricky. *EMDR: Within a Phase Model of Trauma-Informed Treatment* (New York: Routledge, 2007).

Hafsteinsson, Sigurjon Baldur, and Marian Bredin. *Indigenous Screen Cultures in Canada* (Winnipeg: University of Manitoba Press, 2010).

Hartley, John, and Alan McKee. *The Indigenous Public Sphere: The Reporting and Reception of Indigenous Issues in Australia* (New York: Oxford University Press, 2000).

Healey, Jo. *Trauma Reporting: A Journalist's Guide to Covering Sensitive Stories* (London and New York: Routledge, 2019).

Herman, R.D.K. (ed.). *Giving Back: Research and Reciprocity in Indigenous Settings* (Baltimore: Project Muse, 2018).

imagineNATIVE. *On-Screen Protocols and Pathways: A Media Production Guide to Working with First Nations, Métis and Inuit Communities, Cultures, Concepts and Stories* (Toronto: imagineNATIVE, 2019).

Joseph, Bob, and Cynthia. *Working Effectively with Indigenous Peoples* (Port Coquitlam: Indigenous Relations Press, 2017).

Joseph, Robert. *21 Things You May Not Know about the Indian Act* (Port Coquitlam: Indigenous Relations Press, 2018).

Kelly, John, and Miranda Brady. *We Interrupt This Program: Indigenous Media Tactics in Canadian Culture* (Vancouver: UBC Press, 2016).

King, Thomas. *The Truth about Stories: A Native Narrative* (Toronto: House of Anansi Press, 2003).

King, Thomas. *The Inconvenient Indian: A Curious Account of Native People in North America* (Toronto: Doubleday, 2012).

Kimmerer, Robin Wall. *Braiding Sweetgrass* (Minneapolis: Milkweed Editions, 2013).

Knight, Tim. *The Television Storyteller* (Toronto: CBC Training and Development, 1994).

Kovach, Margaret. *Indigenous Methodologies: Characteristics, Conversations, and Contexts* (Toronto: University of Toronto Press, 2000).

Kovach, Bill, and Tom Rosenstiel. *The Elements of Journalism: What Newspeople Should Know and the Public Should Expect* (New York: Three Rivers Press, 2007).

Kukutai, Tahu, et al. *Indigenous Data Sovereignty and Policy* (New York: Routledge, 2020).

Linklater, Renee. *Decolonizing Trauma Work: Indigenous Stories and Strategies* (Halifax: Fernwood Press, 2020).

Mander, Jerry. *In the Absence of the Sacred: The Failure of Technology and the Survival of the Indian Nations* (San Francisco: Sierra Club, 1991).

Maracle, Lee. *My Conversations with Canadians* (Toronto: BookHug Press, 2017).

McGregor, Deborah, J-P Restoule, and Rochelle Johnston (eds.). *Indigenous Research: Theories, Practices, and Relationships* (Toronto: Canadian Scholars, 2018).

Meadows, Michael. *Voices in the Wilderness: Images of Aboriginal People in the Australian Media* (Westport: Greenwood Press, 2001).

Mongibello, Anna. *Indigenous Peoples in Canadian TV News: A Corpus-Based Analysis of Mainstream and Indigenous News Discourses* (Napoli: Paolo Loffredo iniziative editoriali, 2018).

Murray, Stuart. *Images of Dignity: Barry Barclay and Fourth Cinema* (Wellington: Huai Publishers, 2008).

Native American Journalists Association. *100 Questions, 500 Nations: A Guide to Native America* (Front Edge Publishing, LLC, 2014).

National Inquiry into Missing and Murdered Indigenous Women and Girls. *Reclaiming Power and Place: The Final Report of the National Inquiry into Missing and Murdered Indigenous Women and Girls* (The National Inquiry: Canada, 2019).

Rice, Waubgeshig. *Moon of the Crusted Snow: A Novel* (Toronto: ECW Press, 2018).

Ross, Rupert. *Dancing with a Ghost* (Markham: Octopus Publishing, 1992).

Roth, Lorna. *Something New in the Air: The Story of First Peoples Television Broadcasting in Canada* (Montreal and Kingston: McGill-Queen's University Press, 2005).

Saint-Exupéry, Antoine de. *Le Petit Prince* (New York: Harcourt, Brace & World, 1943).

Seesequasis, Paul. *Blanket Toss Under Midnight Sun: Portraits of Everyday Life in Eight Indigenous Communities* (Toronto: Alfred A. Knopf, 2019).

Tator, Carol, and Frances Henry. *Racist Discourse in Canada's English Print Media* (Toronto: The Canadian Race Relations Foundation, 2000).

Taylor, Drew Hayden. *Me Funny* (Vancouver: Douglas & McIntyre, 2006)

Teillet, Jean. *The North-West Is Our Mother: The Story of Louis Riel's People, the Métis Nation* (Toronto: Harper Collins, 2019).

Thistle, Jesse. *From the Ashes: My Story of Being Métis, Homeless, and Finding My Way* (Toronto: Simon & Schuster Canada, 2019).

Trahant, Mark N. *Pictures of Our Nobler Selves. a History of Native American Contributions to News Media* (Nashville: The Freedom Forum First Amendment Centre, 1995).

Treuer, David. *The Heartbeat of Wounded Knee: Native America from 1890 to the Present* (New York: Riverhead Books, 2019).

Truth and Reconciliation Commission of Canada. *Truth and Reconciliation Commission of Canada interim report* (Winnipeg: Truth and Reconciliation Commission of Canada, 2012).

Truth and Reconciliation Commission of Canada. *Canada's Residential Schools: Reconciliation: The Final Report of the Truth and Reconciliation Commission of Canada, Volume 6.* (Montreal and Kingston: McGill-Queen's University Press, 2015).

Truth and Reconciliation Commission of Canada. *Final Report of the Truth and Reconciliation Commission of Canada: Summary: Honouring the Truth, Reconciling for the Future* (Montreal and Kingston: McGill-Queen's University Press, 2015).

Vandell, Kay. *Telegraphies: Indigeneity, Identity, and Nation in America's Nineteenth-Century Virtual Realm* (New York: Oxford University Press, 2020).

Vizenor, Gerald. *Manifest Manners: Narratives on Postindian Survivance* (Lincoln: Nebraska, 1999).

Vowel, Chelsea. *Indigenous Writes: A Guide to First Nations, Métis and Inuit Issues in Canada* (Winnipeg: Highwater Press, 2016).

Younging, Gregory. *Elements of Indigenous Style: A Guide for Writing by and about Indigenous Peoples* (Edmonton: Brush Education, 2018).

Articles and Reports

Ahtone, Tristan. "Telling Indigenous Stories," *Nieman Reports*, June 7, 2017.

American Press Institute, "The Lost Meaning of 'Objectivity.'" Retrieved at: https://www.americanpressinstitute.org/journalism-essentials/bias-objectivity/lost-meaning-objectivity/

American Press Institute, "What Is Journalism?" Retrieved at: https://www.americanpressinstitute.org/journalism-essentials/what-is-journalism/

American Society of Newspaper Editors, "Statement of Principles" (1923). Retrieved at: https://accountablejournalism.org/ethics-codes/american-society-of-newspaper-editors-statement-of-principles

Arnaquq-Baril, Alethea (@Alethea_Aggiuq). "I Am Gutted by How Bad This Article Is, and That I Ever Welcomed the Author into My House. She Arrived in the North Having No Idea What to Even Write About, and I Gave Her a Bazillion Ideas. Instead She Chose to Reinforce Stereotypes." Tweet thread, October 26, 2019. Retrieved at: https://twitter.com/alethea_aggiuq/status/1188086699743698944?lang=en

Assembly of First Nations. "It's Our Time: The AFN Education Toolkit." Retrieved at: https://education.afn.ca/afntoolkit/

Atwood, Margaret. "A Double-Bladed Knife: Subversive Laughter in Two Stories by Thomas King," *Canadian Literature* 124–25 (1990): 243–253.

Australian Broadcasting Corporation Editorial Policies. "ABC Indigenous Content." October 8, 2015. Retrieved at: https://edpols.abc.net.au/guidance/abc-indigenous-content/

Australian Broadcasting Corporation, Elevate: Reconciliation Action Plan July 2019–June 2022. Retrieved at: https://about.abc.net.au/wpcontent/uploads/2019/11/ABCElevateRAP201922.pdf

Azocar, Cristina. "Native Americans," in *The Diversity Style Guide*, ed. Rachele Kanigel (San Francisco: Wiley-Blackwell, 2018): 61–84.

Baker III, Oscar. "Canadian Journalism Schools Respond to the TRC's Calls to Action," *CBC Indigenous*, June 4, 2016.

Balkisson, Denise. "Objectivity: Trust and Truth in an Age of Disinformation." 2020 Atkinson Lecture at Ryerson University. Retrieved at: https://www.ryerson.ca/journalism/news-events/2020/10/atkinson-2020-objectivity-trust-and-truth-in-an-age-of-disinformation/

Barclay, Barry. "The Vibrant Shimmer," *The Contemporary Pacific* 11.2 (1999): 390–413.

Barclay, Barry. "Celebrating Fourth Cinema," *Illusions Magazine* 35 (2003): 1–11.

Barnhart, Brent. "Social Media and Journalism: How to Effectively Reach the Public," *Spout Social*, May 11, 2020. Retrieved at: https://sproutsocial.com/insights/social-media-and-journalism/

Bascaramurty, Dakshana. "Power at Their Fingertips: Indigenous People Turn to Social Media to Expose Injustice," *Globe and Mail*, November 7, 2020.

Beers, David. "A Truly Influential Question: What Might Go Right Tomorrow?" *SPARC BC News*, Spring 2005, 5–7.

Beers, David. "The Public Sphere and Online, Independent Journalism," *Canadian Journal of Education* 29.1 (2006): 109–130.

Belcourt, Billy-Ray. "Dear Media: I Am More Than Just Violence." Personal blog, November 24, 2015. Retrieved at: https://nakinisowin.wordpress.com/2015/11/24/dear-media-i-am-more-than-just-violence/

Berube, Kevin. "The Intergenerational Trauma of First Nations Still Runs Deep," *Globe and Mail*, February 16, 2015.

Bisson, Jonathan, Suzanna Rose, Rachel Churchill, and Simon Wessely. "Psychological Debriefing for Preventing Post Traumatic Stress Disorder (PTSD)," *Cochrane Database of Systematic Reviews* 2 (2002): 1–38.

Blatchford, Christie. "Canada's Native Reserves Deserve Foreign Correspondent," *Globe and Mail*, February 2, 2008.

Blatchford, Taylor. "A More Diverse Student Newsroom Will Make Your Publication Stronger. Here's How to Get Started," *Poynter Institute*, June 17, 2020.

Braganza, Chantal. "Why We Decided to Capitalize Black, Aboriginal and Indigenous," *TVO*, October 7, 2016.

Brant, Clare. "Native Ethics and Rules of Behaviour," *Canadian Journal of Psychiatry* 35 (1990): 534–539.

Brant, Clare. "Native Ethics and Principles," Lecture, 1982. Retrieved at: https://www.cbu.ca/indigenous-affairs/mikmaq-resource-centre/mikmaq-resource-guide/essays/native-ethics-principles/

Brave Heart, Maria Y.H. "The Return to the Sacred Path: Healing the Historical Trauma Response among the Lakota," *Smith College Studies in Social Work* 68.3 (1998): 287–305.

Brave NoiseCat, Julian. "Apocalypse Then and Now," *Columbia Journalism Review*, Winter 2020.

Brean, Joseph. "'The Experiment of Colonization in Canada, It Damaged You Too': Wab

Kinew on His New Memoir," *National Post*, September 18, 2015.
Brousseau, Alanna. "Wab Kinew: The Politics of Power and Language." Blog, October 17, 2015. Retrieved at: https://www.theeditingco.com/blog/10188/wab-kinew-the-power-and-politics-of-language
CBC Indigenous. "Beyond 94: Truth and Reconciliation in Canada." March 19, 2018. Retrieved at: https://newsinteractives.cbc.ca/longform-single/beyond-94
CBC-Radio Canada, *CBC-Radio Canada Employment Equity Annual Report 2019*, Retrieved at: https://cbc.radio-canada.ca/en/impact-and-accountability/diversity-and-inclusion/equity-reports
CBC Radio, "Qanurli: TV Show Part Inuktitut Language Preservation, Part Laughter as Medicine," *CBC Unreserved*, June 6, 2019.
CBC Radio, "Objectivity Is 'The View from Nowhere' and Potentially Harmful: Expert," *The Sunday Edition*, July 10, 2020.
CBC Radio, "'An Enormous Change in the News Agenda': How Trauma-Informed Reporting Is Transforming Journalism," *The Sunday Edition*, August 23, 2019.
Callison, Candis, and Alfred Hermida. "Dissent and Resonance: #Idlenomore as an Emergent Middle Ground," *Canadian Journal of Communication* 40 (2015): 695–716.
Callison, Candis, and Mary Lynn Young. "It's Time for a New Approach to Journalism," *Toronto Star*, June 7, 2020.
Campbell, Tara. "A Copy Editor's Education in Indigenous Style," *The Tyee*, January 17, 2020.
Canadian Association of Journalists "On the Record: Is It Really Informed Consent without Discussion of Consequences?," February 10, 2014. Retrieved at: https://caj.ca/blog/informed-consent
Canadian Press. "'A Role for Humour in Reconciliation': Satire News Site Walking Eagle Taking Off," CBC Manitoba, November 28, 2017.
Canadian Resource Centre for Victims of Crime. "If the Media Calls: A Guide for Victims and Survivors." Retrieved at: https://crcvc.ca/publications/if-the-media-calls/
Carlson, Bronwyn. "Why Are Indigenous People Such Avid Users of Social Media?" *The Guardian*, April 27, 2017.
Carlson, Bronwyn. "The 'New Frontier': Emergent Indigenous Identities and Social Media," in *The Politics of Identity: Emerging Indigeneity*, eds. Michelle Harris, Martin Nakata, and Bronwyn Carlson (Sydney: University of Technology Sydney E-Press, 2013): 147–168.
Carlson, Bronwyn, and Ryan Frazer. *Social Media Mob: Being Indigenous Online* (Sydney, Australia: Macquarie University, 2018).
Carlson, Bronwyn, and Ryan Frazer. "'They Got Filters': Indigenous Social Media, the Settler Gaze, and a Politics of Hope," *Social Media + Society* 6.2 (2020)
Carpenter, Lenny, et al. *"Style Guide for Reporting on Indigenous People"* (Toronto: Journalism for Human Rights, 2017). Retrieved at: https://jhr.ca/wp-content/uploads/2017/12/JHR2017-Style-Book-Indigenous-People.pdf
Castellano, Marlene Brant, and Linda Archibald. "Healing Historic Trauma: A Report from the Aboriginal Healing Foundation" (2007). *Aboriginal Policy Research Consortium International (APRCi)*, 111.
Centre for Suicide Prevention. "Trauma and Suicide in Indigenous People." Retrieved at: https://www.suicideinfo.ca/resource/trauma-and-suicide-in-indigenous-people/
Childers, Nicole. "The Moral Argument for Diversity in Newsrooms Is Also a Business Argument—And You Need Both," *NiemanLab*, November 24, 2020.
Chowdhury, Radiyah. "The Forever Battle of a Journalist of Colour: Dalton Camp Award Winning Essay," *Toronto Star*, July 11, 2020.
Chrona, Jo-Anne. "First Peoples Principles of Learning." Personal blog, 2014. Retrieved at: https://firstpeoplesprinciplesoflearning.wordpress.com/
Cobham, Kari. "How Journalists Can Take Care of Themselves while Covering Trauma," *Poynter*, May 29, 2019.
Cukier, Wendy, John Miller, Kristen Aspevig, and Dale Carl. "Diversity in Leadership and Media: A Multi-Perspective Analysis of the Greater Toronto Area, 2010," *The International Journal of Diversity in Organizations, Communities, and Nations: Annual Review* 11.6 (2012): 63–78.
Cunningham, Brent. "Rethinking Objectivity," *Columbia Journalism Review*, July/August 2003.
Daubs, Katie. "The Man Behind the Satirical Walking Eagle News Finally Says the Things He Never Could as a Journalist," *Toronto Star*, January 10, 2020.
Deer, Ka'nhehsí:io. "Quebec Political Cartoonist 'Sorry' for Feathers and Fringe Portrayal of Wilson-Raybould," *CBC Indigenous*, March 1, 2019.

De Souza, Mike. "A 'Recovering Journalist' Explains What Led Him to Launch the Satirical Walking Eagle News," *National Observer*, November 7, 2018.

Dyer, John. "Is Solutions Journalism the Solution?" *Nieman Reports*, June 11, 2015.

Elliot, Patricia. *Decolonizing the Media: Challenges and Obstacles on the Road to Reconciliation*. Canadian Centre for Policy Alternatives (Saskatchewan Office), October 2016. Retrieved at: https://www.policyalternatives.ca/sites/default/files/uploads/publications/Saskatchewan%20Office/2016/11/Decolonizing%20the%20Media%20%28final%29.pdf

English, Kathy. "Respect, Dignity and Fairness Conveyed in Capital Letters: Public Editor," *Toronto Star*, May 26, 2017.

Environics Institute. "Canadian Public Opinion on Aboriginal Peoples: Final Report, June 2016." Retrieved at: https://www.environicsinstitute.org/docs/default-source/project-documents/public-opinion-about-aboriginal-issues-in-canada-2016/final-report.pdf?sfvrsn=30587aca_2

Facing History and Ourselves. "How Journalists Minimize Bias." Retrieved at: https://www.facinghistory.org/resource-library/facing-ferguson-news-literacy-digital-age/how-journalists-minimize-bias

Fast, Elizabeth, and Delphine Collin-Vézina. "Historical Trauma, Race-Based Trauma and Resilience of Indigenous Peoples: A Literature Review," *First Peoples Child and Family Review* 5.1 (2010): 126–136.

Femifesto and Collaborators. "Use the Right Words: Media Reporting on Sexual Violence in Canada," (2015). Retrieved at: https://www.femifesto.ca/wp-content/uploads/2015/12/UseTheRightWords-Single-Dec3.pdf

Fenlon, Brodie. "Uncivil Dialogue: Commenting and Stories about Indigenous People," *CBC News*, November 13, 2015.

Fontaine, Tim (@anishinaboy). "Chisk Deiter, protester." *Twitter*, February 8, 2020. https://twitter.com/anishinaboy/status/1226147250637811717

Ghosh, Ilana. "Covering Aboriginal Issues: Tips from TRC Commissioner Marie Wilson." *Ryerson Journalism Research Centre*. February 23, 2016. Retrieved at: https://ryersonjournalism.ca/2016/02/23/covering-aboriginal-issues-tips-from-trc-commissioner-marie-wilson/

Giago, Tim. "If You Come Out to Indian Country to Write about Us, Do Your Damned Homework," *Nieman Reports*, July 2, 2019.

Gilmore, Meagan. "Long Journey of Reconciliation Ahead at Canada's Journalism Schools," April 20, 2018.

Gilpin, Emilee. "Indigenous Journalists Speak Up," *National Observer*, December 11, 2018.

Goldberg, Sally. "For Decades Our Coverage Was Racist. To Rise Above Our Past, We Must Acknowledge It," *National Geographic*, March 13, 2018.

Goldman, Jordana. "Lack of Transparency in Newsroom Diversity," *Ryerson Review of Journalism*, April 4, 2019.

Gonzales, Antonia, and Sarah Gustavus, "For Stories on Solutions to Native Health Problems, Reporters Take Pains to Avoid Outside-Looking-In Trap." *USC Annenberg Centre for Health Journalism*, December 2017. Retrieved at: https://centerforhealthjournalism.org/resources/lessons/stories-solutions-native-health-problems-reporters-take-pains-avoid-outside

Government of Nunavut. "Iviqtippalliajut: In the Process of Falling into Place, 2018–2023." https://www.gov.nu.ca/sites/default/files/ch_-_iviqtippalliajut_report_en_rev05.pdf

Government of Nunavut. *Iviqtippalliajut Ally Brochure*. Retrieved at: https://www.gov.nu.ca/sites/default/files/ally_brochure_rev07_withedits.pdf

Grabowski, Mark. "Objectivity Didn't Fail Journalism. Journalists Failed It," *Washington Examiner*, June 17, 2020.

Green, Elon. "Using True Crime to Teach Indigenous History: Reporter Connie Walker on 'Finding Cleo,'" *Columbia Journalism Review*, July 5, 2008.

Gregoire, Lisa. "Nunavut Must Move beyond Paying Lip Service to Traditional Values, Says Glassco Fellow," *Nunatsiaq News*, May 19, 2020.

Hamilton, Wawmeesh. "How Can Journalism Support Reconciliation with Indigenous Peoples?" *The Discourse*, June 17, 2016.

Hanusch, Folker. "Charting a Theoretical Framework for Examining Indigenous Journalism Culture," *Media International Australia Incorporating Culture and Policy*, 149 (2013): 82–91.

Hanusch, Folker. "Cultural Forces in Journalism: The Impact of Cultural Values on Māori Journalists' Professional Views," *Journalism Studies* 16.2 (2015): 191–206.

Harding, Robert. "Aboriginal Child Welfare: Symbolic Battleground in the News Media," in *Indigenous Canada Revisited,* ed. Kerstin Knopf (Ottawa: University of Ottawa Press, 2008), 290–328.

Harding, Robert. "The Media, Aboriginal People and Common Sense," *The Canadian Journal of Native Studies* XXV.1 (2005): 311–335.

Harding, Robert. "Historical Representations of Aboriginal People in the Canadian News Media," *Discourse and Society* 17.2 (2006): 229.

Harper, Stephen. "Indian Residential Schools Statement of Apology—Prime Minister Stephen Harper." *Indigenous and Northern Affairs Canada*, June 11, 2008. Retrieved at: https://www.aadncaandc.gc.ca/eng/1100100015677/1100100015680.

Harris, Johnny. "7 Things I've Learned about Journalism in 7 Years of Being a Journalist." Retrieved at: https://www.youtube.com/watch?v=Rr7povAInwQ&feature=youtu.be

Hartley, John. "Their own media in their own language," in Catharine Lumby and Elspeth Probyn (eds.), *Remote Control: New Media, New Ethics* (New York: Cambridge University Press, 2003)

Hatfield, Samantha Chisholm, Elizabeth Marino, et al. "Indian Time: Time, Seasonality, and Culture in Traditional Ecological Knowledge of Climate Change," *Ecological Processes* 7.25 (2018): 1–11.

Hendriksen, Helen. "5 Reasons to Talk about Trauma," *Psychology Today*, March 27, 2019.

Herrera, Tim. "How to Successfully Pitch the *New York Times* (Or, Well, Anyone Else)," *Nieman Lab*, October 22, 2018.

Historica Canada. *Indigenous Perspectives Education Guide.* Retrieved at: https://fb.historicacanada.ca/education/english/indigenous-perspectives/IndigenousPerspectives/assets/common/downloads/publication.pdf

Hopkins, John. "A Look at Indian Time," *Indian Country Today*, September 13, 2018.

Howard, Ross. *Conflict Sensitive Journalism: A Handbook* (International Media Support/IMPACS: Vancouver, 2009)

Huang, Tom. "6 Questions Journalists Should Be Able to Answer Before Pitching a Story," *Poynter Institute*, August 22, 2012.

Hume, Stephen. "Seems No One's without Sin in the Practice of Self-Government," *Vancouver Sun*, March 1, 2006.

ICT Staff. "10 Hilarious 'You Might Be An Indian' Lines From Don Burnstick," *Indian Country Today*, September 13, 2018.

Indian and Northern Affairs Canada. "Words First: An Evolving Terminology Relating to Aboriginal Peoples in Canada." Communications Branch (October 2002). Retrieved at: http://publications.gc.ca/collections/Collection/R2-236-2002E.pdf

Ingram, Matthew. "Objectivity Isn't a Magic Wand," *Columbia Journalism Review*, June 25, 2020.

Jamil, Sukaina. "How Journalists Should Reframe Their Perspectives on Objectivity," *Ryerson Review of Journalism*, November 26, 2019.

Jones, Allison. "Territory Acknowledgement." Native Land Digital. Retrieved at: https://native-land.ca/resources/territory-acknowledgement/

Jones, Alex S. "An Argument Why Journalists Should Not Abandon Objectivity," *Nieman Reports*, Fall 2009. Retrieved at: https://niemanreports.org/articles/an-argument-why-journalists-should-not-abandon-objectivity/

Joseph, Robert. "Use These Culturally Offensive Phrases, Questions at Your Own Risk," *Indigenous Corporate Training Blog*, September 22, 2015. Retrieved at: https://www.ictinc.ca/blog/culturally-offensive-phrases-you-should-use-at

Joseph, Robert. "Value of Engaging with Indigenous Communities via Social Media," *Indigenous Corporate Training Blog*, August 22, 2016. Retrieved at: https://www.ictinc.ca/blog/value-of-engaging-with-indigenous-communities-via-social-media

Joseph, Robert. "Indigenous Cultural Competency Self-Assessment Checklist." *Indigenous Corporate Training Blog*, March 29, 2016. Retrieved at: https://www.ictinc.ca/blog/indigenous-cultural-competency-self-assessment-checklist

Journalism for Human Rights. *Buried Voices: Changing Tones.* Retrieved at: https://jhr.ca/wp-content/uploads/2019/10/JHR-IRP-Report-v3online.pdf

Karmali, Shahzeer, Kevin Laupland, et al. "Epidemiology of Severe Trauma among Status Aboriginal Canadians: A Population-Based Study," *CMAJ* 172.8 (2005): 1007–1011.

Karki, Arun. "6 Tips for Protecting Your Mental Health When Reporting on Trauma," *International Journalists Network (IJNet)*, November 1, 2017.

Kirkness, V.J., and Barnhardt, R. "First Nations and Higher Education: The Four R's—Respect, Relevance, Reciprocity, Responsibility," *The Journal of American Indian Education* 30 (1991): 1–15.

Klein, Peter, Britney Dennison, et al. "Turning Points." Global Reporting Centre. https://globalreportingcentre.org/turning-points/about/

Knott, Helen. "The Indigenous People I Read about as a Kid Were Nothing Like Me—So I Became a Writer," *Chatelaine*, June 21, 2017.

Korff, Jens. "Aboriginal Use of Social Media," *Creative Spirits*, February 8, 2021. Retrieved at: https://www.creativespirits.info/aboriginalculture/media/aboriginal-use-of-social-media#benefits-

Krebs, Andreas. "'Number One Tool' for First Nations? Facebook," *The Tyee*, May 30, 2011.

Leddy, Shannon. "In a Good Way: Reflecting on Humour in Indigenous Education," *Journal of the Canadian Association for Curriculum Studies (JCACS)* 16.2 (2018): 10–20.

Lefkowich, Maya, Britney Dennison, and Peter Klein. "Empowerment Journalism," *Journalism Studies* 20.12 (September 10, 2019): 1803–9.

Lewis, Seth C., Avery E. Holton, and Mark Coddington. "Reciprocal Journalism," *Journalism Practice* 8.2 (March 4, 2014): 229–41.

Lievano, Wilson. "How to Write Compelling Solutions Journalism Stories," *The Groundtruth Project*, January 31, 2019.

Linnit, Carol. "Who Tells the Story of the Present? Candis Callison on Redefining Journalism in Canada," *The Narwhal*, June 17, 2020.

Lisk, Shelby. "Creating Space for Indigenous Journalism amid the Whiteness of Canadian Media." *TVO*, September 3, 2020.

Lisk, Shelby. "Rewriting Journalism: 'Get Indigenous Voices Involved.'" *TVO*, September 3, 2020.

Loyer, Jessie. "Indigenous TikTok Is Transforming Cultural Knowledge," *Canadian Art*, April 23, 2020.

MacAdam, Alison. "What Makes a Good Pitch? NPR Editors Weigh In," *NPR Training*, January 24, 2017.

Mahtani, Minelle. "Racializing the Audience: Immigrant Perceptions of Mainstream Canadian English-Language TV News," *Canadian Journal of Communication*, 33 (2008): 639–660.

Mahtani, Minelle. "Representing Minorities: Canadian Media and Minority Identities," *Canadian Ethnic Studies Journal* 33.3 (2001): 99+.

Maslin, Crystal Lynn. "Social Construction of Aboriginal People in the Saskatchewan Print Media." Unpublished thesis, 2002. Retrieved at: https://harvest.usask.ca/handle/10388/etd-06202008-130404

McCreadie, Danielle. "When the News Breaks the Journalist," *The Signal*, February 14, 2018.

Media Smarts. "Aboriginal People in the News." Retrieved at: https://mediasmarts.ca/digital-media-literacy/media-issues/diversity-media/aboriginal-people/aboriginal-people-news

MediaSmarts. "Common Portrayals of Aboriginal People." Retrieved at: https://mediasmarts.ca/diversity-media/aboriginal-people/common-portrayals-aboriginal-people

Mental Health America. "Racial Trauma." Retrieved at: https://www.mhanational.org/racial-trauma#:~:text=Racial%20trauma%2C%20or%20race%2Dbased,and%20hate%20crimes %20%5B1%5D

Merina, Victor. "The Internet: Continuing the Legacy of Storytelling," *Nieman Reports*, September 15, 2005.

Millar, Erin. "Reconciling Journalism," *The Discourse*, May 26, 2016. Retrieved at: https://thediscourse.ca/urban-nation/reconciling-journalism

Miller, John. "Who's Telling The News? Racial Representation Among News Gatherers in Canada's Daily Newsrooms," *The International Journal of Diversity in Organizations, Communities, and Nations: Annual Review* 5.4 (2006): 133–142.

Miller, John. "Ipperwash and the Media: A Critical Analysis of How the Story Was Covered," *The International Journal of Diversity in Organisations, Communities and Nations* 8.3 (2005): 1–10.

Monkman, Lenard. "Indigenous Meme Creators Point Out Harsh Truths with Dark Humour," *CBC Indigenous*, September 19, 2018.

Monkman, Lenard (@LenardMonkman1). "Instant @cbc classic from 'Tugguy Lawrenchuk.' Can't take these Crees anywhere" *Twitter*, July 25, 2019. https://twitter.com/lenardmonkman1/status/1154488630355857409?lang=en.

Monkman, Lenard (@LenardMonkman1). "Plude Choochman gets a shoutout in CTV." *Twitter*, February 12, 2020. https://twitter.com/lenardmonkman1/status/1227728280675061762?lang=en

Moore, Michael. "Taking Time to Understand the Story to Be Told," *Nieman Reports*, September 15, 2005.

National Archives of Canada, Record Group 10, vol. 6810, file 470-2-3, vol. 7, 55 (L-3) and 63 (N-3).

National Indigenous Television (NITV). "Indigenous Cultural Protocols: What Media Needs to Do when Depicting Deceased Persons," July 27, 2017. Retrieved at: https://www.sbs.com.au/nitv/article/2017/07/27/indigenous-cultural-protocols-what-media-needs-do-when-depicting-deceased-persons

Native American Journalist Association. "Reporting and Indigenous Terminology," 2017. Retrieved at: https://najanewsroom.com/wp-content/uploads/2018/11/NAJA_Reporting_and_Indigenous_Terminology_Guide.pdf

Native Women's Association of Canada, "Aboriginal Lateral Violence." Factsheet, 2011. https://www.nwac.ca/wp-content/uploads/2015/05/2011-Aboriginal-Lateral-Violence.pdf

Neason, Alexandria. "On Atonement," *Columbia Journalism Review*, January 28, 2021.

Nelson, Sarah E., and Kathi Wilson. "The Mental Health of Indigenous Peoples in Canada: A Critical Review of Research," *Social Science and Medicine* 176 (2017): 93–112.

Nieman Foundation for Journalism at Harvard University. "Covering Indian Country," *Nieman Reports* 59.3 (2005): 5–39.

Nixon, Lindsay. "Writing Indigenous Truths: Trauma Ethics," *QWF Writes*, February 28, 2019. Retrieved at: https://qwfwrites.wordpress.com/2019/02/28/trauma-ethics-by-lindsay-nixon/

Nobel, Carmen. "10 Rules for Reporting on War Trauma Survivors," *The Journalist's Resource*, August 9, 2018. Retrieved at: https://journalistsresource.org/politics-and-government/10-nixon-rules-interviewing-trauma-survivors/

O'Donnel, Ginger. "Journalists as First Responders: Educators Teach Trauma-Informed Reporting, Self-Care," *Insight into Diversity*, March 16, 2020. Retrieved at: https://www.insightintodiversity.com/journalists-as-first-responders-educators-teach-trauma-informed-reporting-self-care/

Plener, Abigail. "How Discourse Media Is Addressing Reconciliation," *Ryerson Review of Journalism*, December 19, 2016.

Porter, Jody. "Pathfinding," *Maisonneuve*, October 20, 2020.

Powers, Patricia. "Native Americans and the Public: A Human Values Perspective," from "Hear Our Story: Communications and Contemporary Native Americans" symposium, Washington, DC, March 2–3, 2006. Retrieved at: https://www.scribd.com/document/224015334/Native-Americans-and-the-Public

Pressé, Michelle. "Last Call Is Over for the Hard-Drinking Journalist," *The Signal*, December 11, 2015.

Pritchard, David, and Florian Sauvageau. "The Journalists and Journalisms of Canada," in *The Global Journalist: News People Around the World*, ed. David Weaver (Cresskill: Hampton Press, 1998), 373–393.

Pugliese, Karyn. "Reconciliation," in Royal Canadian Geographical Society, *Indigenous Peoples Atlas of Canada: Atlas des Peuples Autochtones du Canada*, 2018. Retrieved at: https://indigenouspeoplesatlasofcanada.ca/article/reconciliation/

Pugliese, Kayrn. "Silent No More: What Indigenous Women Journalists in Canada Face, and What Can Be Done to Help Them," in *Half the Story Is Never Enough: Threats Facing Women* (Canadian Commission for UNESCO, World Press Freedom Canada and Journalists for Human Rights, 2020).

Randall, Melanie, and Lori Haskell. "Disrupted Attachments: A Social Context Complex Trauma Framework And the Lives of Aboriginal Peoples in Canada," *Journal of Aboriginal Health* 5 (November 2009): 48–99.

Rave, Jodi. "Keeping It Real: Accurate Coverage of Native Culture," *Poynter*, Aug. 9, 2006.

Rice, Waubgeshig. "Letter to a Young Indigenous Journalist," *The Walrus*, August 31, 2020.

Rollmann, Rhea. "Protesters? Or Land Protectors," *The Independent*, October 28, 2016.

Rosen, Jay. "The View from Nowhere: Questions and Answers," *Press Think*, November 10, 2010.

Rosen, Jay (@jayrosen_nyu): "1/Time for Another Report from Berlin, Midway in My Stay at @BoschAcademy. I'm Studying German Pressthink This Summer. This Thread Is My Notebook on What Objectivity Seems to Mean in German Journalism. to an Outsider. So If That Title Excites You, You're in the Right Place." Tweet thread, July 28, 2018. Retrieved at: https://twitter.com/jayrosen_nyu/status/1023271188309700608?lang=en

Rosenstiel, Tom (@Tom Rosenstiel). "1... I'm Not Avid on Twitter, But at Others' Urging I Want to Offer a Thread in Response to @wesleylowery'S Powerful Essay in the @nytimes on Objectivity, Which I Liked. But the Call for 'Moral Clarity' I Believe Could Use More Clarity... Please Be Patient. This Is 1 of 22." Tweet thread, June 24, 2020. Retrieved at: https://twitter.com/TomRosenstiel/status/1275773988053102592

Sand, Stine Agnete. "Indigenous Television for the Majority: Analyzing NRK Sapmi's Muitte Mu (Remember Me)," *Television and New Media*, 2019. Retrieved at: https://www.researchgate.net/publication/333932025_Indigenous_Television_for_the_Majority_Analyzing_NRK_Sapmi's_Muitte_Mu_Remember_Me

Scire, Sarah. "Five Do-Them-Now Steps to Making Your Newsroom (and Coverage) More Representative," *Nieman Lab*, June 12, 2020.

Sehra, Rohina Katoch. "26 Indigenous Instagram Accounts to Follow Right Away," *HuffPost*, November 10, 2020.

Seymour, Ruth. "Eight Steps toward Cultural Competence," *Poynter*, November 14, 2002.

Sheridan-Burns, Lynette, and McKee, Alan. "Reporting on Indigenous Issues: Some Practical Suggestions for Improving Journalistic Practice in the Coverage of Indigenous Affairs," *Australian Journalism Review* 21.2 (1999): 103–116.

Shin, Laura. "How Journalists Can Work Well with Interpreters when Reporting Stories," *Poynter*, November 12, 2012.

Simanovych, Olga. "How Journalists Can Deal with Trauma while Reporting on COVID-19," Global Investigative Journalism Network, March 24, 2020. Retrieved at: https://gijn.org/2020/03/24/how-journalists-can-deal-with-trauma-while-reporting-on-covid-19/

Sinclair, Murray. "If You Thought Truth Would Be Hard, Reconciliation Will Be Harder." Knight Lecture, University of Manitoba, October 30, 2014. Retrieved at: https://news.umanitoba.ca/if-you-thought-the-truth-was-hard-reconciliation-will-be- harder/

Sinclair, Niigaan. "Idle No More: Where Is the Movement 2 Years Later?" *CBC Indigenous*, December 7, 2014.

Society for Professional Journalists. "Diversity Toolbox." Retrieved at: https://www.spj.org/dtb.asp

Stevens, Mark. "*Stuff*'s Apology to Māori—Our Truth, Tā Mātou Pono," *Stuff*, November 30, 2020.

Stewart, Heather, Michael Williams, Trevor Cullen, Michelle Johnston, Gail Phillips, Pauline Mulligan, Leo Bowman, and Michael Meadows. "Teaching Journalism Students How to Tell Indigenous Stories in an Informed Way: A Work-Integrated Learning Approach," *Asia Pacific Media Educator* 22.1 (2012): 55–67.

Storm, Hannah. "My Mental Health Journey: How PTSD Gave Me the Strength to Share My Story," *Poynter*, July 24, 2020.

"Stuff's Charter: A brave new era for NZ's largest media company" *Stuff*, November 30, 2020. https://www.stuff.co.nz/pou-tiaki/our-truth/300168692/stuffs-charter-a-brave-new-era-for-nzs-largest-media-company

Sweet, Melissa. "Is the Media Part of the Aboriginal Health Problem, and Part of the Solution?" *Inside Story*, March 3, 2009.

Talaga, Tanya. "Reconciliation Isn't Dead. It Never Truly Existed," *Globe and Mail*, February 29, 2020.

TallBear, Kim. "Standing with and Speaking as Faith: A Feminist-Indigenous Approach to Inquiry," *Journal of Research Practice* 10.2 (2014): Article N17.

TallBear, Kim. "Indigenous Bioscientists Constitute Knowledge across Cultures of Expertise and Tradition: An Indigenous Standpoint Research Project," in *Re:Mindings: Co-Constituting Indigenous, Academic, Artistic Knowledges*, eds. Johan Gärdebo, May-Britt Öhman, and Hiroshi Maruyama (Uppsala: The Hugo Valentin Centre, Uppsala University, 2014): 173–191.

Taylor, Drew Hayden. "Ipperwash, on Indian Time," *NOW Magazine*, January 3, 2008.

Taylor, Drew Hayden. "Narrating Indigenous Stories with a Pinch of Humour Isn't Odd. It's a Part of Healing," *Globe and Mail*, January 7, 2021.

Tennant, Zoe. "Subverting True Crime: Connie Walker on the Ethics of Storytelling," *CBC Unreserved*, November 1, 2019.

Todorova, Miglena S. "Co-Created Learning: Decolonizing Journalism Education in Canada," *Canadian Journal of Communication* 41.4 (2016): 673–692.

Torres, Joseph, Alicia Bell, Collette Watson, et al. "Media 2070: An Invitation to Dream Up Media Reparations," October 2020. Retrieved at: https://mediareparations.org/

Truong, Doris. "Indigenous Issues Get Long-Overdue Mainstream Coverage," *Nieman Journalism Lab*, 2020. Retrieved at: https://www.niemanlab.org/2020/12/indigenous-issues-get-long-overdue-mainstream-coverage/

UBC Brand/UBC. First Nations House of Learning. *Indigenous Peoples: Language Guidelines* (Vancouver: University of British Columbia, 2018). Retrieved at: https://indigenous.ubc.ca/indigenous-engagement/featured-initiatives/indigenous-peoples-language-guideline/

UBC First Nations and Indigenous Studies Program. "Terminology." Indigenous Foundations, 2009. Retrieved at: https://indigenousfoundations.arts.ubc.ca/terminology/

Various. "Aboriginal Media, Aboriginal Control," *Cultural Survival Quarterly Magazine* 22.2 (June 1998). Retrieved at: https://www.culturalsurvival.org/publications/cultural-survival-quarterly/22-2-aboriginal-media-aboriginal-control

Venn, David. "Searching for Solutions," *Ryerson Review of Journalism*, October 30, 2019.

Walker, Chad. "Journalists Covering Indigenous Peoples in Renewable Energy Should Focus on Context and Truth, Not Click-Bait," *The Conversation*, January 22, 2020.

Ward, Steven. "Pragmatic News Objectivity: Objectivity with a Human Face." The Joan Shorenstein Center on the Press, Politics and Public Policy, 1999. Retrieved at: https://shorensteincenter.org/wp-content/uploads/2012/03/d37_ward.pdf

Ward, Stephen J.A. "Engagement and Pragmatic Objectivity." *Centre for Journalism Ethics*, March 27, 2017. Retrieved at: https://ethics.journalism.wisc.edu/2017/03/27/engagement-and-pragmatic-objectivity/

Warhover, Tom. "Against Objectivity," *Poynter*, June 15, 2017.

Watson, H.G. "Canadian Press Style Now Capitalizes Aboriginal and Indigenous," *J-source*, July 4, 2017.

Weeber, Christine. "Why Capitalize Indigenous?" *SAPIENS*, May 19, 2020.

Wells, Jennifer. "A Warrior, a Soldier and a Photographer," *Toronto Star*, August 22, 2015.

Wilkes, Rima, et al. "Packaging Protest: Media Coverage of Indigenous People's Collective Action," *Canadian Review of Sociology* 47 (2010):349–379.

Wilson, Christopher. "A Side-Bar on 'Objectivity,'" 2020. Retrieved on "Reading Narrative Journalism" website: https://mediakron.bc.edu/readingnarrativejournalism/exercise-on-attribution/interludes-some-preliminary-tips-for-students/a-side-bar-on-objectivity

Wood, Stephanie. "Inuit, Reporters Call Out *New York Times* for 'Trauma Porn,'" *National Observer*, November 9, 2019.

Zerehi, Sima Sahar. "*Qanurli*, Nunavut's Inuktitut TV Show, Travels to Other Inuit Regions," *CBC North*, February 20, 2016.

Websites

The Canadian Encyclopedia. "Timeline: Indigenous Peoples." Retrieved 4 May 2022. https://www.thecanadianencyclopedia.ca/en/timeline/first-nations.

Historica Canada. "Key Moments in Indigenous History Timeline." Retrieved 4 May 2022. http://education.historicacanada.ca/en/tools/495.

Index

ABC Indigenous, 24
Aboriginal Peoples Television Network (APTN), 24; *APTN National News*, 162; Barnsley and, 192n8; Deverell and, 192n7; Fontaine and, 194, 202; Jackson and, 193n11; Pugliese and, 182–91; Truth and Reconciliation Commission (TRC) and, 230
Aboriginal people: Barnsley and, 192n8; customs and, 56, 61–62; legal issues and, 103; objectivity and, 116; positive vs. negative stories and, 28; Pugliese and, 182, 185; residential schools and, 234–36; Royal Commission on Aboriginal Peoples (RCAP), 10–12, 127; stereotypes and, 10–13; story-takers and, 87; terminology and, 99, 102–6; title claims and, 16n4; Truth and Reconciliation Commission (TRC) and, ix, xvii, 230–31
abuse: bullying, 118–19, 189–90; child, 75, 122; online, 118–20; physical, 77; priests and, 151, 154; sexual, 75, 89–90, 110, 118, 131–32, 151, 153–54, 222, 235; substance, 77, 91; trauma and, 88
Academy of Broadcasting, 162
accountability, 5; Ahtone and, 217–21; Fontaine and, 201; positive vs. negative stories and, 28; reciprocity and, 112–14; Rice and, 148; social media and, 115, 119–20; trauma and, 80; tribal, 220–21
agency, 71–73
Ahtone, Tristan: accountability and, 217–21; avoiding historical analysis, 217; awards of, 215; background of, xiii, 215; bias and, 216; ceremonies and, 221; colonialism and, x, 217, 224; context and, 217–18; crime and, 217; data journalism and, 223–24; education and, 218; ethics and, 218, 221; Indian Country and, 216–24; invisibility of Native Americans in media and, 215–17; maintaining relationships and, 221–22; on Native people, 215–23; non-Indigenous people and, 219, 222; Nunavut and, 216; pitching and, 218–20; police and, 217; reserves and, 217–18; sovereignty and, 223–24; statistics and, 217, 223; stereotypes and, 216; *Texas Observer* and, 215; tough questions and, 222–23; violence and, 217–18; white people and, 216–17, 220
Alberta, 23, 68, 102
Alcatraz Island, 158, 161n9
alcohol: context and, 110; customs and, 65; drunkenness, 4, 7, 10–12, 110; Fontaine and, 203; Rice and, 150; stereotypes and, 10–11; Taylor and, 164; trauma and, 83, 86n19
Algonquins, 143, 182, 191, 192n5, 214n1
Al Jazeera America, 215
All Our Relations: Finding the Path Forward (Talaga), 172
American Academy of Arts and Sciences, 151
American Indian Movement (AIM), 161n9
American Society of Newspaper Editors, 40, 47n9
Anaya, James, 100
Anderson, Jethro, 181n2
Anderson, Leah, 140n5
Anderson, Mark, 11–13, 124
Anishinaabe, 8; Brass and, 214n2; Fontaine and, 194; Indian time and, 52; Ipperwash Crisis and, 186, 192n6; Neechie and, 176, 181n4; objectivity and, 41; as Ojibways, 21, 24, 100, 191, 214n3; Rice and, 41, 141, 143–45; Sagkeeng First Nation, 194; Talaga and, 172; Taylor and, 167; terminology and, xi, 99–100, 204n5; trauma and, 75, 78
Anishinabek News, 23
Apache (Purépecha), 100
Apple Canada, 131
Arizona Republic, The, 151–52, 157–58, 161n7
Aspevig, Kristen, 42
Atwood, Margaret, 91
Australian Broadcasting Corporation (ABC), 125
Avatar (film), 71

Baby Yoda, 198
backstory, 110–11
Bacon, Kevin, 225n4
Baffin Island, 103
Bannock, 151
Barnsley, Paul, 188, 192n8
BBC, 77

Beaver, The (magazine), 8
Beaverton, The (TV show), 194
Because News (TV show), 194
Beers, David, 32
Belcourt, Billy-Ray, 75
Best Serialized Story award, 131
bias: Ahtone and, 216; customs and, 57, 62; Fiddler-Potter and, 210–11; Fontaine and, 199, 202; Indigenous perspective and, 68; invisibility of Native Americans in media, 215–17; objectivity and, 39–46, 47n3; Pugliese and, 184, 187, 190–91; reciprocity and, 114; stereotypes and, 13–14; story choice and, 18; trauma and, 76; Walker and, 136
Bill C-31, 13
bingo card, 18–20, 216
BIPOC, 42, 178
Blackfoot (Siksiká), 100, 161n3
Black Lives Matter, ix, 41
Blatchford, Christie, 56
blockades: CTV Regina and, 204n3; Kokumville, 192n5; land defenders and, 185–87; positive vs. negative stories and, 28; Pugliese and, 185–87; Rice and, 149; stereotypes and, 8–9; terminology and, 204n3
Boushie, Colton, 138, 140n7
Boyden, Joseph, 208, 214n3
Brant, Clare, 52, 64–66, 92
Brass, Mervin, 206–7, 214n2
Brave Heart, Maria, 76, 86n8
British Columbia, 11, 23, 68, 102
bullying, 118–19, 189–90
Burnstick, Don, 94
Bushie, Reggie, 181n3

calendar journalism, 27
Callison, Candis, 39, 42, 44–45, 117
Cameron, Christine, 134–35, 140n4
Campbell, Tara, 99
Canadian Association of Journalists (CAJ), 182
Canadian Broadcasting Corporation (CBC), vii, , 24; Brass and, 214n2; comment submission guidelines and, 119; employment equity and, 42; Fiddler-Potter and, xiii, 8–9, 194–96, 202, 205; Fontaine and, 194–96, 202; Latimer and, 214n1; Missing and Murdered database and, 140n3; Pugliese and, 182; Rice and, 141–42, 147–48; style guides and, 43; Talaga and, 172; Taylor and, 162, 165, 167; Truth and Reconciliation Commission (TRC) and, 124, 230; Walker and, 131, 134, 138
Canadian Journalism Foundation, 79
Canadian Screen Awards, 182
Carl, Dale, 42
Carlson, Bronwyn, 115–16, 119
casinos, 12, 161n11
CBC Indigenous, 24
CBC Unreserved, 24
ceremonies: Ahtone and, 221; customs and, 56–61; Fiddler-Potter and, 207; filming, 57–58; Indian time and, 51, 53; Indigenous perspective and, 68; Pugliese and, 188–89; reconciliation and, 126; Rice and, 141, 143; social media and, 118; Talaga and, 175
Cheam First Nation, 186, 192n4
Chicago Sun-Times, 79
Chiefs: customs and, 66; Fiddler, 181n6; Fiddler-Potter and, 210; hereditary, 69, 187, 192n1; Indian time and, 51–52, 54; Indigenous perspective and, 69; Pugliese and, 183, 186–89; stereotypes and, 10; Taylor and, 163–64, 167; terminology and, 103, 106
child abuse, 75, 122
Chippewas, xi, 192n6
Choochman, Plude, 197, 204n5
Circle News, The (newspaper), 24
Cleo, 131, 134–35, 140n4
Coastal GasLink, 192n1
Code Talkers, 161n6
Colbert Show, The (TV show), 92
Cole, Desmond, 45
colonialism: Ahtone and, 217, 224; context and, 109–11; Fiddler-Potter and, 205, 208–9; objectivity and, 45; Porter and, 225n2; Pugliese and, 185; reconciliation and, 122–27; Rice and, 146; solutions and, 31; stereotypes and, 11–13; story choice and, 20; story-takers and, 87; Talaga and, 178–79; terminology and, 99; Trahant and, 153; trauma and, 75, 77; Walker and, 138
Columbia Journalism Review, 131
Columbus, Christopher, 104
Confederated Tribes of the Colville Reservation, 161n12
contacts, 20, 24n3, 54, 117, 199–201

context: Ahtone and, 217–18; backstory and, 110–11; colonialism and, 109–11; *Indian Act* and, 137; land claims and, 109; language and, 100, 102–3, 106; legal issues and, 109–10; Native people and, 110; Pugliese and, 184–85; racism and, 110; residential schools and, 109–10, 137–38; shrinking attention span and, 109; sidebars and, 109–10; Sixties Scoop and, 137; statistics and, 111; Talaga and, 178–80; Walker and, 137–39
councils: ethics and, 66; Fiddler-Potter and, 208; Indian time and, 51; Indigenous perspective and, 69; MacDonald and, 161n6; media and, 23; Métis National Council (MNC), 102; objectivity and, 46; solutions and, 32; stereotypes and, 7; Talaga and, 173; Trahant and, 159–60
COVID-19, 153, 165
Crazy Horse, 58
Cree: Boushie and, 140n7; Brass and, 214n2; *Finding Cleo* and, 140n4; Harper and, 161n1; Indigenous perspective and, 68; Ontario and, 23, 64; Quebec and, 64; Rice and, 143; Starr and, 214n6; story choice and, 23–24; Swampy (Mushkegowuk), 100; terminology and, 100, 103, 204n3–4; trauma and, 75
crime: Ahtone and, 217; Jackson and, 193n11; stereotypes and, 13; Talaga and, 179; trauma and, 75; U.S. statistics on, 225n3; Walker and, 137–39
criticism, 83, 109, 114, 201, 225n2
CTV, 182, 194, 197, 204n3, 204n5, 214n1
Cukier, Wendy, 42
Custer Died for Your Sins (Deloria), 94
customs: Aboriginal people and, 56, 61–62; alcohol and, 65; bias and, 57, 62; ceremonies and, 56–61; Chiefs and, 66; dancing, 7, 10, 57; deadlines and, 60; death and, 60–62; displays of anger, 65; drumming, 7, 9–10, 26, 58, 103, 148; education and, 59; Elders and, 58–60, 66; ethics and, 60–66; eye contact, 62; Facebook and, 58, 61; feasts and, 57; First Nations and, 58–59, 61; food and, 56, 60, 65; gifts, 56, 59–60, 66, 167, 188; health and, 60, 64; Indian Country and, 57, 60; Inuit and, 61, 63–64, 69; language and, 56–57, 62–63; Native people and, 56–66; non-Indigenous people and, 57, 62, 64; non-interference and, 64–65; Nunavut and, 63–64; Ontario and, 64; opinion and, 58, 60; photographs and, 57–62; protocols and, 56–67; Quebec and, 64; reserves and, 56; respect and, 59–63, 66, 227; sharing, 65–66; statistics and, 65; white people and, 65–68; withdrawal reaction and, 66

Daily Show with Trevor Noah, The (TV show), 92
Dakota, 46, 101, 151
Dakota Access Pipeline, 161n8
Dallas W. Smythe Chair, 205
Dances With Wolves (film), 71
dancing, 7, 10, 57
Dart Centre for Journalism and Trauma, 74, 77–78, 84
data journalism, 223–24
deadlines: customs and, 60; Indian time and, 52–54; objectivity and, 41; Rice on, 147; Talaga on, 173; trauma and, 78
death: Anderson and, 181n2; Boushie and, 138; Bushie and, 181n3; customs and, 60–62; Echaquan and, 181n7; Highway of Tears and, 140n6; MacDonald and, 161n6; pandemic and, 153; Pugliese and, 189–90; residential schools and, 234; stereotypes and, 7, 11, 17n5, 178–79, 203; trauma and, 81; Walker and, 138; Williams and, 140n6; women and, 140n6, 178–79, 181n2; young people and, 178–79, 181n2–3, 181n5
decolonizing journalism: Ahtone and, 224; ethics for, 89n2; OCAP and, 232; reconciliation and, 124, 126–27
defiance: Angry Warrior, 12; blockades, 8–9, 28, 149, 185–87, 192n5, 204n3; land defenders, 43, 118, 185–87, 189; marches, 8, 28; Mohawks and, 8–9; protests, 8–10, 43, 118, 149, 158, 161n8, 161n10, 185–87, 189, 192n2–3, 192n6, 197, 204n5; Red River Resistance, 205; stereotypes and, 8–9
Deloria, Vine, Jr., 94
Dene, 23, 68, 102, 167
Dene and Métis Comprehensive Land Claim, 102
Deverell, Rita, 188, 192n7
Dieter, Chisk, 196, 204n3
Discourse, The (newspaper), 23
diversity: Indigenous perspective and, 70; objectivity and, 42; pitching and,

36–37; positive/negative stories and, 27; reconciliation and, 125; stereotypes and, 12; UNDRIP and, 229
Dockstader, Karl, 189, 192n9
"Drawn from Poverty" (*New York Times*), 216
drugs: customs and, 66; Fiddler-Potter and, 209; humour and, 91; solutions and, 31; Taylor and, 164; trauma and, 77, 83
drumming: customs and, 7, 9–10, 26, 58, 103, 148; stereotypes and, 7, 9–10
drunkenness, 4, 7, 10–11, 110

Eagle Feather News, 23
Eastern Door, The (newspaper), 23
Echaquan, Joyce, 181n7
education: Ahtone and, 218; customs and, 59; Fiddler-Potter and, 210, 212; Indian time and, 51–52; lack of, 31; Pugliese and, 184; residential schools and, 234; social media and, 117; solutions and, 31, 33; stereotypes and, 13–14; Talaga and, 172, 178, 180; Truth and Reconciliation Commission (TRC) and, 13, 231
Elders: customs and, 58–60, 66; elected leadership and, 69; Indian time and, 51–53; opinions of, 60; Pugliese and, 186; Rice and, 147–50; role of, 60; stereotypes and, 7; Talaga and, 173, 175; Taylor and, 166–67; terminology and, 106; traditional, 69
Elements of Journalism, The (Kovach and Rosenstiel), 43
Environics, 38n1
Eskimos, 4, 58, 103
ethics: Ahtone and, 218, 221; councils and, 66; customs and, 60–66; importance of, 3; non-interference and, 64–65; objectivity and, 40–41, 43, 46; OCAP and, 89n2; positive vs. negative stories and, 28; reciprocity and, 112–13; story-takers and, 89n2; trauma and, 77, 83; Truth and Reconciliation Commission (TRC) and, 232
Evans, Heather, 136
Evarts, Hal G., 115
Exxon Valdez (oil tanker), 161n2
eye contact, 62

Facebook: access to, 116–17; customs and, 58, 61; Echaquan and, 181n7; Fontaine and, 199; Rice and, 149; story choice and, 20; Talaga and, 176; Taylor and, 169–70; Trahant and, 158; user demographics of, 117; Walker and, 134
"Face to Face" photo, 8, 15
feasts, 57, 188
Fiddler, Alvin, 177, 181n6
Fiddler-Potter, Merelda: awards of, 205; background of, xiii, 205; bias and, 210–11; Canadian Broadcasting Corporation (CBC) and, 8–9, 194–96, 202, 205; ceremonies and, 207; Chiefs and, 210; colonialism and, 205, 208–9; councils and, 208; education and, 210, 212; First Nations and, 205–6, 211; identity politics and, 207–8; informed conversation and, 211–12; knowledge-based journalism and, 212–13; language and, 208, 210; legal issues and, 212; Métis and, 205–8; Mohawks and, 206, 208; non-Indigenous people and, 206–7, 211, 213; opinion and, 210; reconciliation and, 209–11; reserves and, 207, 210–11; residential schools and, 206, 208, 212–13; Saskatchewan and, 205–6, 210–11; Sixties Scoop and, 206–9, 212; status and, 206; teaching history and, 208–9; Truth and Reconciliation Commission (TRC) and, 209, 213; women and, 205, 209
Finding Cleo podcast, 140n4
First Nations: agency and, 72; Boyden and, 214n3; customs and, 58–59, 61; Fiddler-Potter and, 205–6, 211; Indigenous perspective and, 68–69; legal issues and, 101; objectivity and, 42–43, 46, 47n2; OCAP and, 232; Pugliese and, 183, 190; residential schools and, 234; Rice and, 149; solutions and, 32–33; stereotypes and, 11, 15; story choice and, viii, 23–24; story-takers and, 89n2; Talaga and, 179, 181n4; terminology and, 99–102; trauma and, 81; Treaty Land Entitlement (TLE) agreements and, 210, 214n4; Walker and, 131
First Nations Drum (newspaper), 24
First Nations Forward, 23
First Nations Information Governance Centre, 232
First Nations University of Canada, 205–6, 214n2
"Five Ds Rule", 8–11, 35, 223

500+ Years of Rage, 87–90, 113, 158
Floyd, George, 41
Fontaine, Tim: accountability and, 201; alcohol and, 203; Anishinaabe and, 194; APTN and, 194, 202; background of, xiii, 194; bias and, 199, 202; Canadian Broadcasting Corporation (CBC) and, 194–96, 202; cultivating sources and, 201; expanding Indigenous voices and, 203; health and, 202; humour and, 194–99; Indigenous perspective and, 203; mistakes and, 201–2; photographs and, 196, 203; protests and, 197; respect and, 195–96, 200–203; social media and, 195, 197, 199; teasing and, 195–98; transparency and, 199–201; *Walking Eagle News* and, 92–93, 194, 201–2; white people and, 198
food: customs and, 56, 60, 65; feasts and, 57, 188; health and, 82; positive vs. negative stories and, 27; Pugliese and, 188; reciprocity and, 113; stereotypes and, 10; Trahant and, 158
Ford, John, 225n1
forestry industry, 7, 192n5
Francis, Daniel, 4
Frazer, Ryan, 115
Frontline (TV show), 151, 153

Gannett Foundation, 215
George, Dudley, 186, 192n6
Georgina Island, xi
Gerard, Forrest, 161n3
gifts, 56, 59–60, 66, 167, 188
Gimlet Media, 131
Gitxsan, 16n4
Globe and Mail, 172, 178
Goldberg, Sally, 124–25
graphics, 109–11, 218
Grey Owl, 10

Haida, 68, 143
Haraway, Donna, 44
Harding, Robert, 12, 109
Harper, Elijah, 152, 161n1
Harris, Johnny, 44
Hartley, John, 28
Harvard University, 182, 215
health: agency and, 72; customs and, 60, 64; Echaquan and, 181n7; Fontaine and, 202; food and, 82; health care system, 33, 90, 153, 177, 181n7; medicine, 58–59, 81, 151, 229; mental, 52, 64, 66, 76–77, 81–84, 92, 136, 175–76; objectivity and, 43–44; psychiatrists and, 52, 64, 66, 76, 92; Pugliese and, 190; Rice and, 149; solutions and, 31, 33; statistics on, 31; story choice and, 91; Talaga and, 172, 175–77; Trahant and, 153; trauma and, 74, 76–77, 81–84, 133, 149, 175; Walker and, 133, 136
Healy, Jo, 77
High Country News, 215, 219
Highway of Tears, 140n6
Hill, Charlie, 91, 95n2
Hollywood, 9, 26, 71
honorariums, 59, 66, 166–67
Howard, Ross, 29
Hume, Stephen, 7
humility: Rice and, 145–46, 149–50; transparancy and, 145–46; trauma and, 78
humour: Atwood and, 91; dark, 83, 194; Fontaine and, 194–99; Indian time and, 52; Inuit and, 92–94; Métis and, 92; Mohawks and, 92; Native people and, 91–92; non-Indigenous people and, 95n3; offence and, 94; opinion and, 94; photographs and, 94; proper use of, 94; Pugliese and, 191; punching up and, 197–98; *Qanurli* and, 92–93; as reconciliation, 198–99; self-deprecating, 93; status and, 91; stereotypes and, 94; stoicism and, 12, 91, 94, 196; Taylor and, 52, 92; teasing and, 57, 92–94, 158, 191, 195–98; understanding Indian, 92–94; *Walking Eagle News* and, 92–93, 194, 201–2; white people and, 91, 94

iChannel, 182
"Idle No More" movement, viii–ix, 118, 158, 161n10
Imaginary Indian, The (Francis), 4
Inconvenient Indian (film), 214n1
Indian Act, x, xvi–xvii; context and, 137; Indigenous perspective and, 69; objectivity and, 46; solutions and, 32–33; Talaga and, 179–80; terminology and, 104–5
Indian Country: Ahtone and, 216–24; avoiding historical analysis, 217; customs and, 57, 60; data journalism and, 223–24; legal issues and, 18, 105, 161n4; Marshall Trilogy and, 161n4; Pugliese and, 188; Reporting in Indian Country bingo card, 18–20, 216; *Royal Proclamation of 1763*, x, xv, 105;

terminology and, ix, 105; Trahant and, 151–52, 156, 158–60, 161n4; use of term, ix
Indian Country Today (ICT), 24, 151–52
Indian problem, 32–33
Indian Residential Schools Settlement Agreement, 236
Indian time: Anishinaabe and, 52; ceremonies and, 51, 53; Chiefs and, 51–52, 54; councils and, 51; deadlines and, 52–54; delays, 53; early, 53; education and, 51–52; Elders and, 51–53; humour and, 52; Inuit and, 54n2; late, 53; non-Indigenous people and, 54n2; photographs and, 53; plan for, 52–53; press releases and, 51–52; proper use of term, 54n2; reserves and, 51, 54; respect and, 53; Rice and, 147–48
Indigenous "beat", 22
Indigenous perspective: bias and, 68; ceremonies and, 68; Chiefs and, 69; councils and, 69; Cree and, 68; divisions and, 69; factions and, 69; First Nations and, 68–69; Fontaine and, 203; *Indian Act* and, 69; leadership forms and, 69; Métis and, 68–69; Native people and, 69; as not homogenous, 68–69; opinion and, 69–72; Quebec and, 68; reserves and, 68; status and, 68
IndigiNews, 23
informed consent, 78–79, 132–34
Innu, 42, 103, 171n2
Instagram, 20, 117, 149, 169, 199
Inuinnaqtun, 103
Inuit, x; agency and, 72; customs and, 61, 63–64; humour and, 92–94; Indian time and, 54n2; Indigenous perspective and, 69; Inuk, 68, 103, 106, 162, 164–65, 168, 171n2; Jones and, 171n2; Nunangat of, 103; objectivity and, 46; Porter and, 225n2; residential schools and, 234; Rice and, 143; solutions and, 33; stereotypes and, 11; story choice and, 24; Talaga and, 179; Taylor and, 162–69; terminology and, 100–106
Inuit Qaujimajatuqangit (IQ), 63–64
Inuit Tapiriit Kanatami, 103
Inuktitut: customs and, 64; humour and, 92, 95n5; media and, 24; Taylor and, 164–65, 171n1; terminology and, 103
Inuktut, 102–3
Inuvialuit, 24, 103

Ipperwash Crisis, 186, 192n6
Iqaluit, 162
Iroquois, 64

Jackson, Kenneth, 191, 193n11
John S. Knight Journalism Fellowships, viii, xii
Johnston, Thomas Anguti, 92
Jones, Yvonne, 171n2
Journalists for Human Rights (JHR), 128n6, 182

Karektak, Vinnie, 93
Kasabonika Lake First Nation, 181n2
Kelly, Geoffrey, 54n2
Kettle and Stoney Point First Nation, 192n6
King, Thomas, 92, 227
Kitigan Zibi, 214n1
Kokumville, 192n5
Komulainen, Shaney, 8
Kovach, Bill, 43
Kovach, Margaret, 112
Ku'Ku'kwes website, 23
Kwakwaka'wakw, 14, 42

Labrador, 103, 171n2, 205
Labradorimiut, 103
Labrador Métis Nation, 171n2
Lakota: Crazy Horse, 58; *Dances with Wolves* and, 71; Rice and, 143; trauma and, 76, 78, 86n8
LandBack Lane, 192n9
land claims: Caledonia, 192n2; comprehensive, 102, 214n5; context and, 109; Dene and Métis Comprehensive Land Claim, 102; Dockstader and, 192n9; NunatuKavu, 171n2; objectivity and, 42–43; pitching and, 36; stereotypes and, 4, 19; terminology and, 102–3; treaties and, 13, 21, 124, 155, 185, 210, 214n4–5, 231; violence and, 192n2
land defenders, 43, 118, 185–87, 189
"Land You Live On, The" (worksheet), 20–22
language: context and, 100, 102–3, 106; customs and, 56–57, 62–63; English, 12, 62; erasure of, 76; Fiddler-Potter and, 208, 210; French, 62; governing narratives and, 208–9; interpretation, 62–63, 103; Inuinnaqtun, 103; Inuktitut, 24, 64, 92, 95n5, 103, 164–65, 171n1; Inuktut, 102–3; media and, 23–24; Métis, 102, 234; Pugliese and, 184;

reconciliation and, 122, 125; residential schools and, 234–35; Rice and, 149; social media and, 116–19; story choice and, 21–22; Taylor and, 165–66, 171n1; trauma and, 76; Truth and Reconciliation Commission (TRC) and, 230; UNDRIP and, 229
La Rose, Jean, 189
Latimer, Michelle, 206–8, 214n1
LA Times, 215
La Verendrye Park, 192n5
Lawrenchuk, Tugguy, 197, 204n4
lawsuits, 109, 153
Legacy (Rice), 141
legal issues: Aboriginal people, 103; Anaya and, 100; context and, 109–10; court decisions, 111; federal laws, 218–20; Fiddler-Potter and, 212; First Nations and, 101; *Indian Act*, 32–33, 46, 69, 104–5, 137, 179–80; Indian Country and, 18, 105, 161n4; Indian Residential Schools Settlement Agreement and, 236; lawsuits, 109, 153; Marshall Trilogy and, 161n4; Native people, 105; objectivity and, 43; residential schools and, 109; *Royal Proclamation of 1763*, x, xv, 105; terminology and, 100–105; Treaty Land Entitlement (TLE) and, 214n4
le Journal de Québec/Journal de Montréal, 14
Lemay, Yannick, 14
"Letters to a Young Indigenous Journalist" (Rice), 146
Little Big Man (film), 71
Lone Ranger (TV show), viii
Luke, Marnie, 136

MacDonald, Peter, 161n6
McEachern, Allan, 16n4
Makwa Creative, Inc., 172
Mandalorian, The (TV show), 198
Manitoba: Fontaine and, 194–98; Indigenous perspective and, 68; Métis and, 102; Trahant and, 161n1; Walker and, 140n5
Māori, 122–24
Maracle, Lee, 181n1
marches, 8, 28
Marshall Trilogy, 161n4
Maslin, Crystal, 12
Massey Lecturer, 172
Mears, Ray, 195, 204n1
Media Indigena (podcast), 24
MediaSmarts, 26

medicine, 58–59, 81, 151, 229
Meech Lake Accord, 152, 161n1
mental health: customs and, 64; psychiatrists and, 52, 64, 66, 76, 92; PTSD, 175; Talaga and, 175–76; trauma and, 76–77, 81–84; Walker and, 136
Métis: Boyden and, 214n3; Fiddler-Potter and, 205–8; humour and, 92; Indigenous perspective and, 68–69; language and, 102, 234; Latimer and, 214n1; objectivity and, 42, 46; Ontario and, 102; residential schools and, 234; Rice and, 143; social media and, 115; stereotypes and, 7; Talaga and, 179; terminology and, 100–106
Métis National Council (MNC), 102, 208
Métis Voyageur newsletter, 23
Michener Award, 172
Midnight Sweatlodge (Rice), 141
Mi'kmaw, 68
Miller, John, 42
Ministry of Indigenous Affairs, 69
Missing & Murdered (podcast), 131, 137, 140n3, 140n6
MMIWG, 118, 200, 208, 219
Moccasin Telegraph, The (Evarts), 115
Mohawks: defiance and, 8–9; Fiddler-Potter and, 206, 208; humour and, 92; Kanien'kehá:ka, 52, 100; Oka Crisis and, 204n2; stereotypes and, 4; Tyendinaga, 64
Moon of the Crusted Snow (Rice), 75, 141
Moore, Michael, 51
moral issues, 13, 125
Muskrat Magazine, 23

NAFNIP question, 99
National, The (TV show), 131
National Congress of American Indians, 222
National Geographic, 124
National Indigenous Peoples Day, 27
National Indigenous Times (NIT), 24
National Native News, 215
National Newspaper Awards, 172
National Observer, 182
Nation Magazine, The, 23
Native American Journalists Association (NAJA), 18–19, 182, 215–16
Native Communications Society of the NWT, 23
"Native Ethics and Rules of Behaviour" (Brant), 64

Native people: Ahtone on, 215–23; bingo and, 18–20, 216; context and, 110; customs and, 56–66; humour and, 91–92; Indigenous perspective and, 69; legal issues and, 105; Pugliese and, 182, 184, 186; reconciliation and, 124; social media and, 115, 118; stereotypes and, 11–13; terminology and, 99, 103, 105; Trahant and, 151–59, 161n3, 161n9; trauma and, 75
Navajo, 156–57, 161n6–7
Navajo Times Today, The, 151, 157
Neechie, 176, 181n4
Neekan, Craig, 181n5
neutrality, 146–47
New Brunswick, 192n3, 234
Newfoundland, 234
news hook, 36
New York Times, 151, 215–17, 225n2
Nieman Fellowship, 182, 215
Nishnawbe Aski Nation (NAN), 177, 181n6
NITV, 24
non-Indigenous people: agency and, 72–73; Ahtone and, 219, 222; customs and, 57, 62, 64; diversity and, 12, 27, 36–37, 42, 70, 125, 229; Fiddler-Potter and, 206–7, 211, 213; humour and, 95n3; Indian time and, 54n2; Jackson and, 193n11; pitching and, 36, 38n1; positive vs. negative stories and, 26–27; Pugliese and, 183, 188; reconciliation and, 122–27; solutions and, 33; stereotypes and, 10–11, 16n2; story choice and, 21, 27; story-takers and, 4; Talaga and, 180; trauma and, 81, 89n2; UNDRIP and, 229
Non-Status Indian, 104
Northern News Services Limited, 23
Northwest Territories (NWT), 23, 89, 102–3, 163–64
NPR, 215
NRK Sápmi, 24
Nunatsiaq News, 23
Nunatsiavut, 103
NunatuKavut, 103, 171n2
Nunavik, 23, 103
Nunavimmiut, 103
Nunavummiut, 103
Nunavut: Ahtone and, 216; Baffin Island, 103; customs and, 63–64; media and, 23; Porter and, 225n2; Qaqqaq and, 171n2; Taylor and, 162, 164, 168, 171n1

objectivity: Aboriginal people and, 116; accountability and, 115, 119–20; Anishinaabe and, 41; bias and, 39–46, 47n3; concept of, 40–41; councils and, 46; deadlines and, 41; ethics and, 40–41, 43, 46; fairness and, 44–45; First Nations and, 42–43, 46, 47n2; harmful, 41–43; health and, 43–44; *Indian Act* and, 46; Inuit and, 46; land claims and, 42–43; legal issues and, 43; Métis and, 42, 46; neutrality and, 146–47; opinion and, 26, 31, 38n1, 40–41, 43, 58, 60, 69–72, 94, 169, 187, 210; origins and, 39–40; photographs and, 42; point of view and, 46; police and, 41; protests and, 43; racism and, 41–42; respect and, 44, 120, 124, 126; Rice and, 41–42; sovereignty and, 43; statistics and, 42; transparency and, 43–46; usefulness of, 43–44; white people and, 41–45, 115, 119
OCAP (ownership, control, access, and possession), 89n2, 232–33
Ojibways. *See* Anishinaabe
Oka Crisis, 8, 13, 15, 196, 204n2
Okanese First Nation, 131
Oneida, 95n2, 192n9
Ontario: Anderson death and, 181n2; Bushie death and, 181n3; Cree and, 23, 64; customs and, 64; George death and, 192n6; land reclamation and, 192n2; media and, 23–24, 128n6; Métis and, 23, 102; Neekan death and, 181n5; Porter and, 81; Pugliese and, 182; Rice and, 141; Talaga and, 172, 179; Trahant and, 152; Walker and, 131
opinion: customs and, 58, 60; Elders and, 60; Fiddler-Potter and, 210; humour and, 94; Indigenous perspective and, 69–72; objectivity and, 26, 31, 38n1, 40–41, 43, 58, 60, 69–72, 94, 169, 187, 210; positive vs. negative stories and, 26; public, 38n1, 48n22; Pugliese and, 187; range of, 169; solutions and, 31; Taylor and, 169

PBS, 151, 215
photographs, 61; customs and, 57–62; "Face to Face", 8, 15; Fontaine and, 196, 203; humour and, 94; Indian time and, 53; objectivity and, 42; pitching and, 36; Pugliese and, 186; reciprocity and, 113;

reconciliation and, 9, 124; social media and, 118; story-takers and, 4; Top Five News Photos That Changed Canada, 8; Trahant and, 158; trauma and, 78
pipelines: Dakota Access Pipeline, 161n8; Fontaine and, 204n5; protest and, 66, 149, 161n8, 187, 192n1, 204n5; Pugliese and, 187, 192n1
pitching: Ahtone and, 218–20; backstory and, 110–11; diversity, 36–37; "Five Ds Rule", 35; news hook, 36; non-Indigenous people and, 36, 38n1; photographs and, 36; Pugliese and, 182–84; research and, 35–36
podcasts: resources of, 24; Talaga and, 172, 175; Walker and, 131–32, 136–39
police: Ahtone and, 217; Anderson murder and, 181n2; objectivity and, 41; Pugliese and, 186–89; RCMP, 138, 164, 192n3; sock rounds and, 192n2; Talaga and, 176; tear gas and, 192n2; Trahant and, 158, 161n6; violence and, 9, 158, 186, 192n2, 192n6; Williams murder and, 140n6
Porter, Catherine, 225n2
Porter, Jody, 81–82
positive vs. negative stories: Aboriginal people and, 28; blockades and, 28; burying "good news" and, 27; calendar journalism and, 27; controversial subjects, 28; ethics and, 28; food and, 27; Hollywood and, 26; looking beyond conflict, 28–29; non-Indigenous people and, 26–27; opinion and, 26; range and, 27
poverty, 4, 216–17, 225n2
powwows, 4, 10, 27, 59
priests, 151, 154
Prince Edward Island, 234
Pritchard, David, 42
progress, 9, 13, 68
protests: Caledonia, 192n2; defiance and, 8–10, 43, 118, 149, 158, 161n8, 161n10, 185–87, 189, 192n2–3, 192n6, 197, 204n5; Fontaine and, 197; Idle No More, viii–ix, 118, 158, 161n10; land defenders and, 43, 118, 185–87, 189; objectivity and, 43; pipeline, 66, 149, 161n8, 187, 192n1, 204n5; Pugliese and, 185–87, 189; Rice and, 149; shale gas, 192n3; social media and, 118; Standing Rock, 158–59, 161n8; stereotypes and, 8–10; Trahant and, 158; violence and, 192n6

protocols: customs and, 56–67; OCAP and, 232–33; Pugliese and, 184; Rice and, 143–44; social media and, 118; Taylor and, 166; trauma and, 79, 83
psychiatrists, 52, 64, 66, 76, 92
PTSD, 175
Public Policy Forum, 182
Public Radio News Directors Incorporated, 215
Pugliese, Karyn: Aboriginal people and, 182, 185; APTN and, 182–91; awards of, 182; background of, xiii, 182; bias and, 184, 187, 190–91; blockades and, 185–87; bullying and, 189–90; Canadian Broadcasting Corporation (CBC) and, 182; ceremonies and, 188–89; challenge of female journalists, 189–90; Chiefs and, 183, 186–89; colonialism and, 185; context and, 184–85; death and, 189–90; education and, 184; Elders and, 186; fairness and, 188–89; First Nations and, 183, 190; food and, 188; health and, 190; humour and, 191; Indian Country and, 188; language and, 184; Native people and, 182, 184, 186; non-Indigenous people and, 183, 188; Ontario and, 182; opinion and, 187; photographs and, 186; pitching and, 182–84; police and, 186–89; protests and, 185–87, 189; protocols and, 184; racism and, 190; reconciliation and, 122, 190–91; residential schools and, 190; respect and, 188; teasing and, 191; Truth and Reconciliation Commission (TRC) and, 190; violence and, 186; white people and, 187, 190

Qanurli (TV show), 92–93
Qaqqaq, Mumilaaq, 171n2
Quebec, 8, 14; Crees and, 64; customs and, 64; Echaquan and, 181n7; Indigenous perspective and, 68; Innu and, 103; Kelly and, 54n2; Kitigan Zibi and, 214n1; Kokumville, 192n5; media and, 23; Meech Lake Accord and, 161n1; Nunavik and, 103; Nunavut and, 103

racism: Black Lives Matter movement and, ix, 41; bullying and, 118–19; context and, 110; Floyd murder, 41; Ford and, 225n1; inferiority and, 13; *National*

Geographic and, 124; news prose and, 13; objectivity and, 41–42; Pugliese and, 190; reconciliation and, 122–24; Rice and, 149; social media and, 118–19; stereotypes and, 13, 15; *Stuff* and, 122–24; supremacists, 119; Talaga and, 177–78; trauma and, 76; workplace demographics and, 47n8
Radio Television Digital News Association of Canada, 205
rape, 75, 189–90
Ray Mears Goes Walkabout (BBC), 204n1
RCMP, 138, 164, 192n3
reciprocity, 112–14
Reckoning (Callison and Young), 44
reconciliation: ceremonies and, 126; colonialism and, 122–27; community relationships and, 126; decolonizing journalism and, 124, 126–27; Fiddler-Potter and, 209–11; hiring more Indigenous people, 125–26; humour as, 198–99; language and, 122, 125; *National Geographic* and, 124; Native people and, 124; non-Indigenous people and, 122–27; as ongoing process, x; photographs and, 9, 124; Pugliese and, 190–91; racism and, 122–24; respect and, 236; rules for, 199; stereotypes and, 123–24; *Stuff* magazine and, 122–24; Truth and Reconciliation Commission (TRC) and, 124, 126–27, 209–10; white people and, 122, 125, 190–91
Reconciliation Action Plan (RAP), 125
"Reconciliation in the Media" conference, 138
Red River Resistance, 205
Reporting in Indian Country bingo card, 18–20, 216
Reporting in Indigenous Communities (RIIC), viii
reserves: Ahtone and, 217–18; blockades and, 192n4; Colville, 161n12; customs and, 56; Fiddler-Potter and, 207, 210–11; Indian time and, 51, 54; Indigenous perspective and, 68; Kanesatake, 8; social media and, 116–17; solutions and, 31; stereotypes and, 4; terminology and, 103–5, 105; Trahant and, 152, 156; Treaty Land Entitlement (TLE) and, 214n4; violence on, 217
residential schools, 36; Aboriginal people and, 234–36; apology for, 234–36; churches and, 234; context and, 109–10, 137–38; customs and, 62; deaths in, 234; education and, 234; Fiddler-Potter and, 206, 208, 212–13; First Nations and, 234; Indian Residential Schools Settlement Agreement and, 236; Indian time and, 51; Inuit and, 234; language and, 234–35; legal issues and, 109; Métis and, 234; Pugliese and, 190; Rice and, 149; stereotypes and, 13; story-takers and, 88; survivors of, 43; Talaga and, 179; Taylor and, 164; trauma and, 76, 81; Truth and Reconciliation Commission (TRC) and, 230–31, 236
resilience: love and, 177–78; Talaga and, 177–78; Trahant and, 154; trauma and, 75–76, 80, 85; Walker and, 137, 139
respect: building trust and, 20; community and, 176–77; customs and, 59–63, 66, 227; "do no harm" and, 174–75; Fontaine and, 195–96, 200–203; humility and, 145–46; importance of, 227; Indian time and, 53; informed consent and, 78–79, 132; objectivity and, 44; OCAP and, 232; Pugliese and, 188; reciprocity and, 114; reconciliation and, 236; Rice and, 15–20, 142, 144–48; social media and, 120, 124, 126; southern attitude and, 163–64; story-takers and, 87–90; Talaga and, 173, 175, 177; Taylor and, 163–65, 167, 170; terminology and, 100, 106; trauma and, 74, 80–81, 85; Walker and, 132
Rice, Waubgeshig: accountability and, 148; alcohol and, 150; Anishinaabe and, 41, 141, 143–45; awards of, 141; background of, xiii, 141–42; blockades and, 149; Canadian Broadcasting Corporation (CBC) and, 141–42, 147–48; ceremonies and, 141, 143; colonialism and, 146; covering internal conflicts and, 157–58; Cree and, 143; deadlines and, 147; Debwewin Citation, 141; Elders and, 147–50; fallacy of neutrality and, 146–47; First Nations and, 149; health and, 149; humility and, 145–46, 149–50; independent media and, 157; Indian time and, 147–48; Inuit and, 143; language and, 149; *Legacy*, 141; Métis and, 143; *Midnight Sweatlodge*, 141; *Moon of the Crusted Snow* and, 75, 141; objectivity and, 41–42; Ontario and, 141; political beat and, 155–56; protests and, 149; protocols

and, 143–44; racism and, 149; residential schools and, 149; respect and, 15–20, 142, 144–48; social media and, 149; Standing Rock and, 158–59, 161n8; status and, 145; stereotypes and, 143, 145, 148; transparency and, 144–46; trauma and, 149–50; tribal sovereignty and, 156–57; video journalism and, 141–44; violence and, 146; white people and, 146, 149
Rick Mercer Report, The (TV show), 92
Robertson, Carmen, 11–13, 124
Rolling Stone, 131
Roosevelt, Theodore, 17n5
Rosen, Jay, 41
Rosenstiel, Tom, 43
Royal Commission on Aboriginal Peoples (RCAP), 10–12, 127
Royal Proclamation of 1763, x, 105

Sagkeeng First Nation, 194
Salish, 179
Salt Lake Tribune, 151
Saskatchewan: Balcarres, 214n6; Boushie death and, 138, 140n7; Brass and, 214n2; Fiddler-Potter and, 205–6, 210–11; Fontaine and, 196; land allocations and, 214n4; Métis and, 102; Okanese First Nation, 131; "Reconciliation in the Media" conference, 138; stereotypes and, 8, 12; Taylor and, 162, 171n1
Sauvageau, Florian, 42
Scott, Duncan Campbell, 32
Seattle-Post-Intelligencer, 151
Seattle Times, The, 151
Seeing Red: A History of Natives in Canadian Newspapers (Anderson and Robertson), 11–13, 124
self-care: Talaga and, 175–76; trauma and, 74, 81; Walker and, 135–36
Semaganis, Johnny, 134–35, 140n4
Seven Fallen Feathers (Talaga), 172
sharing, 65–66
Sho-Ban News, 151
Shoshone, 151
sidebars, 109–10
"Silence, The" (Frontline), 151
Sinclair, Murray, 126
Sioux, 94, 101, 161n8
Sixties Scoop, x, xvi; context and, 137; Fiddler-Potter and, 206–9, 212; Talaga and, 179; Walker and, 131, 137

SNC-Lavalin scandal, 13–14
social media: access to, 116–17, 121n3; accountability and, 28; anger and, 65; benefits of, 116–17; bullying and, 118–19; ceremonies and, 118; colonialism and, 45; Echaquan and, 181n7; education and, 117; Facebook, 20, 58, 61, 116, 134, 149, 158, 169–70, 176, 181n7, 199; First Nations and, 115–17; Fontaine and, 195, 197, 199; Instagram, 20, 117, 149, 169, 199; language and, 116–19; Métis and, 115; Native people and, 115, 118; online abuse and, 118–20; online relationships and, 119–20; photographs and, 118; protests and, 118; protocols and, 118; Qaqqaq and, 171n2; racism and, 118–19; reserves and, 116–17; Rice and, 148–49; stereotypes and, 116; Talaga and, 176; Taylor and, 169–70; TikTok, 20, 116–17, 120; Trahant and, 158–60; Twitter, 20, 117, 159, 171n2, 195, 197, 199; upside/downside for journalists, 117–19; user demographics of, 117; verifying information on, 118–19; violence and, 26–27, 118–19; Walker and, 134; women and, 116; YouTube, 117
sock rounds, 192n2
solutions: colonialism and, 31; councils and, 32; education and, 31, 33; First Nations and, 32–33; health, 31, 33; *Indian Act* and, 32–33; Indian problem and, 32–33; Inuit and, 33; non-Indigenous people and, 33; opinion and, 31; reserves and, 31; statistics and, 31; suicide and, 31; white people and, 32–33
southern attitude, 163–64
sovereignty: Ahtone and, 223–24; "Idle No More" and, viii–ix, 118, 158, 161n10; objectivity and, 43; terminology and, 100; Trahant and, 156–57
Standing Rock, 158–59, 161n8
Stanford University, viii
Stanley, Gerald, 140n7
Starr, Tenelle, 214n6
statistics: Ahtone and, 217, 223; context and, 111; customs and, 65; health, 31; objectivity and, 42; solutions and, 31; stereotypes and, 11; story-takers and,

88; terminology and, 104; U.S. Bureau of Justice, 225n3; Walker and, 134
status: Fiddler-Potter and, 206; humour and, 91; Indigenous perspective and, 68; Latimer and, 214n1; Rice and, 145; terminology and, 100–101, 104–5
status quo, 12, 43–44, 72
Steinberg, Neil, 79
stereotypes: Aboriginal people and, 10–13; Ahtone and, 216; alcohol and, 10–11; Angry Warrior, 12; bias and, 13–14; blockades and, 8–9; Chiefs and, 10; colonialism and, 11–13; councils and, 7; crime and, 13; dancing, 7, 10; death and, 7, 11, 17n5, 178–79, 203; defiance and, 8–9; drums, 7, 9–10; drunkenness, 4, 7, 10–11, 110; "Ds" of, 7–11, 35; education and, 13–14; Elders and, 7; First Nations and, 11, 15; food and, 10; good Indian, 11–12, 17n5; Hollywood and, 9, 26, 71; humour and, 94; imagery and, 4; Inuit and, 11; land claims and, 4, 19; list of, 4; Métis and, 7; Mohawks and, 4; NAJA bingo card and, 18–20, 216; Native people and, 11–13; Noble Environmentalist, 12; non-Indigenous people and, 10–11, 16n2; Pathetic Victim, 12; Porter and, 225n2; poverty, 225n2; protests and, 8–10; racism and, 13, 15; reconciliation and, 123–24; repetition of, 5; replacement by more complex, 11–14; reserves and, 4; residential schools and, 13; Rice and, 143, 145, 148; social media and, 116; statistics and, 11; stoicism and, 12, 91, 94, 196; suicide and, 4, 10, 91; Troublemaker, 12; Truth and Reconciliation Commission (TRC) and, 13; violence and, 8, 13, 139, 225n1–2
Stevens, Mark, 124
stoicism, 12, 91, 94, 196
Stolen: The Search for Jermain (podcast), 131
Sto:lo, 181n1
story choice: bias and, 18; bingo card of, 18–20, 216; colonialism and, 20; Facebook and, 20; First Nations and, viii, 23–24; "Five Ds Rule", 8–11, 35; health and, 91; Inuit and, 24; "It bleeds, it leads", 11; language and, 21–22; looking beyond conflict, 28–29; non-Indigenous people and, 21, 27; positive vs. negative stories and, 26–30;

research and, 20, 35–36; social media and, 20; stereotypes and, 7–17 (*see also* stereotypes); worksheet for, 20–22
story-takers, 4, 87–89
Strategic Alliance of Broadcasters for Aboriginal Reflection (SABAR), 107n2
Stuff magazine, 122–24
suicide: restriction of reporting, 61; solutions and, 31; stereotypes and, 4, 10, 91; Talaga and, 172–73; trauma and, 75–76; Walker and, 164
supremacists, 119

Tahltan, 42, 68, 117
Talaga, Tanya: *All Our Relations: Finding the Path Forward*, 172; Anishinaabe and, 172; awards of, 172; background of, xiii, 172; building trust and, 172–73; Canadian Broadcasting Corporation (CBC) and, 172; ceremonies and, 175; colonialism and, 178–79; community and, 176–77; context and, 178–80; councils and, 173; crime and, 179; education and, 172, 178, 180; Elders and, 173, 175; First Nations and, 179, 181n4; health and, 172, 175–77; *Indian Act* and, 179–80; Inuit and, 179; love and, 177–78; Métis and, 179; non-Indigenous people and, 180; Ontario and, 172, 179; podcasts and, 172, 175; police and, 176; racism and, 177–78; residential schools and, 179; resilience and, 177–78; respect and, 173, 175, 177; self-care, 175–76; *Seven Fallen Feathers*, 172; Sixties Scoop and, 179; social media and, 176; suicide and, 172–73; trauma and, 173–76; violence and, 173; white people and, 180
TallBear, Kim, 44, 46, 48n23
Taylor, Drew Hayden, 52, 92
Taylor, Juanita: advice for Southern journalists, 162–64; alcohol and, 164; Anishinaabe and, 167; background of, xiii–xiv, 162; Canadian Broadcasting Corporation (CBC) and, 162, 165, 167; Chiefs and, 163–64, 167; Elders and, 166–67; humour and, 92; Inuit and, 162–69; language and, 165–66, 171n1; Nunavut and, 162, 164, 168, 171n1; opinion and, 169; protocols and, 166; residential schools and, 164; respect and, 163–65, 167, 170; social media and, 169–70; southern attitude and,

163–64; voices of women, 168–69; white people and, 167
Te Ao Māori News, 24
tear gas, 192n2
teasing: Fontaine and, 195–98; humour and, 57, 92–94, 158, 191, 195–98; Pugliese and, 191
Teen Vogue, 131, 151
terminology, xi, 56; Aboriginal people and, 99, 102–6; affiliation and, 100; Anishinaabe and, xi, 99–100, 204n5; blockades and, 204n3; capitalization, 106; Chiefs and, 103, 106; colonialism and, 99; Cree and, 100, 103, 204n3–4; Elders and, 106; Eskimos, 4, 58, 103; First Nations, 99–106; Indian, 3–4, 16n2, 104–5; *Indian Act* and, 104–5; Indian Country, ix, 105; Indigenous, 100–101; Inuit, 100–106; land claims and, 102–3; legal issues and, 100–105; Métis, 100–103, 105–6; NAFNIP question and, 99; Non-Status Indian, 104; people/peoples, 105–6; proper use of, 99–106; reserves and, 103–5; respect and, 100, 106; sovereignty and, 100; statistics and, 104; Status Indian, 100–101, 104–5; terms to avoid, 101; Treaty Indian, 104–5; UNDRIP and, 100; white people and, 104, 122
Texas Observer magazine, 215
Third Coast International Audio festival, 131
This Hour Has 22 Minutes (TV show), 92
Thunderheart (film), 71
TikTok, 20, 116–17, 120
Tonto, viii
Top Five News Photos That Changed Canada, 8
Toronto Metropolitan University, 42
Toronto Star, 172
Tragedies and Journalists: A Guide for More Effective Coverage (Dart Centre), 77
Trahant, Mark: Alaska and, 151–53; background of, xiv, 151; colonialism and, 153; councils and, 159–60; food and, 158; health and, 153; Indian Country and, 151–52, 156, 158–60, 161n4; *Indian Country Today* and, 151–52; Native people and, 151–59, 161n3, 161n9; Ontario and, 152; photographs and, 158; police and, 158, 161n6; protests and, 158; reporting across medicine line and, 151–52; reserves and, 152, 156; resilience and, 154; sexual abuse stories, 153–54; social media and, 158–60; sovereignty and, 156; treaties and, 155
transparency: Fontaine and, 199–201; humility and, 145–46; objectivity and, 43–46; openness and, 135–36; Rice and, 144–46; trauma and, 78; Walker and, 131–33, 136–37
trauma: abuse and, 88; accountability and, 80; alcohol and, 83, 86n19; Anishinaabe and, 75, 78; bias and, 76; caring for interviewees and, 77–81; colonialism and, 75, 77; Cree and, 75; crime and, 75; Dart Centre for Journalism and Trauma, 74, 77–78, 84; deadlines and, 78; death and, 81; disclosure of, 132–33; distrust of media and, 74–75; "do no harm" and, 174–75; ethics and, 77, 83; First Nations and, 81; health and, 74, 76–77, 81–84, 133, 149, 175; historical, 75–77; humility and, 78; informed consent, 78–79, 132; informed reporting and, 74–86; intergenerational, 76–77; language and, 76; Native people and, 75; non-Indigenous people and, 81, 89n2; photographs and, 78; preparing interviewees and, 131–32; protocols and, 79, 83; racism and, 76; residential schools and, 76, 81; resilience and, 75–76, 80, 85; respect and, 74, 80–81, 85; Rice and, 149–50; suicide and, 75–76; Talaga and, 173–76; transparency and, 78; Truth and Reconciliation Commission (TRC) and, 81; violence and, 74–77, 173; Walker and, 131–40
Trauma Reporting: A Journalist's Guide to Covering Sensitive Stories (Healy), 77
treaties: colonialism and, 13; land claims and, 13, 21, 124, 155, 185, 210, 214n4–5, 231; Trahant and, 155
Treaty Indian, 104–5
Treaty Land Entitlement (TLE) agreements, 210, 214n4
Trudeau, Justin, 14
Trump, Donald, 161n5
Truth and Reconciliation Commission (TRC): Aboriginal people and, ix, 230–31; Calls to Action of, 13, 124, 213, 230–31; Canadian Broadcasting Corporation (CBC) and, 124,

230; education and, 13, 231; ethics and, 232; Fiddler-Potter and, 209, 213; language and, 230; Pugliese and, 190; reconciliation and, 124, 126–27, 209–10; residential schools and, 230–31, 236; Sinclair and, 126; stereotypes and, 13; trauma and, 81; as wake-up call, ix
Tusaayaksat Magazine, 24
TVO Indigenous, 24
Twitter: Fontaine and, 195, 197, 199; Qaqqaq and, 171n2; story choice and, 20; Trahant and, 159; user demographics of, 117
"2-for-1" deal, 111
Two Row Times, The, 23
Tyendinaga, 64

UN Declaration on the Rights of Indigenous Peoples (UNDRIP): Articles of, 229; residential schools and, 240; sovereignty and, 156; terminology and, 100, 105; Truth and Reconciliation Commission (TRC) and, 231
Up North (radio program), 141
U.S. Bureau of Justice, 225n3
Uvagut TV, 24

Vanier Canada Graduate Scholarship, 205
View from Somewhere, 44–45
violence, 227; abuse, 75, 77, 88, 91, 110, 118–19, 122, 131–32, 151, 153–54, 222, 235; Ahtone and, 217–18; Belcourt and, 75; death, 60–61 (*see also* death); family, 173; Floyd murder, 41; Ford and, 225n1; George killing, 192n6; Highway of Tears and, 140n6; land claims and, 192n2; lateral, 118; murder, 41, 116, 131, 179, 182, 205; police, 9, 158, 186, 192n2, 192n6; positive vs. negative stories and, 26–27; protests and, 192n6; Pugliese and, 186; rape, 75, 189–90; Rice and, 146; social media and, 118–19; stereotypes and, 8, 13, 139, 225n1-2; Talaga and, 173; trauma and, 74–77, 173; U.S. Capitol and, 161n5; U.S. statistics on, 225n3; Walker and, 133–33, 139; women and, 75, 116, 131, 133–34, 139, 179, 182, 189–90, 205
VisionTV, 182

Vizenor, Gerald, 75–76
Vulture magazine, 131

Walker, Connie: awards of, 131; background of, xiv, 131; bias and, 136; Canadian Broadcasting Corporation (CBC) and, 131, 134, 138; colonialism and, 138; consent and, 133–34; context and, 137–39; crime and, 137–39; death and, 138; Facebook and, 134; First Nations and, 131; health and, 133, 136; Ontario and, 131; podcasts and, 131–32, 136–39; post-interview actions, 134–35; preparing interviewees and, 131–32; resilience and, 137, 139; respect and, 132; Saskatchewan and, 162, 171n1; self-care, 135; sharing with team and, 136; Sixties Scoop and, 131, 137; social media and, 134; statistics and, 134; suicide and, 164; transparency and, 131–33, 136–37; trauma and, 74, 131–40; violence and, 133–33, 139
Walking Eagle News, 92–93, 194, 201–2
Ward, Stephen, 43–44
Wasauksing First Nation, 141
Wawatay News, 24
Wet'suwet'en, 16n4, 118, 186–87, 192n1
whistleblowers, 222–23
Whiteduck, Mary, 186
white people, 4; agency and, 71–73; Ahtone and, 216–17, 220; Boyden and, 214n3; customs and, 65–68; Fontaine and, 198; humour and, 91, 94; objectivity and, 41–45; as Pākehā, 122; Pugliese and, 187, 190; reconciliation and, 122, 125, 190–91; Rice and, 146, 149; social media and, 115, 119; solutions and, 32–33; supremacists, 119; Talaga and, 180; Taylor and, 167; terminology and, 104, 122
Williams, Alberta, 138, 140n6
Wilson, Marie, 81, 138
Wilson-Raybould, Jody, 14
Windspeaker (AMMSA), 24, 192n8
Winfrey, Oprah, 35
withdrawal reaction, 66
women: bullying of, 189–90; challenge of female journalists, 189–90; death of, 140n6, 178–79, 181n2; Fiddler-Potter and, 205, 209; Highway of Tears and, 140n6;

missing, 116, 131, 134, 179, 182, 205; MMIWG and, 118, 200, 208, 219; murder of, 116, 131, 179, 182, 205; rape and, 75, 189–90; social media and, 116; status and, 104; violence against, 75, 116, 131, 133–34, 139, 179, 182, 189–90, 205

Women of Distinction award, 131

Young, Mary Lynn, 39, 42, 44–45
YouTube, 117
Yukon, 103, 115, 164
YWCA, 131